Fodor's

AMSTERDAM

FODOR'S AMSTERDAM

Writers: Floris Dogterom, Karina Hof, Liz Humphr Melzer, Tim Skelton

Editor: Robert I.C. Fisher

Editorial Contributor: Stephen Brewer

Production Editor: Jennifer DePrima

Maps & Illustrations: Mark Stroud, Moon Street Car l Lindroth, *cartographers;* Rebecca Baer, *map editor;* William V *phics*

Design: Fabrizio La Rocca, *creative director;* Tina M , Jessica Ramirez, *designers;* Melanie Marin, *associate director of photography;* Jennifer Romains, *photo research*

Cover Photo: Front cover: (Keizersgracht) SIME/eStock Photo; Back cover: gado gado1 by boo lee http://www.flickr.com/photos/71284893@N00/3164811049/ Attribution-NonCommercial License; Jan Kranendonk/Shutterstock; Amsterdam Tourism & Convention Board. Spine: lillisphotography/iStockphoto.

Production Manager: Angela L. McLean

914.
9235
FOD
2013

3rd Edition

ISBN 978-0-89141-941-9

ISSN 0883-6043

SPECIAL SALES

This book is available at special discounts for bulk purchases for sales promotions or premiums. Special editions, including personalized covers, excerpts of existing books, and corporate imprints, can be created in large quantities for special needs. For more information, write to Special Markets/Premium Sales, 1745 Broadway, MD 3-1, New York, NY 10019, or e-mail specialmarkets@randomhouse.com.

AN IMPORTANT TIP & AN INVITATION

Although all prices, opening times, and other details in this book are based on information supplied to us at press time, changes occur all the time in the travel world, and Fodor's cannot accept responsibility for facts that become outdated or for inadvertent errors or omissions. So **always confirm information when it matters,** especially if you're making a detour to visit a specific place. Your experiences—positive and negative— matter to us. If we have missed or misstated something, **please write to us.** Share your opinion instantly through our online feedback center at fodors.com/contact-us.

PRINTED IN COLOMBIA

10 9 8 7 6 5 4 3 2

CONTENTS

MAPS

ABOUT THIS GUIDE

Fodor's Ratings

Everything in this guide is worth doing—we don't cover what isn't—but exceptional sights, hotels, and restaurants are recognized with additional accolades. Fodor's Choice ★ indicates our top recommendations; ★ highlights places we deem highly recommended. Care to nominate a new place? Visit Fodors.com/contact-us.

Trip Costs

We list prices wherever possible to help you budget well. Hotel and restaurant price categories from **$** to **$$$$** are noted alongside each recommendation. For hotels, we include the lowest cost of a standard double room in high season. For restaurants, we cite the average price of a main course at dinner or, if dinner isn't served, at lunch. For attractions, we always list adult admission fees; discounts are usually available for children, students, and senior citizens.

Hotels

Our local writers vet every hotel to recommend the best overnights in each price category, from budget to expensive. Unless otherwise specified, you can expect private bath, phone, and TV in your room. For expanded hotel reviews, facilities, and deals visit Fodors.com.

Restaurants

Unless we state otherwise, restaurants are open for lunch and dinner daily. We mention dress code only when there's a specific requirement and reservations only when they're essential or not accepted. To make restaurant reservations, visit Fodors.com.

Ratings

- ★ Fodor's Choice
- ★ Highly recommended
- 👶 Family-friendly

Listings

- ✉ Address
- ✉ Branch address
- ☎ Telephone
- 📠 Fax
- 🌐 Website
- 📧 E-mail
- 🎟 Admission fee
- 🕒 Open/closed times
- [M] Subway
- ✥ Directions or Map coordinates

Hotels & Restaurants

- 🏨 Hotel
- 🛏 Number of rooms
- 🍽 Meal plans
- 🍴 Restaurant
- ✍ Reservations
- 👔 Dress code
- 💳 Credit cards
- [$] Price

Other

- ⇨ See also
- ☞ Take note
- 🏌 Golf facilities

Credit Cards

The hotels and restaurants in this guide typically accept credit cards. If not, we'll say so.

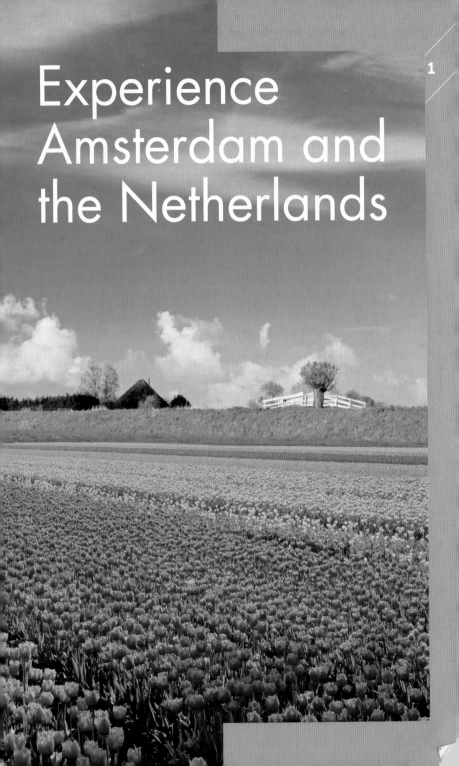

1

Experience Amsterdam and the Netherlands

AMSTERDAM TODAY

Welcome to Amsterdam! Built on a latticework of concentric canals like an aquatic rainbow, this remains the City of Canals—but Amsterdam is no Venice, content to live on moonlight serenades and former glory. While many images are imprinted on your consciousness even before you arrive—the gabled roofs of its mansions, the Rembrandts hypnotizing all viewers in the Rijksmuseum, the splendor of its 17th-century Golden Age—time does not stand still in this city. Indeed, there's an undercurrent of significant changes happening here that might not be immediately apparent. Ask the savvy locals and they will tell you that Amsterdam . . .

. . . is less red.

Or better said, the world's most nice-on-vice neighborhood is no fewer than 50 shades of red—and other Pantone swatches. Since 2007, when Amsterdam unveiled a plan to clean up its Red Light District, surveillance cameras began rolling 24/7, whole bordellos were bought out, and lights went down on a hundred prostitute windows (and counting). Meanwhile, in a move of gentrification par excellence, many spaces were turned over to studio-seeking artists and designers. Project 1012, named for the area's postal code, was initiated to counter rising rates of human trafficking and derivative forms of illegal ickiness. In so doing, the city's historic center was meant to return to "the people," though whether the creatives in residence fairly represent them is up for debate. Still, for inhabitants and visitors both, the de-sleazing efforts have made room for unique, unabashedly boho opportunities—vinyl-record shopping, bespoke pottery, courses for aspiring cordwainers, and wine tastings, to name a few.

. . . is more tasty.

Sex, scatology, assisted suicide: little is difficult for the Dutch to discuss. But to see an Amsterdammer go all awkward, you might raise the issue of dining. Up until a few years ago, besides the pre-theater brasserie deal or a few Indonesian and Surinamese establishments, a quality-seeker's best bet was a traditional brown café, akin to a pub. But there the meal would be formulaic: meat or fish, salad, fries. For such a pleasure-permissive city, how could a side of mayonnaise be the only opportunity for Burgundian indulgence? Clearly, others asked this, too. Today, food quality, variety of venues, and, yes, even the

WHAT'S NEW: WEED-WACKING

"Amster-damaged." "Good girls go to heaven, bad girls to Amsterdam." Slogans on gift-store T-shirts are testament that, more than anything else, the city's decadent reputation is a self-perpetuated industry largely fueled by tourism. While your average Dutchman wouldn't balk at a joint, theirs, in fact, is the last language you'll hear at one of the city's coffee shops, famed for their soft-drug use and sale. In 2012, legislation was drafted to prohibit *blowen* (smoking pot) in coffee shops if you're not a native Hollander.

The shut-down began with a rule enforcing the closure of all coffee shops located within 1,000 feet of a school, a particularly ominous proviso for Amsterdam, the country's most coffee shop–friendly city. By May 2012, the Limburg, North Brabant, and Zeeland provinces

historically depraved customer service all get an A for effort; many deserve at least a B for substance. Amsterdam currently counts nine Michelin-starred restaurants and hosts a twice-yearly restaurant week. National grocer Albert Heijn now has an eco-friendly Puur & Eerlijk ("pure & honest") line, and basic Dutch cable is proud of its very own food network. Not unrelatedly, gym culture is growing.

. . . is more comfy.

Not unlike the gastronomy sitch, Amsterdam's offerings for accommodations long lacked Goldilocksian middle ground. For luxury, you'd have to spend oodles of euros on a Dutch five star that would still charge for "extras" like gym use and Wi-Fi. For comfort, you'd settle on a ho-hum chain. Enter the boutique hotel. More and more of these small, stylish lodgings are appearing—and in prime spots. The design-catalog-worthy rooms are exciting enough, and their personable, polyglot hosts, Apple-inclined workstations, and organic breakfast spreads are definitely something to write home about.

. . . is less cushy.

Bezuiniging. Don't bother trying to say it; every Dutch person and their boss already does. This, by now soporific, word—a fancy term for "cuts"—has been uttered over and over to explain the butchering of budgets since late 2010. The conservative government that began the movement blamed global recession and the euro crisis. *Bezuiniging* has closed arts foundations, shrunk public broadcasters, caused small businesses to go bankrupt, and is responsible for many a hard-working do-gooder getting sacked.

. . . is more connected.

The Dutch will never not be ready to talk about the weather, but to really ignite conversation among Amsterdammers, try this: "Noord-Zuidlijn." Completion of the metro's latest addition is delayed till at least 2017 and is costing an extra €1.5 billion. Yet when ready, the 10 km (6 miles) spanning the hipster-happening borough of Noord and the chichifying Zuidas business hub will be but a 16-minute *poof!* On Tuesday through Sunday afternoons, you can check on the progress yourself at the city's underground observation station, the Uitkijkpunt (Rokin 92). Better mobility is happening, thanks to the improved tram network, the refillable swipe-n-go OV-chipkaart, and announcements in English at stops of main attractions.

began requiring coffee shops to become "members-only." Meaning? To purchase marijuana or hash, their customers had to hold a *wietpas.* Only catch? To get a "weed pass" you must be a Dutch resident. On January 1, 2013, it was decided this regulation would take effect for all 12 provinces, including North Holland, home to largely pro-pot Amsterdam. BUT. The wietpas experiment only caused more drug dealing on the streets, coffee shops the size of supermarkets, and enormous traffic jams. So, in October 2012 Amsterdam's New Labor/Liberal government canceled the wietpas, and the city will keep welcoming all visitors and will not deny tourists access to coffee shops. This also goes for the major towns of the Randstad, like Rotterdam and Haarlem.

WHAT'S WHERE

Numbers refer to chapter numbers.

2 **Amsterdam.** If only those 13th-century fishermen who decided to dam up the Amstel could see what became of their erstwhile marsh. It's the capital and spiritual "downtown" of a nation, where Gothic monuments interface with digital billboards and Golden Age drinking holes neighbor hip coffee shops. Wander just outside the city center and you'll find tree-lined canals, hidden courtyards, and wood-paneled cafés—a panoply of painting-perfect images.

7 **Day Trips.** How could you visit Holland and not trod through the tulip fields? Or take in some of the Netherlands' folkloric towns famous for their centuries-old wooden houses, fishing boats, and locals in traditional costume? This country is so manageably small, there's no excuse not to take a day trip from Amsterdam to visit a couple of countryside villages.

8 **The Randstad.** Rotterdam, The Hague, Haarlem, and Delft make up just a few of the towns and cities whose borders almost overlap each other, to such an extent that the entire region is now called the Randstad, or Border City, as locals consider it one

North Sea

IJmuiden

H

Lisse

Leiden

Den Haag
(The Hague) ✪

Hoek van
Holland

Delft

8

Rotterdam

Voorne

Overflakkee

Beijerland

Schouwen

Duiveland

Tholen

Noord
Beveland

Oosterschelde

Roosendaal

Walcheren

Bergen
op Zoom

Middelburg

Zuid
Beveland

Vlissingen

Westerschelde

Terneuzen

Antwerpen
(Antwerp)

0   20 miles

0   30 km

mammoth megalopolis. That, indeed, is true of Rotterdam, bombed to the ground in World War II, it has nevertheless become one of the world's busiest industrial ports, with a phenomenal skyline and a keepin'-it-real appreciation for the latest culture.

Over in The Hague, government, international courts, criminal tribunals, and embassy rows make their home, along with fabulous museums including the Mauritshuis, address of Vermeer's *Girl with a Pearl Earring*. The place has a buttoned-up nightlifelessness, so don't head here to party.

By contrast, the historically well-preserved Haarlem and Delft are sweet dollhouselike cities. It is just a short step from the ocean of annual color of "Die Bloemen Route" (The Flower Route) to a haven of perennial color, the city of Haarlem, the earliest center of Dutch art, where you'll find excellent Frans Hals and Teylers museums. Delft is a wonderland of tree-lined canals, humpbacked bridges, and step-gabled houses and preserves the atmosphere of Holland's Golden Age better than any other city in the country.

QUINTESSENTIAL AMSTERDAM

Canals

Amsterdam's canals are constant reminders that man—or the Dutch, anyway—can control nature and actually make a nice life off it. More than 97 km (60 miles) of canals, 400 stone bridges, and 90 islands have been created since the 17th century. Today, the *Grachtengordel* is a UNESCO World Heritage Site, not to mention prime real estate. On days with even the slightest sun, cafés with canalside seating become a game of musical chairs. In warmish weather, the waterways truly come to life, as locals hop in their boats, taking anyone and anything normally welcome in their living room for a riparian wine-and-cheese soiree. Once associated with 1970s antiestablishment types, houseboats are increasingly a more affordable option for domicile-desperate locals, as well as visitors seeking quaint lodging (and not minding unpredictable plumbing).

Gezelligheid

If you listen carefully to local speech and detect what sounds like a mild throat clearing, no doubt you're hearing one of the most cherished words in Lowlands parlance—*gezellig*. The term is frequently translated as "cozy," though anyone who has had the chance to experience Dutch *gezelligheid* ("coziness") will confirm that cozy doesn't quite cut it. From the word *gezel* meaning "mate," gezelligheid quite literally refers to the general conviviality of a place or a person.

Even if you don't have the chance to snuggle up on an Amsterdammer's couch, you can still witness signs of the spirit in lingering café conversations, those unsolicited cookies alongside your coffee, little lights along the canals at night, and house cats meowing out the window.

According to 19th-century French writer Joris-Karl Huysmans, Amsterdam is "a dream, an orgy of houses and water." More than 100 years later, that's true, though one might venture to say the orgy's components have expanded.

Tolerance

"Tolerance" has long been a buzzword of the historical live-and-let-live approach to governance in the Netherlands. The nation as a whole has been seen as liberal and left-leaning, though "tolerate" is a simplistic translation for the Dutch verb *gedogen*, which suggests something more like "turn a blind eye to." Problems are increasingly zoned to their own neighborhoods (e.g. prostitutes) or regulated (e.g. pot). One famous Amsterdammer notorious for refusing to sugarcoat anything he found intolerable, notably organized religion, was filmmaker Theo van Gogh. In 2003, he was brutally murdered by a fellow Dutchman associated with a home-grown Islamic terrorist group. To many, the event marked a cataclysmic shift in the tides of so-called tolerance. So while a progressive paradise compared with many other places, the Netherlands today is warier than ever.

Vices

Although their heyday has faded, cannabis and call girls are still relatively plentiful, professionalized, and, most remarkably, permitted. But this open society does, however, have protocol apropos. First, use with caution. Don't consume more marijuana or hash than you can handle, whether smoked or ingested in the form of a "space cake" (a pot brownie).

Likewise, legally employed, tax-paying prostitutes are likely to insist on condom use but, if they do not, you should. Second, do not take photos. Doing so while socializing with prostitutes could result in your being literally kicked to the curb, if not by your subjects than by their surveillant superiors. Vice visitors are advised to check for the latest updates, per city, on evolving legislation, althought the 2012 laws still permit the purchase of soft drugs.

AMSTERDAM
TOP ATTRACTIONS

Albert Cuypmarkt

(A) Check out the city's most popular market as much for its vibrant, varied products as for the multicultural, pan-capitalist production. Since 1905, Albert Cuypstraat has hosted the now 300+ cluster of stalls and stores behind them, selling everything from fresh-cut flowers and hot-off-the-griddle *stroopwafels* (honey-filled wafers) to Tupac T-shirts and Moroccan wedding dresses.

Amsterdam Museum

Though given relatively little marquee space, this is one of the best museums in which to invest your time and attention. Amsterdam's history is engagingly displayed all under one roof, from medieval times until the Golden Age, through the radical '60s up to life in the current millennium.

Anne Frankhuis

(B) Not only is this the home of the most widely read Dutch author, but the setting of her famous book. Some might be too haunted by the story's tragic ending to relish a visit, but many can appreciate the foundation's efforts to raise awareness about Europe's anti-Semitic past and discrimination everywhere.

Begijnhof

(C) The city's most famous *hofje* (small courtyard) was established in the 14th century for vow-taking religious women known as beguines. A community of spiritually devout women still inhabits the surrounding homes today, sharing their neat little space with two churches, a famously old wooden house from the early 1500s, and tourists seeking a quadrant of quiet.

Canal Cruise

No visit is complete without gliding along the 97 km (60 miles) of canal that concentrically ring around Amsterdam. For a

standard hourlong daytime cruise, simply walk up to any one of the various boating companies docked in the city center. Inquire further to arrange a private tour, a candle-lit dinner cruise, or any number of special themed sails.

Heineken Experience

(D) The most obvious enthusiasts here are young gents traveling (or stumbling) in groups, but the Heineken Experience has been suitable for the entire family ever since on-site brewing stopped in 1988. Learn the brand's history, observe beer being made, lose yourself in the 4-D film, and of course, taste-test.

Hermitage Amsterdam

(E) Since its grand reopening in 2009, the Hermitage Amsterdam has had lines out the door and acclaim audible almost all the way to St. Petersburg. This largest dependency of the famous Russian museum has two permanent presentations

detailing its own historic premises, while also hosting a splendid rotation of art.

Rijksmuseum

(F) With a €374 million renovation project rounding off in spring 2013, the state museum, as its name means, is just revving up to show visitors—in a brand new light—7,500 artworks from its 900,000-piece permanent collection. Rembrandt's *The Night Watch* and *The Kitchen Maid* by Vermeer are but a couple.

Van Gogh Museum

Two hundred paintings, 500 drawings, and 750 letters by the post-Impressionist make the Van Gogh Museum an imperative stop for even the merely cocktail-conversant among art appreciators. Though for *The Starry Night* you'll have to hit the MoMA in New Amsterdam, stellar masterpieces abound (as do their souvenir posters and umbrellas).

NETHERLANDS TOP ATTRACTIONS

Delfshaven, Rotterdam

(A) What better way to appreciate Rotterdam's uniquely modern silhouette than by spending time in the one district spared from World War II bombing and the city's subsequent reconstruction? Situated along the River Maas, Delfshaven is a favorite neighborhood among locals and visitors for its easygoing, twinkle-lit entertainment.

Delft

(B) It doesn't get any Dutcher than Delft. This picturesque city, Vermeer's hometown nestled between The Hague and Rotterdam, is famous for its signature blue-and-white pottery. The last remaining Delftware factory of the 32 once in operation, De Koninklijke Porceleyne Fles, is still flourishing, as it has since it was established in 1653.

Escher in Het Paleis Museum, The Hague

(C) Superbly repurposed, this former queen's palace is now a museum devoted to the Dutch graphic artist M. C. Escher. Besides the exhaustive collection of his paintings and prints, you'll be treated to thoughtfully curated biographical material and an interactive exhibition of various optical illusions starring none other than you.Kröller-Müller Museum, Otterlo

The Keukenhof Park, Lisse

(D) One of the largest open-air flower exhibitions in the world, the Keukenhof park is most famed for its 7 million tulips, which draw huge crowds when they bloom here every spring. Some of the planting is of the rather gaudy tulip varieties, but there's no holding back on the bulb-buying opportunities.

Kröller-Müller Museum, Otterlo

(E) Located in the Hoge Veluwe National Park in the province of Gelderland, the Kröller-Müller may have the most fantastic museum backyard on the Continent. Yet its contents are even more impressive; the world's second-largest Van Gogh collection hangs alongside Picassos, Gauguins, Mondrians, and Seurats.

The Storybook Holland Towns

(F) Hans Brinker would have no problem walking into any of the Storybook Holland towns—Volendam, Market, Monnickendam, or Broek-in-Waterland—and fitting right in. Set with cobblestone streets paved with nostalgia and punctuated with curiosity shops and postcard-pretty harbors, each of these villages is an open-air museum, an invitation to explore the Holland of your dreams.

Mauritshuis, The Hague

(G) Expansion and renovation are expected to keep the Mauritshuis closed until mid-2014, though during that time one hundred of that museum's best Rembrandts, Rubens, Vermeers, and Holbeins will be on view at the nearby Gemeentemuseum.

Frans Hals Museum, Haarlem

(H) Many consider this Golden Age 17th-century artist to be the first modern painter. A fantastically adept and naturally gifted man, he could turn out a portrait in an hour, and each captured the emotions of a moment, a smile or a grimace, in a sort of proto-Impressionism.

Museumpark, Rotterdam

Beginning in 1994, celebri-techt Rem Koolhaas (a native Rotterdammer himself) transformed it into a swath of tree-happy green connecting the Netherlands Architecture Institute, Kunstal, the Chabot, the Natural History, and the Boijmans van Beuningen Museum.

AMSTERDAM WITH KIDS

For each racy adult attraction Amsterdam offers, there's another dozen that deserve a PG (Pure Goodness) mark to entice the entire family. It's not for nothing that UNICEF identified Dutch children as the most fortunate in the world. Alongside exceptional infant care and happy dairy cows, the peaceful, open-minded society produces chill parents who tend to raise remarkably well-adjusted little ones. Here are tips on what to do with your own.

Um, Museums? Yes!

Some cultural catchalls are exceptionally child-friendly: the Rijksmuseum offers special audio tours for 6- to 12-year-olds, and the Amsterdam Museum recently opened Het Kleine Weeshuis, a wing recreating life in a 17th-century orphanage, geared toward 4- to 10-year-olds. But if the olden days bore them, go find NEMO. The Netherlands' biggest science center is sure to entertain and educate multiple generations with five floors of clever exhibits and live demos, plus, from the pitched roof deck, a spectacular view of city and shore. If that view stirs the nascent mariner within, visit the newly renovated Scheepvartmuseum, 500 years of Dutch naval history, with everything from sea-battle paintings and old-fashioned sailing compasses to a walk-in whale and a replica of the *Amsterdam*, a Dutch East India Company 18th-century cargo ship.

Where the Wild Things Are

Compared with other metropolitan zoos, Artis is small, but the animal-sensitive surroundings represent the sensibilities of the first country to elect an animal-rights party to Parliament. From apes to zebras, all the major species are present, plus there are regular sea lion shows, butterfly expos, and spectacular (read: slightly gruesome) feeding sessions. Your ticket will also grant you entrance next door to the planetarium and the not-to-be-missed aquarium.

For those with shorter attention spans, various neighborhoods have free public petting zoos. At the local *kinderboerderij*, kids not only rub elbows with farm animals but are often allowed to bottle-feed them. If your fellow travelers wish to find their own bottle, Kinderboerderij de Pijp (⊕ *www.kinderboerderijdepijp.nl*), open weekdays 11–5 and weekends 1–5, is a stone's throw from the champagne bar atop the Okura Hotel.

To Tucker Them Out

If little ones want to swim, public pools are open year-round and don't require a membership. The Zuiderbad on Museumplein is a local favorite, while the Brediusbad in Westerpark has an outdoor pool in summer. Rather stay dry? Tun Fun (⊕ *www.tunfun.nl*) is a giant indoor playground with mega-slides, ball pools, inflatable bouncers, and laser games.

Meanwhile, the restaurant quiets adults with espresso and Wi-Fi. With no mountains to speak of, the Netherlands has some avid climbing clubs. Klimmuur Amsterdam (⊕ *www.deklimmuur.nl*), which caters to first-timers, boasts its own kids' climbing club. Prefer to stay grounded? Monday through Saturday before 5, those 15 or younger are welcome to strike out at Knijn Bowling (⊕ *www.knijnbowling.nl*).

Last but not least, soccer lovers won't want to miss a World of Ajax tour (⊕ *www.amsterdamarena.nl*) through the city's famous *voetbol* stadium.

FREE OR ALMOST FREE

Regardless of the fluctuating dollar-to-euro exchange rate, the Netherlands is an expensive country to visit. Besides flowers, cheese, and wine, everything seems pricier in Amsterdam than in an American city. Here, though, are some cost-free exceptions.

Music to the Ears

Give your ears a free tune-up at one of the many free lunchtime concerts scheduled during the cultural season (which is generally considered year-round minus July and August).

Classical performances are usually at 12:30 on Tuesdays in the Muziktheater and the Muziekgebouw and on Wednesdays in the Concertgebouw.

Arrive a half hour early to guarantee your seat. Less in demand, though a no less lovely way to pass 30 minutes, the Conservatorium van Amsterdam and various churches also hold recitals for the public.

Cultural Collateral

Linger in the glassed-in corridor outside the Amsterdam Museum (entrance at Kalverstraat 92), known as the Schuttersgalerij, where the city's wealthy civic guards, peers of those in Rembrandt's *The Night Watch*, gaze down at you from 15 huge Golden Age paintings.

Even if you're not searching for your Dutch ancestors in its 35 km (20 miles) of records, the Amsterdam City Archives merits a visit.

A permanent exhibition of artifacts and ephemera documenting the city is displayed throughout the premises; the former bank is in itself worth the tour.

There's a modest €2.50 suggested donation for entrance to the Hollandsche Schouwburg, commemorating the 104,000 Dutch Jews who were killed in World War II.

The building was a popular theater, then became a Jewish deportation center, and a visit is a somber experience, albeit a salient way to learn about this dark chapter in Amsterdam's history.

Ferry Merry

A guided canal cruise is the finest way to appreciate Amsterdam's inner waterways, but to really ride a local's wave, hop on a free ferry behind Centraal Station.

Commuters shuttling between the city center and the borough of Noord rely on the three main lines, though the boats are open to anyone—pedestrian or cyclist—looking for a breezy, horizon-expanding cruise over the IJ (yes, that damnable diphthong of a name for the lake connecting the city to the North Sea).

The NDSM-Werfveer line offers the longest ride, 14 minutes, and leaves every 15 minutes on weekdays and every half hour on weekends. If time permits, do get off: this is a perfect chance to explore the rusty postindustrial bliss of NDSM Wharf, where creative offices and art studios neighbor old sea vessels, abandoned freight cars, and lifting equipment.

Free Spirit

Seeking a meditative moment? By day any of Amsterdam's public parks is ideal for a stretch or a stroll. The centrally located Vondelpark is a visitor's favorite (outfitted with its own Picasso sculpture), though Saphartipark in the Pijp has an impressive jungle gym for adults who like to exercise al fresco.

The city's man-made forest, the Amsterdamse Bos, is an oasis for cyclists, Nordic walkers, kayakers, and even some urban tent-toters.

BICYCLING IN AMSTERDAM

Join the "Rack Pack"

Stand at any intersection in any Dutch city and you're guaranteed to see bicycles. Getting around on two wheels has long made sense for Lowlanders. They're proud of their rep as frugal, efficient, sporty, and eco-conscious—qualities all embodied in and on a bike. That their country is flat and that petrol and parking are dear commodities also make the *fiets* a no-brainer.

Where does that leave you, footloose holidaymaker? It depends. Experienced cyclists will glide around Amsterdam, feeling they've died and gone to . . . Portland, Oregon. After all, bike lanes abound, motorists yield to cyclists, and trams are vigilant of the little guys who pedal. This just might be the place where you can satisfy that need for speed. Visitors with little to no metropolitan biking background, however, might think twice.

Steady Wins the Race

Getting stuck behind a swerving slowpoke can create problems: some speedy Amsterdammers lose their cool and forget their regular traffic obedience. If you're mounting a bike to help nurture that inner child who misses the joys of a banana seat, it might be best to work through that desire in a residential neighborhood, a park, or smaller town. But if you feel you're enough of a biking pro and want to go native, join the rest of the bike snobs who make up downtown Amsterdam's "rack pack." Slow? Fast? Actually, everyone knows that when it comes to city biking, steady wins the race. At any speed, you'll quickly realize that cycling in Amsterdam is, foremost, a means to easy mobility.

Renting Your Ride

Getting a bike in Amsterdam is even easier than getting on one. Tourist-friendly rental shops dot the city center. Walk in, have the shopkeeper size you, hand over a bit of collateral (usually a credit card or your passport plus €50), and you're ready to roll.

Although small shops are popping up, citywide chains MacBike and Yellow Bike have dominated the market for decades. Both are obvious choices for guided group tours within Amsterdam or its surrounds. A must-mention drawback is that both have prominent logos and crazy-bright-colored frames (Mac's in Betty Boop red, Yellow Bike's in . . . you guessed it), so everyone on the road will know you're an out-of-towner. Then again, riding around in what is essentially the equivalent of a Student Driver car might be prudent if you're a newbie. Approaching road-racers will know to exercise caution, though may also exercise their bell-ringing behind you. Prefer to go more incog? Rent from the all-around excellent chain Het Zwarte Fietsenplan. Staff are exceptionally amicable. And—should careening canal-side prove so delightful that you stay a while—new and secondhand bikes are sold here, too.

CONTACTS

Het Zwarte Fietsenplan Centrum ✉ *Nieuwezijds Voorburgwal 146* ☎ *020/670–8531* ✉ *Eerste Constantijn Huygensstraat 88* ☎ *020/412–1440* ✉ *Beethovenstraat 86* ☎ *020/670–8531* ✉ *Lijnbaansgracht 282, Amsterdam, North Holland, Netherlands* ☎ *020/670–8531* ⊕ *www.hetzwartefietsenplan.nl* ⊙ *Mon.–Fri. 8–8, weekends 10–6.*

MacBike Centraal Station Oost ✉ *Stationsplein 5* ☎ *020/624–8391* ⊕ *macbike.nl* ⊙ *Daily 9–5:45* ✉ *Weteringschans 2* ☎ *020/528–7688.*

Yellow Bike Nieuwezijds Kolk ✉ *Marnixstraat 220* ☎ *020/620-6940* ⊕ *www.*

yellowbike.nl ☾ *Sun.–Mon. 9:30–5 (later hours in the summer)* ✉ *Oudezijds Armsteeg 22.*

What to Wear

Although the Dutch are notoriously underdressed, what they—notably of the fairer sex—pull off wearing and bearing while cycling is impressive. Don't be surprised to see stilettos, panty-flashing miniskirts, full-on flowing Goth regalia, with dogs in handlebar baskets, *sundroffspring* straddled on child seats, plus an umbrella, iPhone, and/or dinner party-bound bouquet of flowers in hand or underarm. Let comfort guide your own cycling wardrobe choices, though note some pointers.

Basic rental bikes have back-pedal foot brakes, not hand brakes. Shoes with no heels whatsoever (canvas sneakers and ballerina flats, for instance) make it dangerously easy for your foot to slide off the pedal and lose control of your stop reflex.

Nothing like a pair of drawstring palazzos to get into that no-counting-calories vacation mode, right? And nothing like billowy pants cuffs to get caught in your bicycle chain! Ditto on sweats, flowing skirts, and dresses.

Chances are you will be precipitated on in the Netherlands. A fine idea is thus to pack water-resistant wear. Forgot it? Durable, affordable raingear can be bought at any branch of HEMA, the Dutch equivalent of Target.

Road Rules: Do

■ Hand-signal: extend right arm before turning right; vice-versa for left.

■ Ride in all available bike lanes (not amidst auto traffic or on sidewalks).

■ Beware of parked cars with doors swinging open.

LOOK, DAD! NO HANDS!

Kids from 7 months to 45 pounds can sit on a child's seat; those 6 and up might consider joining their keepers on a tandem bike.

■ Use bike lights in the dark; otherwise, face a ticket.

■ Lock your two-wheeler to something fixed; a bike rack is best.

Road Rules: Don't

■ Call, text, chat, or surf while cycling.

■ Blow a red light; otherwise, face a ticket.

■ Stop suddenly mid–bike lane.

■ Ring your bell unless an audible being dangerously obstructs your path.

■ Cycle if you're chemically impaired.

Bike Aboard!

Worry not. If you need to get to another section of the city or another town altogether—but don't want to pedal all the way there and back—there are options.

TO BRING A BIKE ON THE AMSTERDAM METRO:

Buy a supplementary €1.60 *fietskaartje* (bike ticket), enter the car with the blue circular bike logo, and look for the special hooks to which you affix your front wheel. If all designated spots are taken (not unlikely on a rainy day), stay in the same car, doing your best to stand with your bike. For more information, consult Amsterdam's transport authority (☎ *0900/8011* ⊕ *en.gvb.nl*).

TO BRING A BIKE ON A NATIONAL DUTCH TRAIN:

Buy a €6 *dagkaart fiets* (bike day card) and—so long as it's during off-peak hours (weekdays 7:30 pm–6:30 pm and 9 am–4 pm and weekends)—hop on.

OR NOT TO BRING A BIKE:

If glutes are groggy by the time you get to the train station, store your bike. You'll never need to look far for a rack to lock your bike cost-free. Larger stations offer a €5 daily locker service.

For more information, consult the Dutch railroad (☎ *0900/9292* ⊕ *www.ns.nl/en*).

Waterland-Ho!: A Great Bike Trip

If you're jonesin' for green, consider a bike ride in the nearby country. A mere five-minute sail from Centraal Station, Amsterdam Noord offers inhabitants—and visitors—quieter and roomier ways of the road with plenty of tree-lined waterways to keep the Zen in motion.

If you like your nature interspersed with a bit of folkloric kitsch, check out any or all of the 10 villages forming the region known as Waterland.

The former fishing communities graciously cater to tourists, with easy-to-navigate cycling paths.

Within a matter of meters, you can zoom—or laze—past polders and windmills, small wooden houses, and draw bridges, churches, and cafés.

A good point to begin your northern exposure is Buiksloterweg, which you can reach by the same-named ferry crossing the IJ every 12 minutes.

Best City Bike Trails

The Dutch touch is behind most nature in the Netherlands: along with their damming, sluicing, and poldering skills, turns out they're talented landscapers, too.

LIFE IS HARD, ROADS TOO!

No laws require bicyclists in the Netherlands to wear helmets. Should you seek one for yourself or your child, simply inquire at a rental shop. Yes, you will stick out, but peace of mind feels nicer than a concussion.

Amsterdam's man-made parks are oxygen-emitting testament to this, making for some very pleasant cycling. While locals frequent Vondelpark, Oosterpark, and Westerpark for jogs and picnics, a biker's best bet is the Amsterdamse Bos. The 80-year-old forest, also man-made, has 50 km (31 miles) of cycling paths that snake through Amsterdam's southern Buitenveldert neighborhood and the nearby suburb of Amstelveen.

Besides rentals, Fietsverhuur Amsterdamse Bos offers tips on navigating within the woods as well as routes to the city center and, if you ever wanted to ride along a plane runway, neighboring Schiphol Airport.

Planning Your Own Bike Trip

Map your trip in advance by consulting the Amsterdam Tourist Office (⊕ *www.vvvfietsrouteplanner.nl*) or visiting a route-planning website such as that of the Dutch Cyclist Union.

Their online service (⊕ *www.fietsersbond.nl/fietsrouteplanner*) not only maps out the most efficient way to pedal, but specifies how many calories a ride burns and how much CO_2 is saved by taking two wheels instead of four.

AMSTERDAM FAQS

What's the best way to pay for things?
The Netherlands is notoriously credit card–phobic, with locals using their European bank–issued debit cards to pay even for a cup of coffee.

While larger establishments will accept your Visa (and sometimes other major credit cards), to avoid surcharges, cash is your safest bet. Either come with bills or use your bank card to take out a lump sum at a compatible ATM. Don't expect small shops or restaurants to accept your €100 or €500 bills (best to change them at the airport) and pocket at least a euro's worth in coins to pay your entrance into public restrooms.

How should I dress?
Anything goes in Amsterdam. OK, the most uppity of restaurants might cater to a sport coat and high-heeled clientele, and some of the more hair gel–prone dance clubs have a no-sneakers policy, but sartorial rules are nearly nil.

After all, jeans are worn to the opera, drag to the grocery store, and butt cracks regularly peekaboo from bike seats. If you want to fit in, be yourself—individualism is far more fashionable than any monogram—and pack rain gear.

What's the difference between Holland and the Netherlands?
The Netherlands is the country's official name. Holland is its colloquial, albeit erroneous, appellation that metonymically refers to North Holland, the province in which Amsterdam is located.

Can I get around without a bike?
All major cities in the Netherlands have an efficient tram-and-bus network, and Amsterdam has an ever-expanding metro system. Taxis are more expensive, but worth taking if you're walking-impaired,

traveling in a group, or a state of mind too altered to read a map.

Can I have fun without being high?
If you like art, cycling, scenic water views, a lively café culture, paid sex, and/or beer, yes.

But if you choose to experience part of your trip in a haze, remember to purchase any soft drugs in controlled zones: selling or purchasing on the street is illegal and punishable.

While softness may stymie some hired services, note that when it comes to drugs, hard is forbidden—so be sure to say *Nee* to cocaine, ecstasy, heroin, etc.

Will our children be exposed to sleaze left and right?
No. Amsterdam is far more Mother Goose than *Kama Sutra*. If you need to shield impressionable eyes, however, it's best to avoid the Red Light District, where bikinied prostitutes are on display alongside graphically merchandised sex shops and live sex-show marquees.

A warning, too, about late-night channel surfing: topless telephone-sex operators get more air time than Leno or Letterman.

When will those endless museum renovations ever get finished?
Happily, the mecca of modern art in Amsterdam—the Stedelijk Museum—unveiled their spectacular renovation in the Fall of 2012, right on time. Unhappily, the renovation at the top museum—the Rijksmuseum—was so major that another delay was announced: they will now open their doors in April 2013 (months after we went to press). Our write-up has the main aspects of their exciting refurbishment, but many of the details will need to be discovered on your visit.

GREAT ITINERARIES

AMSTERDAM, HAARLEM, DE HOGE VELUWE, DELTA WORKS, THE HAGUE, AND SCHEVENINGEN

Day 1: Canal-crawling in Amsterdam

Make your first acquaintance with Amsterdam in the garden-themed Jordaan, with its perfectly arced canals, hidden courtyards, and politely moored houseboats.

Begin your journey on the corner of Raadhuisstraat and Prinsengracht. If you don't mind a quick cardio workout, climb to the top of the 279-foot Westerkerk tower, which offers a sublime view of the city.

Whether on foot or wheels, continue your canal crawl northward, peeking into artists' galleries, antiques stores, and clothing boutiques. Work up your appetite for a satellite dish–size pancake at the Pancake Bakery.

And when it's time to turn those bike lights on, make your way to the buzz of Leidseplein. For concerts and dancing to your favorite decade, head to Paradiso or Melkweg, or listen to live riffs at Jazz Café Alto. Conclude with a nightcap in the Art Deco dining room of the American Hotel.

Day 2: Pedaling to Haarlem

With Amsterdam's Haarlemmerplein as your starting point, hop on the bike path and forge westward to the metropolis for which the square is named. The approximately 19-km (12-mile) ride to Haarlem is one super-Dutch sight after another: a medieval dike, a windmill, a steam-pumping station-turned-museum, an old sugar mill, sand dunes, and little towns in between.

By the time you spot the tower of Haarlem's Town Hall, get ready to dismount—a stroll is in order. The city is renowned for its elegant square, church organs played by Haydn and Mozart, and the nation's oldest museum.

If *zadelpijn* (sore butt) has set in, you and your bike can always take the train back to Amsterdam.

Day 3: Cycling and Cubism in De Hoge Veluwe

Now that you've had a taste of Dutch urban life, get ready for a whiff of nature. Keep in mind, though, that most scenes of green in the Netherlands are the work of man. Years spent tweaking dams, dikes, and polders have made the Lowlands an inhabitable landscape today.

De Hoge Veluwe, in the province of Gelderland, is the finest the country has to offer by way of a national park. Plus, it provides free bikes for navigating modest hills and dips through 13,590 acres of woodlands, plains, heather fields, and sand drifts. Besides the fellow sentient beings zooming by on shiny white two-wheelers, you might spot a wild boar or sheep.

After getting your cardio for the day, make your way to the Kröller-Müller Museum, which has a serious collection of Picassos, Mondriaans, and Seurats, as well as a superb sculpture garden to which Rodin is no stranger.

Logistics: Once within the park, the distance to the museum depends on your starting point: 2½ km (1½ miles) from the Otterlo entrance, 4 km (2½ miles) from Hoenderloo, and a little more than 10 km (6 miles) from Schaarsbergen.

Day 4: Cruising Along the Afsluitdijk

Trade in your bike for something motorized and take the scenic route southward to witness a sublime example of technology trumping nature.

The Delta Works is a massive dam and flood barrier—24-foot-high banks stretch 20 miles (32 km) along the A7 motorway. Give yourself at least a kilometer to get used to driving on the concrete tendril engulfed by blue. On your right, you'll see the North Sea's inlet, known as the Zuiderzee, while to your left, fishermen bespeckle the freshwater banks of the IJselmeer.

Logistics: Budget and Avis have convenient locations in Amsterdam and throughout the country. You can also join a group tour by visiting almost any tourist information center.

Day 5: Museum-Hopping in The Hague

No one will try to convince you otherwise if your impression of The Hague is that of super sobriety—what with all the royalty, diplomats, international judges, and civil servants running around. But don't forget that the Count's Hedge (as the city's official Dutch name actually means) also does justice to arts and culture.

The Gemeetemuseum holds the most Mondriaans under one roof (and currently masterpieces from the under-renovation Mauritshuis) and the Escher Museum is, in a word, awesome.

For when you get peckish, there's a veritable embassy row's worth of eateries, from kiddie menu–friendly Dutch cafés to posh hotel dining rooms, and one of the most prominent Chinatowns in the country. The Hague's Indonesian restaurants are said to be hemisphere-altering.

A FEW TIPS

Even if you're new on two wheels, biking the car-free Hoge Veluwe is relaxing. Until January 2014, more than 30 pieces from the Mauritshuis collection—including *Girl with a Pearl Earring*—will be on a U.S. tour. That's a reminder that if your heart is set on seeing a particular artwork, first check that it's in house.

Day 6: Sun and Fun in Scheveningen

Once you've had your fill of The Hague's manicured gardens and stately buildings, take a side trip to Scheveningen, the Netherlands' most popular esplanade. Restaurants, clubs, casinos, bungee jumps, ice cream stands, and trinket shops create an almost American ethos, though dip into the frigid waters of the North Sea and you'll be quickly reminded that the Jersey Shore is far away.

Logistics: For optimum safety and security, park your car in one of Scheveningen's public garages or open car parks.

BEATING THE EURO

To go Dutch is a native practice indeed, but don't think your host country will be footing half your vacation bills. The Netherlands is an expensive place to visit. Here, however, are ways to save.

Travel Off-Season

To save on airfare, book your trip in the fall or winter (except around Christmas) when neither tulips nor tourism are abloom.

Lodge Like a Local

You may well find many Dutch hotels to be overpriced and underwhelming. If you're used to American luxury, be ready to recalibrate your rating system by at least one star, meaning a five-star Amsterdam hotel feels more like a New York City four-star, and even fancy suites tend to be space challenged. Particularly if you're staying over two nights, consider a more affordable, more personal short-term apartment rental. While you're at it, go for that canalside home or houseboat you've always dreamed of.

Move Like a Local

If your hotel is away from the city center or you plan to cover lots of ground, rent a bike. Visitors less comfortable on two wheels should take public transportation. If you plan to ride more than once, buy a refillable OV-chipkaart.

Self-Hydrate

For a country that's spent centuries diking and damming, getting a drink of water should be no biggie, right? Think again. To prevent an extra €2 (or more) from being added to your restaurant tab, be sure to ask specifically for *glaasje kraanwater* ("a glass of tap water"). Some ignoble establishments will refuse, but if you find a compassionate server, a small (even shot-size!) glass of lukewarm liquidity will appear. In any case, BYO H2O in your travel bag.

Cultural Cost-Cutting

The electronic I amsterdam Card provides free or discounted admissions to many of Amsterdam's top museums, a free canal cruise, unlimited public transport use, and 25% off lots of star-turn attractions and restaurants. A one-day pass costs €40, a two-day costs €50, and a three-day costs €60. It can be purchased at the Netherlands Board of Tourism & Conventions at Schiphol Airport's Arrivals Hall 2, the Centraal Station branch of the Netherlands Board of Tourism (VVV), various City Transport Company (GVB) points, at some hotels and museums, and online (⊕ *www.iamsterdamcard.com*). The Last Minute Ticket Shop offers tickets for comedy clubs, the ballet, opera, symphony, and theater at a 50% discount. Though you must make your purchase on performance day in person at the office, you can preview the daily selection online (⊕ *www.lastminuteticketshop.nl*). Sales begin at noon.

If you travel to the Netherlands frequently or plan on visiting several museums within a year's time, consider investing in a *Museumkaart* (museum card). This gives you 365 days of free entry to more than 440 museums nationwide. It can be purchased at participating museums and online (⊕ *www.museumkaart.nl*) for €44.95 or, if you're under 25, for €22.50.

CONTACTS

Last Minute Ticket Shop Centraal Station
✉ *Stationsplein 10, Amsterdam, Netherlands* ☎ *020/201–8800* ⊕ *www.vvv.nl* ◷ *Mon.–Sat. 9–7, Sun. 9–5* ✉ *Leidseplein 26, Amsterdam, Netherlands* ⊕ *www.amsterdamsuitburo.nl* ◷ *Mon.–Sat. 10–6, Sun. 12–6.*

Exploring Amsterdam

WORD OF MOUTH

"We sat at a table outside, in Amsterdam, next to a canal—how could it get any better?"

—T4TX

"It took me a day or so to gauge the rhythm of the place, but when you start to harmonize, it's a supremely well-balanced way of life."

—Fashionista

WELCOME TO AMSTERDAM

TOP REASONS TO GO

★ **Golden Age Canals:**
This is a city you have to get to know from the water in order to be properly introduced, so hop aboard one of those glass-roof boats that tour the city's 17th-century canals to glide past gabled mansions or under bridges twinkling with fairy lights at night.

★ **Those Hidden Hofjes:**
Head to the Begijnhof to feel the gentle breeze of history in the solitude of a serene courtyard (*hofje*) that has hardly changed since the Pilgrim Fathers worshipped here five centuries ago.

★ **Rembrandt & Company:** For a giant gasp of Golden Age glory, explore the Rijksmuseum, home to hundreds of famed Dutch Old Masters, including Rembrandt's legendary *The Night Watch*.

★ **Two Wheels Good:**
Trundling through the Jordaan district on a sit-up-and-beg Dutch bike, with narrow alleys on one side, leafy canals on the other, with the wind in your hair, is transporting in more ways than one.

1 **The Old City Center.**
Heritage mixes with hustle here, as church towers soar above medieval defenses, and in the center, the infamous Red Light District.

2 **The Waterfront.** Across the IJ and along the water, a shiny, new Amsterdam is emerging.

3 **The Canal Ring.** Amsterdam at its most "viewtiful," this is the Golden Age city of beautiful waterways and 17th-century mansions.

4 **Jordaan and the Leidseplein.** Eat, drink, and sing in neighborly Jordaan or party in nightlife HQ Leidseplein.

5 **Museum District.**
Amsterdam's culture zone where high heels clack down the PC Hooftstraat for luxury retail relief.

6 **De Pijp.** An arty, bohemian, global village where you can taste a multitude of multicultural treats.

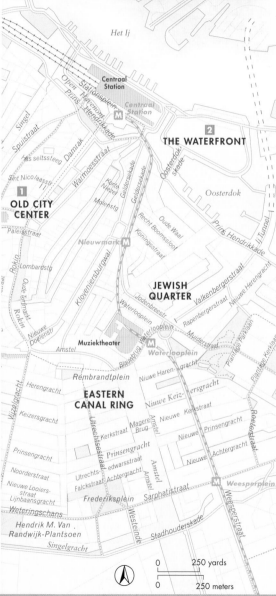

GETTING ORIENTED

Once understood that there are no straight lines in central Amsterdam, you'll find it to be an easy city to navigate (or purposely get lost in). For starters it is teeny. Think of it as an onion with Centraal Station as the stem and the city folding out as layers, each on a somewhat circular path under the guidance of the Canal Ring. To stay oriented, just follow each onion layer around. We seriously advise you to do your exploring with map in hand. The concentrically circular nature of the city's layout makes it terribly easy to unwittingly walk in exactly the opposite direction from the one you thought you were heading. To stay safe, always watch out for bikes and trams. Keep off the bike paths, which are well paved and often mistaken for sidewalks. Bikers have the right-of-way, so if you hear a bell, move quickly. Trams function similarly, and will also ring their bell before they move. Just look both ways, and look both ways again before crossing streets.

Updated by Floris Dogterom

Perhaps Amsterdam's greatest charm is also its greatest enigma: How can such a gracious cultural center with an incomparable romance also multitask as the most offbeat metropolis in the world?

Built on a latticework of concentric canals like an aquatic rainbow, this remains the City of Canals—but Amsterdam is no Venice, content to live on moonlight serenades and former glory. Rather, on nearly every street you'll find old and new side by side: quiet corners where time seems to be holding its breath next to neon-lit Kalverstraat, Red Light ladies strutting under the city's oldest church.

Indeed, Amsterdam has as many facets as a 40-carat diamond polished by one of the city's gem cutters, from the capital, and spiritual "downtown," of a nation ingrained with the principles of tolerance to a veritable Babylon of old-world charm. While impressive gabled houses bear witness to the Golden Age of the 17th century, their upside-down reflections in the city's canal waters below symbolize and magnify the contradictions within the broader Dutch society.

With a mere 730,000 friendly souls, 179 nationalities, and with almost everything a scant 10-minute bike ride away, Amsterdam is actually more of a village—albeit a largish global one—that happens to pack the cultural wallop of a megalopolis. There are scores of concerts every day, numerous museums, summertime festivals, and a legendary party scene. It's vibrant, but not static (which is why the entry of the Grachtengordel canal ring into the UNESCO World Heritage Site list has not been greeted with universal joy). The city is making concerted efforts to broaden its appeal with initiatives like Project 1012, which aims to diversify the economy of the Red Light District. Just like construction in the rest of the city, Project 1012 is a work in progress, but there is light at the end of the tunnel. The scaffolding has come down around Museumplein, and new architectural landmarks, such as the EYE Film Institute across the IJ, are up.

Despite the disruptions, it's impossible to resist Amsterdam's charms. The French writer J-K Huysmans fell under its spell when he called Amsterdam "a dream, an orgy of houses and water."

So true: the city of Amsterdam, when compared with other major European cities, is uniquely defined by its houses—not by palaces, estates, and other aristocratic folderol. With 7,000 registered monuments, most of which began as the residences and warehouses of humble merchants, set on 160 man-made canals (stretching 75 km [50 miles]), and traversed by 1,500 or so bridges, Amsterdam has the largest historical inner city in Europe. Its famous circle of waterways, the Grachtengordel, is a 17th-century urban expansion plan for the rich and a lasting testament to the city's Golden Age, the 17th century.

REMBRANDT TO ROCK-N-ROLL

If we often take stereotypes with a grain of salt, in the case of Amsterdam, believe them; but at the same time, we need to remember that there's so much more. To find the "more," one must be deliberate in planning explorations; otherwise some visitors may find themselves looping back—as have sailors for centuries—to the city's gravitational center, the Red Light District. After all, as a visitor you are hopefully here, at least partly, to unburden yourself of some misconceptions. Certainly this town is endearing because of its kinder, gentler nature—but a reputation for championing sex, drugs, and rock 'n' roll cannot alone account for Amsterdam's being the fourth most popular destination in Europe (after London, Paris, and Rome).

Carrying far greater weight—cultural, moral, social—is the fact that within a single square mile the city harbors some of the greatest achievements in Western art. Is there a conscious inmate of our planet who doesn't revere Rembrandt, who doesn't love Van Gogh?

THE JOY IS IN THE DETAIL

Just remember as you tour all the must-sees that Amsterdam is such a great walking city because so many of its real treasures are untouted details: tiny alleyways barely visible on the map, hidden garden courtyards, shop windows, sudden vistas of church spires and gabled roofs that look like so many unframed paintings.

And don't forget that the joy is in the detail: elaborate gables and witty gable stones denoting the trade of a previous owner, floating houseboats and hidden *hofjes* (courtyards with almshouses).

Before tying on your weatherproof shoes, go efficiently local by toting an umbrella, for Amsterdam has a propensity toward sudden bursts of rain. A cloudy day should inspire a more lingering exploration of the Museum District, rich with other cultural refugees from rain.

Chances are you'll be rewarded with a sunny late afternoon and your walk along the Prinsegracht canal will shine at this time with the kind of glow you witnessed earlier that day in a Golden Age painting at the Rijksmuseum. With any luck, your best photo-op will probably wind up being a sidewalk artist putting the finishing touch on his version of Vermeer's *Milk Maid*.

PLANNING

WHEN TO GO

There's no bad time to visit Amsterdam, but there are two big seasons. Tulip time is mid-March to mid-May, when the global rush to the bulb fields is matched by a springtime surge in hotel bookings and the line for the Anne Frank House. It is also bustling in the summer months when there's an enormous variety of cultural events and festivals. Queen's Day (April 30) and Museum Night (first week in November) are worth visits in their own right. Take advantage of Tulip Days (third weekend in April), Open Garden Days (third weekend in June), and Open Monument Day (second weekend in September) for seeing heritage properties and some extraordinary gardens rarely open to the public.

HOW'S THE WEATHER?

Amsterdam is only 7 feet above sea level, so the city is always a little damp. There is high humidity in the summer and a fair amount of rain, especially in the winter, but, moisture aside, Amsterdam's weather is ultimately comfortable. The temperatures are rarely extreme, and there are lots of balmy days, especially in June, July, and August. November to April is overcast and windy with a bit of snow and ice around the New Year.

Whatever the weather, it doesn't hang about for long, so plan for every eventuality. Wear layers to put on or take off, have sturdy shoes for your explorations on foot, and bring a good umbrella.

GETTING AROUND

The best way to see Amsterdam is by bike or on foot, but the city's public transport system, GVB, is extremely reliable. It operates the buses, trams, metro, and ferries with service 24 hours a day. The ticket system used is the OV-chipkaart, a credit-card-size smart card that you use to check in and out of the transport network. There are GVB one-day or multiday versions, but if there's a sudden deluge you can leap on a tram or bus and pay on board—you'll receive a disposable ticket valid for an hour—although it's the least value-for-money option. For discounted travel (ages 4–11, 65+, student), you need to buy a personalized card with a photo that you load with credit. There's a one-off fee (about the same as a one-day pass to Amsterdam) for this card.

WATER TAXIS

A bright yellow water taxi provides a novel, if expensive, means of getting about, but the price is per trip, not per person, so the cost can be split amongst a group (each boat carries up to eight people). The cost is €1.75 per minute within the center, with a pickup charge of €7.50. Centraal Station (west side—look for the Rederij Lovers landing stage) to the Anne Frank House, for example, takes 15 minutes. There are landing stages throughout the city where you might find one waiting, or you can book by telephone.

Contact **Water Taxi** ☎ 06/41230005 ⊕ www.water-taxi.nl.

HOURS OF OPERATION

Restaurants are usually open evenings 6–11, although some kitchens close as early as 10, and many are closed on Sunday or Monday.

Queen's Day (the Queen's birthday), Amsterdam's biggest street party, happens every year on April 30.

Major sights, such as Amsterdam's Koninklijk Paleis (Royal Dam Palace) have summer opening hours; some parks are open dawn to dusk, others 24/7; the scenic courtyard hofjes are usually open at the discretion of the inhabitants.

Museum hours vary; to give some instances, the city's famous Van Gogh museum is open 10–6 (and on Friday, 10–10), and the Anne Frank House is open 9–9 mid-March–mid-September (Saturday, 9–10) and until 10 in July and August, and 9–7 mid-September–mid-March (Saturday, 9–9).

Note that when this book refers to summer hours, it means approximately Easter (between March 22 and April 25) to October; winter hours run from November to Easter.

MONEY-SAVING TIPS

The **I amsterdam City Card** provides free and discount admissions to many of Amsterdam's top museums (but not the Anne Frank House), plus a free canal ride, free use of public transport, and a 25% discount on various attractions and restaurants; savings can be very substantial. A 24-hour pass costs €40, a 48-hour costs €50, and a 72-hour costs €60. The pass comes with a booklet in Dutch, English, French, German, Italian, and Spanish. It can be purchased at branches of the VVV (Netherlands Board of Tourism information offices), the GVB (both at Centraal Station), and through some hotels and museums.

If you are here for a few more days or intend to visit museums in other parts of the Netherlands, such as Haarlem, a *Museumkaart* (museum card) might offer better value. This gives you free entry to more than 440 museums throughout the country for a year, including the top draws in

AN EMBARRASMENT OF RICHES

Amsterdam's history as a commercial hub began in 1275, when Floris V, count of Holland, decreed that the fledgling settlement would be exempt from paying tolls. Consequently, the community, then called "Aemstelredamme," was soon taking in tons of beer from Hamburg, along with a lot of thirsty settlers. The beer profits opened up other fields of endeavor, and by the 17th century Amsterdam had become the richest and most powerful city in the world.

It had also produced the world's first-ever multinational company: the East India Company (VOC), which shipped spices, among other goods, between Asia and Europe. Amsterdam was, in Voltaire's words, "the storage depot of the world." While the rest of Europe still felt it necessary to uphold the medieval tags of "honor" and "heroism," Amsterdam had the luxury of focusing just on money—and the consequent liberty it created.

Amsterdam (except the Anne Frank House). It is available, upon showing ID, at VVV offices and participating museums for €44.95.

VISITOR INFORMATION

The VVV has several offices around Amsterdam. The office in Centraal Station is open daily 8–8; the one on Stationsplein, opposite Centraal Station, is open daily 9–5 (high season); on Leidseplein (ticket bureau), daily 10–7; and at Schiphol Airport, daily 7 am–10 pm. Stop by any of the offices for tour recommendations, maps, and calendars of events. The helpful staff can speak many languages. For a small fee, they can book hotel rooms or other accommodation. The rates change daily, and VVV gets details from the hotels every morning.

In the summer, there are also a few extra helpers outside Centraal Station and key tourist spots like the Museumplein who can help with basic inquiries and directions. Look for people wearing bright red T-shirts and caps with the I amsterdam logo.

Contact VVV—Netherlands Board of Tourism ⊠ *Stationsplein 10, Centraal Station* ⊕ *www.iamsterdam.com* ⊠ *AUB Ticketshop, Leidseplein 26(terrace-side), Leidseplein* ⊠ *Schiphol Airport, Arrivals 2 Building, Luchthaven Schiphol.*

2

THE OLD CITY CENTER: HET CENTRUM

A city with a split personality, Amsterdam is both a historic marvel and one of the most youthful metropolises in the world—and you'll get complete servings of both sides of the euro coin in this first, introductory tour.

In fact, a full blast of its two-faced persona will be yours simply by walking into Amsterdam's heart (if not soul): the Dam. For, as the very center of the Centrum, or center city, this gigantic square has hosted many singular sights: Anabaptists running nude in the name of religious freedom, the coronation of kings and queens, stoned hippies camping out under the shadow of its surrealistically phallic National Monument.

The Dam is just one showpiece of the western side of the historic center, known as the Nieuwe Zijde (New Side) and which occupies the district between Damrak (and its extension Rokin) and the Singel canal, just to the west of the sector known as the Oude Zijde (Old Side).

The Dam (Dam Square) remains a useful landmark bridging the older (east) and newer (west) sides of the Centrum. From here you can head off to worship naval heroes in the Nieuwe Kerk or, for some retail therapy, pop into the De Bijenkorf (which lives up to its name—the beehive—during big sales). The core of the oldest part of the city is Amsterdam's most famous area, the Red Light District, known locally as *de Wallen*, with the aptly named Oude Kerk, its oldest church, bang in the middle. Business in the two main canals and narrow alleyways leading off them is conducted against an implausibly scenic backdrop (porn emporiums and coffee shops at ground level, gables on the top) with atmospheric views from the bridges. (Although this is relative; there's no comparison with the non–Red Light District leafy environs of the southern sections of these same canals below the Damstraat). Its eastern perimeter is Zeedijk, which leads from Centraal Station through Amsterdam's little Chinatown.

There's a bit more in Gelderskade and Nieuwmarkt, where the street opens up into a vibrant square packed with cafés and dominated by the hulking presence of ex–weigh house and medieval gateway, De Waag.

Heading southward along the Kloveniersburgwal is a rewarding wander with diversions on both sides of the water: look for churches, chapels, attractive canals, and some notable historic buildings that today house departments of the University of Amsterdam. Farthest west, running parallel to Rokin, is the Nes theater district; heading east is the Old Jewish Quarter, which includes the synagogue complex of the Joods Historisch Museum, Amsterdam's most famous flea market behind the City Hall/Music Theater complex on Waterlooplein, and behind all that, the Rembrandthuis. But if you get lost, even the worst student of foreign languages can easily get help by asking for "Dam Square."

TIMING

You can walk around the center of Amsterdam easily in a few hours if you want a brief immersion into these very different districts, but there are enough sites and museums to last several days. The joy of the city is in the details, so factor in time for meandering.

WESTERN HALF OF THE CENTER

As you walk down the Damrak from Centraal Station, you're heading toward the commercial center of the city—and the place where most visitors organically converge—the Dam, the heart of the city since a dam was built over the Amstel in the 12th century. Home to the Royal Palace, the Nieuwe Kerk, and the oddly phallic National Monument, it's actually rather dull in itself, but it fulfills the role of focal point for protests and celebrations. There's a lot of shopping of the chain-store variety in the pedestrianized Nieuwendijk and Kalverstraat leading off the Dam. On weekends, at the Muntplein end, football fans might be tempted by the enthusiastic Oranje Voetbal Museum while non-football fans have coffee with a view at the café atop the Kalvertoren shopping mall nearby. The top cultural stops in this district are the Amsterdam Museum and the peaceful Begijnhof, the best known of the almshouses built round a central courtyard or hofje. The entrance to this can be found off graceful Spui, which is the literary headquarters of the city. It's a beautiful square with a clutch of great bookshops, and it hosts famous book and art markets.

TOP ATTRACTIONS

Fodor'sChoice ★ ☯ **Amsterdam Museum** (*Amsterdam Historical Museum*). Any city that began in the 13th century as a boggy swamp to become the trading powerhouse of the world in the 17th century has a fascinating story to tell, and this museum does it superbly. It's housed in a rambling amalgamation of buildings, once a convent, which was used as Amsterdam's Civic Orphanage. Before visiting the actual museum, walk past the entrance and check out the glassed Schuttersgalerij (Civil Guards Gallery) lined with huge portraits of city militias—though not in the same league as *The Night Watch*, you can see them for free. Recently, 21st-century renditions of civil guard paintings have been added to the collection, notably one featuring the "Maid of Amsterdam," with a joint in one hand and Rembrandt's face tattooed on her chest. ⊠ *Kalverstraat 92 and Sint Luciënsteeg 27, Centrum* ☎ *020/523–1822* ⊕ *www.amsterdammuseum.nl* 🎫 *€10* ☯ *Daily 10–5.*

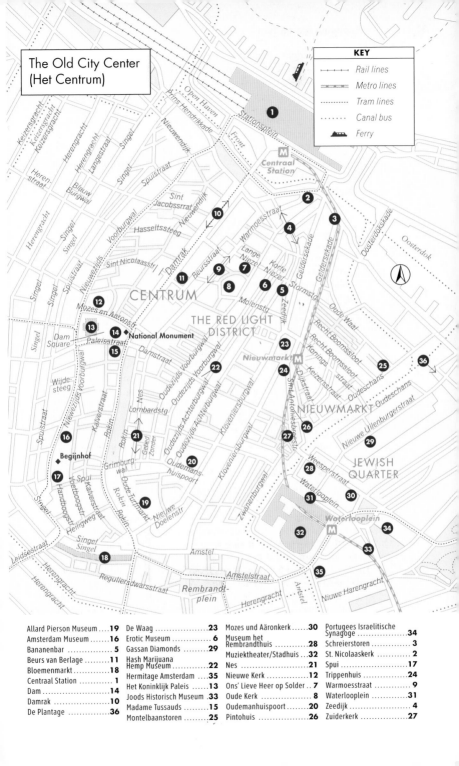

The Old City Center (Het Centrum)

Open Haven

Prins Hendrikkade

Stationsplein

Centraal Station

Keizersgracht
Keizersgracht
Keizersgracht

Herengracht
Herengracht
Langestraat

Herenstraat

Singel

Blauw
Bluaw

Nieuwendijk

Singel

Spuistraat

Sint Jacobsstraat

Nieuwendijk

Warmoesstraat

Oosterdokskade

Oosterdok

Herengracht

Singel

Singel

Voorburgwal

Sint Nicolaasstr

Damrak

Beursstraat

Hasseltssteeg

Lange Niezel

Korte Niezel

Geldersekade

Gelderskade

Storms

Oude Waal

Singel
Singel
Singel

Spuistraat

Nieuwezijds

Molensteg

Zeedijk

Recht Boomssloot

Recht Boomssloot

CENTRUM

THE RED LIGHT DISTRICT

Oudezijds Voorburgwal

Oudezijds Voorburgwal

Oudezijds Achterburgwal

Oudezijds Achterburgwal

Kloveniersburgwal

Konings

Kerzerstraat

Oudeschans

Oudeschans

NIEUWMARKT

Mozes en Aaronstr

Dam Square

Singel

Paleisstraat

National Monument

Damstraat

Nieuwmarkt

Dijkstraat

Sint Antoniesbreestraat

Nieuwe Uilenburgerstraat

Oudeschans

JEWISH QUARTER

Wijdesteeg

Kalverstraat

Nes

Lombardstg

Rokin

Gelder

Zonder

Nieuwezijds Voorburgwal

Spuistraat

Oudezijds Achterburgwal

Kloveniersburgwal

Weesperstraat

Waterlooplein

Begijnhof

Grimburgwal

Oudemanshuispoort

Zwanenburgwal

Waterlooplein

Spui

Voetboogstr

Kalverstraat

Heiligeweg

Handboogstr

Oude Turfmarkt

Rokin

Nieuwe Doelenstr

Amstel

Waterlooplein

Leidsestraat

Singel
Singel

Herengracht

Reguliersdwarsstraat

Herengracht

Amstel

Amstelstraat

Rembrandtplein

Nieuwe Harengracht

Herengracht

Amstel

Oosterdok

★ **Beurs van Berlage** (*Berlage's Stock Exchange*). Down otherwise tacky Damrak is the old stock-exchange building that received a hostile reception when it was first built but is now revered as Amsterdam's first modern building and the country's most important piece of 20th-century architecture. Built between 1898 and 1903 by H.P. Berlage, the building became a template for the style of a new century. Gone were all the ornamentations of the 19th-century "Neo" styles. The new Beurs, with its simple lines and the influence it had on the Amsterdam School architects who followed Berlage, earned him the reputation of being the "Father of Modern Dutch Architecture."

The building is in fact a political manifesto that preaches the oneness of capital and labor. Built upon 4,880 wooden piles, each of the Beurs van Berlage's 9 million bricks is meant to represent an individual, who together form a strong and democratic whole. Berlage showed particular respect for the labor unions by exposing their works and accenting the important structural points with natural stone. Today, the Beurs serves as a true Palazzo Publico with concert halls (home to the Dutch Philharmonic Orchestra) and space for exhibitions of architecture and applied arts. The small museum has exhibits about the former stock exchange and its architect and offers access to the lofty clock tower and strong room, but these can be viewed only by taking part in a bi-weekly tour (every second Saturday from mid-January to mid-June, €14.50, reservations 020/531–3355) or on an architecture tour organized by Artiflex (020/620–8112). Stop in at the café to admire the stunning symbolist mosaics by Jan Toorop over a coffee (*Mon.–Sat. 10–9, Sun. 11–9*). ✉ *Damrak 277, Centrum* ☎ *020/530–4141* ⊕ *www.beursvanberlage.nl* 📷 *Varies based on exhibition* ☉ *Varies based on exhibition.*

Bloemenmarkt (*Flower Market*). This is the last of the city's floating markets. In days gone by, merchants would sail up the Amstel loaded down with blooms from the great tulip fields to delight patrons and housewives. Today, the flower sellers stay put, but their wares are still offered on stalls-cum-boats along with fridge magnets and other cheesy Amsterdamorabilia. ✉ *Singel (between Muntplein and Koningsplein), Centrum* ☉ *Mon.–Sat. 9–5:30, Sun. 11–5:30.*

Centraal Station (*Central Station*). The main train station of the Dutch capital, this building was designed as a major architectural statement by P.J.H. Cuypers. Although sporting many Gothic motifs (including a unique wind vane disguised as a clock in its left tower), it is now considered a landmark of Dutch Neo-Renaissance style. (Cuypers also designed the city's other main gateway, the Rijksmuseum, which lies like a mirrored rival on the other side of the late 19th century town.) The building of the station required the creation of three artificial islands and the ramming of 8,600 wooden piles to support it. Completed in 1889, it represented the psychological break with the city's seafaring past, as its erection slowly blocked the view to the IJ. Another controversy arose from its Gothic detailing, which was considered by uptight Protestants as a tad too Catholic—like Cuypers himself—and hence earned the building the nickname the "French Convent" (similarly, the Rijksmuseum became the "Bishop's Castle"). Currently sections of Centraal Station are under construction with the new North/South metro

The Royal Palace (Het Koninklijk Paleis) was originally built as a city hall during the Dutch Golden Age, when the government could afford such luxuries.

line. The new bus station is on the IJ side. If you are visiting the restaurant on Platform 2b, wander down to look at the magnificent golden gate of the Queen's Waiting Room (alas, you can't go in, but scan the QR code at the entrance with your smartphone for a 360° virtual tour). ⊠ *Stationsplein, Centrum* ☎ *0900–9292 (public transport information).*

QUICK BITES

1e Klas. A particularly stylish place to wait for a train is 1e Klas, whose original Art Nouveau brasserie interior, no longer restricted to first-class passengers, is perfect for lingering over coffee, a snack, or a full-blown meal accompanied by fine wine. Whatever the hour, it's a fine place to savor the sumptuousness of *fin de siècle* living. Opening hours: daily, 8:30 am–11 pm. ⊠ *Platform 2B, Centraal Station, Stationsplein 15, Centrum* ☎ *020/625–0131.*

Dam (*Dam Square*). Home to the Koninklijk Paleis (Royal Palace) and the Nieuwe Kerk, Dam Square (or just Dam), is Amsterdam's main square. It traces its roots to the 12th century and the dam built over the Amstel (hence the city's name). The waters of the Damrak (the continuation of the Amstel) once reached right up to the Dam, with ships and barges sailing to the weigh house. Folks came here to trade, talk, protest, and be executed. In the 17th century it was hemmed in by houses and packed with markets. Behind the Nieuwe Kerk there's an atmospheric warren of alleys with *proeflokaal* (liquor tasting house) De Drie Fleschjes (the Three Small Bottles) on Gravenstraat dating from 1650. In the 19th century the Damrak was filled in to form the street leading to Centraal Station, and King Louis, Napoléon's brother, demolished the weigh house in 1808 because it spoiled the view from his bedroom window in the Royal Palace. Today the Dam is a bustling meeting point with street performers and fairs on high days and holidays.

National Monument. The towering white obelisk-shaped object opposite the Palace on the other side of Damrak, the National Monument was erected in 1956 as a memorial to the Dutch soldiers who died in World War II. Designed by architect J. J. P. Oud (who thought that De Stijl minimalism was in keeping with the monument's message), it's the focal point for Remembrance Day (on May 4th) that commemorates Dutch lives lost in wars and peacekeeping missions around the world. Every year, the Queen walks from the Koninklijk Paleis to the monument and lays flowers. The monument contains 12 urns: 11 are filled with earth from all the Dutch provinces, and the 12th contains earth from the former colonies (Indonesia, Surinam, and the Antilles). Oud designed the steps to be used as seating, and today it's still a favored rest spot and a great place to watch the world go by. ⊠ *Follow Damrak south from Centraal Station. Raadhuisstraat leads from Dam behind the Palace to intersect main canals.*

> **BUILDING IN A SWAMP**
>
> In order to build the Royal Palace, architect Jacob van Campen had to dig deep in search of solid ground using the standard local technique of driving wooden piles down through layers of swamp and sand to anchor the foundation. What was less standard was the sheer number of piles—a figure that every Dutch child knows—13,659.

Fodor'sChoice ★ **Het Koninklijk Paleis** (*Royal Palace*). From the outside, it is somewhat hard to believe that these ponderous premises were declaimed by poet and diplomat Constantijn Huygens as the "Eighth Wonder of the World." It was built between 1648 and 1665 as the largest secular building on the planet. From the inside, its magnificent interior inspires another brand of disbelief: this palace was actually built as a mere city hall. Golden Age artistic greats such as Ferdinand Bol, Govert Flinck and Jan Lievens were called in for the decorating (Rembrandt's sketches were rejected). In the building's public entrance hall, the **Burgerzaal,** the world was placed quite literally at one's feet: two maps inlaid in the marble floor show Amsterdam as the center of the world, and as the center of the universe.

The building has remained the Royal Palace ever since Napoléon's brother squatted there in 1808, and it's one of three palaces at the disposal of Queen Beatrix, who hosts official receptions and state visits here. Royal memories of Amsterdam are probably a bit mixed. Her wedding in 1966 was disrupted by a radical student group throwing smoke bombs at her carriage, and in 1980 her coronation was derailed by riots on the Dam. And at the 2010 Dodenherdenking (Remembrance of the Dead) ceremony by the National Monument, a man screamed during the two-minute silence prompting a panic and stampede among the crowd, who no doubt feared a rerun of the 2009 Queen's Day tragedy, when a gunman drove through the route of the royal procession killing seven. The Palace hosts art exhibitions and displays on the history of the building itself. Official occasions mean opening times can vary. ⊠ *Dam, Centrum* ☎ *020/620–4060* ⊕ *www.koninklijkhuis. nl* ⌑ *€7.50* ⊙ *Daily 11-5 (closed during royal events; check website for details of current opening hours).*

Het Scheepvaartmuseum (*Maritime Museum*). Designed by Daniël Stalpaert in 1656 as a storehouse for the Amsterdam war fleet, this impossible-to-overlook example of Dutch Classicism became the new home of the Maritime Museum in the 1970s. Even if you're not much of a nautical fan, the building alone is worth a visit. During the recent, extensive renovation, the courtyard of the biggest remaining 17th-century storehouse (free admission) was roofed over with a 200-ton glass-and-steel construction, the design of which is a reference to compass roses and lines of longitude and latitude on old nautical charts. In the daytime, the roof casts ever-changing shadows on the courtyard floor (weather permitting); at night, hundreds of led lights on the rafters create the fairy-tale illusion of a star-spangled sky. ⊠ *Kattenburgerplein 1, Centrum* ☎ *020/523–2222* ⊕ *www.hetscheepvaartmuseum.nl* ⌑ *€15* ⊙ *Daily 9-5.*

★ **Nieuwe Kerk** (*New Church*). Begun in the 15th century, the Nieuwe Kerk (it celebrated its 600th birthday in 2010) is a soaring Late Gothic structure whose tower was never completed because the authorities blew all their money on the building of the Palace next door. Whereas the Oude Kerk had the blessing of the Bishop of Utrecht, the Nieuwe Kerk was supported by the local well-to-do merchant class—the result was an endless competition between the two parochial factions. Don't miss the magnificently sculpted wooden pulpit by Albert Vinckenbrinck constructed after the Great Fire of 1645. It took him 19 years to complete, though there is now a bit missing: the scales from a Lady of Justice were an impulsively generous gift to the Canadians, who liberated Amsterdam. Other features include the unmarked grave of the poet Vondel (the "Dutch Shakespeare") and Rombout Verhulst's extravagantly sculpted eulogy to naval hero Admiral Michiel de Ruyter (you can peer through a glass to see his actual coffin in the crypt). ⊠ *Dam, Centrum* ☎ *020/638–6909* ⊕ *www.nieuwekerk.nl* ⌑ *€5 (admission varies according to exhibition)* ⊙ *Daily 10-6 (special exhibition times vary).*

Spui (*Spui Square*). This beautiful and seemingly tranquil tree-lined square hides a lively and radical recent past. Journalists and bookworms have long favored its many cafés, and the Atheneum News Center (No. 14–16) and its adjoining bookstore are the city's best places to peruse an international array of literature, magazines, and newspapers. More cultural browsing can be enjoyed on the Spui's book market on Friday and its art market on Sunday. ⊠ *Bounded by Spuistraat and Kalverstraat, Centrum.*

QUICK BITES | **Hoppe. Several of the bar-cafés and eateries on Spui are good places to take a break. The ancient Hoppe has been serving drinks between woody walls and on sandy floors since 1670.** ⊠ *Spui 18–20, Centrum* ☎ *020/420–4420.*

Broodje van Kootje. If you just want to eat and run, try Broodje van Kootje for a classic Amsterdam *broodje* (sandwich). ✉ *Spui 28, Centrum* ☎ *020/626–9620.*

WORTH NOTING

Damrak (*Dam Port*). This unavoidable and busy street leading up to Centraal Station, which is being smartened up as the "red carpet" to the city, is lined with a mostly tawdry assortment of shops, attractions, hotels, and greasy-food dispensers. It's a shame, because behind the neon signs are some beautiful examples of lovely Dutch architecture. Damrak, and its extension, Rokin, was once the Amstel River, bustling with activity, its piers loaded with fish and other cargo on their way to the weigh house at the Dam. Now the only open water that remains is a patch in front of the station that provides mooring for canal tour boats. ✉ *Centrum.*

Madame Tussauds Amsterdam. This branch of the world-famous wax museum, above the Peek & Cloppenburg department store, depicts Holland's glitterati, including Golden Age celebrities—there's a life-size, 3-D rendering of a painting by Vermeer (alas, the lighting is dubious), and an understandably displaced-looking Piet Mondriaan. Of course, there is also a broad selection of international superstars, including Barack Obama. Bring your own ironic distance, or skip it altogether: people-watching on Dam Square is much more entertaining than an hour and a half (their recommended tour time) wax-watching in Madame Tussauds. ✉ *Dam 20, Centrum* ☎ *020/523–0623* ⊕ *www. madame-tussauds.nl* ✇ *€22* ☽ *Sept.–June, daily 10–5:30; July and Aug., daily 10–7:30.*

THE RED LIGHT DISTRICT: DE WALLEN

As the oldest part of Amsterdam, the Oude Zijde (Old Side) has been very old and very Dutch for a long time. It stands to reason, then, that you'll find, in this mirror quadrant to the Nieuwe Zijde, the entire galaxy of Amsterdam here—everything from the archaeological treasures of the Allard Pierson Museum to the famous "Our Lord in the Attic" chapel to, well, acres of bared female flesh. Yes, here within the shadow of the city's oldest church is the most famous Disneyland of Sex in the world: the Red Light District.

Forming a rough triangle from Centraal Station bordered by Warmoesstraat, Damstraat, and Zeedijk, this famous district incorporates the two oldest canals in the city and its oldest building (the Oude Kerk). It has been an area for prostitution since the 14th century, but it is changing fast. Through Project 1012 (the postal code for the district), the city is aiming to halve the numbers of coffee shops and windows for prostitution (around 200) to combat organized crime. They are well on the way. If you decide to take a stroll around *de Wallen* (as the Red Light District is called) don't let a little sleaze scare you away. Even in the reddest of sections, the Walletjes ("little walls") area (defined by Oudezijds Voorburgwal canal and Oudezijds Achterburgwal canal north of Damstraat and their interconnecting streets), this area is also essentially the oldest and once poshest part of town.

In the 16th century, the residents of the Oudezijds Voorburgwal were so rich that the area was nicknamed "the Velvet Canal." And even before the recent cleanup, it has always been a real district with families and tradespeople, students and professionals living alongside the sex shops, bars, churches, and brothels. Even the cops come across as cute and cuddly, often distributing flyers that hype them as being "used to weird things" and offering such canny advice as "if you visit one of the women, we would like to remind you, they are not always women." The new city goal here is more economic diversity, with cutting-edge art and fashion for sale in the windows; the message is buy the dress, not the woman. Edit out the garish advertising and the sweaty breasts hypnotically sandwiched against the red-neon framed windows, and you have some very pretty buildings indeed. But have no fear: this area is also blessed with the city's Chinatown and large sections—as the vast majority of this tour will attest—of pure, unadulterated old worldness.

TOP ATTRACTIONS

Bananenbar (*Banana Bar*). Since the 1970s, this supersleazy bar has featured naked barmaids doing "now you see it, now you don't" tricks that involve fruit, which hardly merits landmark status, although along with Caso Rosso across the canal, whose show is deemed to be slightly classier, it is a Red Light institution. ⊠ *Oudezijds Achterburgwal 137, Centrum* ☎ *020/627–8954.*

Fodor'sChoice ★ **Ons' Lieve Heer op Solder** (*Our Lord in the Attic Museum*). With its elegant gray-and-white facade and spout gable, this appears to be just another lovely 17th-century canal house, and on the lower floors it is. But tucked away in the attic is a clandestine place of Catholic worship, a *schuilkerk* (hidden church), one of the very few to survive more or less in its original state. Catholic masses were officially forbidden from 1578, but the Protestant authorities in Amsterdam turned a blind eye provided the churches were not recognizable as such from the outside. The Oude Kerk was decatholicized and stripped of its patron, St. Nicholas, so this little church, consecrated in 1663, was dedicated to him until the St. Nicolaaskerk opened in 1887. The chapel itself is a triumph of Dutch classicist taste, with magnificent marble columns, gilded capitals, a colored-marble altar, and the *Baptism of Christ in the Jordan* (1716) painting by Jacob de Wit presiding over all.

The grandeur continues through the house, which was renovated by merchant Jan Hartan between 1661 and 1663. Even the kitchen and chaplain bedroom remain furnished in the style of the age, and the drawing room, or *sael*, looks as if it were plucked from a Vermeer painting. With its gold chandelier and Solomonic columns, it's one of the most impressive 17th-century rooms left in Amsterdam. Besides boasting canvases by Thomas de Keyser, Jan Wynants, and Abraham de Vries, the house also displays impressive collections of church silver and sculptures. The new part of the museum, on the other side of the alley, hosts temporary exhibitions. ⊠ *Oudezijds Voorburgwal*

Even if you have no plans to patronize, Amsterdam's Red Light District is like no other place on earth. Don't miss this once-in-a-lifetime window-shopping experience.

40, *Centrum* ☎ 020/624–6604 ⊕ *www.opsolder.nl* ✉ €8 ⊗ *Mon.–Sat. 10–5, Sun. 1–5.*

★ **Oude Kerk** (*Old Church*). Amsterdam's oldest church has evolved over three centuries to look as it does today. What began as a wooden chapel in 1306 was built up to a hall church and then a cross basilica between 1366 and 1566 (and fully restored between 1955 and 1979). It was violently looted during the Reformation and stripped of its altars and images of saints—though the looters did leave the 14th-century paintings still visible on its wooden roof, as well as the Virgin Mary stained-glass windows that had been set in place in 1550. The famed Vater-Müller organ was installed in 1726. Don't miss the carved choir stalls that illustrate proverbs relating to cardinal sins, among other things. Within this open, atmospheric space, there's a gravestone for Rembrandt's wife Saskia van Uylenburgh and also for Kiliaen van Rensselaer, one of the Dutch founders of what is now New York, and by the door, a bronzed hand cupping a naked breast. This is one of a series of sculptures placed throughout Amsterdam in 1982 by an anonymous artist. The Oude Kerk is as much exhibition space as a place of worship, hosting the annual World Press Photography competition and top-notch modern-art shows. Its carillon is played every Tuesday at 2 and every Saturday at 4—the best place to listen is the bridge in front of the church. ✉ *Oudekerksplein 23, Centrum* ☎ 020/625–8284 ⊕ *www. oudekerk.nl* ✉ €5 ⊗ *Mon.–Sat. 11–5, Sun. 1–5:30.*

★ **Schreierstoren.** Amsterdam's distinctive defense tower began life around 1487 as the end point of the city wall. The term *schreien* suggests the Dutch word for wailing. As lore would have it, this "Weeping Tower" was where women came to cry when their sailor husbands left for sea and to cry again when they did not return (there's a gable stone from 1569 of a woman and a boat on the Gelderskade side). But the word *schreier* actually comes from an Old Dutch word for "sharp" and since the old city wall made

> ## A SECOND HOME
>
> Prior to the Reformation, the Oude Kerk was known as the "living room" because peddlers displayed their goods in the church and beggars slept there.

a sharp corner here, it is a rather more accurate derivation for the tower's name. It's also famous as the point from which Henry Hudson set sail to America. A plaque on the building tells you that he sailed on behalf of the Dutch East India Company to find a shorter route to the East Indies. In his failure, he came across Canada's Hudson Bay and later—continuing his unlucky streak—New York harbor and the Hudson River. He eventually landed on Manhattan and named it New Amsterdam. The VOC café attached has a lovely view and serves *jenever* and other delights. On the next floor up, there's a nautical shop for modern-day sailors. ⊠ *Prins Hendrikkade 94–95, Centrum* ⊕ *www.schreierstoren.nl.*

Warmoesstraat. This touristy strip of hostels, bars, and coffee shops began life as one of the original dikes along the Amstel before evolving into today's busy shopping street. It's here that the famous 17th-century poet Vondel did business from his hosiery shop at No. 101, and where Mozart's dad tried to unload tickets for his son's concerts in the area's upscale bars. It entered a decline in the 17th century when the proprietors decamped for fancier digs on the Canal Ring; sailors (and the businesses that catered to them) started to fill in the gaps. In the 19th century, the street evolved, along with its extension **Nes,** into the city's primary debauchery zone. Karl Marx was known to set himself up regularly in a hotel here, not only to write in peace but to ask for the occasional loan from his cousin-in-law, Gerard Philips, founder of that capitalist machine Philips. ⊠ *Between Dam and Nieuwe Brugsteeg, Centrum.*

QUICK BITES

Snackbar Bird. Zeedijk offers a number of the best quick meal stops in town. Considered the best noodles in town, Snackbar Bird offers wok-fried-in-front-of-your-eyes dishes from Thailand; for a less cramped meal, try its restaurant across the street. ⊠ *Zeedijk 77, Centrum* ☎ *020/420–6289.*

De Amsterdamsche Visch Handel. Raw herring—the ultimate Dutch snack—can be enjoyed at this landmark eatery (est. 1938) in local fashion; just grab the fish by the tail, tilt your head backwards, and let the slippery, salty sea creature find its way down the red lane, green lights all the way. ⊠ *Zeedijk 129, Centrum* ☎ *020/624–2070* ⊕ *www.zeedijk129.nl.*

Latei. A Zeedijk and students' fave, Latei combines a dense interior of high-quality kitsch (all of it for sale) with the serving of coffee, open-face sandwiches, and healthy snacks. ⊠ *Zeedijk 143, Centrum* ☎ *020/625–7485.*

The Leaning Houses of Amsterdam

Ever wonder why all of Amsterdam's old houses lean like drunken sailors on a Saturday night? After the great fires of 1421 and 1452, which swept through and destroyed nearly three-quarters of the city, building regulations became stricter and wooden structures were forbidden. Only two early timbered examples remain in Amsterdam, though others might be lurking behind more "modern" facades: the Houten Huis (Wooden House) at the Begijnhof built in the second half of the 15th century, and No. 1 Zeedijk, completed in 1550. Since brick is a substantially heavier material than wood (and the city is still sinking into the mud at a slow and steady pace), all structures were built on wooden pilings slammed deep into the sand. Without enough depth (and Jordaan construction was particularly suspect), or with fluctuating water-table levels, the wooden pilings begin to crumble and the house tilts. Today, rotten wooden pilings can be replaced with cement ones, without tearing down the building.

Zeedijk. Few streets have had a longer or more torrid history than Zeedijk, which has been around since Amsterdam began life as a boggy hamlet. In the 15th and 16th centuries, its businesses serviced the lonely, thirsty sailors disembarking from the ships of the East India Company. By the 1970s, the only traffic Zeedijk saw was drug traffic. Tourists were advised to avoid the neighborhood at night because of the junkies and high crime rates. A few years back, the city started cracking down, and it's now much easier to accept the stray, dubious-looking character as merely part of the scenery as opposed to its definition.

There are several interesting sights along the Zeedijk. The 17th-century **Sint Olofskapel** (St. Olaf Chapel), named after the patron saint of dikes, sports a life-affirming sculpture: grains growing out of a supine skeleton (this used to be a positive message). It's now a conference center for the NH Barbizon Palace Hotel.

Across the street at No. 1 is one of only two houses with timbered facades left in the city. Dating from around 1550, **In't Aepjen** (In the Monkeys) provided bedding to destitute sailors if they promised to return from their next voyage with a monkey. Each floor juts out more than the one below so rainwater falls directly onto the street and goods can be hauled up easily. Café 't Mandje at No. 65 was the first openly gay bar run by legendary lesbian biker chick Bet van Beeren (1902–67). It reopened in 2008, with much of the original interior restored, complete with trophy ties Bet snipped off customers.

The Chinese community dominates the end of the street, where street signs are in Dutch and Mandarin. There are around 10,000 Chinese in Amsterdam, a 20th-century presence much younger than the Dutch in China (Taiwan came under Dutch control in 1624). The highlight is the Lotus Flower Buddhist Temple **Fo Guang Shan He Hua** (No. 118). Chinatown extends into Geldersekade and Nieuwmarkt and every year there are small (but colorful) Chinese New Year celebrations. ⊠ *Oudezijds Kolk (near Centraal Station) to Nieuwmarkt, Centrum.*

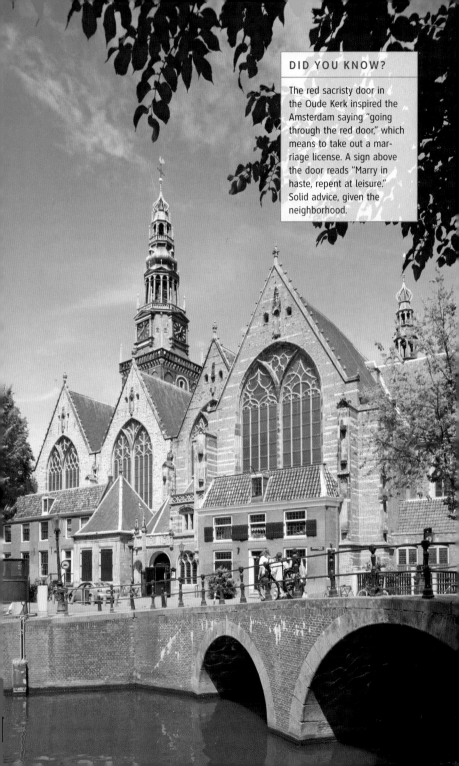

WORTH NOTING

Erotic Museum. "Five floors of highly suggestive trinkets and photos" is probably a better description than "museum." Beatles fans may like the original and satisfyingly suggestive sketches by John Lennon, perhaps rendered when he and Yoko did their weeklong bed-in for peace at the Amsterdam Hilton. There's a cultural aspect on the third floor in La Gallery Provocatrice that encompasses a wide range of artistic genres. ⊠ *Oudezijds Achterburgwal 54, Centrum* ☎ *020/624–7303* ⊕ *www.erotisch-museum.nl* ☒ *€7* ☉ *Mon.–Thurs. 11 am–1 am; Fri.–Sun. 11 am–2 am.*

Hash Marihuana & Hemp Museum. Here's your chance to suck back the 8,000-year history of hemp use. **Cannabis College,** at No. 124, covers similar territory and is free, though they ask for a donation if you want to tour the garden (⊕ *www.cannabiscollege.com*). ⊠ *Oudezijds Achterburgwal 148, Centrum* ☎ *020/624–8926* ⊕ *www.hashmuseum.com* ☒ *€9* ☉ *Daily 10 am–11 pm.*

St. Nicolaaskerk (*St. Nicholas Church*). The architect A. C. Bleys designed this church, built in 1887, with its dark and eerie interior as a replacement for all the clandestine Catholic churches that operated during the Reformation. After the Oude Kerk and "Our Lord in the Attic" chapel, this church became the third and (probably final) Sint Nicolaas church. The all-purpose patron saint of children, thieves, prostitutes, sailors, and the city of Amsterdam, transforms into Sinterklaas in mid-November when he arrives from "Spain" on a "steamboat" with his helper Zwarte Piet (Black Pete). The eve of his birthday on December 6 is celebrated as a family feast when everyone exchanges presents and poems. Note that the church is open only when volunteer custodians are available. It hosts a Gregorian chant vesper service September to June on Sunday at 5. ⊠ *Prins Hendrikkade 76, Centrum* ☎ *020/624–8749* ⊕ *www.nicolaas-parochie.nl* ☒ *Free* ☉ *Tues.–Fri. 11–4, Mon. and Sat. 12–3.*

HARTJESDAGEN

The third weekend in August is the time for an annual Amsterdam tradition, the Hartjesdagen (Heart Days) on the Zeedijk. An arts festival with cross-dressing overtones, you can drop your jaw at spectacular stiletto-heeled running races, swing to Latin American street bands, compete in a song festival for new talent, and enjoy opera performances and other acts. The highlight is on Sunday when a drag-queen parade traipses across a central podium. Intimate and relaxed, Hartjesdagen is unpretentious and welcoming and embodies that delightful Dutch shared coziness called *gezelligheid*.

NIEUWMARKT AND ENVIRONS

At the bottom of the Zeedijk and bordering the Red Light District lie Nieuwmarkt and the brooding Waag, ex-gatehouse to the city. It's been a marketplace since the 17th century, selling cheese, herbs, cloth, and fish, as well as spices brought back from the ships of the Dutch East India Company. Public executions and other gruesome punishments took place here as well, supplying cadavers to the Surgeon's Guild for dissection. This is where Rembrandt came to watch Professor Tulp in action before painting *The Anatomy Lesson*. During WWII, it was known for a flourishing black market and as a collection place where Jews were held before being shipped off to concentration camps. Today it's an upscale local gathering place, ringed by restaurants, cafés, jazz clubs, and a microbrewery. There's a farmers' market every Saturday and more occasional antiques and curiosities sales.

> **SUPER SKINNY**
>
> There are a few other hyper-narrow houses in Amsterdam besides the Little Trip House. The narrowest rear gable is at Singel 7 at only 1 meter wide. The building on Oude Hoogstraat 22 is only 2.02 meters (7 feet) wide and 6 meters (19 feet) deep.

After the hustle (literally) of the Red Light District, the neighborhood provides a refreshing break. Due east is a cluster of less-touristy, quiet little canal-lined streets (the Rechtboomsloot is especially scenic). Directly south, straight up the Kloveniersburgwal, is the University of Amsterdam, housed in a myriad of lovely old buildings along and between the canals.

QUICK BITES

In De Waag. Although you may wish to sniff out your own favorite among the many café-restaurants that line this square, only In De Waag occupies such historic surrounds and, at night, even highlights its epic medieval roots with candlelight. ⊠ *Nieuwmarkt 4, Centrum* ☎ *020/422–7772.*

't Loosje. An arty and studenty option is 't Loosje, which is graced with tile tableaux that are more than 80 years old. ⊠ *Nieuwmarkt 32–34, Centrum* ☎ *020/627–2635.*

TOP ATTRACTIONS

Allard Pierson Museum. Once the repository of the nation's gold supply, this former National Bank with its stern Neoclassical façade is now home to other treasures. Dynamite helped remove the safes and open up the space for the archaeological collection of the University of Amsterdam in 1934, and the museum traces the early development of Western civilization, from the Egyptians to the Romans, and of the Near Eastern cultures (Anatolia, Persia, Palestine) in a series of well-documented (if old-fashioned) displays. It links internally to the University of Amsterdam's Bijzondere Collecties (Special Collections) showcase with interesting exhibitions and a stylish café. ⊠ *Oude Turfmarkt 127, Centrum* ☎ *020/525–2556* ⊕ *www.allardpiersonmuseum.nl* ☎ *€6.50* ⊗ *Tues.– Fri. 10–5, weekends 1–5.*

De Waag (*Weigh House*). Built in 1488, the Waag functioned as a city gate, Sint Antoniespoort, until 1617. It would be closed at exactly 9:30 pm to keep out not only bandits but also the poor and diseased who built shantytowns outside the city's walls. When Amsterdam expanded, it began a second life as a weighing house for incoming goods. The top floor of the building accommodated the municipal militia and several guilds, including the stonemasons who did the evocative decorations that grace each of the seven towers' entrances. One housed a teaching hospital for the Surgeons' Guild. The Theatrum Anatomicum (Anatomy Theater), with its cupola tower covered in painted coats of arms, was the first place in the Netherlands to host public autopsies. For obvious reasons, these took place only in the winter. Now the building is occupied by a café-restaurant and the Waag Society (a.k.a. the Society for Old and New Media). ⊠ *Bounded by Kloveniersburgwal, Geldersekade, and Zeedijk, Centrum* ⊕ *www.waag.org.*

★ **Trippenhuis** (*Trip House*). As family home to the two Trip brothers, "Purveyors of Waepens, Artilleree, Shotte, and Amunition of Werre," who made their fortune during the 17th-century Golden Age, this noted house's buckshot-gray exterior and various armament motifs—including mortar-shaped chimneys—designed by Justus Vingboons, are easily explained. But the Corinthian-columned facade actually covers two symmetrical buildings (the dividing wall is positioned behind the middle windows), one for each brother, making it the widest residence (at 22 meters) in Amsterdam. From 1815 to 1885 it housed the national museum or Rijksmuseum and is now the home of The Royal Netherlands Academy of Arts and Sciences (though they weren't allowed to call it "Royal" under German occupation in the war). Be sure to look across the canal to No. 26, the door-wide white building topped with golden sphinxes and the date of 1696, which is known as the "Little Trip House" or "House of Mr. Trip's Coachman." The story goes that the coachman remarked that he would be happy with a house as wide as the Trippenhuis door. By way of response, Mr. Trip built just that with the leftover bricks. ⊠ *Kloveniersburgwal 29, Centrum.*

WORTH NOTING

Nes. Nes is a refreshingly quiet corridor filled with theaters and restaurants; in earlier days it was packed with monasteries and convents, until the Alteration (or Protestant changeover), which kick-started Amsterdam's march toward the Golden Age. The Frascati Theater (No. 59–65) began life as a coffeehouse in the 18th century, but it wasn't until the 1880s that the Nes really blossomed with cafés filled with dance, song, and operetta performances; stars often represented the less uptight segment of the Jewish community. Adjacent to the southern end of the Nes is **Gebed Zonder End,** the "Prayer Without End" alleyway, which got its name because it was said you could hear prayers from behind the walls of the convents that used to line this alley. ⊠ *Between Langebrugsteeg and Dam, Centrum.*

Oudemanhuispoort (*Old Man's House Gate*). Landmarked by its famous chiseled pair of spectacles set over the Oudezijds Achterburgwal pediment—a sweet reference to old age—this passage led to a pensioners' house, an "Oudemannenhuis," first built in 1754. Today, bikes, not canes, are in evidence, as this former almshouse is now part of the

University of Amsterdam. One charming relic from its founding days is the covered walkway, which would have been lined with tiny shops whose rents helped subsidize the 18th-century elderly. Adorned with red shutters, the stalls now house an array of antiquarian booksellers. At the Kloveniersburgwal end stands a statue of Mother Amsterdam protecting two elders, sculpted by Anthonie Ziesenis in 1786. ⊠ *Between Oudezijds Achterburgwal, and Kloveniersburgwal, Centrum.*

QUICK BITES

De Brakke Grond. As to be expected from a theatrical neighborhood, the Nes offers some prime eating and drinking holes. Fans of Belgian beer should certainly stop at the patio of De Brakke Grond, part of the Flemish Cultural Center, to partake in one or two of the dozens of options. ⊠ *Nes 43, Centrum* ☎ *020/422–2666.*

Kapitein Zeppos. On the "Prayer Without End" alley, which runs parallel to Nes's south end, is Kapitein Zeppos, which is named after a 1960s Belgian TV star. This former cigar factory is soaked with jazzy old-world charm. ⊠ *Gebed Zonder End 5, Centrum* ☎ *020/624–2057.*

THE JEWISH QUARTER: JOODSE BUURT

While Amsterdam has been Calvinist, Protestant, and Catholic for varying chunks of its history, it has been continuously considered a Jerusalem Junior of sorts by migrating populations of Jews from the medieval to the modern era. In fact, the city came to be known as Mokum (the Hebrew word for place), as in *the* place for Jews. And when the Jewish population arrived, so did much of Amsterdam's color and glory.

Just witness the legendary diamond trade and feast your eyes upon Rembrandt's *Jewish Bride* in the Rijksmuseum, just one of many canvases the artist painted when, searching for inspiration and Old Testament ambience, he deliberately set up a luxurious household near the heart of the Jewish Quarter.

Since the 15th century, the *Joodse Buurt* (Jewish Quarter) has traditionally been considered the district east of the Zwanenburgwal. The Quarter got its start thanks to the Inquisition, which was extremely efficient in motivating many Sephardic Jews to leave Spain in 1492. Holland's war with Spain inspired the 1597 Union of Utrecht—it was formulated to protect Protestants from the religious oppression that came with Spanish invasions, but essentially meant that all religions were tolerated. This provided a unique experience for Jewish people because, unlike elsewhere in Europe, they were not forced to wear badges and live in ghettos. These and other freedoms helped attract many Yiddish-speaking Ashkenazi Jews from Eastern Europe who were escaping pogroms.

Jews were still, however, restricted from joining guilds and being registered as tradesmen. The only exceptions were in the up-and-coming trades where no guild mafia had arisen, such as diamond cutting and polishing, sugar refining, silk weaving, and printing. These slim advantages also helped attract many Yiddish-speaking Ashkenazis from

Eastern Europe escaping pogroms. By the end of the 19th century, the rise of the diamond industry meant the spreading of the community away from the old Jewish Quarter. By 1938, 10% of Amsterdam's population was Jewish. They had hugely influenced the city's culture and language (the Yiddish word *mazzel*, meaning "good luck," is still used as a standard farewell). Today what remains much more painfully ingrained in the city's psyche is what happened during the Nazi occupation, when the Jewish population was reduced to one-seventh of its size. There were many examples of bravery and the opening of homes to hide Jewish people, but there are many more—and less often told—stories of collaboration. Although the current Jewish population has risen to 20,000, the Jewish community itself exists largely beneath the surface of Amsterdam, and most place Dutch identity before Judaism.

To see locate these sights on a map, see The Old City Center map near the front of the chapter.

TOP ATTRACTIONS

Joods Historisch Museum (*Jewish Historical Museum*). Four Ashkenazi synagogues (or *shuls,* as they are called in Yiddish), dating from the 17th and 18th centuries, were combined with glass-and-steel constructions in 1987 to create this warm and impressive museum commemorating the four-century history of the Jewish people in Amsterdam and the Netherlands. Back in the 17th century, Ashkenazi Jews fled the pogroms in Central and Eastern Europe. They weren't exactly welcomed with open arms by the already settled Sephardic Jews, who resented the increased competition imposed by their often poorer brethren; consequently separate synagogues were built.

Four of them make up this complex: the **Neie Sjoel** (New Synagogue, 1752) shows the history of Jews in the Netherlands from 1900 until today; the **Grote Sjoel** (Great Synagogue, 1671) presents the tenets of Judaism as well as the history of Jews in the Netherlands before 1900; the **Obbene Sjoel** (Upstairs Synagogue, 1685) is home to the children's museum; and the **Dritt Sjoel** (Third Synagogue, 1700/1778) houses the museum's offices. The museum also features a resource center and one of the city's few purely kosher cafés. Whether or not you tour the collections or regular exhibitions, check out the excellent tours of the Jewish Quarter conducted by this museum. ⊠ *Nieuwe Amstelstraat 1, Centrum* ☎ *020/531–0310* ⊕ *www.jhm.nl* ▨ *€12 (combination ticket, also valid for Hollandsche Schouwburg and Portuguese Synagogue)* ☉ *Daily 11–5.*

Fodor's Choice ★ **Museum het Rembrandthuis** (*Rembrandt House Museum*). This is the house that Rembrandt bought, flush with success, for 13,000 guilders (a princely sum) in 1639, and where he lived and worked until 1656 when declared bankrupt. The inside is a remarkable reconstruction job, as the contents have been assembled based on inventories made when Rembrandt was forced to sell everything, including an extravagant collection of art and antiquities (a contributing factor in his money troubles). He originally chose this house on what was then the main street of the Jewish Quarter, to experience firsthand the faces he would use in his Old Testament religious paintings.

The house interior has been restored with contemporaneous elegant furnishings and artwork in the reception rooms, a collection of rarities that match as closely as possible the descriptions in the inventory, and the main studio, occasionally used by guest artists, which is kept fully stocked with paints and canvases. But it doesn't convey much of the humanity of Rembrandt himself. When he left here, he was not only out of money, but also out of favor with the city after relationships with servant girls following the death of his wife, Saskia.

The little etching studio is perhaps the most atmospheric. Littered with tools of the trade, a printing press, and a line hung with drying prints (there are demonstrations), it's easy to imagine Rembrandt finding respite here, experimenting with form and technique, away from uncomfortable schmoozing for commissions (and loans) in the grander salon.

The museum owns a huge collection of etchings with 260 of the 290 he made represented, and a changing selection is on permanent display. His magisterial "Hundred Guilder" and the "Three Crosses" prints show that Rembrandt was almost more revolutionary in his prints than in his paintings, so this collection deserves respectful homage, if not downright devotion, by printmakers today. ⊠ *Jodenbreestraat 4–6, Centrum* ☎ *020/520–0400* ⊕ *www.rembrandthuis.nl* ⊠ *€10* ⊙ *Daily, 10-5.*

QUICK BITES

Grand Café Amstelhoeck. On the corner of the Stopera complex, hard by a statue of local hero Spinoza, Grand Café Amstelhoeck has incomparable views over the Amstel. ⊠ *Zwanenburgwal 15, Centrum* ☎ *020/620–9039.*

Soup en Zo. Hands down, many say, Soup en Zo has the best soup in Amsterdam; there's a second branch in Spiegelstraat, opposite the Rijksmuseum. ⊠ *Jodenbreestraat 94A, Centrum* ☎ *020/422–4243.*

Muziektheater/Stadhuis (*Music Theater/City Hall*). Universally known as the Stopera—from the combining of "Stadhuis" (City Hall) and "Opera"—the brick-and-marble complex, opened in 1986, has been described as a set of dentures, and there were moans that its "two for one" nature was a tad too typical of the bargain-loving Dutch. Before the first brick was in place, locals protested over the razing of historic houses in the old Jewish Quarter and around Nieuwmarkt to make way for it (in particular, look for the moving memorial that marks the spot of a Jewish orphanage, which honors the saga of how, in 1943, three teachers voluntarily accompanied 100 children to the extermination camp of Sobibor: "None of them returned. May their memory be blessed"). ⊠ *Waterlooplein 22 or Amstel 3, Centrum* ☎ *020/551–8117* ⊕ *www.stopera.nl* ⊠ *Tours €5.00* ⊙ *Mon.-Fri. 12-6; Sat.-Sun. 12-3; tours Sat. noon or by arrangement (020/551-8103).*

★ **Pintohuis** (*Pinto House*). Scholar and grandee Isaac de Pinto escaped the Inquisition in Portugal to become a significant investor in the Dutch East India Company in Amsterdam. He bought this Italian Renaissance–style house in 1651. It was grandly renovated by his son, together with architect Elias Bouwman, in the 1680s. In the 1960s it was almost demolished so that the street could be widened, but activist squatters saved the building. The interior is lushly decorated, particularly the

Rembrandt: Magnificence and Misery

Dutch art speaks with many voices, but in the case of Rembrandt van Rijn (1606–69)—the greatest painter of Holland's 17th-century Golden Age—it is often magically silent. Standing before his reticent and meditative masterpieces, one is aware of a painter who grew great at the art of suggesting rather than laying bare on canvas. Born in Leiden, the fifth child of a miller, Rembrandt quickly became rich from painting.

As the years went by, he dug deeper and deeper into the essence of his subjects and portrayed the incessant metaphysical struggle for inner beauty and reason. When his whole material world crashed about him, he unaccountably continued to turn out art that grew bolder and stronger. His greatness as a painter has tended to eclipse the spectacular rags-to-riches-to-rags saga of his life.

Heralded as a budding genius, the young Rembrandt arrived in Amsterdam in 1632 to live with Hendrich van Ulyenburgh, an art dealer who helped Rembrandt land his first commissions. Before long, he had married Ulyenburgh's cousin, a rich lass named Saskia, in 1634. Heady with her large dowry and swamped by patrons, Rembrandt announced his "arrival" by buying an exceedingly patrician mansion on the Breestraat (today the Museum het Rembrandthuis).

The aristocrats of the area had decamped for the newly chic district of the Grachtengordel, allowing the immigrant set, mostly Portuguese Jews, to colonize the quarter. If Rembrandt's patrons were clamoring for biblical scenes, what better place to set up shop than in the midst of this "New Jerusalem"?

The young couple moved in on May 1, 1639, along with cartloads of Tournai tablecloths, marble fireplaces, busts of Roman emperors, and one beribboned pet monkey. The year 1642 saw the peak of Rembrandt's fame, with *The Night Watch* unveiled at the Kloveniersdoelen but, before long, its peat-burning fireplaces had darkened the canvas—a bad omen. Then, on June 14, Saskia died from tuberculosis and the 1641 birth of their son, Titus. Shortly thereafter, Rembrandt's romance with Geertje Dircx, hired as a babysitter, soured with her lawsuit against his broken promise of marriage.

As for his new housekeeper, Hendrikje Stoffels, by 1654, the Reformed Church fathers had declared that she "confesses that she has engaged in fornication with Rembrandt the painter, is therefore severely reprimanded, and is forbidden to take part in the Lord's Supper." Unmarried though they stayed, a child was born, and Amsterdam was scandalized.

Then Rembrandt wound up at insolvency court, forced to auction his belongings and decamp to a simple house on the Rozengracht canal. While patrons still knocked on his door (although he had become "unfashionable" with the chic new Neoclassical style), Hendrikje's death in 1663, Titus's early demise in 1668, and pressing creditors meant Rembrandt spent his last years in penury. What he would have made of the fact that one of his smaller, minor portraits of a dour old lady was auctioned several years ago for nearly $24 million we will never know.

See the ingredients Rembrandt used to mix oil paints, as well as huge collection of etchings, at Museum het Rembrandthuis.

painted ceilings by 17th-century master Jacob de Wit, with more recent additions by the entrance: spot the little cherub reading a book, a reference to the building's current manifestation as a public library. ⊠ *Sint Antoniebreestraat 69, Centrum* ☎ *020/624–3184* ⌨ *Free* ⊗ *Mon. 2–8, Wed. and Fri. 10–5:30, Sat. 11–4.*

Portugese Synagoge (*Portuguese Synagogue*). With Jerusalem's Temple of Solomon as inspiration, Elias Bouman designed this noted synagogue between 1671 and 1675 for the Sephardic Jewish community, the first Jews to settle in the Netherlands. They were descendants of Spanish and Portuguese Jews (Sepharad is Hebrew for the Iberian peninsula), escaping the inquisitions or forced conversion to Catholicism in the 15th and 16th centuries. On its completion it was the largest synagogue in the world, and its spare, elegantly proportioned wood interior has remained virtually unchanged through the centuries. It is still magically illuminated by hundreds of candles in two immense candelabra during services. The buildings around the synagogue house the world-famous Ets Haim ("Tree of Life") library, one of the oldest still-functioning Jewish libraries in the world. ⊠ *Mr. Visserplein 3, Centrum* ☎ *020/531–0380* ⊕ *www.esnoga.com* ⌨ *€12* ⊗ *Apr.–Oct., Sun.–Fri. 10–4; Nov.–Mar., Sun.–Thurs. 10–4, Fri. 10–2.*

Waterlooplein. Amsterdam's most famous flea market was once an area bordered by the Leper and Peat canals that often took the brunt of an overflowing Amstel River and therefore housed only the poorest of Jews. In 1893 it became the daily market for the surrounding neighborhood—a necessity, since Jews were not allowed to own shops at the time. It became a meeting place whose chaos of wooden carts

and general vibrancy disappeared along with the Jewish population during World War II. And yet it still provides a colorful glimpse into Amsterdam's particular brand of pragmatic sales techniques. Its stalls filled with clothes, bongs, discarded electronics, and mountains of Euro knickknacks can be a battle—although sometimes a worthwhile one—to negotiate. ⊠ *Waterlooplein, Centrum* ⊕ *www.waterloopleinmarkt.nl* ☉ *Mon.–Sat. 9–6.*

★ **Zuiderkerk** (*South Church*). Gorgeous enough to have inspired both Sir Christopher Wren and Claude Monet, this famous church was built between 1603 and 1611 by Hendrick de Keyser, one of the most prolific architects of Holland's

Golden Age (he chose to be buried here). It was one of the earliest churches built in Amsterdam in the Renaissance style and was the first in the city to be built for the (Protestant) Dutch Reformed Church. In 1944 during the hunger winter, it was a morgue. The church's hallowed floors, under which three of Rembrandt's children are buried, are now rented out as events location. You can visit the church, although the serious redecorations that have taken place have deprived it of its charm. The church tower however—a soaring accumulation of columns, brackets, and balustrades—is one of the most glorious exclamation points in Amsterdam; its bells are played every Thursday and it is open for climbing from April to September or by prior arrangement (www.westertorenamsterdam.nl). ⊠ *Zuiderkerkhof 72, Centrum* ☎ *020/308–7987* ⊕ *www.zuiderkerkamsterdam.nl.*

WORTH NOTING

★ **De Plantage.** Only a short walk away from Waterlooplein (follow the tram tracks) is Amsterdam's famed Plantage neighborhood. Compared with many parts of the city, there's a gracious and spacious feel to the Plantage with its wide boulevards, parks, and elegant 19th-century architecture making it similar to the Museum District. It's a nice wander with a handful of family attractions and some excellent museums.

Its earliest roots are in the 17th century, when the area was divided into 15 parks and it was a recreational zone for the wealthy. Rare plants brought back on VOC ships were taken to the **Hortus Botanicus**, one of the oldest botanical gardens in the world, where famous botanists like Linnaeus researched. On the corner of Linnaeusstraat (the street where Theo van Gogh was murdered), the **Tropenmuseum** provides insight into the many tropical cultures, some of which Holland once colonized. Top draw in the area is **Artis Zoo** and its Neoclassical aquarium built in 1882, which you can also appreciate from the roadside.

Eco Architecture

Dutch architecture is known for its creative approach to practical problems, and right now eco-architecture (bringing environmental awareness to building design) is hot. With its focus on sustainability, the renewal of the Eastern Docklands and NDSM, a former dockyard on the northern IJ bank, is a perfect example of this trend. Amsterdam's newest zone, IJburg—a complex of eight islands (seven of them created from scratch) that will eventually house 45,000 people—is a work in progress, but the combination of floating homes, eco-effective houses, and planning tussles between dense housing versus the need for green spaces, has sustainability at its core. The transformation of industrial spaces to cultural places just keeps on going. In 2013, a cultural center opens in Zeeburgeiland in and on top of two former sewage-treatment silos. It's cutting-edge and incredibly clever.

Opposite the zoo is the marvelous **Verzetzmuseum** (Resistance Museum). There are other poignant reminders that, from the late 19th century up to the Second World War, this was a neighborhood for wealthier Jewish families. In little Wertheim park is the **Auschwitz Memorial** with its engraved message: *Nooit Meer* (Never Again). After German occupation in 1941, Jews were forbidden to assemble in public places, and the **Hollandsche Schouwburg** became the Jewish theater where weddings (banned from the Town Hall) could take place (there's a film of one of the last in the exhibition upstairs). When the Germans requisitioned the theater in 1942, Jews were gathered here to be sent to their death. Between 1941 and 1944, 104,000 Jews were deported from the Netherlands; 1,169 survived.

Also opposite the zoo, but on the other side, is the new **Amsterdam Tattoo Museum,** that is centered on global tattoo legend Henk Schiffmacher's huge collection of tattoo-related objects from all over the world.

Along the Amstel river, the enormous **Hermitage Museum** has been a big cultural hit since it reopened in 2009 with artworks direct from its base in Russia. ⊠ *Centrum* ⊕ *www.deplantageamsterdam.nl.*

Gassan Diamonds. By the beginning of the 18th century, Amsterdam had a virtual monopoly in the diamond industry in Europe, so when diamonds were discovered in South Africa in 1869, there was a windfall for Amsterdam's Jewish communities, a third of whom worked in the diamond trade. Built in 1879, Gassan Diamonds was once home to the Boas diamond-polishing factory, the largest in the world, where 357 diamond-polishing machines processed 8,000–10,000 carats of rough diamonds a week. Today, Gassan offers polishing and grading demonstrations and free one-hour tours, in more than 27 languages, of the building and its glittering collection of diamonds and jewelry. ⊠ *Nieuwe Uilenburgerstraat 173, Centrum* ☎ *020/622–5333* ⊕ *www.gassan.com* 🗲 *Free* ☉ *Daily 9–5.*

★　**Hermitage Amsterdam.** Taking advantage of 300 years of historical links between Amsterdam and St. Petersburg, Professor Mikhail Piotrovsky,

The world-class Hermitage Amsterdam often hosts blockbuster temporary exhibitions.

director of the State Hermitage Museum in St. Petersburg, and Ernst Veen, director of the Nieuwe Kerk museum in Amsterdam, chose this spot on the Amstel for a new outpost. In 2009, the final refurbishment stage of the Amstelhof was complete and ever since the place has had lines out the door and acclaim audible almost all the way to St. Petersburg. Inside, huge, high, white interiors and smaller side rooms connected by long unadorned corridors give ample rooms for art treasures, although the allocation for exhibition space is actually much smaller than you might imagine from the outside, but the size of the shop and café are not. But when the material on show is of the highest quality, this matters not a bit, for this venue has welcome many of Amsterdam's biggest museum blockbusters and highest ticket prices. Past shows included babysitting all the great Van Goghs from the Van Gogh Museum while it was being renovated, along with a big Impressionism show. As for the 2013 calendar, March to September will see an exhibition devoted to Peter the Great while 2014 sees a show on Gauguin and his contemporaries, Pierre Bonnard and Maurice Denis. ⊠ *Amstel 51* ☎ *020/530–7488* ⊕ *www.hermitage.nl* ⬛ *€15, I amsterdam Card €3, children under 17 free* ☉ *Daily 10–5; Wed. 10–8.*

★ **Montelbaanstoren** (*Montelbaans Tower*). Rembrandt loved to sketch this slightly leaning redbrick tower, which was built in 1516 as part of the city's defenses. In 1606, the ubiquitous Hendrick de Keyser oversaw the building of a new tower complete with clockworks that was known as Malle Jaap ("Crazy Jaap") by locals, since the bells pealed at odd times. The year 1610 saw the tower embark on a lean too far, and with lots of manpower and ropes it was reset on a stronger foundation. From 1878 till 2006, it housed the City Water Office. After a thorough renovation, the tower is now rented out to Secret Garden, a foundation for lesbian, gay, bisexual, and transgender Muslims. ⊠ *Oude Schans 2, Centrum* ☎ *020/778–6120.*

QUICK
BITES

Café Sluyswacht. The best place to view the Montelbaanstoren is from the patio of the crooked Café Sluyswacht overlooking Oudeschans. But beware of the slant. You don't want to tumble into the water after a few beers. ⊠ *Jodenbreestraat 1, Centrum* ☎ *020/625–7611* ⊕ *www.sluyswacht.nl.*

Mozes en Aäronkerk (*Moses and Aaron Church*). Landmarking the eastern corner of the Waterlooplein flea market, this rarely used church was originally built in the 1640s, then rebuilt in 1841 by architect T. F. Suys. Today it is an adult education center. ⊠ *Waterlooplein 205, Centrum* ☎ *020/622–1305* ⊕ *www.mozeshuis.nl* ☉ *Hrs vary.*

2

THE WATERFRONT

Amsterdam was built on water—it's the source of the city's wealth and cultural history. Before Centraal Station was built, the center of the city was open to the sea. International shipping routes ended here, sluicing bounty into the city via the Amstel and the man-made canals that loped around. Today, the area is experiencing a renaissance. With the massive development around the station and landmark buildings going up east, west, and north across the water (North being the city's most populous but least glamorous district), a shiny new Amsterdam is being built on the waterfront.

Directly to the west of Centraal Station are the **Westelijke Eilanden** (Western Islands), which housed the heavy and polluting industries of the 17th century: shipbuilders, pickling factories, and smokehouses for fish. The old warehouses give this neighborhood a special "village within the city" feel. It borders one of the city's main green areas, the Westerpark, which runs parallel with the train lines coming out of Centraal Station. In the park, the Westergasfabriek (⇨ see *Nightlife and the Arts*) is the place to go for funky international festivals, art cinema, clubbing and cafés, conferences, music, and experimental exhibits.

The opposite direction will bring you to the **Eastern Docklands**, also an area that has been completely redeveloped since the 1990s. Architectural highlights of this former squatters' paradise include the swoopy-roofed (like a wave) cruise ship Passenger Terminal Amsterdam, the Muziekgebouw aan 't IJ (Music Building on the IJ) (⇨ see *Nightlife and the Arts*), Amsterdam's amazing new library—the biggest in Europe!—and some startling bridges and futuristic housing projects.

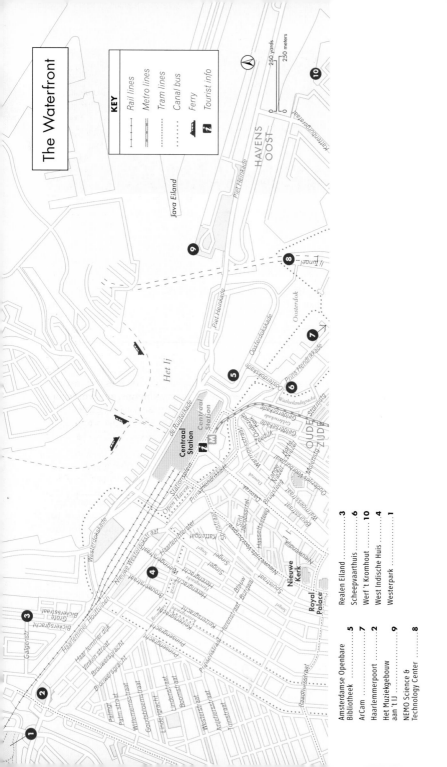

The Waterfront

KEY

——— Rail lines

——— Metro lines

········· Tram lines

········· Canal bus

Ferry

🛈 Tourist info

250 yards

250 meters

The waterfront in **Amsterdam North** on the other side of the IJ, once a bleak industrial no-man's-land, is buzzing with new international art spaces, restaurants and clubs, and a new architectural landmark, the EYE Film Institute Netherlands.

TOP ATTRACTIONS

Fodor's Choice ★ **Muziekgebouw aan 't IJ** (*Music Building on the IJ*). Just 200 meters from Centraal Station and built on a peninsula on the IJ, this spectacular building's design (compliments of Danish architects 3XN) was based on the shape of a ship. Since opening in 2005, it has become a main concert hall for both classical and jazz fans: the black box jutting out is the legendary jazz venue, Bimhuis. The glass building is architecturally stunning with its ship's ramp entrance and the Zen-like simplicity of its three natural colors (concrete, black, and light maple wood). The floor-to-roof glass walls provide angular transparency and spectacular views into the building and out onto the IJ. Weather variations—clouds, rain, sunshine, and light— organically change the atmosphere inside. Its multifunctional main auditorium seats 725; a smaller auditorium seats 120 people, and foyers and extensive conference and catering facilities lure in business visitors who are not strictly here for the music. There are regular exhibitions, and workshops for kids (ages 7+) in the educational Klankspeeltuin (sound garden). Pay a lunchtime visit to chill out in café-restaurant Zouthaven and enjoy the waterfront terrace. ⊠ *Piet Heinkade 1, Centrum* ☎ *020/788-2000* ⊕ *www.muziekgebouw.nl.*

Fodor's Choice ★ ♻ **NEMO Science & Technology Center.** Opened in 1997, this green copper-clad building designed by Renzo Piano—co-creator of the Pompidou Center in Paris—is an international architectural landmark: a ship's hull rising colossally out of the middle of the water, over the Coen Tunnel entrance to Amsterdam North. A rooftop café and summer "beach" terrace (*Boven*NEMO or "above NEMO") offer a superb panorama of the area. It's worth a visit, just for the view (June–September, 10–7, free). Inside, there are five floors of fantastical, hands-on, high-tech fun making this a science wonderland. Attractions range from the giant "bubbles" on the ground floor to experiments in the wonder lab and interactive exhibitions like Teen Facts. Kids love it. ⊠ *Oosterdok 2, Centrum* ☎ *020/531-3233* ⊕ *www.e-nemo.nl* ⊡ *€13.50* ☉ *Sept.–May, Tues.–Sun. 10–5; June–Aug., daily 10–5.*

★ ♻ **Openbare Bibliotheek Amsterdam** (*Amsterdam Public Library*). Europe's biggest public library offers a multifarious collection of information to around 5,000 visitors per day. The €75 million building (the "bieb," as locals call it), designed by architect Jo Coenen, has a big theater, seminar and conference rooms, an art space, and an extensive music library. A superb children's section is set below a terraced central lounge

2

UNDER CONSTRUCTION

While the city remains dedicated to preserving ancient buildings, it is fundamentally altering the center and the area around Centraal Station with the construction of a new north–south subway line. The line, which is extremely over-budget, highly controversial, and not due to be completed until 2017, continues to create chaos in many parts of Amsterdam.

area. Park yourself in the comfy designer furniture and peruse a mind-boggling international magazine collection. With 1,000 desks, half of them with PCs connected to the Internet, you can study and surf in peace, for free, but only if you are a member. Others pay €1 per half hour. The seventh-floor La Place restaurant has an outside terrace with a spectacular view over the city. Amsterdam Conservatory is right next door with regular free recitals by students. ⊠ *Oosterdokskade 143, Centrum* ☎ *020/523–0900* ⊕ *www.oba.nl* ⊙ *Daily 10–10.*

Fodor'sChoice
★ **Realeneiland** (*Reals Island*). About a dozen blocks to the west of Centraal Station, there are three off-the-beaten-track islands built on landfill back in the 17th century. These Western Islands—known in Dutch as De Westelijke Eilanden—were constructed as a safe warehouse zone. The nautical ambience is particularly beloved by Amsterdammers, who all seem to have recreational boats, and other seafaring folk. From the smallest island, Prinseneiland, follow the Galgenstraat (Gallows Street), which once offered a vista of bodies (or bits of bodies—sometimes the heads were placed elsewhere) on the town's gallows across the water. Bickerseiland is a jumble of modern housing, boats, and in the little farm, bunnies. Across the white wooden drawbridge, is Realeneiland, renowned for the little row of 17th-century merchant's houses with biblical gables on Zandhoek. "De Gouden Reael" is the name the governor-general of the Dutch East Indies, Laurens Reael, gave to his house, now a waterside bar and restaurant serving regional French cuisine. It wittily refers to his namesake; a golden *real* was a Spanish coin from the 16th century. It's a perfect spot to raise a toast to the old days and watch boats sail along the Westerdok. ⊠ *Zandhoek 14, Centrum* ⊹ *Follow Haarlemmerstraat/Haarlemmerdijk from Centraal Station and go under the railway tracks at Buiten Oranjestraat or at Haarlemmerplein.*

WORTH NOTING

ARCAM. Architecture Centrum Amsterdam is dedicated to promoting modern Dutch architecture and organizes exhibitions, lectures, and tours (there's an extensive list of specialist tour companies and individuals on their website), and publishes a wide range of maps and guides both print and online, including ARCAM's selection of the contemporary essential for Amsterdam: 25 Buildings You Should Have Seen. Its swoopy and silver building has already become an architectural icon in itself. ⊠ *Prins Hendrikkade 600, Centrum* ☎ *020/620–4878* ⊕ *www. arcam.nl* ⊡ *Free* ⊙ *Tues.–Fri. 1–5.*

Het West-Indisch Huis (*West Indies House*). These former headquarters of the Dutch West India Company (WIC) has major historical significance. Although not as sovereign as the VOC, it was essentially given free rein to trade on Africa's west coast, the Americas, and all the islands of the West Pacific and New Guinea, and to oversee the infamous export of 275,000 slaves from West Africa to the Caribbean in the 17th century. In these rooms, the decision was made to buy Manhattan for 60 guilders. Silver bullion, piled up by Piet Pieterszoon Heyn (or Piet Hein), was collected here in 1628 after Piet won another of his infamous sea battles. Now used as a location for events and marriage ceremonies, you can come into the courtyard of the building via its side entrance

The Nemo Science Museum (next to a fun replica of an old VOC ship) was designed by starchitect Renzo Piano, of Centre Pompidou fame.

on Herenmarkt to see the statue of Peter Stuyvesant. ⊠ *Herenmarkt 93–7, Jordaan.*

Scheepvaarthuis (*Shipping Office*). With its extravagantly phantasmagoric zinc-roof detailing spilling over various sculpted sea horses, boat anchors, sea gods (Neptune and his four wives), dolphins, and even shoals of fish, this is one of Amsterdam's most delightful turn-of-the-20th-century structures. Built in the 1910s to sport a suitably prow-shaped front, it was used as the headquarters for the major shipping firms that brought back all that booty from Java and the Spice Islands during the final Dutch colonial years. It's now a five-star hotel, the Grand Hotel Amrâth Amsterdam. 20th-century master architects Piet Kramer, Johan van der Mey, and Michel de Klerk all contributed to the design of the building; their structure was one of the opening salvos by the fantastic Amsterdam School. After admiring all the ornamentation on the facade, amble around the sides to take in the busts of noted explorers, such as Barentsz and Mercator, along with patterned brickwork and strutting iron tracery. Wander inside to check out the Seven Seas restaurant design, enjoy a drink at the classically restored bar, or book a private tour of the upper floors of the building, with its equally lavish interior (via Museum Het Schip, www.hetschip.com, 020/418–2885). ⊠ *Prins Hendrikkade 108, Centrum.*

★ **Westerpark.** Just beyond the Jordaan is one of contemporary Amsterdam's most cherished spaces. It's a park, first and foremost, with lawns, playgrounds, water fountains, a fabulous designer paddling pool, and a couple of tennis courts. Here you'll also find the sprawling terrain of the city's old gas works—the Westergasfabriek. Cafés, galleries, clubs, and a great arthouse cinema occupy the former industrial landscape that has been lovingly detoxed, replanted, and refurbed, building by building. And even more delightfully (and unlike the Vondelpark), behind it lies some natural wilderness with a community farm, a children's farm, a natural playground for kids, and some polder areas with footpaths between them. Plus a lovely late-19th-century cemetery. ⊠ *Haarlemmerweg 8–10, Jordaan* ⊕ *www.westergasfabriek.nl.*

THE CANAL RING

Forming an area of unparalleled historical beauty, the famous Grachtengordel, or Canal Ring, is located to the west and south of the city center. Call it a "belt" or a "girdle," the Golden Age landmark actually exists of three main encircling canals: Prinsengracht (Princes' Canal), Keizersgracht (Emperors' Canal), and Herengracht (Gentlemen's Canal). They became the premier addresses—the Fifth Avenues, the Avenue Fochs, the Park Lanes—of historic Amsterdam when wealthy bankers and famous merchants ordered homes built in the latest fashionable styles, ranging from Baroque to Neoclassical.

The Grachtengordel is quintessential Amsterdam. As you explore, keep in mind that when these impressive canal houses were built for the movers and shakers of the 17th-century Golden Age, home owners were taxed on their houses' width, not height. A double frontage and staircase (two adjacent lots) displayed wealth and prestige, as did the number of windows facing the canal, and ornate gables and decorative features (such as finely wrought railings). While there's considerable scrolling variation from one house to the next, creating that attractive higgledy-piggledy, gabled skyline for which Amsterdam is famous, it's very harmonious, and from a historic point of view, remarkably intact. Sixteen hundred buildings in these canals have protected heritage status, and as of July 2010 the Canal Belt is officially on the UNESCO World Heritage List.

The first canals were developed for defense and then transport, but in the 17th century came an original piece of town planning (and epic job-creation scheme) to deal with the need for expansion: a girdle of canals wrapping right round the city center. The first phase of the construction of the Canal Belt began with the **Herengracht** (Gentlemen's Canal) in 1612. This was followed some 50 years later with a second phase—the **Keizersgracht** (Emperor's Canal) and **Prinsengracht** (Prince's Canal). Developing from west to east (like a giant windshield wiper, according to historian Geert Mak), the innermost canal, the **Singel,** was widened, and the main canals were intersected with radial canals like the **Brouwersgracht, Leliegracht,** and **Leidsegracht** (all of which are well worth a diversion). The grandest stretch of the grandest canal is supposedly along the Herengracht between Leidsestraat to the Amstel, which is known as the **Gouden Bocht** ("Golden Bend").

When it comes to touring the canals, there are many boats that depart and leave from the piers near the Centraal Station with numerous stops throughout the city. *For full information see the section on "Amsterdam Tours" in the Travel Smart chapter.*

The marble-lined interiors are no less spectacular and surprisingly deep. Be sure to visit one of the canalside museums to get a fuller appreciation. Open Gardens Weekend (⊕ *www.opentuinendagen.nl*) in June and Open Monument Weekend (⊕ *www.openmonumentendag.nl*) in September offer additional chances to see inside properties rarely open to the public. Early morning, before the cruise boats churn up the water, can be a special time. Look out for the special Amsterdam light that turns the windows of the Keizersgracht and Herengracht lilac.

TIMING

A wander along one of these canals will provide some of the most memorable images of your trip, so allocate at least a morning or afternoon for exploring; die-hard lovers of historic Amsterdam could easily spend a day or two here.

WESTERN CANAL RING

The section leading from the Brouwersgracht, where the grand canals start, to the Leidsestraat, includes fine views and excellent shopping opportunities, particularly south of the Rozengracht in the Negen Straatjes (Nine Little Streets) that run between the canals.

TOP ATTRACTIONS

Fodor's Choice ★ **Anne Frankhuis** (*Anne Frank House*). Anne Frank, one of the most famous authors of the 20th century, wrote the inspiring diary of a Jewish girl who was forced to hide with her family here in a hidden apartment from the Nazis. In the pages of *The Diary of Anne Frank* (published posthumously in 1947 as *The Annex* by her father—the title she chose) young Anne recorded two increasingly fraught years living in secret in a warren of rooms at the back of this 1635 canal house. Anne Frank was born in Germany in 1929; when she was four her family moved to the Netherlands to escape growing anti-Jewish sentiment. Otto Frank operated a pectin business and decided to stay in his adopted country when the war finally reached the Netherlands in 1940. In July 1942 he took his wife and daughters, Anne and her sister, Margo, into hiding, and a week later they were joined by the Van

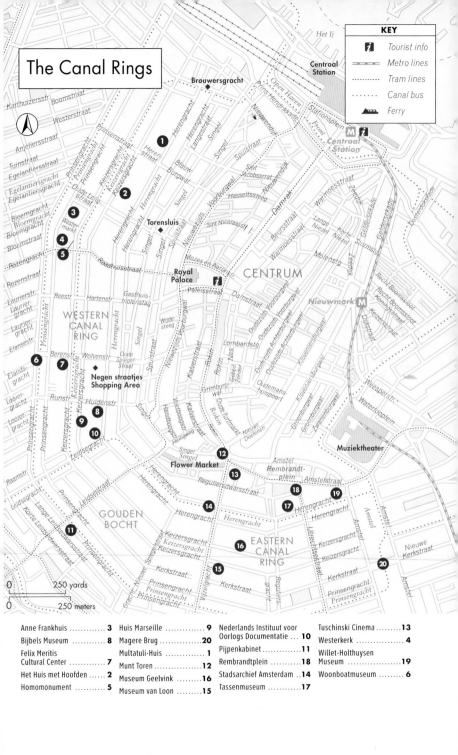

The Canal Rings

Het Ij

Centraal Station

Brouwersgracht

Open Haven Front

Stationsplein

Centraal Station

Torensluis

CENTRUM

Royal Palace

Nieuwmarkt

WESTERN CANAL RING

Negen straatjes Shopping Area

Muziektheater

Flower Market

Amstel Rembrandt-plein

GOUDEN BOCHT

EASTERN CANAL RING

Nieuwe Kerkstraat

0 — 250 yards

0 — 250 meters

Lanskroon, a classic Amsterdam café on the Singelgracht and the Heisteeg, serves fantastic *stroopwafels* (treacle waffles).

Pels family: Auguste, Hermann, and their son, Peter. Four months later, dentist Fritz Pfeffer moved in.

The five adults and three children sought refuge in the attic of the rear annex, or *achterhuis*, of Otto's business in the center of Amsterdam. The entrance to the flat was hidden behind a hinged bookcase. Here, like many *onderduikers* ("people in hiding") throughout Amsterdam, Anne dreamed her dreams, wrote her diary, and pinned movie-star pictures to her wall (still on view). Five trusted employees provided them with food and supplies. In her diary, Anne chronicles the day-to-day life in the house: her longing for a best friend, her crush on Peter, her frustration with her mother, her love for her father, and her annoyance with the petty dentist, who was called Dussel in her diary. In August 1944, the Franks were betrayed and the Gestapo invaded their hideaway. All the members of the annex were transported to camps. Anne and Margot died of typhoid in Bergen-Belsen a few months before the liberation. Otto Frank was the only survivor of the annex. Miep Gies, one of the friends who helped with the hiding, found Anne's diary after the raid and kept it through the war. Now, millions of people read it and its tale of humanity's struggle with fascism. ■ TIP→ The line to get into the Anne Frank House is extremely long, especially in the summer. It moves (sort of) quickly, but it's best to arrive early or book tickets online to avoid the worst crowds. ✉ *Prinsengracht 263–267, Centrum* ☎ *020/556-7105* ⊕ *www. annefrank.nl* 🎫 *€9* ⊗ *Mar.–Sept., daily 9–9 (Sat. until 10); July–Aug., daily 9–10; Sept.–Mar., daily 9–7 (Sat. until 9).*

★ **Het Huis met de Hoofden** (*The House with the Heads*). The Greek deities of Apollo, Ceres, Mars, Minerva, Bacchus, and Diana welcome you—or rather busts of them do—to this magnificent example of Dutch Renaissance architecture, one of the three houses in Amsterdam with a side house, the forerunner of the double house. (The Bartolotti House, Herengracht 170–172 and De Dolfijn (The Dolphin), Singel 140–142 are the other spectacular examples.) This 1622 mansion is attributed to architect Pieter de Keyser, son of the more famed Hendrick. One story attached to the house relates to a maid and a crew of burglars: as they emerged from some hiding place, she chopped off their heads one by one and then (maybe) married the seventh. In 2007 the mansion was bought by Joseph R. Ritman, owner of a world-famous collection of spirituality literature, the Hermetic Philosophy Library (open to the public at Bloemstraat 13). ⊠ *Keizersgracht 123, Centrum.*

Multatuli Huis. This museum honors the beliefs and work (and continues the legacy) of Eduard Douwes Dekker (1820–87), a.k.a. Multatuli (from the Latin, meaning "I have suffered greatly"), who famously wrote *Max Havelaar, or the Coffee Auctions of the Dutch Trading Company,* a book that uncovered the evils of Dutch colonialism. The son of an Amsterdam sea captain, Dekker accompanied his father to the Dutch East Indies (Indonesia) and joined the Dutch civil service. After years of poverty and wandering, in 1860 he wrote and published his magnum opus, denouncing and exposing the colonial landowners' narrow minds and inhumane practices. Today, Dutch intellectuals and progressive thinkers respect him mightily. ⊠ *Korsjespoortsteeg 20, Centrum* ☎ *020/638–1938* ⊕ *www.multatuli-museum.nl* ☉ *Weekends noon–5 and Tues. 10–5.*

Fodor's Choice ★ **Westerkerk** (*Western Church*). Built between 1620 and 1631 by (you guessed it) Hendrick de Keyser, the Dutch Renaissance–style Westerkerk was the largest Protestant church in the world until St. Paul's Cathedral in London was built in 1675. Its 85-meter tower, the tallest in the city, is topped by a gaudy copy of the crown of the Habsburg emperor Maximilian I, who gave Amsterdam the right to use his royal insignia in 1489 in gratitude for support given to the Austro-Burgundian princes.

The church is renowned for its organ and carillon (there are regular concerts). The carillon is played every Tuesday between noon and 1 by a real person (a *carillonneur*) but is automated at other times with different songs tinkling out on the quarter hour, day and night (it drives some locals nuts). Anne Frank described the tunes in her diary. Rembrandt, who lived on Rozengracht 188 during his poverty-stricken last years, and his son, Titus, are buried (somewhere) here. Rembrandt's posthumous reputation inspired some very surreal television three centuries later, when a body was unearthed that was mistakenly thought to be his: while exposed to the glare of the news cameras, the skull turned to dust. The Westertoren (Westerkerk Tower) is a fun climb from April to the end of October. ⊠ *Prinsengracht 281(corner of Westermarkt), Centrum* ☎ *020/624–7766* ⊕ *www.westerkerk.nl* ⎙ *Free for interior; €6 for Westertoren.* ☉ *Apr.–June, weekdays 10–6, Sat. 10–8; July and Aug., Mon.–Sat. 10–8; Sept., weekdays 10–6, Sat. 10–8; Oct., weekdays 10–4, Sat. 10–6.*

WORTH NOTING

★ **Bijbels Museum** (*Bible Museum*). Although this museum does indeed have a massive collection of Bibles—as well as exhibits with archaeological finds from the Middle East and models of ancient temples that evoke biblical times—what probably draws more people is the building itself and its beautifully restored interior and garden.

> **INTERNATIONAL CELEBRITY**
>
> Anne Frank's diary has been translated into more than 65 languages and has sold more than 30 million copies, making her the international celebrity she always dreamed of being.

The two classical canal houses built in 1662 by Philips Vingboons were known as the Cromhout Houses after their first owner, rich merchant Jacob Cromhout (The crooked leg on the gable stone is a play on his name, which means bent wood in Dutch). Highlights include the kitchens, garden rooms and garden, and 18th-century painted ceilings by Jacob de Wit. ⊠ *Herengracht 366–368, Centrum* ☎ *020/624–2436* ⊕ *www.bijbelsmuseum.nl* ☑ *€10* ◷ *Mon.–Sat. 10–5, Sun. 11–5.*

Felix Meritis Cultural Center. The recently restored home of the former Felix Meritus Society ("happiness through achievement"), is a typical building of the Enlightenment, and indeed its Neoclassical architecture arose one year before the French Revolution, 1788. It housed a society dedicated to the study and promotion of economics, science, painting, music, and literature. It has an observatory and concert hall (Robert and Clara Schumann performed here twice). After the dissolution of the society in 1888, it was owned by printers, occupied by the Communist Party, and then became a venue for performing arts under the name Shaffy Theater. It's now a European Centre for Arts, Culture, and Science (and that's Culture with a very big C). Readings, panels, and discussions are hosted here with the aim of promoting international cultural exchange. Drop by to pick up a program or a coffee in its café with huge windows overlooking the canal. ⊠ *Keizersgracht 324, Centrum* ☎ *020/623–2321* ⊕ *www.felixmeritis.nl.*

Homomonument (*Homosexual Monument*). This, the world's first memorial to persecuted gays and lesbians, designed by Karin Daan, was unveiled in 1987. Three huge triangles of pinkish granite—representing past, present, and future—form a larger triangle. On May 4 (Remembrance Day), there are services here commemorating all homosexual victims in history, with emphasis on the victims of World War II, when thousands were killed (the 50,000 sentenced were all forced to wear pink triangles stitched to their clothing). Flowers are laid daily for lost friends, especially on the descending triangle that forms a dock of sorts into Keizersgracht. The points of the triangles point to the Anne Frank House, the National Monument on Dam Square, and the COC Center, the gay-and-lesbian organization founded in 1946, discreetly called the Center of Culture and Leisure Activities. ⊠ *Westermarkt, Centrum.*

Pink Point. Near the Homomonument is the kiosk housing Pink Point, the best source of information on gay and lesbian Amsterdam. It is open daily 10–6 (July–August 9:30–7). ☎ *020/428–1070* ⊕ *www. pinkpoint.org*

Huis Marseille (*Marseille House*). This cutting-edge, contemporary photography museum is housed in six exhibition rooms of a 17th-century canal house originally owned by a rich merchant with business interests in Marseille (the warehouse at number 403 also belonged to the house). The widest possible range of genres is covered with new shows every three months. They also have around 2,000 photographic books which can be consulted in the library. ⊠ *Keizersgracht 401, Centrum* ☎ *020/531–8989* ⊕ *www.huismarseille.nl* ⊡ *€5* ☉ *Tues.–Sun. 11–6.*

> **TOWERS BRIDGE**
>
> **Torensluis** (*Tower Bridge*). A top photo-op in this district, the Torensluis is the oldest (and the widest) bridge in Amsterdam. It was originally built over a 17th-century sluice gate and book-ended with towers. The rooms with barred windows that you see at the base of the bridge were used as a lockup for drunks and have now been turned into an art space called brug9. ⊠ *Singel between Torensteeg and Oude Leliestraat, Centrum.*

QUICK BITES

The Pancake Bakery. A Dutch way of keeping eating costs down is to pack one's belly with pancakes. The Pancake Bakery remains one of the best-known places in Amsterdam to try them, with a menu that offers a near infinite range of topping possibilities—from the sweet to the fruity to the truly belly-gelling powers of cheese, pinapple, and bacon. ⊠ *Prinsengracht 191, Centrum* ☎ *020/625–1333* ⊕ *www.pancake.nl.*

Spanjer en Van Twist. This popular spot, only five minutes from the Anne Frank House, is great for lunch under the trees. ⊠ *Leliegracht 60, Centrum* ☎ *020/639–0109* ⊕ *www.spanjerenvantwist.nl.*

🐾 **Woonbootmuseum** (*Houseboat Museum*). There are around 2,250 houseboats in Amsterdam (and one especially for cats—the Poezenboot [Cat Boat] asylum that floats opposite Singel 38). The converted 1914-built sailing vessel, the *Hendrika Maria*, provides a glimpse into this unique lifestyle. It almost feels as if you are visiting grandma, and there's even a special child-play zone. ⊠ *Prinsengracht opposite No. 296, Centrum* ☎ *020/427–0750* ⊕ *www.houseboatmuseum.nl* ⊡ *€3.75* ☉ *Mar.–Oct., Tues.–Sun. 11–5; Nov.–Feb., Fri.–Sun. 11–5.*

EASTERN CANAL RING AND REMBRANDTPLEIN

Amsterdam's 17th-century Golden Age left behind a tidemark of magnificent buildings to line its lovely canals. The point where these canals intersected with Nieuwe Spiegelstraat became known as the "Golden Bend"—the Gouden Bocht—since houses here were occupied by the richest families of Amsterdam, where elaborate gables, richly decorated facades, finely detailed cornices, colored marbles, and heavy doors created an imposing architecture that suits the bank headquarters of today as well as it did the richest grandees of yore. This tour takes in such time-burnished marvels, but—to an even greater degree than with the

CLOSE UP

The Crowning Touch: Gables and Hooks

2

Amsterdam's famous neck gables. Keep an eye peeled for bell and step gables.

The gabled houses on the Canal Ring are Amsterdam's most picture-perfect historic feature. The infinite array of gables on the city houses dominates the city's postcard-perfect image and is a carefully preserved asset.

Starting in the 16th century, the different gable types were used to camouflage the end of sharp, pitched roofs and architectural idiosyncrasies. The lack of firm land meant that Amsterdam houses were built on narrow, deep plots, and one of the only ways to make a property distinctive was at the top, with a decorative gable. The most famous design was the step gable, which rises to a pinnacle, and was also used in Flemish architecture, as seen in the Belgian town of Bruges. Gable variants include spout, step, neck, elevated neck, Dutch, bell, and cornice, and they often include splendid scrollwork and ornamentation.

Styles came and went, so the type of gable can reflect how old a house is (provided they are both the same age; nowadays, sometimes the

gable is saved and the house behind redeveloped). The Brouwersgracht (Brewers' Canal) has colorful facades harking back to Amsterdam's brewing trade with the towns of the Hanseatic League. Some gables include decorative panels that show what was being stored: grain, wood, gold, or coffee. Others have symbolic pictorial decorations, and many carry the merchant family's shield.

One thing all canal houses have in common is the hook in the gable, to which a pulley wheel and rope can be attached. This handy manual elevator system was developed from medieval shipping techniques; it's pretty impossible to move bulky goods up and down the precariously steep staircases found inside most Amsterdam houses. Boxes, pianos, couches, or whatever are winched up using the rope and pulley, and hauled in through exceptionally wide removable windows. Keep your eyes peeled as you walk through the city and you may see a few Dutch movers in action.

2

tour of the Western Canal Ring and the Jordaan—this remains a city area of contrasts. Amsterdam's richest stretches of canals, the Eastern Canal Ring, which still glitters with the sumptuous pretensions of a Golden Age past, will be put against the more "street" (albeit quickly gentrifying) realities of two commercial avenues with busy pitches, Leidseplein and Rembrandtplein, that fully reflect Amsterdam's present as a truly global village.

As for the area's "back story," in 1660 city planners decided to continue the western half-ring of canals that had been rising since 1613 and had already been proven as a prime and scenic living location for the well-heeled. But the mega-well-heeled observed that the allotments there were too narrow and therefore now had an opportunity to buy two adjoining allotments in the east; this excess is the reason why this area is currently much less residential and much more taken over by banks, businesses, and hotels. Add museums to this list, as you will find assorted treasures on view hereabouts, including Baroque-era interiors on view at the magnificent 17th-century Willet-Holthuysen Museum and the period-room-rich Museum van Loon. Then also add in scenic pleasures like the Munt Toren tower and the famed Magere Brug ("Skinny") bridge, plus even a stretch or two of canal benches (fairly rare, in fact) to help drink in the canal views, and you have a wonderfully rich exploring district.

To the north of the Golden Bend is the western half of the Grachtengordel (i.e., west of the arterial Leidsestraat and heading up to the magnificent reinvented warehouses of Brouwersgracht). This was the first canal sector to be built and harbors not only miles of gabled residences that reflect most sweetly and surreally in the canal waters below but also intersecting streets that harbor a plethora of high-quality, quirky shopping and eating, especially on the "Nine Streets."

TOP ATTRACTIONS

Fodor'sChoice **Magere Brug** (*Skinny Bridge*). Of Amsterdam's 60-plus drawbridges, ★ the Magere Brug is the most famous and provides gorgeous views of the Amstel and surrounding area. It was purportedly first built in 1672 by two sisters living on opposite sides of the Amstel who wanted an efficient way of sharing that grandest of Dutch traditions: the *gezellige* (socially cozy) midmorning coffee break. Walk by at night when it's spectacularly lit. Many replacements to the original bridge have come and gone, and this, dating from 1969, is just the latest. ⊠ *Between Kerkstraat and Nieuwe Kerkstraat, Centrum.*

Fodor'sChoice **Museum van Loon.** Once home to one of Rembrandt's most successful ★ students, Ferdinand Bol, this house and its twin, No. 674 next door (home of the Kattenkabinet; a five-room museum dedicated to cats), were built in 1672 by Adriaan Dortsman and extensively remodeled in the 18th century by Abraham van Hagan and his wife, Catherina Tripp, whose names are entwined in the brass balustrade on the staircase. The Van Loon family occupied it from 1886 to 1960. After extensive restoration to its 18th-century glory, it was opened as a museum in the 1970s. The elegant salons include many Van Loon portraits and possessions, including paintings known as *witjes*, illusionistic depictions of

Amsterdam's Hofjes—the Historic Almshouses

Claes Claeszhofje

Hidden behind innocent-looking gateways throughout the city center, most notably along the main ring of canals and in the Jordaan neighborhood, are some of Amsterdam's most charming houses.

There are more than 40 *hofjes* (little courtyards surrounded by almshouses), mainly dating back to the 18th century when the city's flourishing merchants established hospices for the elderly.

Their philanthropy was supposed to be rewarded by a place in heaven. But be warned (and be prepared for disappointment): today's hofje residents like their peace and quiet, and often lock their entrances to keep out visitors.

The most notable examples on the Grachtengordel can be viewed only on open days.

Begijnhof (*Beguine Court*). Here, serenity reigns just feet away from the bustle of the city. The Begijnhof is the

tree-filled courtyard of a residential hideaway where women lived a spiritual and philanthropic life from 1150 onwards. Documents from the 14th century mention the "Beghynhuys" with some rules and regulations for membership. They were simple: no hens, no dogs, and no men. Free lodging was provided in return for caring for the sick and educating the poor.

No. 34 is one of two remaining wooden houses in the city following 15th-century fires that consumed three-quarters of the city. The small **Engelse Hervormde Kerk** (English Reformed Church) dates from the 14th century, when it was a place of worship for the Begijnen. Its pulpit panels were designed by a young Piet Mondriaan in 1898. After the Alteration of 1578 the church was relinquished to Protestants (and used by the Pilgrim Fathers visiting in 1607). When senior Begijn Cornelia Arents died in 1654, she said she'd rather be buried in the gutter of the Begijnhof than in the—now Protestant—church. Her wish was granted the following year when her remains were moved; look for the granite slab and plaque on the wall between the church and lawn. The replacement chapel, **Begijnhofka-pel** (Begijn Chapel) was designed by Philips Vingboons and approved by the city (as was the mode), provided it didn't look like a church from the outside. ☒ *Entrances on the north side of Spui and on Gedempte Begijnensloot opposite Begijnensteeg, Centrum* ⊕ *www.begijnhofamsterdam. nl* ⊙ *Begijnhof-Kapel, Mon. 1–6:30, Tues.–Fri. 9–6:30, weekends 9–6.*

The Begijnhof is by far the most famous hofje, but there are a few other little gems to explore that are generally open.

Sint Andrieshofje. Built in 1614, this is the oldest courtyard almshouse in Amsterdam and famous for its Delftware entry. ☒ *Egelantiersgracht 105–141, Jordaan.*

Claes Claeszhofje. This charmer is actually two joined hofjes: the Zwaardvegershofje (Sword Makers' Hofje) and the three-house hofje founded in 1616 by the Anabaptist draper Claes Claesz. Anslo (note his coat of arms atop one entry). Today's tenants are artists and music students. Don't miss the **Huis met de Schrijvende Hand** ("House with the Writing Hand"), topped by a six-stepped gable. ☒ *Junction of Egelantiersstraat 28–54, Eerste Egelantiersdwarsstraat 1–5, and Tuinstraat 35–49, Jordaan.*

Zevenkeurvorstenhofje. Though the houses standing today are from the 18th century, the Zevenkeurvorstenhofje was actually founded around 1645. ☒ *Tuinstraat 197–223.*

The Karthuizerhof and a happy occupant.

Karthuizerhof. Founded in 1650, the courtyard has two 17th-century pumps. ☒ *Karthuizersstraat 21–131, Jordaan.*

On the Prinsengracht, between the Prinsenstraat and the Brouwersgracht, are two hofjes very close to one another. The **Van Brienenhofje** (Prinsengracht 85–133, closed to the public) and the **Zon's Hofje** (Prinsengracht 159–171, open weekdays 10–5) both have plaques telling their stories.

Suykerhoff-hofje. For a moment of peace, visit the Suykerhoff-hofje and take in its abundantly green courtyard. These houses opened their doors in 1670 to Protestant "daughters and widows" (as long as they behaved and exhibited "a peace-loving humor") and provided each of them with free rent, 20 tons of turf, 10 pounds of rice, a vat of butter, and some spending money each year. If only the same were done today. ☒ *Lindengracht 149–163, Centrum.*

Seeing "the Venice of the North" by boat is an unforgettable experience.

landscapes and other scenes. The symmetrical garden is a gem. Facing the rear of the house, the recently restored Grecian-style coach house holds exhibitions and in the future (hopefully) will serve teas. ⊠ *Keizersgracht 672, Centrum* ☎ *020/624–5255* ⊕ *www.museumvanloon.nl* ☑ *€7* ⊗ *Wed.–Mon. 11–5.*

★ **Stadsarchief Amsterdam** (*City Archives*). Established in 1914, the city's archives comprise millions of maps, drawings, prints, books, photography, and film about Amsterdam; a staggering 35 km worth, the biggest in the world. But (like the Rijksmuseum), there's a manageable highlights taster with 300 of the "most attractive, unusual, valuable, and moving" items on permanent display in the Treasury, former bank vaults that look like the tomb of an Egyptian pharaoh. The epic checkerboard building, completed in 1926 and named in honor of its theosophist architect Karel de Bazel, is also fascinating and infused with its creator's religious beliefs. In theosophy, a building is an art form that can express a higher message using mathematical principles to achieve total harmony. Have deep thoughts over lunch in the café or browse the excellent on-site bookstore. The additional exhibitions (for which there is usually a small charge) are also terrific. ⊠ *Vijzelstraat 32, Centrum* ☎ *020/251–1511* ⊕ *www.stadsarchief.amsterdam.nl* ☑ *Free* ⊗ *Tues.–Sat. 10–5, Sun. 11–5.*

Tuschinski Cinema. Although officially the architect of this "Plumcake"— as it was described when it first opened in 1921—was H. L. De Jong, the financial and spiritual force was Abram Icek Tuschinski (1886–1942), a Polish Jew who after World War I decided to build a "unique" theater. And because interior designers like Pieter den Besten, Jaap Gidding, and

Chris Bartels came up with a dizzying and dense mixture of Jugendstil, Art Deco, and Amsterdam styles, it is safe to say he achieved his goal. The frescoes of elegant women by Pieter den Besten were only discovered in 2000 under layers of paint. To this day, watching movies from one of the extravagant private balconies remains an unforgettable experience—especially if you are in the "love seats" with champagne. Sobering note: Tuschinski died in Auschwitz. ⊠ *Reguliersbreestraat 26–28, Centrum* ☎ *0900–1458* ⊕ *www.tuschinski.nl.*

Fodor's Choice   **Willet-Holthuysen Museum.** Here's a rare chance to experience what it was
★   like to live in a gracious mansion on the Herengracht in the 18th century. In 1895, widow Sandrina Louisa Willet-Holthuysen bequeathed this house and its contents to the city. It was actually built in 1687 but has been renovated several times and is now under the management of the Amsterdam Museum. Take an hour or so to discover its interiors and artwork, including a sumptuous ballroom and a rarities cabinet. Complete the luxury experience by lounging in the French-style garden in the back. ⊠ *Herengracht 605, Centrum* ☎ *020/523–1822* ⊕ *www. willetholthuysen.nl* ⊒ *€8* ⊗ *Weekdays 10–5, weekends 11–5.*

WORTH NOTING

Munttoren (*Mint or Coin Tower*). This tower received its name in 1672, when French troops occupied much of the surrounding Republic, and Amsterdam was given the right to mint its own coins here for a brief two-year period. Hendrick de Keyser added the spire in 1620, and the weather vane on top in the shape of a gilded ox is a reference to the calves market close by: Kalverstraat. The guardhouse, which now houses a porcelain shop, has a gable stone above its entrance, which portrays two men and a dog in a boat. This is a symbolic representation of the city, where warrior and merchant, bonded by loyalty—that would be the dog—are sailing toward the future. ⊠ *Muntplein, Centrum.*

★   **Museum Geelvinck Hinlopen Huis.** Don't miss this canal-house museum with an unusual entrance on the Keizersgracht. Access is via the tradesmen's entrance (the old coach house) and then through the garden to the rear of the house, which has its front door on the golden bend of the Herengracht. Built in 1687 for Albert Geelvinck and his much younger wife, Sara Hinlopen, it's been home to Amsterdam's most notable families. The interiors are reconstructions though no less interesting for that; enthusiastic curators will be happy to fill you in on some of the details. There are regular concerts, as the Sweelinck musical instruments collection is housed here. ⊠ *Keizersgracht 633, Centrum* ☎ *020/715–5900* ⊕ *www.museumgeelvinck.nl* ⊒ *€8* ⊗ *Wed.–Mon., 11–5.*

Rembrandtplein (*Rembrandt Square*). Smaller than the Leidseplein, this touristy square (which used to be the city's butter market) is the focus for hotels, restaurants, cafés, and nightlife venues. After recent refurbishment, the statue of the man himself in the middle of the square looks even more imposing. Café Schiller at No. 26 is an Art Deco haven from the scrum. ⊠ *One block south of the Amstel River, Centrum.*

THE JORDAAN AND THE LEIDSEPLEIN

The northern sectors of the Grachtengordel canal ring center around Amsterdam's beloved Jordaan (pronounced Yore-*dahn*). Although this cozy, scenic, and singular neighborhood's working-class roots have long sprouted branches of gentrification, it remains an area rich in picturesque canals and historic courtyards—a wanderer's paradise.

While this once-poor district has had one of the city's most colorful histories, today the Jordaan (the name probably derives from the French for garden, *jardin*) has moved steadily upmarket. Its 1895 population of 80,000, which made it one of the densest in Europe, has declined to a mere 14,000, and the whole area has been greatly gentrified. But in many ways, the Jordaan will always remain the Jordaan, even though its narrow alleys and leafy canals are now lined with quirky specialty shops, excellent restaurants, galleries, and designer boutiques, especially along the streets of Tweede Anjeliersdwarstraat, Tuinstraat, and Egelanteirsstraat. Directly south of the Jordaan, marking the midpoint of the Grachtengordel, is the bustling Leidseplein, Amsterdam's vortex for the performing arts, with street performers, music venues, theaters, and jazz bars.

The Leidseplein is the tourist center of the city and, like Rembrandtplein, is surrounded by cheap eateries and bars, their terraces packed with visitors and shoppers set for the Leidsestraat. Cafés like Reijnders (⊠ *Leidseplein 6*), Eijlders (⊠ *Korte Leidsedwarsstraat 47*), and the Art Deco American Hotel (keep an eye out for the statue of the woodcutter in the trees nearby) are more authentic, less tacky respites.

If you walk down the alleyway to the right of the white Stadsschouwberg theater (⊠ *Leidseplein 26*), past the Melkweg and Sugar Factory (nighttime music/theater/happening venues) and over the Leidsegracht, you have reached the southern perimeter of the Jordaan. Built to house canal-belt construction workers in the 17th century, the city's smellier industries such as tanning and brewing were also banished here. Living conditions were overcrowded and squalid, and the inhabitants gained a reputation for rebelliousness and community spirit. Elandsgracht was one of several canals hereabouts that were filled in for sanitary reasons in the 19th century. Today, fancy shops have moved in, including, at the other end of the street, De Looier Indoor Antiques Market (⊠ *Elandsgracht 109*). North of the Rozengracht, the Jordaan becomes even more scenic. Once home to the lumpenproletariat, the neighborhood is now a gentrified paradise.

TOP ATTRACTIONS

★ **Bloemgracht** (*Flower Canal*). Lined with suave "burgher" houses of the 17th century, this canal has been termed the "Herengracht of the Jordaan" (Gentlemen's Canal of the Jordaan). It was a center for paint and dye manufacturers, which made sense, because the Jordaan was populated with Golden Age artists: Rembrandt ran a studio here. Although modern intrusions have been made, Bloemgracht is still proudly presided over by "De Drie Hendricken," three houses set at No. 87 to 91 owned by the Hendrick de Keyser heritage organization, with their gable stones for the farmer, a city settler, and a sailor. ⊠ *Between Lijnbaansgracht and Prinsengracht, Jordaan.*

Fodor'sChoice **Brouwersgracht** (*Brewers' Canal*). Regularly voted Amsterdam's most
★ beautiful street, this wonderful canal at the northern border of the Jordaan is lined by residences and former warehouses for brewers, fish processors, and tanneries who traded here in the 17th century when Amsterdam was the "warehouse of the world." Without sacrificing the ancient vibe, most of the buildings have been converted into luxury apartments. Of particular note are Nos. 204–212 and their trapezium gables. At No. 162, there are two dried fish above the door. This decoration on a metal screen was the forerunner of the gable stone denoting occupation. The canal provides long views down the grand canals that are perfect for photo-ops. The Brouwersgracht runs westward from the end of the Singel (a short walk along Prins Hendrikkade from Centraal Station) and forms a cap to the western end of the Grachtengordel. On top of the old canal mansions dotting the Brouwersgracht are symbols referring to the breweries that used this waterway to transport their goods to thirsty drinkers hundreds of years ago. ⊠ *Jordaan.*

Egelantiersgracht (*Eglantine Canal*). Named for the "eglantine rose" (the floral names for canals in the district are certainly at odds with the fragrance emanating from them in their early days), this is one of the loveliest canals in the area. Many of the houses along this canal and the streets around it were first occupied by Golden Age painters and artisans, including the legendary mapmaking Blaeu family. Hidden here is the **St. Andrieshofje,** famous for its Delftware entryway. Certainly not hidden (it is usually jammed with people) is the famed **Café 't Smalle** (on the corner of the Prinsengracht). This *bruin café* ("brown bar"), covered with eglantine roses and complete with waterside terrace, was where Pieter Hoppe began his jenever distillery in 1780, an event of such global significance that 't Smalle is recreated in Japan's Holland Village in Nagasaki. ⊠ *Between Lijnbaansgracht and Prinsengracht, Jordaan.*

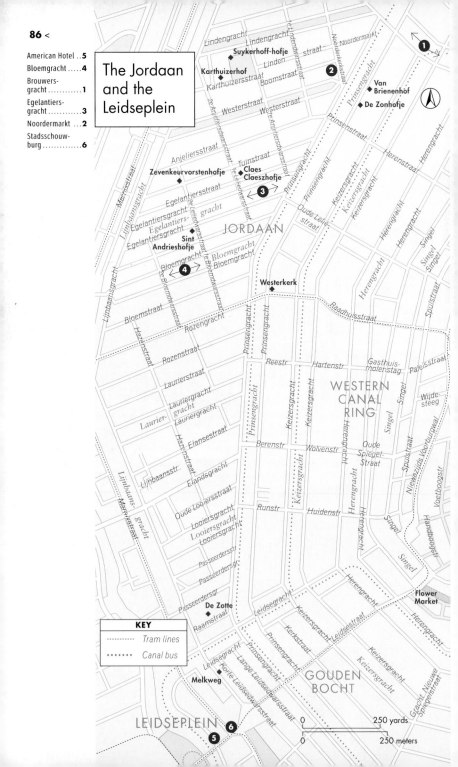

The Jordaan
and the
Leidseplein

KEY

.... Tram lines

•••••• Canal bus

Catch a show and laugh out loud at the Boom Chicago.

QUICK
BITES

Winkel 43. The city's best apple pie can be had at Winkel 43. ✉ *Noordermarkt 43, Centrum* ☎ *020/623–0223* ⊕ *www.winkel43.nl.*

Café Chris. If you're more thirsty than hungry, try the "brown bar" Café Chris, which has been pouring beverages since 1624. Its coziness is taken to absurd lengths in its tiny men's bathroom, whose urinal position outside the door means that pranksters can easily shock you out of your reveries with a quick pull of the flusher. Be warned. ✉ *Bloemstraat 42, Centrum* ☎ *020/624–5942* ⊕ *www.cafechris.nl.*

Noordermarkt (*Northern Market*). In 1620, as the Jordaan expanded, city planners decided to build a church at this end of town for poorer residents. The **Noorderkerk** (Northern Church) designed by Hendrick de Keyser (who else?) and completed after his death by his son Pieter, was built on egalitarian lines in the form of a Greek cross (four equal arms) with the pulpit in the middle. Until 1688 the surrounding square, Noordermarkt, was a graveyard whose residents were moved to make room for a market, and the commerce is still notable. On Mondays, there's a flea market, with a textile market on Westerstraat, and on Saturdays, there's a popular organic farmers' market with a general market along Lindengracht. There are excellent eating opportunities around the square, including a foodies' favorite, Bordewijk (✉ *Noordermarkt*). Other restaurants on Westerstraat, including **De Buurman** (✉ *Westerstraat 30* ☎ *020/625–2428*), are also top-notch. ✉ *Bounded by Prinsengracht, Noorderkerkstraat, and Noordermarkt, Centrum.*

WORTH NOTING

Eden Amsterdam American Hotel. This landmark was designed by Willem Kromhout in 1902. He grafted Neo-Gothic turrets, Jugendstil gables, Art Deco windows, and a charming freestyle clock tower onto a proto–Amsterdam School structure. Its famed Art Deco–style Café Americain, where Mata Hari held her wedding reception, went from bohemian to being boycotted when it banned hippies in the 1960s. Today, it remains the perfect place for a spot of tea. ⊠ *Leidsekade 97, Jordaan* ☎ *020/556–3200* ⊕ *www.edenamsterdamamerican.com.*

Stadsschouwburg (*Municipal Theater*). After burning down and being rebuilt several more times, the current Neo-Renaissance facade that dominates Leidseplein, with its lushly Baroque-style horseshoe interior, was created in 1894. The nation's theater scene was somewhat staid until 1968, when, during a performance of the *Tempest,* the actors were showered with tomatoes. The nationwide protest, the "tomato campaign," showed people's discontent with the established theater's lack of social engagement. It resulted in subsidies for newer theater groups—many of which now form the old guard who regularly play here. Today, Dutch theater is dynamic, strongly physical and visual, often with a hilarious, absurdist sense.

Although the majority of the programming is in Dutch, there's also a constant stream of visiting theater and dance companies. The International Theater & Film Books store downstairs next to the entrance also comes highly recommended by theater lovers. The Uitburo, where you can buy tickets for all cultural events, is also located here; pick up a free copy (in Dutch) of the listings newspaper *Uitkrant.* ⊠ *Leidseplein 26, Jordaan* ☎ *020/624–2311* ⊕ *www.ssba.nl; www. theaterandfilmbooks.com.*

QUICK BITES

Boom Chicago. Americans will feel right at home at the hilarious improv café Boom Chicago, where people can enjoy a decent dinner before seeing Boom's later evening show. In summer there is a terrace option. ⊠ *Leidseplein 12, Museum District* ☎ *020/423–0101 tickets* ⊕ *www.boomchicago.nl.*

Wildschut. One of Amsterdam's first grand cafés, Wildschut is an elegant respite after culture or shopping. ⊠ *Roelof Hartplein 1–3, Museum District* ☎ *020/676–8220.*

2

THE MUSEUM DISTRICT

In short, the history of art is here at your fingertips (not to mention your potentially blistered toetips), as Rembrandts, Van Goghs, and Bill Violas are all on evocative display in the city's three main art museums: the Rijksmuseum, the Vincent van Gogh Museum, and the Stedelijk Museum of modern art.

The sheer quantity of quality on display in the museums located around Museumplein offers a remarkably complete lesson in the history of Western art. But remember that when it comes to art, as with all good things in life, moderation is the key. Happily, what saves this neighborhood from drowning in its own rarefied air is the not-to-be-missed people's park and city's lung, the Vondelpark, where you can neutralize your art-soaked eyes with the restful greens of grasses and trees while sipping on a beverage or scoffing down a picnic. When you regain your energy, remember that this neighborhood also harbors the most elitist shopping options along the country's most famous fashion strip, P. C. Hooftstraat. And the antiques shops along Nieuwe Spiegelstraat are everything a shopaholic could wish for.

It's always been a plush district. At the end of the 19th century, the city wanted a zone for luxury housing here, but dithered on how to develop it even as the cultural institutions were being put in place: the Rijksmuseum (1885), the Concertgebouw (1888), and the Stedelijk (1895). Eventually the decision to create an open space was agreed. In 1973, the Van Gogh Museum joined the square. The past few years have seen some well-publicized cultural chaos with delays and confusion over the redevelopment of the Stedelijk and the Rijksmuseum. After what felt like forever (but was in fact only a decade), both museums reopened in 2013 and 2014 respectively. The question remains: were they worth the wait?

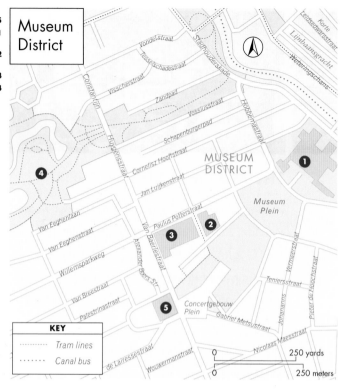

TIMING

With 70% more exhibition space the new Stedelijk is rather big, and the completely refurbished Rijks is huge. Doing all three museums, including the Van Gogh, is probably achievable in a day, but it doesn't allow much time to linger. It also depends on the queues, for which the Van Gogh is especially notorious. Visit on a Wednesday and you can sandwich in a free lunchtime concert at the Concertgebouw.

TOP ATTRACTIONS

QUICK BITES

De Hollandsche Manege. Nip into the Neoclassical-era Hollandsche Manege (the oldest riding school in the Netherlands) and enjoy a cup of tea in one of Amsterdam's best-kept secrets. Inspired by the famous Spanish Riding School in Vienna, and a national monument, the building's café is open to the public and overlooks the riding arena where classes are regularly held. ⊠ *Vondelstraat 140, Museum District and Environs* ☎ *020/618–0942* ⊕ *www.dehollandschemanege.nl.*

Fodor's Choice
★

Rijksmuseum (*State Museum*). Rembrandt's *The Night Watch*, Vermeer's *The Love Letter,* Frans Hals's *Portrait of a Young Couple* . . . you get the picture. The Netherlands' greatest museum, the famed Rijksmuseum is home to a near infinite selection of masterpieces by these top

Believe it or not, the Rijksmuseum's celebrated Rembrandt masterpiece, *The Night Watch*, should really be called *The Day Watch*, according to many art historians.

masters along with Steen, Ruisdael, Hobbema, Cuyp, and the rest of their Golden Age ilk. Long the nation's pride, the museum was rent by major changes when it closed for a massive 12-year renovation beginning in 2005. As of Spring 2013, however, the revamped museum will finally open its doors, and viewers will see a lot more than just burnished gold-leafed ceilings and polished terrazzo-stone floors. The big news: the renewed Rijks has abandoned the old art/design/history divisions and has now threaded these three previously disparate collections into one panoply of art and style presented chronologically, from the Middle Ages to the 20th century. Don't be surprised, in other words, if you see a vase in a 17th-century painting by Gerard Dou and the same, real Delft blue-and-white vase next to it.

That is just the largest of changes wrought in the new renovation. The first, however, will be the museum's spectacular exterior. When architect P. J. H. Cuypers came up with a somewhat over-the-top design in the late 1880s, it shocked Calvinist Holland down to its—one imagines—overly starched shorts. Cuypers was persuaded to tone down some of what was thought as excessive (read: Catholic) elements of his Neo-Renaissance decoration and soaring Neo-Gothic lines. During the building's construction, however, he did manage to sneak some of his ideas back in, and the result is a magnificent, turreted building that glitters with gold leaf and is textured with sculpture—all the more spectacular now, thanks to the first-class renovation (much of the building has been restored the way Cuypers intended it to be, including the terrazzo flooring in the Great Hall). This is, truly, a fitting palace for the national art collection.

Dutch Art—Then and Now

Capture of Damietta by Haarlem Crusaders by Cornelis Claesz van Wieringen (ca. 1580–1633).

Few other countries can boast of having fathered so many great artists, but then again, Holland seems almost expressly composed for the artist by nature. Its peaceful dells, rolling dunes, and verdant mantles of foliage seem so alluring they practically demand the artist pick up brush and palette. During the Golden Age of the 17th century, an estimated 20 million paintings were executed and every home seemed to have an oil painting hung on the wall. Even before the arrival of Rembrandt and Vermeer, the country had a rich artistic history.

In the late 16th century, the Netherlands were divided into a Flemish south under Catholic Spanish rule, and an independent northern alliance of Dutch Protestant provinces. Before then, most painters hailed from the southern cities of Gent, Antwerp, and Bruges, and their subject matter was mostly biblical and allegorical— Jan van Eyck (1385–1441) founded the Flemish School, Hieronymus Bosch (1450–1516) crafted meticulous, macabre allegories, and Pieter Bruegel the Elder (1525–69) depicted scenes of Flemish peasant life.

In the north, a different style began surfacing. Around Haarlem, Jan Mostaert (1475–1555) and Lucas van der Leyden (1489–1553) brought a new realism into previously static paintings. In Utrecht, Gerrit van Honthorst (1590–1656) used light and shadow to create realism never seen before on canvas.

From these disparate schools flowed the Golden Age of Dutch painting, and Hals, Rembrandt, and Vermeer all borrowed from each diverse technique. Frans Hals (1581–1666) has been called the first modern painter. A fantastically adept and naturally gifted man, he could turn out a portrait in an hour. He delighted in capturing the emotions—a smile or grimace—in an early manifestation of Impressionism.

Rembrandt van Rijn (1606–69) is regarded as the most versatile artist of the 17th century. Born in Leiden, he grew rich from painting and tuition. His early works were overly ornamental, but as the years went by he dug deeper into the metaphysical essence of his subjects. When his material world collapsed around him—he was blackmailed and ruined—he somehow turned out even greater art, showing off a marvelously skilled use of light and shadow.

Jan Vermeer (1632–72), the third in this triumvirate, was a different case altogether. He produced only 35 known paintings, but their exquisite nature make him the most precious painter of his time. He brought genre art to its peak; in small canvases with overwhelming realism he painted the soft calm and everyday sameness of middle-class life.

Around the middle of the century, Baroque influences began permeating Dutch art, heralding a trend for landscapes. Artists such as Albert Cuyp and Meindert Hobbema's scenes of polder lanes, grazing cows, and windswept canals were coveted by 17th- and 18th-century collectors. Other masters were more playful in tone. Jan Steen's (1625–79) lively, satirical, and sometimes-lewd scenes are imbued with humor.

The greatest Dutch painter of the 19th century is undoubtedly Vincent van Gogh (1853–90). During his short but troubled life, he produced an array of masterworks, although he famously sold only one. He only began painting in 1881, and his first paintings often depicted dark peasant scenes. But in his last four years, spent in France, he produced endlessly colorful and arresting works. In 1890, he committed suicide after struggling with depression. To this day, his legacy continues to move art lovers everywhere.

The 20th century brought confusion to the art scene. Unsure what style to adopt, many artists reinvented themselves. Piet Mondriaan (1872–1944) is someone who evolved with his century. Early in his career he painted bucolic landscapes. Then, in 1909, at the age of 41, he began dabbling, first with Expressionism and then Cubism. He eventually developed his own style, called neo-plasticism. Using only the primary colors of yellow, red, and blue set against neutral white, gray, and black, he created stylized studies in form and color. In 1917, together with his friend Theo van Doesberg (1883–1931), he published an arts magazine called *De Stijl* (*The Style*) as a forum for a design movement attempting to harmonize the arts through purified abstraction. Though it lasted only 15 years, the movement's effect was felt around the world.

The most vibrant movement to emerge after World War II was the experimental CoBrA (artists from Copenhagen, Brussels, and Amsterdam), cofounded by Karel Appel (1921–2006) and Constant (née Constant Nieuwenhuis, 1920–2005). With bright colors and abstract shapes, their paintings have a childlike quality. The artists involved continue to have influence in their respective countries.

Girl with a Pearl Earring, Jan Vermeer (1632–72).

While the collection encompasses both the West and Asia, and ranges from the 9th through the 19th centuries, the bulk is of 15th- to 17th-century paintings, mostly Dutch. But if your time is limited, head directly for the Gallery of Honor to admire Rembrandt's *The Night Watch*, with its central figure, the "stupidest man in Amsterdam," Frans Banningh Cocq. His militia buddies that surround him each paid 100 guilders to be included—quite the sum in those days, so a few of them complained about being lost in all those shadows. It should also be noted that some of these shadows are formed by the daylight coming in through a small window. Daylight? Indeed, *The Night Watch* is actually *The Day Watch*, but it received its name when it was obscured with soot—imagine the restorers' surprise. The rest of this "Best of the Golden Age" hall features other well-known Rembrandt paintings and works by Vermeer, Frans Hals, and other household names.

> ### KRAMER'S BRIDGE
>
> Architectural buffs shouldn't miss the 1925 bridge crossing Singelgracht on the Leidsestraat. Its swoopy, Amsterdam School style was designed by Piet Kramer (1881–1961), along with 220 other Amsterdam bridges. For more information on Amsterdam's historic bridges, visit *www.bmz. amsterdam.nl* (in Dutch).

A progression through the different floors (each floor of the two wings is dedicated to one or more centuries) takes you past works by some of the greatest Dutch painters of the 15th to the 19th centuries. Get ready to browse Mannerist renderings of biblical and mythic scenes where gods and goddesses show an almost yogic ability in twisting their limbs; eerily lifelike portraits with the lighting maximized to flatter the paying subject; landscapes that may either be extravagant and fantastical in both subject and style or conversely dull, flat, and essentially lacking everything but sky; Caravaggio-inspired exercises by the painters of Utrecht School who employed contrast in light and shadow to heighten a sense of drama; straight moralistic paintings of jolly taverns and depraved brothels warning of the dangers of excess; meticulous and shimmering still-lifes of flowers, food, and furnishings; cold mathematical renderings of interiors that could be used as architectural blueprints. All of these works prove that the nouveau riche of the Golden Age had a hunger for art that knew no bounds.

Unmissable masterpieces include Vermeer's *The Little Street*—a magical sliver of 17th-century Delft life—and his incomparable *The Love Letter*, in which a well-appointed interior reveals a mistress and her maid caught in the emotional eddies of a recently opened and read billet-doux. Ostensibly, a more sedate missive is being read in Vermeer's *Woman in Blue Reading a Letter*, on view nearby. But is this just a matronly dress or is the woman pregnant and thinking about a missing husband (note the seafaring map)?

For an institution dedicated to antiquity and art history, the Rijksmuseum has shown a remarkable technical savvy in making its vast collection more accessible via its incredible website. On the sub-site Rijksstudio you can see, download, share, and do basically anything else you like with images of 125,000 works from the museum's collection.

■ TIP → Don't leave the country without visiting the mini-museum at Schiphol Airport (✉ *Holland Boulevard between piers E and F behind passport control* ☎ *020/653–5036* ☉ *Daily, 6 am–8 pm*). ✉ *Stadhouderskade 42, Museum District* ☎ *020/674–7000* ⊕ *www.rijksmuseum. nl* 🎫 *€15* ☉ *Daily 9–5.*

2

Cobra Café. Don't leave the Cobra Café on Museumplein (across from the Rijksmuseum) before checking out the bizarre bathrooms in the basement. ✉ *Hobbemastraat 18, Museum District* ☎ *020/470–0111* ⊕ *www.cobracafe.nl.*

Fodor's Choice
★

Stedelijk Museum of Modern Art. Amsterdam's celebrated treasurehouse of modern art, the Stedelijk finally reopened (in September 2012) following a massive refurbishment of this wedding-cake Neo-Renaissance structure built in 1895. In true Amsterdam fashion, the locals were quick to nickname the futuristic addition by globally acclaimed local architects Benthem/Crouwel the *"Badkuip"* (Bathtub); it incorporates a glass-walled restaurant (which you can visit, along with the museum shop, without a museum ticket). The new Stedelijk boasts twice the exhibition space compared to the old, thanks, in part, to the new Bathub, which will now host temporary shows (watch out for Suprematist Malevich in 2013 and the noted South-African-Dutch painter Marlene Dumas in 2014).

As for the Stedelijk's old building, it is now now home to the museum's own, fabled collection of modern and contemporary art. While this collection harbors many works by such ancients of modernism as Chagall, Cézanne, Picasso, Monet, Mondriaan, and Malevich, there is a definite emphasis on the post-World War II period: with such local CoBrA boys as Appel and Corneille; American Pop artists as Warhol, Johns, Oldenburg, and Liechtenstein; Abstract Expressionists as de Kooning and Pollock; and contemporary German Expressionists as Polke, Richter, and Baselitz; and displays of Dutch essentials like De Stijl school, including the game-changing *Red Blue Chair* that Gerrit Rietveld designed in 1918 and Mondriaan's 1920 trail-blazing *Composition in Red, Black, Yellow, Blue, and Grey.* ✉ *Paulus Potterstraat 13, Museum District* ☎ *020/573–2911* ⊕ *www.stedelijk.nl* 🎫 *€15* ☉ *Tues. and Wed. 11–5; Thurs. 11–10; Sat. and Sun. 10–6.*

Fodor's Choice
★

Van Gogh Museum. Opened in 1973, this remarkable light-infused building—based on a design by famed De Stijl architect Gerrit Rietveld—venerates the short, certainly not sweet, but highly productive career of everyone's favorite tortured 19th-century artist. First things first: Vincent was a Dutch boy and therefore his name is not pronounced like the "Go" in Go-Go Lounge but rather like the "Go" uttered when one is choking on a whole raw herring.

While some of the Van Gogh paintings that are scattered throughout the world's high art temples are of dubious providence, this collection's authenticity is indisputable: its roots trace directly back to brother Theo van Gogh, Vincent's artistic and financial supporter. The 200 paintings and 500 drawings on display here can be divided into his five basic periods, the first beginning in 1880 at age 27 after his failure in finding

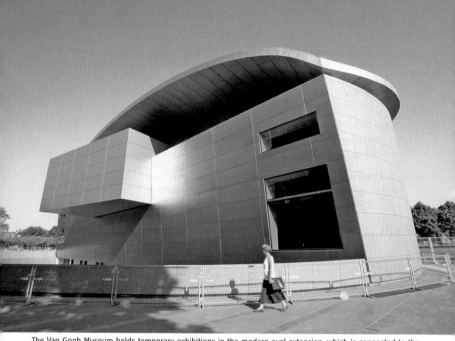

The Van Gogh Museum holds temporary exhibitions in the modern oval extension, which is connected to the main galleries by an underground walkway.

his voice as schoolmaster and lay preacher. *The Potato Eaters* is perhaps his most famous piece from this period.

In 1886, he followed his art-dealing brother Theo to Paris, where the heady atmosphere—and drinking buddies like Paul Signac and Henri de Toulouse-Lautrec—inspired him to new heights of experimentation.

With a broadened palette, he returned to the countryside in 1888 to paint still lifes—including the famous *Sunflowers* series (originally meant to decorate the walls of a single bedroom in the Maison Jaune he had set up to welcome Paul Gauguin)—and portraits of locals around Arles, France. His hopes to begin an artist's colony here with Paul Gauguin were dampened by the onset of psychotic attacks, one of which saw the departure of his ear lobe (a desperate gesture to show respect for Gauguin—in southern France, ears were cut off of bulls by matadors and presented to their lady loves). Recuperating in a mental-health clinic in St-Remy from April 1889, he—feverishly, one is quick to assume—produced his most famous landscapes, such as *Irises* and *Wheatfield with a Reaper,* whose sheer energy in brush stroke makes the viewer almost feel the area's sweeping winds. In May 1890, Van Gogh moved to the artist's village of Auvers-sur-Oise, where he traded medical advice from Dr. Paul Gachet in exchange for paintings and etching lessons. The series of vibrantly colored canvases the pained painter made shortly before he died are particularly breathtaking. These highly productive last three months of his life were marred by depression and, on July 27, he shot himself in the chest while painting *Wheatfield with Crows* and died two days later. That legendary painting remains the iconic image of this collection.

In 1999, the 200th anniversary of Van Gogh's birth was marked with a new museum extension designed by the Japanese architect Kisho Kurokawa; this hosts superbly presented temporary shows of 19th-century art, including changing shows of Van Gogh's drawings (more than 500 are in the collection). With all this new space, you might be tempted to take a break at the museum's cafeteria-style restaurant. ✉ *Paulus Potterstraat 7, Museum District* ☎ *020/570–5200* ⊕ *www.vangoghmuseum. nl* ✉ *€14* ☉ *Sat.–Thurs. 10–6, Fri. 10–10.*

WORTH NOTING

Ⓒ **Vondelpark.** On sunny days, Amsterdam's "green lung" is the most densely populated section of the city. Vondelpark is *the* place where sun is worshipped, joints are smoked, beer is quaffed, picnics are luxuriated over, bands are grooved to, dogs are walked, balls are kicked, lanes are biked, jogged, and rollerbladed on, and bongos are bonged. By evening, the park has invariably evolved into one large outdoor café.

In 1865 the Vondelpark was laid out as a 25-acre "walking and riding park" for residents of the affluent neighborhood rising up around it. It soon expanded to 120 acres and was renamed after Joost van den Vondel, the "Dutch Shakespeare." Landscaped in the informal English style, the park is an irregular patchwork of copses, ponds, children's playgrounds, and fields linked by winding pathways. The park's focal point is the open-air theater, which offers free summer entertainment from Friday through Sunday.

Over the years a range of sculptural and architectural gems have made their appearance in the park. Picasso even donated a sculpture, *The Fish*, on the park's centenary in 1965, which stands in the middle of a field to deter football players from using it as a goalpost. The terraces of the **Blue Teahouse**, a rare beauty of functionalist Nieuwe Bouwen (Modern Movement) architecture, built beside the lake in 1937, are packed throughout the day, starting with dog walkers in the early morning to clubbers by night. ✉ *Stadhouderskade, Museum District* ⊕ *www. openluchttheater.nl.*

DE PIJP: "THE PIPE"

Named for its dirty, narrow streets and even narrower houses, De Pijp ("The Pipe") began at the end of the 19th century as a low-income neighborhood for workers, with cheaply built housing to match. Today it is *the* up-and-coming bohemian part of town, Amsterdam's truly global village.

Many streets in this neighborhood are named after painters, including main thoroughfare Ferdinand Bolstraat, Rembrandt's former pupil who escaped to the grand canals (and what is now the Museum van Loon) when he married money. From the 1890s through the early 1990s, cheap rents attracted poor families, market hawkers, students, artists, and wacky radicals, causing a common comparison with Paris's Latin Quarter. From his De Pijp grotto, the writer Ferdinand Bordewijk depicted Amsterdam during World War I as a "ramshackle bordello, a wooden shoe made of rock"; Piet Mondriaan began formulating the revolutionary art of De Stijl in an attic studio on Ruysdaelkade (No. 75); Eduard Jacobs sang absurd, sharply polemical sketches of the neighborhood's pimps, prostitutes, and disenfranchised heroes that figure in the Dutch musical cabaret called *kleinkunst* (literally 'small art'). The Amsterdam School Diamantbuurt (Diamond Quarter) is an interesting slice of history and the multi-windowed former Royal Asscher Diamond Company on Tolstraat 127 (note the names of surrounding streets: Saffierstraat for sapphires, Smaragdstraat for emeralds, etc.) that housed factory workers.

The Heineken Brewery attracted the first Spanish guest workers to the neighborhood during the early 1960s. Though they no longer brew here, you can still indulge in the Heineken Experience. Later, waves of guest workers from Turkey and Morocco and citizens from the former colonies of Surinam and Indonesia revitalized the area around Albert Cuypstraat with (much-needed) culinary diversity. By the 1980s, De Pijp was a truly global village, with more than 126 nationalities in situ.

Shop like the Dutch at the Albert Cuypstraat Market.

Due to be completed by 2015, construction for a new underground Metro line has literally ripped through this area. That said, De Pijp remains a prime spot for cheap international eats and pub-crawling at local bars and cafés.

TIMING

Dinner here, with an hour or so wandering before and a bit of bar hopping after, is a good way to taste the vibe of the district. Or visit the market in the morning followed by lunch or a picnic in Sarphatipark.

TOP ATTRACTIONS

Fodor's Choice
★

Albert Cuypmarkt (*Albert Cuypstraat Market*). More than 100 years old, the Albert Cuypmarkt is one of the biggest and busiest street markets in Europe. Like the majority of street names in De Pijp, it is named after a Golden Age painter. From Tuesday to Saturday, thousands of shoppers throughout the city flock to its more than 270 stalls selling fruit and vegetables, fish (live lobsters and crabs), textiles, and fashion, with a decades-long waiting list for a permanent booth. Things can get dramatic—if not occasionally violent—from 9 every morning, when the lottery for that day's available temporary spaces takes place. ⊠ *Albert Cuypstraat between Ferdinand Bolstraat and Van Woustraat, De Pijp* ⊕ *www.albertcuypmarkt.nl* ⊗ *Mon.–Sat. 9–6 (but often earlier if the weather is bad).*

QUICK BITES

Albina. The best multicultural snacks can be found around the Albert Cuyp-market. If you want to keep things cheap and speedy, then try Surinamese cuisine at Albina. Fill up on the roti, rice, or noodle dishes. ⊠ *Albert Cuypstraat 69, De Pijp* ☎ 020/675-5135.

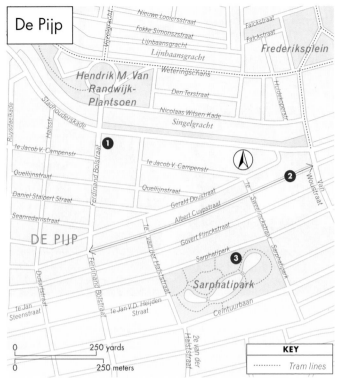

Fodor's Choice
★
Heineken Experience. Founded by Gerard Heineken in 1864, the Heineken label has become one of the world's most famous (and popular) beers. It's no longer brewed here, though you'll see at times that the Heineken horse-drawn dray still clip-clops across town heavy with its kegs. The original brewery has now been transformed into the "Heineken Experience," an interactive center that offers tours of the facilities. Everything from vast copper vats to beer-wagon shire horses are on view, and if you've ever wanted to know what it feels like to be brewed and bottled, the virtual reality ride "Brew U" will clue you in. Others may want to exercise their privilege of drinking multiple beers in a very short time. (Note: this tour is open only to visitors over the age of 18.) ⊠ *Stadhouderskade 78, De Pijp* ☎ *020/523–9222* ⊕ *www.heinekenexperience.com* 🔤 *€17 (€15 online)* ☼ *Daily 11–5:30 (June–Aug. 10:30–7).*

WORTH NOTING

Sarphatipark. This miniature Bois de Boulogne was built by and named after the noted city benefactor Samuel Sarphati (1813–66), whose statue graces the central fountain. With its paths undulating along trees, ponds, and expanses of grass, this park can be considered a big square rather than a small park, but it's a perfect place to picnic on everything you picked up at the Albert Cuypmarkt. ⊠ *Bounded by Ceintuurbaan and Sarphatistraat, De Pijp.*

Where to Eat

WORD OF MOUTH

"If I were to only recommend one restaurant, it would be De Kas. They either grow their own food or buy locally, only cook what's in season, and keep no freezers full of food. The menu is limited, but sensational. Book the Chef's Table and sit in the kitchen watching them cook, chatting with the chef with an unlimited amount of wine, and it will be an experience of a lifetime."

— TheAntiquesDiva

Updated by
Liz Humphreys

Her sons and daughters having ranged the four corners of the earth for several centuries, the Netherlands have long offered visitors a vast variety of cooking, everything from a tongue-tingling Indonesian *rijsttafel* rice banquet to an elegant turbot on a bed of beetroot and nettle leaves. But if you're looking for *real* Dutch cooking, be prepared for sterner stuff—simple, solid nourishment with true belly-packing power.

A prime example is the *erwtensoep*, a thick pea soup fortified with a variety of meats. Let the good local burghers save this magnificent brew for ice-skating time; true aficionados of Dutch cooking like this about 364 days of the year. It can be loaded with spicy sausages and pork fat; it's as thick as diesel oil, as rich as super-condensed cream, as inert as infantry pancakes, and sometimes as indigestible as green sawdust—but is it good!

And one top reason why is because of the astounding quality of fresh ingredients available to Dutch chefs. Holland's national green thumb produces the continent's greatest variety of vegetables and fruits, its Gelderland lush forests yield the finest game, and because Dutch sea dikes are covered with rare herbs that nourishes lambs and calves, this results in exceptionally tasty, tender meats year-round. Of course, the waters of the Netherlands offer up a briny feast of fish and shellfish.

No wonder Amsterdam's top chefs have a no-nonsense obsession in bringing out the best in the ingredients and not drowning them in fusion-for-fashion's-sake finery. For them, "New Dutch Cuisine" has to embrace the traditional grass-roots values of organic farming. As with the Slow Food revolution throughout Europe, it is all about artisanal producers of farmhouse cheeses, great farmer's markets, and locally sourced provisioners. And we are talking local: the city's most forward-thinking chefs are now growing their vegetables and herbs in a plot actually attached to their restaurants. For them, New Dutch Cuisine is defined by farm-fresh, perfectly cooked veggies, and often-organic meat (or fish sourced from nearby areas): garden-to-table cooking, if you will.

But let's not forget *un*local. International urban eating trends make it highly probable, on a walk through Amsterdam, to encounter a sushi shack, a soup shop, a Thai take-out joint, an organic baker of hearty Mediterranean breads, and an olive oil specialist. Most famed are the foods of the former Dutch colonies of Indonesia: the beloved *rijsttafel* (rice table), offering small plates of often-spicy fish, meats, and vegetables served with rice—a culinary experience not be missed.

As for lunch, just follow the locals into one of Amsterdam's iconic cafés or bars (also often called an *eetcafe*, eating cafés) to have a *broodje* (sandwich), *uitsmijter* (fried eggs with cheese and/or ham served on sliced bread), or salad. Ask about the *dagschotel* (daily dish of meat, vegetable, and salad based on what was cheapest and freshest at the market that morning). If you are out only for a cheap, grease-enhanced snack, check out the infinite snack bars where you can buy—sometimes via a heated wall *automaat*—deep-fried meat blobs or french fries that you can order with an amazing range of toppings. Or try the many cheap Suri/Indo/Chin snack bars that serve a combination of Suriname, Indonesian, and Chinese dishes.

The top taste? Head to the many fish stalls—or *haringhandels*—found on the city's bridges. The prime treat is raw *haring* (herring that has been saltwater-cured in vats). This working person's "sushi" variation is at its most succulent—hence, the usual onion and pickle garnish is not required—at the start of the fishing season (late May to early June). If this sounds too radical, there's always a selection of battered and fried fishes, *Noordzee garnalen* (North Sea shrimp, which are tinier, browner, and tastier than most of their brethren) and *gerookte heilbot* (thinly sliced smoked halibut). However, if you decide to indulge, *gerookte paling* (smoked freshwater eel), rich in both price and calories, is the way to go.

PLANNING

EATING-OUT STRATEGY

Where should we eat? With thousands of Amsterdam eateries competing for your attention, it may seem like a daunting question. But fret not—our expert writers and editors have done most of the legwork. The selections here represent the best this city has to offer. Search "Best Bets" for top recommendations by price, cuisine, and experience. Or find a review quickly in the listings, organized alphabetically within neighborhoods. Dive in, and enjoy!

HOURS

One thing you should be aware of is the Dutch custom of early dining; in fact, the vast majority of the city's kitchens turn in for the night at 10 pm—though many of the newer establishments are moving away from this long-held tradition (though not by much). It should also be noted that many restaurants choose Monday—and often Sunday, too—as

PRINSEN
EILAND

BICKERS
EILAND

WESTERDOK
EILAND

NOORD 5

Haarlemmer-Houttuinen

Nieuwe Westerdokstraat

Het Ij

De Ruijterkade

Noord Hollandsch
Kanaal

Open Haven From

Prins Hendrikkade

dokskade

Centraal
Station

Stationsplein

Oosterdok

THE WATERFRONT
Dishes often
inspired by
the sea

Centraal
Station

Nassaukade

Singelgracht

Brouwersgracht

Prinsengracht

Keizersgracht

Herengracht

Singel

THE JORDAAN
Quality cuisine
in the most
distinctive of
neighborhoods

**WESTERN HALF
OF THE CENTRUM**
Student appeal vs.
New Dutch Cuisine

Warmoesstraat

Gelderskade

Egelantiersgracht

JORDAAN

Bloemgracht

Rozengracht

CENTRUM

Damrak

Beursstraat

Warmoesstraat

DE WALLEN
RED LIGHT
DISTRICT

Nieuwmarkt

**THE RED LIGHT
DISTRICT**
From cheap
Asian spots to
the ultraposh

Raadhuisstraat

Spuistraat

Nieuwezijds Voorburgwal

**WESTERN
CANAL RING**

Royal Palace

Paleisstraat

NIEUWMARKT

Berenstr. Wolvenstr.

Marnixstraat

Prinsengracht

Keizersgracht

Herengracht

Singel

**WESTERN
CANAL RING**
Canalside
treasures
with culinary
ambition

Rokin

Rokin

Nieuwe Doelenstr.

Kloveniersburgwal

Oudezijds Voorburgwal

Oudezijds Achterburgwal

Kloveniersburgwal

**NIEUWMARKT
AND ENVIRONS**
Fancy a terrace
or a casual
café?

St. Antoniesbreestr.

Amstel
Amstel

Muziektheater

Waterlooplein

Flower Market

Rembrandt-
plein

THE LEIDSEPLEIN
Late-night
eats and hidden
delights

Herengracht

Keizersgracht

GOUDEN
BOCHT

EASTERN
CANAL RING

Amstel

Wibautstraat

**EAST OF
AMSTEL**
A relaxed
approach
to dining

Vondelpark

Weteringschans

Stadhouderskade

Prinsengracht

Vijzelgracht

**EASTERN CANAL RING
AND REMBRANDTPLEIN**
Posh dining picks

**THE MUSEUM
DISTRICT**
Brasseries
befitting
high culture

Rijksmuseum

Lijnbaansgracht

Singelgracht

Weteringschans

Frederiks-
plein

DE PIJP
From ethnic cheap
to ethnic chic

Paulus Potterstraat

Van Gogh
Museum

Museum
Plein

Hobbemakade

Boerenwetering

Hendrik M. Van
Randwijk-
Plantsoen

Stadhouderskade

900 ft

300 m

their day of rest. Lunches are usually served between noon and 2, but many restaurants in Amsterdam are open for dinner only.

WITH KIDS

As befitting a relaxed town, residents tend to be welcoming toward children in restaurants. In the listings, look for the 👶, which indicates a restaurant that is especially accommodating when eating out with children.

RESERVATIONS

Many Amsterdam restaurants are extremely popular and have limited seating, so making reservations for both the more upscale and the smaller restaurants is always a good idea to avoid disappointment. In the listings we note only when reservations are essential or if they are not accepted.

TIPPING

A 15% service charge is automatically included on the menu prices. However, the trend is for most diners to throw in an extra euro or two on smaller bills and around 10 percent on larger bills.

3

RESTAURANT REVIEWS

Listed alphabetically within neighborhoods. Use the coordinate (✥ 1:B2) at the end of each listing to locate a site on the corresponding map. Prices in the reviews are the average cost of a main course at dinner or, if dinner is not served, at lunch.

THE OLD CITY CENTER (HET CENTRUM)

WESTERN HALF OF THE CENTER

This side of the center has lots of history, but none of the neon of the Red Light District. It's the intellectual heart of Amsterdam and a magnet for after-work revelers and tourists, who often load up at a restaurant around Spui Square before washing it down with some nightlife in an ancient bar or the latest lounge.

$$$ DUTCH

🍴 **Brasserie De Poort.** Restored in the Old Dutch style (complete with polished woods and ceiling paintings), this restaurant—part of the Die Poert van Cleve hotel complex—is, in fact, officially Old Dutch. Its roots as a steak brasserie stretch back to 1870, when it awed the city as the first eatery with electric light. By the time you read this, De Poort will have served nearly 6 million of its acclaimed juicy slabs, served with a choice of five accompaniments. The menu is supplemented with other options such as smoked mackerel, a traditional pea soup thick enough to eat with a fork, and a variety of fish and traditional Dutch dishes. [$] *Average main: €25* ✉ *Nieuwezijds Voorburgwal 176–180, Centrum* ☎ *020/622–6429* 🌐 *www.dieportvancleve.com* 🕒 *No dinner Sun.–Wed.* ✥ *1:A3.*

$$ CAFÉ Fodor's Choice ★

🍴 **Café Luxembourg.** One of the city's top grand cafés, Luxembourg has a stately interior and a view of a bustling square, both of which are maximized for people-watching. Famous for its brunch, its classic café menu includes a terrific Caesar salad, lobster bisque, and excellent Holtkamp

DID YOU KNOW?

Canalside cafés are perfect for a midday break, when you can relax with an afternoon drink and take in Amsterdam's famous scenery. With more than 60 miles' worth of canals in the city, you are sure to find a canal and café to suit your tastes.

BEST BETS FOR AMSTERDAM DINING

With thousands of restaurants to choose from, how will you decide where to eat? Fodor's writers and editors have selected their favorite restaurants by price, cuisine, and experience in the Best Bets lists below. In the first column, Fodor's Choice designations represent the "best of the best" in every price category. You can also search by neighborhood for excellent eats—just peruse the following pages.

Fodor's Choice ★

Bakkerswinkel, p. 111
Bazar Amsterdam, p. 136
Blauw, p. 131
Café Luxembourg, p. 105
De Kas, p. 139
Restaurant Vermeer, p. 113
Toscanini, p. 127

By Price

$

Bakkerswinkel, p. 111
Bazar Amsterdam, p. 136
Bird, p. 112
Café Bern, p. 114
Pancake Bakery, p. 121
Soup en Zo, p. 115
Warung Spang-Makandra, p. 138

$$

Café de Reiger, p. 126
Café Luxembourg, p. 105
La Oliva, p. 126
Moeders, p. 127
OPEN, p. 119
Toscanini, p. 127

$$$

Blauw, p. 131
De Kas, p. 139

$$$$

Beddington's, p. 124
Blauw aan de Wal, p. 112
Bridges, p. 112
La Rive, p. 139
Restaurant Vermeer, p. 113

By Cuisine

DUTCH

Bolenius, p. 131
D' Vijff Vlieghen, p. 109
Greetje, p. 117
Haesje Claes, p. 109
Moeders, p. 127
Pancake Bakery, p. 121

FRENCH

Bord'Eau, p. 114
Ciel Bleu, p. 137
Flo Amsterdam, p. 124
La Rive, p. 139
Restaurant Vermeer, p. 113

INDONESIAN

Blauw, p. 131
Kantjil & de Tijger, p. 111
Sama Sebo, p. 134
Tempo Doeloe, p. 125

By Experience

CHILD-FRIENDLY

Brasserie Witteveen, p. 136

De Taart van m'n Tante, p. 137
Sea Palace, p. 127

MOST ROMANTIC

De Belhamel, p. 121
De Witte Uyl, p. 137
La Rive, p. 139
La Vallade, p. 139

OUTDOOR DINING

Bickers a/d Werf, p. 117
Café Loetje, p. 133
Restaurant As, p. 133
Westergasterras, p. 129
Winkel 43, p. 129

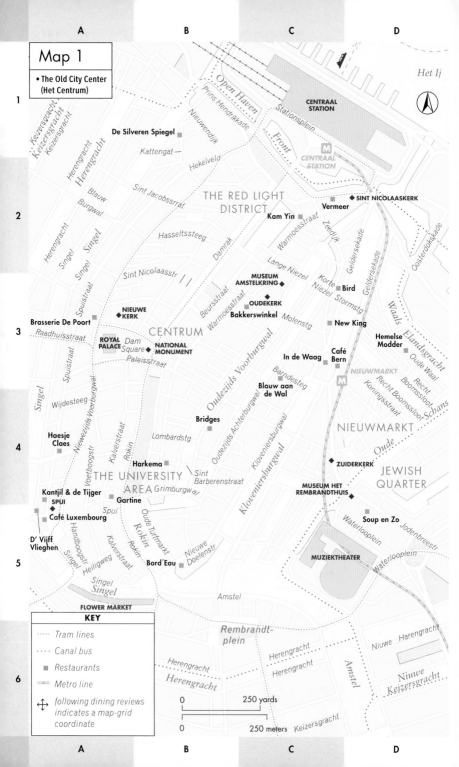

krokets (croquettes, these with a cheese, shrimp, or veal filling). The "reading table" is democratically packed with both Dutch and international newspapers and mags. $ *Average main: €18* ✉ *Spui 24, Centrum* ☎ *020/620–6264* ⊕ *www.luxembourg.nl* ✛ *1:A5.*

$$$ ✕ **De Silveren Spiegel.** Despite appearances, this precariously crooked
DUTCH   building near the solid Round Lutheran Church is here to stay. Designed by the ubiquitous Hendrik de Keyser, it has managed to remain standing since 1614, so it should last through your dinner of contemporary Dutch cuisine. In fact, take time to enjoy their use of famous local ingredients, such as succulent lamb from the North Sea island of Texel and honey from Amsterdam's own Vondelpark. There are also expertly prepared fish plates, such as roasted fillet of red snapper with a homemade vinaigrette. Inside, white walls, wood beams, and the occasional 17th-century painting or antique make for a restful, if not eye-filling, surround. The full five-course menu will set you back €52.50. Lunch is available only for large groups. $ *Average main: €30* ✉ *Kattengat 4–6, Centrum* ☎ *020/624–6589* ⊕ *www.desilverenspiegel.com* ☺ *Closed Sun. No lunch* ✛ *1:B1.*

$$$ ✕ **D' Vijff Vlieghen.** The "Five Flies" is a rambling dining institution
DUTCH   that takes up five adjoining Golden Age houses. Yet the densely evocative Golden Age vibe—complete with bona fide Rembrandt etchings, wooden *jenever* (Dutch gin) barrels, crystal and armor collections, and an endless array of old-school bric-a-brac—came into being only in 1939. You'll find business folk clinching deals in private nooks here, but also busloads of tourists who have dibs on entire sections of the restaurant: book accordingly. The overpriced menu of new Dutch cuisine emphasizes local, fresh, and often organic ingredients in everything from wild boar to pan-fried grey mullet. Lack of choice is not an issue here: the wine list, and the flavored jenever are—like the décor—of epic proportions. $ *Average main: €28* ✉ *Spuistraat 294–302, Centrum* ☎ *020/530–4060* ⊕ *www.thefiveflies.com* ☺ *Closed first two wks in Aug. No lunch* ✛ *1:A5.*

$ ✕ **Gartine.** This intimate and inexpensive breakfast, lunch, and high-tea
CAFÉ   favorite is strewn with flea market finds (such as a gorgeous Portuguese
Fodor'sChoice   chandelier) and often requires a reservation to snag one of its 10 tables.
★   But it's worth planning in advance for their lovely sandwiches and soups—with veggies picked fresh from their own kitchen garden—or their home-baked cakes, cupcakes, and quiches. Afternoon tea in this snug spot, only served from 2 to 5 pm, is a popular choice for catching up with old friends—especially on Amsterdam's notoriously rainy days. $ *Average main: €8* ✉ *Taksteeg 7, Centrum* ☎ *020/320–4132* ⊕ *www. gartine.nl* ✍ *Reservations essential* ▭ *No credit cards* ☺ *Closed Mon. and Tues. Closed three wks in July. No dinner* ✛ *1:A4.*

$$ ✕ **Haesje Claes.** Groaning with pewter tankards, stained glass, leaded-
DUTCH   glass windows, rich historic paneling, Indonesian paisley fabrics, and tasseled Victorian lamps, this restaurant's "Old Holland" vibe and matching menu attract lots of tourists. And why change a winning formula? The Pieter de Hooch–worthy interiors eclipse the food, although the (somewhat overpriced) dishes include an excellent pea soup and a selection of *stamppotten* (mashed dishes that combine potato with

CLOSE UP

Indonesian Rice Tables

Holland's famed *rijsttafel*, or rice table, was the ceremonial feast of the Dutch colonists in Indonesia centuries ago. The Dutch are famously pragmatic; when originally confronted with the many dishes that came from the thousands of islands that made up their former colony of Indonesia, they simply decided to try dozens of different small portions at a time, and serve them with rice. A rice table consists of approximately 10–25 appetizer-size dishes, meant to be shared among a group of people. When you sit down and place your order, the staff will bring a number of hot plates, warmed by candles, to the table. The ritual of describing the dishes is a ceremony in itself, and one should pay heed to which dishes are described as the spiciest. (And perhaps order a tongue-soothing *witbier* to wash it all down.) Once you face the dizzying array of platters, put two spoonfuls of rice in the center of your plate and limit yourself to one small taste of everything. Otherwise, you're licked from the start. Then repeat.

The following is a guide to some of our favorite items.

STARTERS
Soto ajam: a clear chicken broth with vegetables and rice noodles.

Krupuk: crackers of dried fish or shrimp meal fried in oil.

Loempia: deep-fried rolls of bean sprouts, vegetables, and meat; basically a much larger take on the Chinese egg roll.

Saté: a skewer of bite-size morsels of *babi* (pork), *kunding* (lamb), or *ajam* (chicken), drenched in a rich peanut sauce or a sweetened, thick soy sauce.

MEAT
Babi ketjap: pork in soy sauce.

Frikadel goring: fried minced meat. A watered-down sausage version of this has become standard fare in all Dutch snack bars—it's almost as popular as *frites* (french fries).

Rendang: Sumatran spicy meat, often beef, lovingly stewed in no fewer than 11 spices.

VEGETABLES
Gado-gado: a mix of cold, cooked vegetables such as beans and cabbage, drowned in a spicy peanut sauce.

Paksoy: a leafy green that is often steamed and sprinkled with sesame oil.

Sambal boontjes: butter beans or French beans spiced with a chili paste.

Sambal goring tahu: stir-fried wafers of fermented soy beans with a sauce of *sambal* (crushed chili paste).

Sayur lodeh: vegetables cooked in a coconut cream broth, which helps take the bite out of peppery spiciness.

SEAFOOD
Ikan lada hitam: baked fish splashed with black pepper and a spiced soy sauce.

Ikan Bali: baked fish in a Balinese-style sauce.

Oedang blado: baked shrimp in a spicy sauce.

Oedang piendang koening: grilled jumbo shrimp in a sweet-and-sour sauce and lemongrass.

Sambal goreng cumi cumi: baked squid in a spicy sambal made of hot peppers.

Gado-gado, a staple of Indonesian *rijsttafel.*

a variety of vegetables or meats). On cold winter nights, opt for the *hutspot,* a stamppot of mashed potato and carrot supplemented with steamed beef, sausage, and bacon. But nothing could be more "delicious" than the fabulous decor here, certainly in the running for Amsterdam's handsomest historic landmark. [$] *Average main: €18* ✉ *Spuistraat 273, Centrum* ☎ *020/624–9998* 🌐 *www.haesjeclaes.nl* ✥ *1:A4.*

$$$ INDONESIAN 👶 🍴 **Kantjil & de Tijger.** Although you can order à la carte at this large and spacious Indonesian restaurant, the menu is based on four different *rijsttafel* (rice tables), with an abundance of meat, fish, and vegetable options, all varying in flavor from coconut-milk sweet to distressingly spicy (the light local *witbier* beer is an excellent antidote). You can also choose to hit their to-go counter around the corner (✉ *Nieuwezijds Voorburgwal 352*) for cheap noodles. [$] *Average main: €25* ✉ *Spuistraat 291–293, Centrum* ☎ *020/620–0994* 🌐 *www.kantjil.nl* ✍ *Reservations essential* ✥ *1:A4.*

THE RED LIGHT DISTRICT

The city's Red Light District peddles more than just flesh and porn. It's also host to many bargain Asian restaurants and the fine delicacies of some of Amsterdam's most esteemed eateries.

$ EUROPEAN Fodor's Choice ★ 🍴 **Bakkerswinkel.** This genteel yet unpretentious bakery and tearoom evokes an English country kitchen, one that lovingly prepares and serves breakfasts, high tea, hearty-breaded sandwiches, soups, and divine slabs of quiche. The closely clustered wooden tables don't make for much privacy, but this place is a true oasis if you want to indulge in a healthful breakfast or lunch. The convenient location on busy Zeedijk will only be open until 2014, when the original Bakkerswinkel reopens at Warmoesstraat 69 after renovations. There are several other locations: such as one complete with a garden patio in the Museum District and another at Westergasfabriek, plus a takeout-only counter at Warmoesstraat 133. $ *Average main: €8* ⊠ *Zeedijk 37, Red Light District* ☎ *020/489–8000* ⊕ *www. debakkerswinkel.com* ⊗ *No dinner* ✛ *1:C3.*

$ ✕ **Bird.** After many years of success
THAI operating the chaotic and tiny Thai snack bar across the street, Bird's proprietors opened this expansive 100-seat restaurant. Now they have the extra kitchen space to flash-fry their options from an expanded menu, and enough room to place the chunky teak furnishings they have imported from Thailand. The best tables—where you can savor coconut-chicken soup with lemongrass followed by fruity curry with mixed seafood—are at the rear overlooking the canal. $ *Average main: €15* ⊠ *Zeedijk 72–74, Red Light District* ☎ *020/620–1442* ⊕ *www. thai-bird.nl* ✛ *1:C3.*

$$$$ ✕ **Blauw aan de Wal.** In the heart of the Red Light District is a small
MEDITERRANEAN alley that leads to this charming oasis, complete with the innocent
Fodor's Choice chirping of birds. "Blue on the Quay" is set in a courtyard that once
★ belonged to the Bethanienklooster monastery; it now offers a restful environment with multiple dining areas, each with a unique and serene view. Original wood floors and exposed-brick walls hint at the building's 1625 origins, but the extensive and inspired wine list and the open kitchen employing fresh local ingredients in its Mediterranean-influenced cuisine both have a contemporary chic. After starting with a frothy pea soup with chanterelle mushrooms and pancetta, you may want to indulge in a melt-in-the-mouth, herb-crusted lamb fillet. $ *Average main: €31* ⊠ *Oudezijde Achterburgwal 99, Red Light District* ☎ *020/330–2257* ⊕ *www.blauwaandewal.com* ⊗ *Closed Sun. and Mon. No lunch* ✛ *1:C3.*

$$$$ ✕ **Bridges.** When you enter this classy restaurant inside the Sofitel
SEAFOOD Amsterdam hotel, you will pass a Karel Appel wall mural, before getting distracted by the outdoor garden (where you can dine, if you'd like), and a raw bar covered with oysters, sushi, lobster, and fresh fish tartare. The kitchen produces an array of global fish dishes that use few but always fresh ingredients to showcase the natural flavors of the fish, like the monkfish with fois gras and hazelnut, and the halibut with farfalle pasta, green peas, and squid ink. Guests can certainly put their faith in the wine choices coming out of their vinothèque. In short: if you love seafood, Bridges is a fine destination for a celebratory meal. $ *Average main: €34* ⊠ *Sofitel Legend The Grand Amsterdam Hotel,*

Oudezijds Voorburgwal 197, Centrum ☎ *020/555–3560* 🌐 *www.bridgesrestaurant.nl* ✍ *Reservations essential* ✥ *1:B4.*

$$ THAI 🍴 **De Kooning van Siam.** Sitting smack in the middle of the Red Light District, this Thai establishment is favored by local Thai residents. Although the ancient beams and wall panels are still visible in this old canal house, the furniture and wall decorations refreshingly dilute the sense of Old Dutchness. Sensitive to wimpier palates, the menu balances such scorchers as stir-fried beef with onion and chili peppers with milder options. [$] *Average main: €19* ✉ *Oudezijds Voorburgwal 42, Red Light District* ☎ *020/623–7293* 🌐 *www.dekooningvansiam.nl* 🕓 *Closed Sun. No lunch* ✥ *1:C3.*

$$ FRENCH 🍴 **Harkema.** This brasserie along the city's premier theater strip has infused a former tobacco factory with light, color, and general design savvy. The kitchen, which is open between noon and 11, serves reasonably priced lunches and French classics like *croque monsieur* (French-style grilled cheese and ham sandwich), and a wall of wine bottles assures something to appeal to all tastes. [$] *Average main: €17* ✉ *Nes 67, Red Light District* ☎ *020/428–2222* 🌐 *www.brasserieharkema.nl* ✥ *1:B4.*

$ ECLECTIC 🍴 **Kam Yin.** Representative of the many Surinam snack bars found throughout the city, Kam Yin offers this South American country's unique fusion of Caribbean, Chinese, and Indonesian cuisines that arose from its history as a Dutch colony. Perhaps the most popular meal is the *roti,* a flat-bread pancake, which comes with lightly curried potatoes and vegetable or meat additions. If you come for lunch, try a *broodje pom,* a sandwich filled with a remarkably addictive mélange of chicken and cassava root (mmmmm, root vegetable). Basic, clean, convivial, and noisy, Kam Yin shows extra sensitivity with its speedy service, long hours (daily noon–midnight), and a doggy-bag option. [$] *Average main: €9* ✉ *Warmoesstraat 6–8, Red Light District* ☎ *020/625–3115* ✥ *1:C2.*

$$$$ FRENCH Fodor'sChoice ★ 🍴 **Restaurant Vermeer.** With its milk-white walls, dramatic black-and-white patterned floors, Delft plates, fireplace hearths, and old chandeliers, this stately place does conjure up the amber canvases of the great Johannes. Its superposh vibe, however, suggests that no milkmaid will be able to afford the prices here, set within the 17th-century wing of the NH Barbizon Palace Hotel. The way chef Christopher Naylor combines tastes, textures, and temperatures is masterful, may it be sea bass poached in buttermilk with white asparagus, sweet and sour grapefruit, and ginger cream, or lamb with nettles, chicory, and pistachio. And for €110 you can get the full nine-course roller coaster of dishes, or four courses for €80 and five courses for €95. An army of waitstaff is on hand to ensure that the service is always impeccable. [$] *Average main: €65* ✉ *NH Barbizon Palace Hotel, Prins Hendrikkade 59–72, Red Light District* ☎ *020/556–4885* 🌐 *www.restaurantvermeer.nl* 🕓 *Closed Sun. Closed first wk of Jan. and one month in summer* ✥ *1:C2.*

NIEUWMARKT AND THE UNIVERSITY AREA

The Nieuwmarkt and square is an eclectic mix of upscale eateries at the beating heart of Nieuwmarkt, and student-friendly (read reasonably priced) hangouts that surround it. The adjoining streets are dotted with the type of venues that live up to the reputation of Amsterdam as the

The industrial lighting, exposed brick, and glass-box kitchen might fool you into thinking you're in New York, but this is Amsterdam's trendy Tunes.

laid-back, chilled out European capital. Perfect places to linger over a glass of wine or a *pilsje* (a little glass of beer), or indulge in local snacks or full-blown meals.

$$$$ FRENCH Fodor's Choice ★ 🍴 **Bord'Eau.** Newly opened in the regal Hotel de l'Europe, this playfully modern French restaurant is elegant without being stuffy. Of course, the ingredients are top-notch, but what really sets the cooking apart are the inventive preparations, such as the beetroot in salt crust with marinated wild salmon and horseradish ice cream or the blue lobster with a coral and grapefruit broth. Don't miss the stunning desserts, including a huge gold-flecked chocolate balloon that melts down to reveal a scoop of kaffir lime ice cream inside. To avoid breaking the bank (too much), opt for their lunch tasting menus, ranging from €38 for two courses to €58 for four courses. For a view to match the meal, ask for a table overlooking the Amstel River. [$] *Average main: €43* ✉ *Nieuwe Doelenstraat 2–14, Centrum* ☎ *020/531–1619* 🌐 *www.bordeau.nl* 🕒 *Closed Sun. and Mon. Closed three wks in Aug. No lunch Sat.* ✥ *1:B5.*

$ SWISS 🍴 **Café Bern.** This dark, woody, and well-worn café—as evocative as a Jan Steen 17th-century interior—has been serving the same simple cheese fondue for decades. Get salads to start (they offer five types to choose from, for only €5) and then dunk those bread bits into the wonderfully cheesy mess. Besides their cheese fondue, they also offer a steak entrecote that you cook at the table. Don't come for a romantic meal; you'll very likely be sharing a communal table with a group of boisterous locals out to celebrate. [$] *Average main: €15* ✉ *Nieuwmarkt 9, Centrum* ☎ *020/622–0034* 🌐 *www.cafebern.com* ✍ *Reservations essential* 💳 *No credit cards* 🕒 *No lunch* ✥ *1:C3.*

$$ EUROPEAN 🍴 **Hemelse Modder.** This bright, stylish, informal, and vegetarian-friendly restaurant is on one of the city's broadest canals and has a long-standing reputation for high quality at a great price. You can select à la carte or from a nicely priced three- or four-course menu costing €31.50 and €36, respectively. Indulge in, say, a mackerel salad marinated with onions, raisins, and pine nuts, or a Scottish roast lamb with thyme and string beans. The inspired choices show a global sweep but invariably come to rest within the borders of France, Great Britain, and the Netherlands. But do tuck into one of the mountainous grand desserts, including the "heavenly mud" mousse of dark and white chocolate that gives the restaurant its name. [$] *Average main: €19* ✉ *Oude Waal 11, Centrum* ☎ *020/624–3203* 🌐 *www.hemelsemodder.nl* ⏲ *No lunch* ✣ *1:D3.*

TIME FOR APPELTAART

Amsterdammers' favorite dessert, found in nearly every café, has to be the *appeltaart*. Some are more like cake and some more like pie, some chock-full of apples and some heavier on the cinnamon. Find the best at Winkel 43 in the Jordaan and De Taart van m'n Tante in the Pijp.

$$ MEDITERRANEAN Fodor's Choice ★ 🍴 **In de Waag.** A decade ago, the lofty beamed interior of the 17th-century Waag (weigh house) was converted into a grand café and restaurant and has remained a popular option for many reasons, one being a strict dinner-lighting policy of candles only—from a huge wooden candelabra, no less—that nicely helps maintain the building's medieval majesty. The menu is Mediterranean with Dutch touches, including entrées like the entrecote with fries and Dutch lettuce with walnuts, and the deep-fried polenta with spinach, smoked ricotta, and chanterelles. The long wooden tables make this an ideal location for larger groups, and if you happen to belong to a party of eight, you should definitely book the spookily evocative tower room. Daytime hunger pangs are also catered to from 11 on, when you can enjoy a sandwich, a salad, or a snack on the spacious terrace (and you can even breakfast before that, starting at 9 am). [$] *Average main: €24* ✉ *Nieuwmarkt 4, Centrum* ☎ *020/422–7772* 🌐 *www.indewaag.nl* ✣ *1:C3.*

$ VEGETARIAN Fodor's Choice ★ 🍴 **Soup en Zo.** "Soup Etc" bucks Amsterdam's slow-service trend by being particularly speedy (at least between 11 and 8 on weekdays and noon and 7 on weekends), as well as health-conscious. Eight soups are available daily, at least half of which are vegetarian. You can even ask for a taste, but we all know how much the Dutch pride themselves on their soups. Steaming bowls come with chunky slices of whole-grain breads, and the menu also offers salads and exotic fruit juices. Once you're fortified, you can rush back to searching for bargains at the Waterlooplein flea market or window-shopping for arts and antiques around its second, Museum District location. [$] *Average main: €5* ✉ *Jodenbreestraat 94a, Centrum* ☎ *020/422–2243* 🌐 *www.soupenzo.nl* ✍ *Reservations not accepted* 💳 *No credit cards* ✣ *1:D5.*

On the Menu

A typical Dutch meal is often derided for its boldly honest approach to the food groups: meat, vegetable, potato. But all you need is one restaurant meal that seems home cooked by a particularly savvy mother to see that Dutch cuisine is filled with unexpected nuances and can be positively *skeee-rumptious*.

There are usually many different meals on offer, including very traditional winter fare such as *zuurkool met spek en worst* (sauerkraut with bacon and sausage); *hutspot* (a hotchpotch of potato and carrots served with sausage); *stamspot* (a hotchpotch of potato and sauerkraut served with sausage); and *erwetensoup*, also called *snert*, which is a thick pea soup that comes fortified with a variety of meats.

More-summery options are the famed *asperges*, the white and tender local asparagus that comes into season in May, and *mossellen*, or mussels, that are matured by mid-August in the pristine waters of Oosterschelde in Zeeland. Fancier summer starters may be a seasonal salad with smoked salmon or eel, or a carpaccio made with sole.

And although it may be handy to learn that *kip* means "chicken" and *biefstuk* means "beefsteak," a much easier and common shortcut to understanding a Dutch menu is to ask for an English menu (or a quick translation of "recommendations").

Keep in mind one local menu quirk: an entrée is, in fact, a starter and not a main course. Those are called *hoofdgerechten*. For snack and sandwich best bests, see the Close-Up box "Refuel Around Town."

No matter if it's *jong* (young), *belegen* (aged), or *oud* (ancient)—the Dutch live for their cheese. A young Gouda has a creamy flavor and soft consistency; as it matures it acquires a more robust flavor and firmer texture. Edam's red cover means a cheese marked for export; locally, the Edam (as well as Gouda) usually wears a yellow or, if aged, a black coat. Edam is very mild, with slightly salty or nutty flavors.

Other popular Dutch cheeses include *Leidse kaas* (often supplemented with cumin seeds); *Frisian Clove,* a firm-textured cheese spiced with cloves; and the hole-ridden *Maasdammer*, which is similar to Swiss Emmentaler but much creamier.

For a sweet finale, desserts invariably include homemade custards and some version of profiterole, which is a liquor-soaked thin pancake usually filled with ice cream and drowned in dark chocolate. Everyone's homemade favorite is the *appeltaart*, which now comes in many delightful variations.

THE WATERFRONT

Amsterdam's historic harbor is home to some of the most unique restaurants in the city, from a reclaimed TV tower to a floating Chinese pagoda—and perhaps more will soon sprout on the north side of the IJ River with the long-awaited opening of the Eye Film Institute. Lots of construction still going on hereabouts, so it remains to be seen what the future truly holds for this area.

A selection of cheeses at Restaurant Vermeer, one of the city's temples to haute cuisine.

$$ ECLECTIC 🍴 **Bickers a/d Werf.** A true hideaway on Bickers Island, this is a place for which the possibility of getting lost is worth it. With an all-wood terrace, it resembles a harbor with a watery nautical view. The interior is stark and modern. The food is tasty—think shrimp croquettes and chips served in a paper cone and accompanied by an excellent mayonnaise. The portions are considerable. [$] *Average main: €19* ✉ *Bickerswerf 2, Bickers Island, The Waterfront, Centrum* ☎ *020/320–2951* 🌐 *www.bickersaandewerf.nl* 🕒 *Closed Mon. and Tues.* ✥ *2:A1.*

$$ ITALIAN 🍴 **Fifteen.** This franchise of superstar chef Jamie Oliver does exactly the same as the London original: it trains disadvantaged young adults as kitchen team players. It's proven to be a remarkably consistent success, thanks in part to its slightly out-of-the-way but waterfront location in the up-and-coming Eastern Docklands neighborhood. While the kids learn under the tutelage of well-established chefs, diners indulge in such tempting and sophisticated mains as roasted chicken with panzanella and salsa verde, the plaice with fennel, anchovies, and tomato, or the ravioli with egg, ricotta, and black truffle. Dine deliciously, and do a good deed at the same time! [$] *Average main: €19* ✉ *Jollemanhof 9, The Waterfront, Centrum* ☎ *020/509–5015* 🌐 *www.fifteen.nl* 🕒 *No lunch Sun.* ✥ *2:B5.*

$$$ DUTCH ★ 🍴 **Greetje.** If your Dutch food experiences have consisted of bland potatoes with even blander balls of fried dough, Greetje could be your religious awakening. It's certainly not nouvelle: in a truly old-fashioned homey environment, the chef takes rarely seen or forgotten dishes and prepares them with fresh, local, and often organic ingredients. Think grilled sandwiches of Frisian sugar bread (traditional sweet bread from Holland's North) with layers of homemade duck liver terrine and

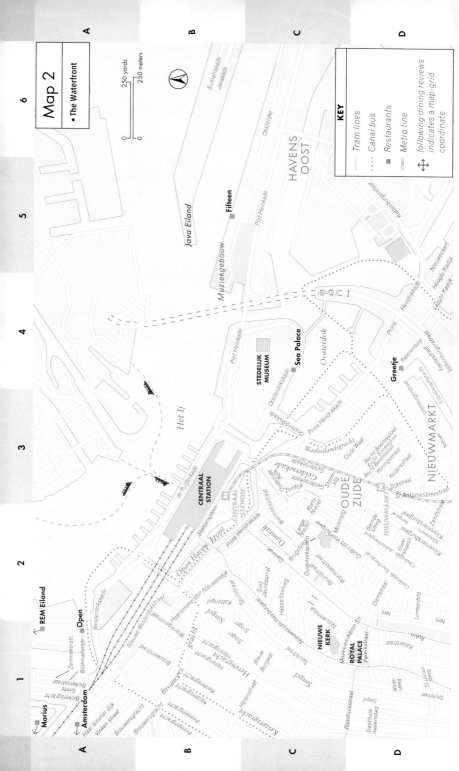

apple syrup, or fillet of plaice with carrots, onion, and Dutch shrimp. Service does veer from Dutch tradition—it's efficient and extremely helpful. If you're a licorice fan, don't miss the over-the-top licorice crème brûlée with Dutch black licorice ice cream. $ *Average main: €25* ✉ *Peperstraat 23, The Waterfront, Centrum* ☎ *020/779–7450* ⊕ *www. restaurantgreetje.nl* ⊘ *No lunch* ✛ *2:D4.*

$$
MEDITERRANEAN

✕ **Marius.** This casual neighborhood bistro in Westerpark draws a relaxed local crowd with its seasonal takes on seafood and meat served with farm-fresh veggies. The dishes change daily—the ingredients are chosen from the morning market by the chef, who trained at Berkeley's Chez Panisse—and may include monkfish with beets and avocado or quail with artichokes, Swiss chard, and polenta, but regulars come for the *vitello tonnato* (sliced veal with tuna sauce) and bouillabaisse that are always on the menu. (Four courses will run you €47.50.) Next door, the owners recently opened Worst, a tiny but welcoming wine, cheese, and charcuterie joint where you can snack while waiting for your table. $ *Average main: €24* ✉ *Barentszstraat 173, The Waterfront, Centrum* ☎ *020/422–7880* ⊕ *www.deworst.nl/marius.html* ⊘ *Closed Sun. and Mon. No lunch* ✛ *2:A1.*

$$
FRENCH

✕ **OPEN.** Just west of Central Station, this sleekly designed glass-and-metal-outfitted restaurant atop an old 1920s railway offers 360-degree views of the IJ river. An open kitchen and a golden bar provide a winning combination of seasonal French- and Italian-inspired dishes; entrées, such as the rack of lamb with shallots and apples, or the cabbage rolls with saffron risotto croquette and smoked garlic sauce, can be ordered as whole or half dishes. However, the views and décor often trump the food. $ *Average main: €22* ✉ *Westerdoksplein 20, The Waterfront, Centrum* ☎ *020/620–1010* ⊕ *www.open.nl* ⊘ *No lunch Sat. and Sun.* ✛ *2:A1.*

$$
ECLECTIC

✕ **REM Eiland.** If you're looking for the most unique dining experience in Amsterdam, this former offshore TV tower transported from the North Sea—and perched (thankfully not precariously) out on the IJ River—delivers. Though the food takes a bit of a backseat to the phenomenal views, you can still enjoy a solid bistro-style lunch of oysters or tabouli salad with Dutch shrimp, or a dinner of roasted chicken with mashed potatoes. And did we mention those views? Depending on where you sit, gaze out across the river to the NDSM wharf or back toward the city skyline. Plan to bike or take a cab to reach REM, though, as it's a hike from the closest tram and bus stops. $ *Average main: €19* ✉ *Haparandadam 45–2, The Waterfront, Centrum* ☎ *020/688–5501* ⊕ *www. remeiland.com* ⊘ *Closed Mon.* ✛ *2:A1.*

THE CANAL RINGS

If you're in Amsterdam for just one meal, head for the canals. In the midst of a storybook setting you'll find all manner of restaurants from glass-walled bistros to dining rooms that play on the city's rich merchant past. In the summer, outdoor terraces put you at the water's edge.

The views are incredible at REM Eiland, a former offshore TV tower, now an exciting, vibrant restaurant.

WESTERN CANAL RING

The intrinsically posh sector of the Grachtengordel ring and its intersecting streets is a foodie paradise. Meals here come equipped with the potential for an after-dinner romantic walk to aid digestion: the arches of the bridges are prettily lit, and their watery reflections pull at the heartstrings of even the most wayworn of travelers.

$$ EUROPEAN

🍴 **Café Van Puffelen.** At the ancient Van Puffelen, on a particularly mellow stretch of canal, the menu is of the modern café variety. But it's the daily specials, such as salmon in an herb crust, that draw so many regulars, including a young, primarily local crowd. If the main dining room gets too boisterous, you can always escape to the more secluded and intimate mezzanine or, in the summer, to the inviting terrace. [$] *Average main: €18* ✉ *Prinsengracht 375–377, Western Canal Ring* ☎ *020/624–6270* 🌐 *www.restaurantvanpuffelen.com* ✍ *Reservations not accepted* 🕒 *No lunch Mon.–Thurs.* ✥ *3:A3.*

$$$$ FRENCH

🍴 **Christophe.** Suave and sleek, the William Katz–designed interior—which evokes this artist's acclaimed ballet scenery (thanks to all the silver ribbons and black-crystal chandeliers)—remains one of the best reasons to visit Christophe. Chef Jean-Joel Bonsens's French-tinged and ever-evolving menu—always with a few vegetarian options—may include entrées such as lobster and orange with saffron, tomato, basil, and vanilla, or roast suckling pig with braised carrots and honey polenta gravy. You can preorder a "boat box" in case you want to take your meal on a canal cruise. [$] *Average main: €36* ✉ *Leliegracht 46, Western Canal Ring* ☎ *020/625–0807* 🌐 *www.restaurantchristophe.nl* ✍ *Reservations essential* 🕒 *Closed Sun. and Mon. No lunch* ✥ *3:A2.*

$$$ EUROPEAN 🍴 **De Belhamel.** Set on the edge of the Jordaan, this restaurant is blessed with Art Nouveau detailing and wallpaper that is so darkly evocative of fin-de-siècle living it may inspire a thirst for absinthe and symbolist poetry. But the views of the Herengracht Canal and the attentive and friendly service create a romantic setting in which to settle down and enjoy the French and Italian–inspired menu. In the winter, hearty game dishes (such as venison with a red wine and shallot sauce) are featured; in summer, lighter fare is offered, and the seating spills out into the street. [$] *Average main: €24* ✉ *Brouwersgracht 60, Western Canal Ring* ☎ *020/622–1095* 🌐 *www.belhamel.nl* ✥ *3:B1.*

$$$ MEDITERRANEAN 🍴 **Envy.** Not too surprisingly, Envy has a sexy look: the dining rooms are peek-a-boo shady, with their sleek furnishings seductively lit by low-hanging spotlights. The menu is "sexy," too, comprised of appetizer-sized dishes (priced around €10 each) that can be shared by the whole table. Each of these dishes—which may include baked lobster with carrot cream and bergamot, and lamb with a pistachio crust—are as gorgeously presented as the waitstaff. Order two to three dishes each, or splurge on the four- or five-course tasting menus. [$] *Average main: €30* ✉ *Prinsengracht 381, The Canal Ring* ☎ *020/344–6407* 🌐 *www.envy.nl* ✍ *Reservations essential* ⏲ *No lunch Mon–Thurs.* ✥ *3:A3.*

$$ CONTEMPORARY 🍴 **Lust.** "Lust" has a slightly different meaning in Dutch, and suggests a less aggressive desire best translated as "appetite." And if you've worked up a lunchy one while wandering the Nine Streets specialty shopping area, this is a truly satiating place for healthful club sandwiches, pastas, and salads. Be sure to visit the wacky washroom before you leave. [$] *Average main: €19* ✉ *Runstraat 13, Western Canal Ring* ☎ *020/626–5791* 🌐 *www.lustamsterdam.nl* ✥ *3:A4.*

$ DUTCH ★ 🦢 🍴 **Pancake Bakery.** It's hard to go wrong when going out for Dutch pancakes in Amsterdam. But the quaint Pancake Bakery rises above the pack of similar eateries with its medieval vibe, canalside patio near the Anne Frank House, and a mammoth menu with more than 75 choices of sweet and savory toppings. There are also omelettes, and a convincing take on the folk dish of *erwtensoep* (a superthick, smoked sausage–imbued pea soup—only available from Oct. to April). But don't rise too early for your pancakes—the bakery doesn't open till noon—and be prepared to wait: reservations are only taken for groups of six or more. [$] *Average main: €11* ✉ *Prinsengracht 191, Western Canal Ring* ☎ *020/625–1333* 🌐 *www.pancake.nl* ✍ *Reservations not accepted* ✥ *3:A2.*

$$ MEDITERRANEAN ★ 🍴 **Pianeta Terra.** Marble-clad, intimate, and softly lighted, this restaurant has a menu that embraces the whole Mediterranean region and that follows the Slow Food philosophy, paying respect to vegetarians and organic farmers. The daily set menus are a sure bet, and may include fillet of mackerel with a confit of cherry tomatoes and capers or cannelloni with buffalo ricotta, wild asparagus, and Parmesan. The pasta, like the bread, is made fresh daily on the premises from organic ingredients. [$] *Average main: €23* ✉ *Beulingstraat 7, Western Canal Ring* ☎ *020/626–1912* 🌐 *www.pianetaterra.nl* ✍ *Reservations essential* ⏲ *Closed Sun. and Mon. No lunch* ✥ *3:A4.*

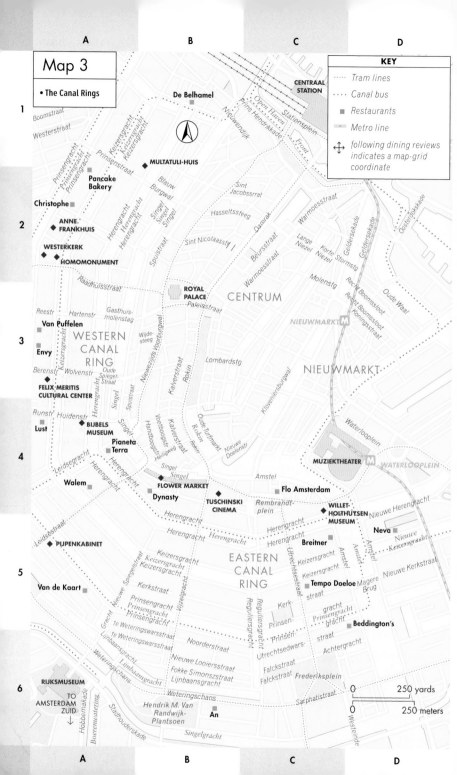

Map 3

- The Canal Rings

KEY
- ······ Tram lines
- ····· Canal bus
- ■ Restaurants
- ▦ Metro line
- ✛ following dining reviews indicates a map-grid coordinate

Boomstraat

Westerstraat

De Belhamel

CENTRAAL STATION

Open Haven
Stationsplein
Front

Prinsengracht
Prinsengracht
Keizersgracht
Keizersgracht
Keizersgracht

Prinsenstraat

Nieuwendijk
Prins Hendrikkade

Nieuwedijk

■ MULTATULI-HUIS

Pancake Bakery

Blauw
Burgwal

Christophe ■

Herengracht
Herengracht
Herengracht

Singel
Singel
Singel

Sint Jacobsstraat

Hasseltssteeg

Warmoesstraat

Gelderskade
Gelderskade

Oosterdokskade

◆ ANNE FRANKHUIS

Sint Nicolaasstr I

Beursstraat

Lange Niezel
Korte Stormstg
Korte Niezel

◆ WESTERKERK

Spuistraat

Warmoesstraat

Rech Boomssloot
Recht Boomssloot

Oude Waal

■ HOMOMONUMENT

Raadhuisstraat

ROYAL PALACE

Paleisstraat

CENTRUM

Molensteg

Koningsstraat

Reestr   Hartenstr

Gasthuismolensteg

NIEUWMARKT Ⓜ

Van Puffelen ■

WESTERN CANAL RING

Wijdesteeg

Nieuwezijds Voorburgwal

Kalverstraat

Rokin

Lombardsteg

NIEUWMARKT

Envy ■

Keizersgracht

Berenstr   Wolvenstr

Oude Spiegelstraat

Singel

Spuistraat

Herengracht

FELIX MERITIS CULTURAL CENTER

Runstr   Huidenstr

Lust ■

◆ BIJBELS MUSEUM

Voetboogstr
Handboogstr
Heiligeweg

Kalverstraat
Rokin

Oude Turfmarkt

Nieuwe Doelenstr

Waterlooplein

Pianeta Terra ■

Amstel

MUZIEKTHEATER Ⓜ   WATERLOOPLEIN

Singel
Singel

Walem ■

◆ FLOWER MARKET

Dynasty ■

TUSCHINSKI CINEMA

■ Flo Amsterdam

Rembrandtplein

◆ WILLET-HOLTHUYSEN MUSEUM

Nieuwe Herengracht

Neva ■

Nieuwe Kerkersgracht

Herengracht

Herengracht

Herengracht

Breitner ■

Utrechtsestr.

Amstel

Nieuwe Kerkstraat

◆ PIJPENKABINET

Leidsestraat

Herengracht
Herengracht

EASTERN CANAL RING

Keizersgracht
Keizersgracht
Keizersgracht

Amstel
Amstel

Kerkstraat

■ Tempo Doeloe

Magere Brug

Van de Kaart ■

Gracht   Nieuwe Spiegelstraat

Kerkstraat

Prinsengracht
Prinsengracht
Prinsengracht

Kerkstraat

Prinsengracht
gracht

Reguliersgracht

Prinsengracht

Beddington's ■

1e Weteringsstraat
1e Weteringswarsstraat

Noorderstraat

Utrechtsedwarsstraat

Achtergracht

Lijnbaansgracht
Lijnbaansgracht

Nieuwe Looiersstraat

Fokke Simonszstraat

Lijnbaansgracht

Falckstraat

Weteringschans

Frederiksplein

RIJKSMUSEUM

TO AMSTERDAM ZUID
↓

Hobbemakade

Boerenwetering

Hendrik M. Van Randwijk-Plantsoen

Weteringschans

Sarphatistraat

■ An

Singelgracht

Stadhouderskade

Lijnbaansgracht

Westeinde

0   250 yards

0   250 meters

$$ ✕**Van de Kaart.** This subcanal-level
MEDITERRANEAN eatery with its peaceful dining room
offers a savvy and stylish balancing
of Mediterranean tastes. Though
the menu is in continual flux, it
may include cuttlefish, prawn, and
crayfish with couscous, or a veal
pastrami with lettuce and bacon,
or a vegetarian pot au feu. You can
also opt for one of three set menus:
€29.50 for the pre-theater surprise
menu between 5:30 and 7 pm; €35
for three courses; and €49.50 for
the four-course Saturday "wine
menu," where you bring your
own bottle or purchase glasses of
wine from a great wine list. $ Av-
erage main: €19 ⊠ Prinsengracht
512, Western Canal Ring ☎ 020/625–9232 ⊕ www.vandekaart.com
⊗ Closed Sun. No lunch ✛ 3:A5.

> ### PANCAKE CRAVINGS
>
> With both sweet and savory top-
> pings, *pannenkoeken* (pancakes)
> are also a mainstay on the menu
> of many cafés. They are a spe-
> cialty at such places as the famous
> **Pancake Bakery**, the **Upstairs
> Pannenkoekenhuis** (⊠ *Grimburg-
> wal 2, Old Side* ☎ *020/626–5603*),
> and the **Boerderij Meerzicht**
> (⊠ *Koenenkade 56, Buitenveldert*
> ☎ *0290/679–2744*), which is an
> out-of-the way petting zoo in
> the heart of Amsterdamse Bos
> (Amsterdam Forest).

$$ ✕**Walem.** As if ripped from the pages of *Wallpaper* magazine, this
ECLECTIC sleekly hip and trendy all-day grand café serves elegant breakfast and
lunch options—as well as plenty of both cappuccino and champagne.
Dinnertime is fusion time, as the chefs create salads of chicken, noodles,
Chinese cabbage, and bean sprouts, or serve grilled vegetable lasagna
with a tomato and basil salsa. In the summer, you can relax in the
formal garden or on the canal-side terrace. Late at night, guest DJs
spin hip lounge tunes for an appreciative crowd. $ *Average main: €17*
⊠ *Keizersgracht 449, Western Canal Ring* ☎ *020/625–3544* ⊕ *www.
walem.nl* ✛ *3:A4.*

EASTERN CANAL RING AND REMBRANDTPLEIN

The Eastern Canal Ring and the Rembrandtplein are packed with some
of the city's poshest restaurants. Main streets of culinary interest include
upscale Utrechtsestraat, which takes you on an around-the-world culinary trip, and the lively Reguliersdwarsstraat, jammed with sidewalk
cafés to satisfy your people-watching urge. Informally dubbed the city's
"Gay Street," Reguliersdwarsstraat is as much known for its eateries
as for its hip gay patrons.

$$ ✕**An.** This long-popular Japanese eatery once offered only takeout; now
JAPANESE you can linger over an evening meal along with some excellent plum
wine (*umeshuu*). Although the menu focuses on sushi, the kitchen also
offers fantastic baked tofu (*atsuage*) and some superdelicious *gyoza*—
steamed or fried dumplings filled with veggies or seafood. You may still
choose to forgo dining in the oddly Mediterranean-style dining room
and take your meal to a nearby bench on the Amstel or to the green
expanses of Saraphatipark. $ *Average main: €20* ⊠ *Weteringschans
76, Eastern Canal Ring and Rembrandtplein* ☎ *020/624–4672* ⊕ *www.
japansrestaurantan.nl* ▭ *No credit cards* ⊗ *Closed Sun. and Mon. No
lunch Sat.* ✛ *3:B6.*

> **WHO'S NEXT IN LINE?**
>
> Most *slagers* (butchers) and *bakkers* (bakers) supplement their incomes by preparing *broodjes* (sandwiches) of every imaginable meat and cheese topping. Traditional lines don't form, so pay attention to who was already there when you arrived.

$$$$ ECLECTIC 🍴 **Beddington's.** Although both the flavor and presentation of dishes here are decidedly French, many of chef Jean Beddington's creations hint at other influences: her youth spent in English country kitchens, the three years she spent mastering macrobiotic cooking in Japan, or any number of other influences she has gleaned from her culinary travels across the globe. The frequently changing menu is prepared with a feather-light touch; you can choose from three prix-fixe courses for €48 or four courses for €55. [$] *Average main: €48* ✉ *Utrechtsedwarsstraat 141, Eastern Canal Ring and Rembrandtplein* ☎ *020/620–7393* 🌐 *www.beddington.nl* ✍ *Reservations essential* ⏲ *Closed Sun. and Mon. No lunch. Closed last wk of July and first two wks of August.* ✥ *3:D5.*

$$$ MEDITERRANEAN 🍴 **Breitner.** Whether for romance or the pure enjoyment of fine contemporary dining, Breitner gets high marks. With a formal interior of rich red carpeting and muted pastel colors, and a view across the Amstel River that takes in both the Muziektheater-Stadhuis (Music Theater–City Hall complex) and the Hermitage Amsterdam, this spot serves Mediterranean-inspired dishes, many of which pack a flavorful punch. The seasonal menu may include starters such as Dutch mackerel with mango and coconut cream, and entrées such as tuna with eggplant and basil or suckling pig with bacon, dried tomatoes, and potato croquettes. Oysters, fabulous desserts, and an innovative wine list allow you to step into the realm of pure culinary decadence. [$] *Average main: €28* ✉ *Amstel 212, Eastern Canal Ring and Rembrandtplein* ☎ *020/627–7879* 🌐 *www.restaurant-breitner.nl* ⏲ *Closed Sun., last wk of July, first wk of Aug. No lunch* ✥ *3:C5.*

$$$ ASIAN 🍴 **Dynasty.** Although its name has nothing to do with the 1980s television show of the same name, this restaurant's regular clientele (showbiz types, football heroes, dangling arm candy) does sometimes resemble a casting call for a soap opera. The interior is certainly fanciful: the Art Deco starting point blurs into an Asian frenzy of rice-paper umbrellas hanging from the ceiling and a supporting chorus of golden Buddhas. In the summer, try for a table on the "dream terrace" majestically set in a Golden Age courtyard. Happily, chef K.Y. Lai's menu, which is full of Cantonese, Thai, Malaysian, and Vietnamese culinary classics, is as ambitious as the décor; his drunken prawns (jumbo shrimp marinated in an intoxicating broth of Chinese herbs and Xiaoxing wine) are reliably excellent, as are many of the other specialties here. [$] *Average main: €30* ✉ *Reguliersdwarsstraat 30, Eastern Canal Ring and Rembrandtplein* ☎ *020/626–8400* 🌐 *www.restaurantdynasty.nl* ⏲ *Closed Tues. No lunch* ✥ *3:B4.*

$$$ FRENCH 🍴 **Flo Amsterdam.** Everything shines here: the copper, the mirrors, the white tablecloths and, of course, the food. Part of a popular chain, Flo is centrally located right off bustling Rembrandtplein and serves classic

The Sea Palace, an opulent floating restaurant, is a feast of authentic dim sum, pork buns, red paper lanterns, and black lacquer ceilings.

French dishes to a devoted crowd. Indulge in their heavenly fish soup, head to their Fruits de Mer bar, or have your waiter prepare steak tartare at your table. (Due to local activism, they did remove foie gras from their menu). [$] *Average main: €24 ⊠ Amstelstraat 9, Eastern Canal Ring and Rembrandtplein ☎ 020/890-4757 ⊕ www.floamsterdam.com ⌂ Reservations essential ☉ No lunch Sat. and Sun. ✛ 3:C4.*

$$$ ✕ **Tempo Doeloe.** For decades, this has been a safe and elegant—albeit
INDONESIAN somewhat cramped—place to indulge in that spicy smorgasbord of the gods, the Indonesian rice table. Stay alert when the waitstaff points out the hotness of the dishes; otherwise you might wind up having to down several gallons of antidotal *witbier*, the sweet local wheat beer. It can get rushed here so it's best to book for a weeknight—though even then, you may still need to wait (a handy time to study the endless menu) for a seat to open up. [$] *Average main: €29 ⊠ Utrechtsestraat 75, Eastern Canal Ring and Rembrandtplein ☎ 020/625-6718 ⊕ www. tempodoeloerestaurant.nl ⌂ Reservations essential ☉ Closed Sun. No lunch ✛ 3:C5.*

THE JORDAAN AND THE LEIDSEPLEIN

THE JORDAAN
Its maze of narrow streets lined with leaning gabled houses makes the Jordaan a unique backdrop for lunch or dinner. The streets most heavily laden with eateries include Westerstraat and Lindengracht. (Don't look for a canal in the case of the latter one, as it has long been paved over.) And most recently, the painfully scenic side streets found in the area between Bloemgracht, Prinsengracht, Westerstraat, and Marnixstraat

have evolved into a culinary 'Little Italy' of sorts.

$ **FAST FOOD** ✕**Burgermeester.** Indeed, they are "burger masters" here. Perhaps one can quibble and say that their bun tends to fall apart when you take a bite, but this just attests to the juiciness of the burger. Burgermeester's tasty range of options includes beef, salmon, and lamb, to name a few (they also have goat cheese and spinach burgers, though vegetarians may be rightfully wary of the cow pictures plastering the walls), plus a number of side dishes like the baked potato, corn on the cob, and a variety of salads. There are two other locations, in De Pijp and the Plantage. $ *Average main: €8* ✉ *Elandsgracht 130, Jordaan* ☎ *020/423–6225* ⊕ *www.burgermeester. eu* ⊟ *No credit cards* ⊕ *4:B5.*

$$ **DUTCH** ✕**Café de Reiger.** This excellent neighborhood brown café ("brown" because of its nicotine-stained woodwork) has a long history of being packed with boisterous drinkers and diners. Its past is reflected in its tile tableaux and century-old fittings. The Dutch fare is of the bold meat-potato-vegetable variety, always wonderfully prepared and sometimes even with an occasional adventurous diversion, such as the sea bass tastily swimming in a sauce of fennel and spinach (but regulars usually just opt for the spare ribs). At lunchtime on Saturdays there is a menu of sandwiches and warm snacks. $ *Average main: €20* ✉ *Nieuwe Leliestraat 34, Jordaan* ☎ *020/624–7426* ⊕ *www.dereigeramsterdam. nl* ⌣ *Reservations not accepted* ⊟ *No credit cards* ☾ *Closed Mon. No lunch Sun.–Fri.* ⊕ *4:C3.*

$ **VEGETARIAN** ✕**De Vliegende Schotel.** The Flying Saucer has been providing tasty, simple, and inexpensive vegetarian fare (they say 80 percent of their ingredients are organic) for a couple of decades now. With a relaxed vibe and a squatter's aesthetic—think a Berkeley café—this is alternative Amsterdam at its best. Try their popular vegetable dish inspired by the Borneo rainforest, a satisfying mixture of veggies with coconut milk, tempeh, and cashews. $ *Average main: €11* ✉ *Nieuwe Leliestraat 162, Jordaan* ☎ *020/625–2041* ⊕ *www.vliegendeschotel.com* ⊟ *No credit cards* ☾ *No lunch* ⊕ *4:B3.*

$$ **SPANISH** ✕**La Oliva.** Its extended name "La Oliva Pintxos y Vinos" describes what's served here: a huge selection of warm and cold *pintxos* (Northern Spanish tapas that run the range from oysters and other shellfish to pata negra with flambéed pears) that can be paired with one of their stellar wines (many of which can be ordered by the glass), along with a smattering of fish- and meat-based larger plates. The friendly waitstaff is ready to help you find your optimum selection. Round out your meal with the chocolate mousse with marinated strawberries before walking it off in the scenic Jordaan. $ *Average main: €23* ✉ *Egelantiersstraat*

WALL-O-FOOD

✕**FEBO.** The ubiquitous FEBO snack-bar chain serves *patat* (french fries) with a stunning variety of toppings (we like the satay sauce and mayo combo), along with mysterious-looking choices of deep-fried meats and cheeses. If you don't want to wait in line, buy your food right out of the wall. It may not be fresh but it's worth sampling for a taste of traditional Dutch snack food. $ *Average main: €3* ⊟ *No credit cards.*

122–4, Jordaan ☎ *020/320–4316* 🌐 *www.laoliva.nl* ✍ *Reservations essential* ✥ *4:C2.*

$ PIZZA ★ 🍴 **La Perla.** It's tough to find good pizza in this town, but the folks at this outpost—tucked away on a happening Jordaan sidestreet—have it pretty darn close. Their brick-oven, thin crust Neapolitan-style pies draw lively crowds of locals and tourists alike who invariably stand in line for a taste of their classic margherita, *quattro formaggi* (four cheeses), or spicy *puttanesca* (no slices, just whole pizzas). Sit at the long communal table or, if you're lucky enough, land one of the few separate tables. Though there's no atmosphere to speak of, you're here for the pie. Others will prefer to head for the roomier La Perla outpost across the street, where you can also sit outside. [$] *Average main: €13* ✉ *Tweede Tuindwarsstraat 14 & 53, Jordaan* ☎ *020/624–8828* 🌐 *www.pizzaperla.nl* ✍ *Reservations not accepted* 💳 *No credit cards* ⏲ *No lunch Mon. and Tues.* ✥ *4:C2.*

$$ DUTCH 🍴 **Moeders.** As can be expected from a place called Mothers, we're talking about Dutch home cooking along with a side of kitsch. In a café-style room alive with conversation and full of antiques and photos of mothers (to which you can contribute your own snapshot), guests are treated to simple homegrown dishes prepared with a refined gusto, even if it's just mashed potatoes with sausage or a steak fried in butter. (Vegetarians be warned: pickings are slim.) They also have a daily dish special for €10 every day until 7 pm. On sunny days ask try to snag a table on their canal-side terrace. [$] *Average main: €17* ✉ *Rozengracht 251, Jordaan* ☎ *020/626–7957* 🌐 *www.moeders.com* ✍ *Reservations essential* ⏲ *No lunch Mon.–Fri.* ✥ *4:A4.*

$$ CHINESE ★ 👶 🍴 **Sea Palace.** You can't miss this over-the-top Chinese floating restaurant, parked on the Oosterdok near Central Station. But in what could easily be a tourist trap, the authenticity and freshness of the dim sum and other dishes often surprise. In fact, inside you'll find a mainly Chinese crowd enjoying nongreasy pork buns and tasty shrimp dumplings—along with more exotic offerings like beef intestines—in an ornate atmosphere of red paper lanterns and red- and black-lacquered ceilings that wouldn't be out of place in Hong Kong or Vancouver. Best of all, Sea Palace serves dim sum every day until 11 pm, or choose from their extensive Canton, Macau, and Peking duck menus. [$] *Average main: €19* ✉ *Oosterdokskade 8, The Waterfront, Jordaan* ☎ *020/626–4777* 🌐 *www.seapalace.nl* ✥ *2:C4.*

$$ ITALIAN Fodor'sChoice ★ 🍴 **Toscanini.** In the heart of Amsterdam's most authentic neighborhood is this true-blue Florentine trattoria, one that is a perennial favorite with professionals and media types. The open kitchen, skylighted ceiling, wooden floors and tables, and attentive service all work to create a sort of "country kitchen" atmosphere. The cooks pride themselves on their ability to create any regional dish, but you will undoubtedly find your favorite already listed on the extensive menu. The risottos are profound, the fish dishes sublime, the desserts delicious, and the wine list inspired. *Buonissimo!* [$] *Average main: €21* ✉ *Lindengracht 75, Jordaan* ☎ *020/623–2813* 🌐 *www.restauranttoscanini.nl* ✍ *Reservations essential* ⏲ *Closed Sun. No lunch* ✥ *4:D1.*

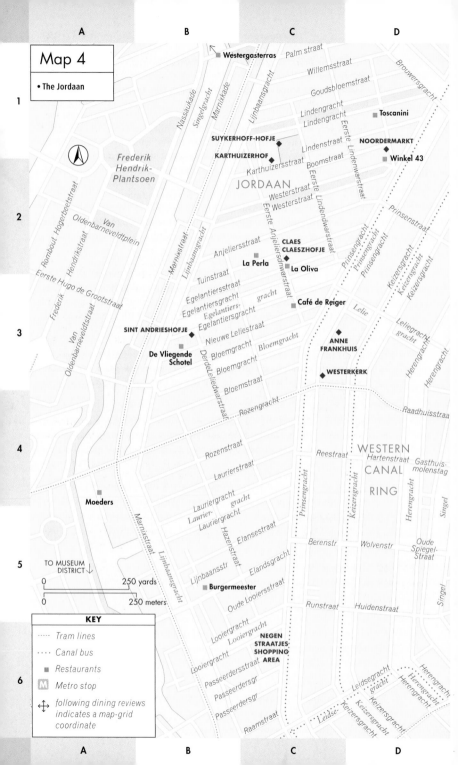

$$
CAFÉ ✕ **Westergasterras.** Located in the Westergasfabriek arts complex (just behind the Jordaan), the Western Gas Terrace restaurant overlooks a park and a former city gas container that is now an industrial-age monument. With its outdoor seating blurred with its indoor seating by retractable glass walls, Westergasterras is a perfect destination—on a lazy afternoon or evening—to enjoy the sun. Their basic but tasty café-style dishes include soups, sandwiches, pastas, tapas, grilled entrecote, and apple pie. On weekends they have been known to start a barbecue, and a DJ spins on Friday evenings in the spring and summer months. $ *Average main: €18* ✉ *Klönneplein 4–6, Westergasfabriek, Jordaan* ☎ *020/684–8496* ⊕ *www.westergasterras.nl* ☉ *Variable hrs in winter* ✛ *4:B1.*

$
CAFÉ
☺ ✕ **Winkel 43.** One word: *appeltaart*. That pretty much sums up the appeal of this popular little café with traditional wood-beamed ceilings. Here, locals, students, and tourists-in-the-know gather for slices of this thick, cake-like Dutch specialty, studded with fresh apples and cinnamon, topped with housemade whipped cream if you'd like, and best washed down with a mug of steaming fresh mint tea. This slice of Netherlandish heaven can be savored on Winkel's large patio—on the edge of busy Westerstraat and continuing across the street into the Noordermarkt—which is especially tempting on sunny days and almost impossible on Saturdays before 5 pm, when crowds spill over from the busy outdoor organic market. Otherwise, wait for a seat and enjoy a tasty sandwich, salad, or pasta dish if you're hungry for more than just sweets. $ *Average main: €11* ✉ *Noordermarkt 43, Jordaan* ☎ *020/623–0223* ⊕ *www.winkel43.nl* ⟋ *Reservations not accepted* ✛ *4:D1.*

THE LEIDSEPLEIN

The bustling square called Leidseplein is the heart of Amsterdam's nightlife. It gets the shortest amount of shut-eye of any neighborhood, explaining its popularity with late-night munchers. Although the eateries on the square require that you dig deep in your wallet, the surrounding streets are packed with more affordable (though not always high-quality) restaurants.

$
INDONESIAN ✕ **Bojo.** There are plenty of mediocre late-night eateries around the Leidseplein, but the bamboo'd and somewhat-cramped Bojo stands out for serving huge portions of enjoyable food. You'll find everything here, from *saté* (skewered and barbecued meats) to vegetarian *gado-gado* (vegetables drowned in a spicy peanut sauce) to their one-plate rice tables where several different small dishes are brought together. Two notes: Bojo is open daily until 2 am and credit cards are only accepted if you spend €35 or more. $ *Average main: €13* ✉ *Lange Leidsedwarsstraat 49–51, Leidseplein* ☎ *020/622–7434* ⊕ *www.bojo. nl* ☉ *No lunch Mon.–Wed.* ✛ *5:C2.*

$$$
FRENCH ✕ **Café Americain.** Though thousands of buildings in Amsterdam are designated historic monuments, few have their *interiors* landmarked as well. This one is, and for good reason: it's an Art Deco extravaganza of arched ceilings, stained glass, leaded-glass lamps, wall paintings, and a huge antique reading table. (Mata Hari had her wedding reception here.) Though the food is less notable than the décor (the menu offers everything from light snacks to full dinners), the coffee and cakes are

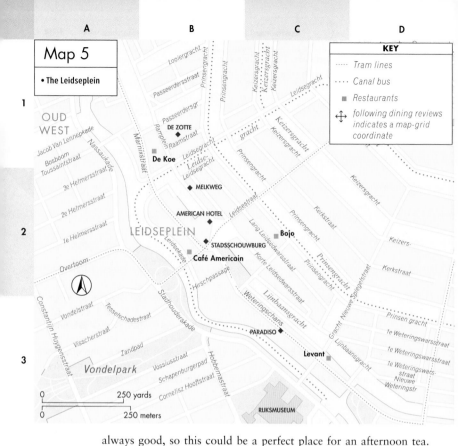

always good, so this could be a perfect place for an afternoon tea. $ *Average main: €23* ⊠ *Eden Amsterdam American Hotel, Leidsekade 97, Leidseplein* ☎ *020/556–3010* ⧄ *Reservations not accepted* ✛ *5:B2.*

$$
MEDITERRANEAN

✕ **De Koe.** Downstairs at "The Cow," the cooks crowded into the tiny kitchen manage to pump out wonderfully prepared dishes. Despite the restaurant's name, the ever-changing menu tends to favor less beef and more fish, ostrich (made with truffle sauce), and vegetarian tortelloni. The crowd is largely local, casual, and friendly. Upstairs from the café is an equally earthy and popular bar. $ *Average main: €17* ⊠ *Marnix-straat 381, Leidseplein* ☎ *020/625–4482* ⊕ *www.cafedekoe.nl* ⊗ *No lunch* ✛ *5:B1.*

$$
TURKISH
☕

✕ **Levant.** Here in a simple and modern setting you can indulge in grilled meats (and the appropriate firewaters with which to wash it all down). All the while, your children will invariably be entertained by the extraordinarily warm staff. This hidden treasure comes with a canal-side terrace (from which, on your way out, you can pay your respects to the bustling kitchen staff). $ *Average main: €19* ⊠ *Weter-ingschans 93, Leidseplein* ☎ *020/622–5184* ⊕ *www.restaurantlevant. nl* ⊗ *No lunch* ✛ *5:C3.*

MUSEUM DISTRICT

With such monuments to culture as the Rijksmuseum, the Van Gogh Museum, and the Concertgebouw, it's no surprise that this ultra-posh area attracts the suited and booted. In keeping with the upper-crust tone, you'll find some of the city's most critically acclaimed, and excruciatingly expensive, restaurants.

BELLY UP TO THE BAR

Most local brown bars and cafés serve a range of snacks meant to be washed down with beer. *Bitterballen* (bitter balls—really just more dainty versions of croquettes), *kaas blokjes* (cheese blocks that are always served with mustard), and *vlammetjes* (pastry puffs filled with spicy beef and served with Thai sweet-chili sauce) all work to keep your belly happy through to dinnertime.

$ FAST FOOD 🍴 **Bagels and Beans.** This low-key, bustling hot spot is just what the good doctor ordered: a wealth of fresh-made bagel choices, along with fresh juices and piping-hot coffee. There are over a dozen locations, but the Museum District location wins with its remarkably pleasant and peaceful back patio. [$] *Average main: €7* ✉ *Van Baerlestraat 40, Museum District* ☎ *020/675–7050* 🌐 *www.bagelsbeans.nl* 🕓 *No dinner* ✣ *6:B2.*

$$$ INDONESIAN Fodor's Choice ★ 🍴 **Blauw.** Located a bit off the beaten track on the other end of Vondelpark sits Blauw, reputedly—many believe—the best rice table (*rijstaffel)* in town. Set along the rising culinary boulevard of Amstelveenseweg, this shrine to one of Holland's favorite taste sensations recently got a make-over: out went the traditional Indonesian batik interior and then arrived an array of lacquered red walls to accent giant blowups of vintage family photos and the like. The result is fun, today, and hip. More color comes from the menu's choices, which range from €26.50 for the vegetarian rijstaffel to €31.25 for the meat, fish, and veggie option; both are fresh, well-spiced, and full of exotic flavors. Note that you can also order a la carte dishes. For those who want memories-in-the-making, ask the waiter to use the staff camera and then check the restaurant's Web site the next day to download a photo of yourself and your party at your table. [$] *Average main: €25* ✉ *Amstelveenseweg 158–160, Museum District* ☎ *020/675–5000* 🌐 *www.restaurantblauw.nl* ✍ *Reservations essential* 🕓 *No lunch* ✣ *6:A2.*

$$$ DUTCH Fodor's Choice ★ 🍴 **Bolenius.** What's "New Amsterdam cuisine," you ask? For your delicious answer, venture to this innovative restaurant (replete with Scandinavian-inspired lacquered wood and angular chairs) way out by the World Trade Center. Luckily, it's right near the Station Zuid metro stop. (Yes, Amsterdam has a metro, and it's pretty good.) Everything at Bolenius is fresh, beautifully composed, and hyper-local; in season, many of their vegetables and herbs come from their very own kitchen garden, one of the largest in Amsterdam. No cream or sugar is used in the innovative dishes like a "risotto" of cauliflower and ricotta, topped with herring eggs, or the 30-day dry-aged beef with parsnip and apple—with an exception for the amusing desserts, including a reinterpretation of old-fashioned Dutch candies. Thank Bolenius for taking the starch out of venerable Dutch cuisine—and giving us a taste of the future.

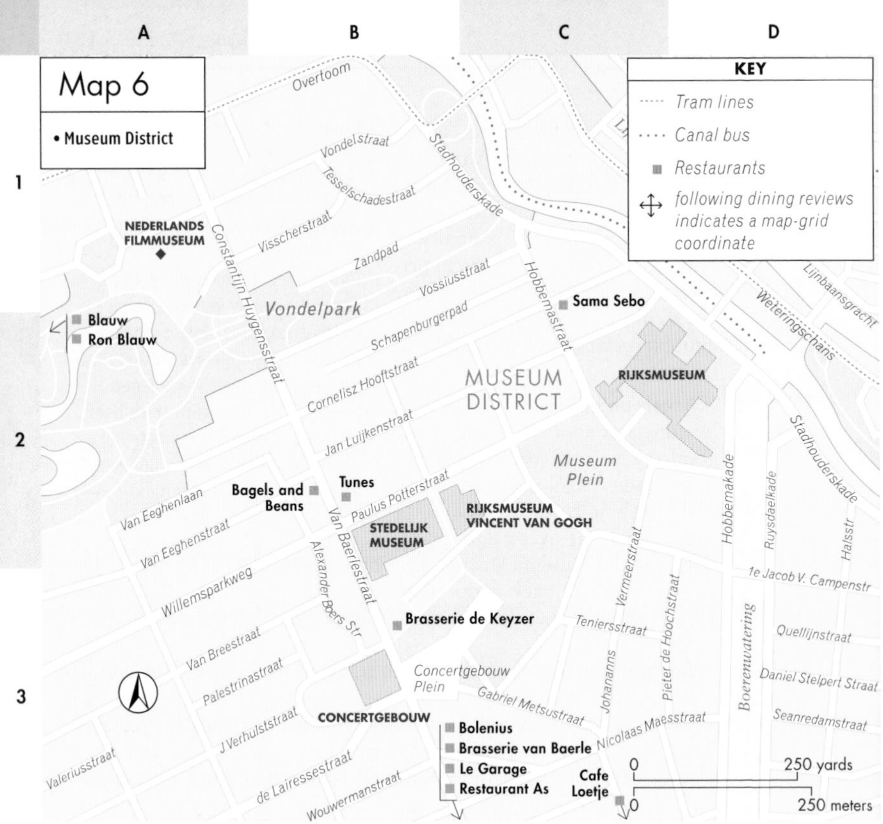
A
B
C
D
1
2
3
Map 6
• Museum District
KEY
Tram lines
Canal bus
Restaurants
following dining reviews indicates a map-grid coordinate
Overtoom
Vondelstraat
Tesselschadestraat
Stadhouderskade
Visscherstraat
Zandpad
Vossiusstraat
Schapenburgerpad
Cornelisz Hooftstraat
Jan Luijkenstraat
Paulus Potterstraat
Constantijn Huygensstraat
Hobbemastraat
Vondelpark
NEDERLANDS FILMMUSEUM
Blauw
Ron Blauw
Sama Sebo
MUSEUM DISTRICT
RIJKSMUSEUM
Weteringschans
Lijnbaansgracht
Museum Plein
Bagels and Beans
Tunes
STEDELIJK MUSEUM
RIJKSMUSEUM VINCENT VAN GOGH
Van Eeghenlaan
Van Eeghenstraat
Willemsparkweg
Van Baerlestraat
Alexander Boers Str
Brasserie de Keyzer
Van Breestraat
Palestrinastraat
J Verhulststraat
Valeriusstraat
de Lairessestraat
Wouwermanstraat
Concertgebouw Plein
CONCERTGEBOUW
Gabriel Metsustraat
Bolenius
Brasserie van Baerle
Le Garage
Restaurant As
Cafe Loetje
Nicolaas Maesstraat
Teniersstraat
Vermeerstraat
Johannes
Pieter de Hoochstraat
Boerenwetering
Hobbemakade
Ruysdaelkade
Halsstr
1e Jacob V. Campenstr
Quellijnstraat
Daniel Stelpert Straat
Seanredamstraat
0
250 yards
250 meters

[$] *Average main: €28* ✉ *George Gershwinlaan 30, Museum District* ☎ *020/404–4411* 🌐 *www.bolenius-restaurant.nl* 🕓 *Closed Sun.* ✛ *6:B3.*

$$ EUROPEAN 🍴 **Brasserie de Keyzer.** In the shadow of the golden lyre that tops the Concertgebouw (Concert Building), this institution has been serving musicians and concertgoers alike for almost a century. You can come here at almost any hour for anything from a drink to a full meal. The appropriately classical, dimly lighted Old Dutch interior—comfortable as an old shoe—is paneled with dark wood and spread with Oriental rugs. The menu leans toward tradition with a classic salade niçoise, rack of lamb, and sole à la meunière, with homemade steak tartare being the house specialty. [$] *Average main: €24* ✉ *Van Baerlestraat 96, Museum District* ☎ *020/675–1866* 🌐 *www.brasseriekeyzer.nl* ✛ *6:B3.*

$$ EUROPEAN 🍴 **Brasserie van Baerle.** If it's Sunday and you want to brunch on the holiest of trinities—blini, caviar, and champagne—look no further than this brasserie. The elegant modern furnishings and the professional yet personal service attracts a business crowd at lunch, as well as late-night diners still on an aesthetic roll after attending an event at the nearby Concert Building. Come to be treated to a French-influenced menu that includes oysters, duck confit, steak tartare, and *boudin noir* (blood sausage). There's outdoor dining when the weather cooperates. [$] *Average main: €25* ✉ *Van Baerlestraat 158, Museum District* ☎ *020/679–1532*

⊕ *www.brasserievanbaerle.nl* ⌂ *Reservations essential* ⊗ *No lunch Sat. or Mon.* ✛ *6:B3.*

$$
STEAKHOUSE

✕ **Café Loetje.** Amsterdam locals closely guard their pick for the best (and cheapest) steakhouse in the city—but that doesn't prevent hoards of diners descending on this bustling bistrolike Dutch institution. Filled with students, hipsters, and families alike, it also allures with a wonderful terrace. Simply choose whether you want a beef fillet for €16.50 or a spicier version called a "bali" for €17.50; extra-large versions cost slightly more. Keep in mind that all steaks are served rare—you can't get them any other way. There's also hamburger, pork schnitzel, and, for the non-beef eater, sole and tuna. Finish your meal with the sticky toffee cake before leaving for a well-deserved nap. $ *Average main: €15* ⊠ *Johannes Vermeerstraat 52, Museum District* ☎ *020/662–8173* ⊕ *www.cafeloetje.nl* ⌂ *Reservations not accepted* ⊗ *No lunch Sat. and Sun.* ✛ *6:C3.*

$$$
FRENCH

✕ **Le Garage.** This former garage is now a brasserie awash with red-plush seating and mirrored walls—perfect for local glitterati who like to see and be seen. This is the home of the celebrity chef Joop Braakhekke, whose busy schedule of TV appearances necessitates his leaving the kitchen in other—very capable—hands. The food uses French haute cuisine as its starting point. Yes, foie gras is one of their favorite ingredients, and they also make a fine steak tartare—Amsterdam's dish of the moment—at your table. Although champagne, fine wines, and caviar accent the essential poshness of it all, the daily, two-course power-lunch menu is quite reasonably priced at €25. $ *Average main: €30* ⊠ *Ruysdaelstraat 54, Museum District* ☎ *020/679–7176* ⊕ *www. restaurantlegarage.nl* ⌂ *Reservations essential* ⊗ *No lunch weekends. No lunch mid-July to late Aug.* ✛ *6:B3.*

$$
MEDITERRANEAN
Fodor's Choice
★

✕ **Restaurant As.** In one of the most unique settings in town—a former chapel, in the round—a Chez Panisse–trained chef whips up frequently changing menus with local ingredients and a Mediterranean flair. If you don't like chatting with your neighbor, this may not be your place, since most seats are at long communal tables. But the three-course menus for €40 are great value and make it worth venturing to Amsterdam's far southern reaches (the No. 5 tram stops a block away); they always feature a choice of meat or fish, and you can add a housemade pasta "in-between" course for €6 more. In the summer, don't miss their gorgeous terrace, with a perfect view of the (believe it or not) outdoor open kitchen. $ *Average main: €40* ⊠ *Prinses Irenestraat 19, Museum District* ☎ *020/644–0100* ⊕ *www.restaurantas.nl* ⌂ *Reservations essential* ⊗ *No lunch Mon.* ✛ *6:B3.*

$$$$
EUROPEAN
★

✕ **Ron Blaauw.** Though the casually funky decor at this two-Michelin-star restaurant—street art on the wall above the open kitchen, star-shaped lamps hanging from the ceiling—seems incongruous with the primarily business-suited clientele, the modern French-meets-Dutch food will please both the hipster and the corporate warrior. Seasonal ingredients meet creative presentation in prix-fixe menu dishes such as a fillet of brill fish with vegetable "flowers," or a lovely dessert of rose yogurt with raspberry sorbet and nasturtium. Wash it all down with a glass of wine from their thoughtfully chosen list, and be sure to sit on the inviting terrace if the sun peeks through. $ *Average main: €75* ⊠ *Sophialaan 55, Museum District* ☎ *020/496–1943* ⊕ *www.ronblaauw. nl* ⌆ *Reservations essential* ⊘ *Closed Sun. and Mon. No lunch Sat.* ✛ *6:A2.*

$$$

INDONESIAN

✕ **Sama Sebo.** This busy but relaxed neighborhood restaurant acts as a not-too-adventurous "Intro to Indo" course. Since 1969, Sama Sebo has gained nearly institution status by dishing out *rijsttafel*, a feast with myriad exotically spiced small dishes, in an atmosphere characteristically enhanced by bamboo walls, miniature wood "spirit houses," and 19th-century-style lamps. During lunch they serve simpler dishes: *bami goreng* (spicy fried noodles with vegetables or meat) and *nasi goreng* (the same, but with rice instead of noodles). At the bar, you can wait for your table while having a beer and getting to know the regulars. $ *Average main: €29* ⊠ *P. C. Hooftstraat 27, Museum District* ☎ *020/662–8146* ⊕ *www.samasebo.nl* ⌆ *Reservations essential* ⊘ *Closed Sun.* ✛ *6:C1.*

$$$$

EUROPEAN

Fodor's Choice

★

✕ **Tunes.** Thanks to the exposed brick, industrial lighting, glass-box kitchen, and young, vibrant crowds, you'll swear you're in a mod New York restaurant at this buzzy new rendezvous in the striking Conservatorium Hotel, across from the Stedelijk Museum. But even as the helpful servers explain each Delft-patterned plate of Spanish-inflected Dutch food, your attention will be focused solely on enjoying the sophisticated fusion cooking (the chef spent years in Spain learning the latest in foams, powders, and playful combinations). Particularly excellent are the sweetbreads with peanut sauce and shrimp crackers—a nod to Holland's colonial past in Indonesia—or the zucchini risotto with Dutch cheese and mushrooms. Choose from a three-course set menu for €68, or regular and vegetarian tasting menus, and pair your meal with wines from the smart list. $ *Average main: €68* ⊠ *Conservatorium Hotel Amsterdam, Van Baerlestraat 27, Museum District* ☎ *020/570– 0000* ⊕ *www.conservatoriumhotel.com/restaurants_and_bars* ⌆ *Reservations essential* ⊘ *Closed Sun. No lunch* ✛ *6:B2.*

DE PIJP

Loud, proud, and bohemian, de Pijp is all things to all people. The original occupants of this once-staunchly working-class area are still around, though they are dwindling in numbers as the area becomes increasingly pricey. Today you'll see more upwardly mobile types, as well as members of the thriving Turkish and Moroccan communities. The mix is mirrored in the choice of dining options, so you can grab a roti, a bowl of *soto ayam* (Indonesian chicken soup), or a plate of seafood linguine.

$$

INDIAN

✕ **Balti House.** If you find yourself craving curry, the dishes at this excellent purveyor of Indian cuisine have an actual subtle variance in flavors. Some of their more addictive choices are any one of their soups or tandooris, the garlic naan bread, and the homemade *kulfi* ice cream. The patio is a lovely place to sit when the sun is out. $ *Average main: €17* ⊠ *Albert Cuypstraat 41, De Pijp* ☎ *020/470–8917* ⊕ *www.baltihouse. nl* ⊘ *No lunch* ✛ *7:A3.*

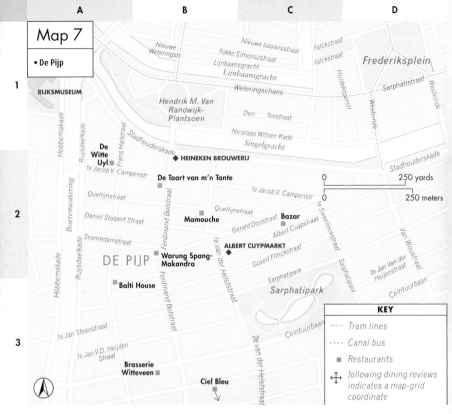

RIJKSMUSEUM

Nieuwe Weteringsstr

Nieuwe Looiersstraat

Falckstraat

Fokke Simonszstraat

Falckstraat

Frederiksplein

Lijnbaansgracht

Lijnbaansgracht

Weteringschans

Hendrik M. Van Randwijk-Plantsoen

Den   Texstraat

Nicolaas Witsen Kade

Singelgracht

Sarphatistraat

Westeinde

Hobbemakade

Ruysdaelkade

Frans Halsstraat

Stadhouderskade

De Witte Uyl ■

◆ HEINEKEN BROUWERIJ

Stadhouderskade

1e Jacob V. Campenstr

De Taart van m'n Tante ■

Te Jacob V. Campenstr

0 ────── 250 yards

0 ────── 250 meters

Boerenwatering

Quellijnstraat

Quellijnstraat

Ferdinand Bolstraat

Daniel Stalpert Straat

Mamouche ■

Gerald Doustraat

Bazar ■

Albert Cuypstraat

Te Sweelinckstraat

Van Woustraat

Seanredamstraat

◆ ALBERT CUYPMARKT

DE PIJP   Warung Spang-Makandra ■

Govert Flinckstraat

2e Jan Van der Heijenstraat

Ruysdaelkade

Hobbemakade

■ Balti House

Ferdinand Bolstraat

1e van der Helststraat

Sarphatipark

Sarphatipark

Ceintuurbaan

1e Jan Steenstraat

1e Jan V.D. Heijden Straat

Brasserie Witteveen ■

Ceintuurbaan

2e van der Helststraat

Ciel Bleu

$ ✕ **Bazar Amsterdam.** A golden-angel-capped church provides the sin-
AFRICAN gular setting for this delightfully flashy restaurant. Cheap and flavor-
Fodor'sChoice ful North African cooking—covering the range from falafel to mixed
★ grilled meats—is served here in an environment of convivial chaos. Since
Bazar is located alongside the country's largest outdoor market, it is also
the perfect place to break for coffee (or for breakfast, lunch, or dinner,
for that matter) in between rounds of market wandering. **$** *Average
main: €13* ⊠ *Albert Cuypstraat 182, De Pijp* 📞 *020/675–0544* ⊕ *www.
bazaramsterdam.nl* ⊕ *7:C2.*

$$ ✕ **Brasserie Witteveen.** Once upon a time this location was a legendary
CAFÉ Dutch grand café complete with Turkish carpeted tables and a distinc-
☺ tive old-world feel. Since its reopening in 2010, the Brasserie Witteveen
is now quite modern with a central bar and brasserie section, mosaic-
tiled floors, a 16-meter chesterfield sofa, wine room, and a separate play
area for children (who also have their own menu). However, it remains
as neighborly as ever as they serve café-style dishes everyday for break-
fast, lunch, and dinner. In particular, their soups (remember that the
Dutch are masters) are delightful: don't miss their Dutch-style pea soup
or their potato soup with smoked eel. **$** *Average main: €15* ⊠ *Ceintu-
urbaan 256–260, De Pijp* 📞 *020/344–6406* ⊕ *www.brasseriewitteveen.
nl* ⊕ *7:B3.*

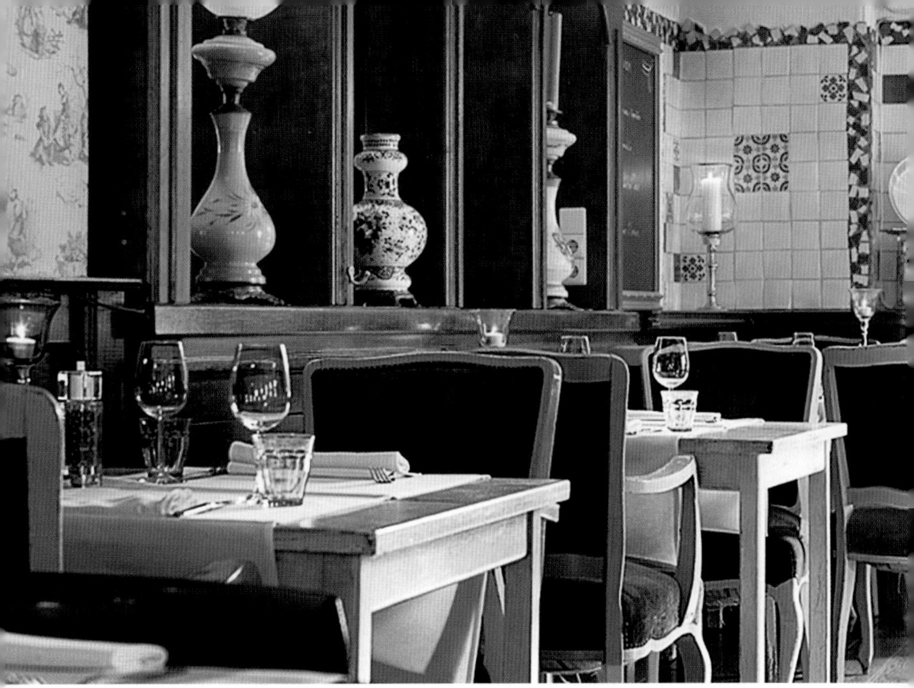

With its quaint decor, Greetje is a leading showcase got the "New Dutch" cuisine. Licorice crème brûlée, anyone?

$$$$ FRENCH Fodor's Choice ★ 🍴 **Ciel Bleu.** One of only two two-Michelin-star restaurants in Amsterdam, this elegant French dining room—renovated about five years ago—concedes to modernity with hip touches like upside-down tulip-shaped lights and a metallic rose chandelier. But the food here at the "Blue Sky" remains resolutely for those with chubby pocketbooks and expansive palates; the five- or seven-course tasting menus (for €95 or €147.50, respectively, with optional wine pairings) are really the way to go for a celebratory meal. Enjoy beautifully presented classic dishes like goose liver with langoustine and fricassée of lobster or the glazed sweetbreads while enjoying the amazing panoramic views from the 23rd floor of the Hotel Okura Amsterdam. [$] *Average main: €85* ✉ *Hotel Okura Amsterdam, Ferdinand Bolstraat 333, De Pijp* ☎ *020/678–7450* 🌐 *www.cielbleu.nl* ✍ *Reservations essential* 🕒 *Closed Sun. Closed three wks in Aug. No lunch* ✣ *7:B3.*

$ CAFÉ 🐤 🍴 **De Taart van m'n Tante.** Looking like the set of a children's television program, "My Aunt's Cake" has funky tables covered with wacky and colorful pies and cakes. In fact, many of these products—which are often developed in cooperation with artists—have side careers as props in Dutch film and television productions. Quiche is the menu's only savory option. This is a perfect place to get pumped up on sugar before taking on Albert Cuyp market. [$] *Average main: €5* ✉ *Ferdinand Bolstraat 10, De Pijp* ☎ *020/776–4600* 🌐 *www.detaart.com* ✍ *Reservations not accepted* 💳 *No credit cards* 🕒 *No dinner* ✣ *7:B2.*

$$$ ECLECTIC Fodor's Choice ★ 🍴 **De Witte Uyl.** Cozy and romantic White Owl offers a truly eclectic menu: a hybrid of Dutch, Mediterranean, and Spanish cooking with interesting combinations that, when they work (more often than not), produce some of the most exciting flavors in Amsterdam. As an added

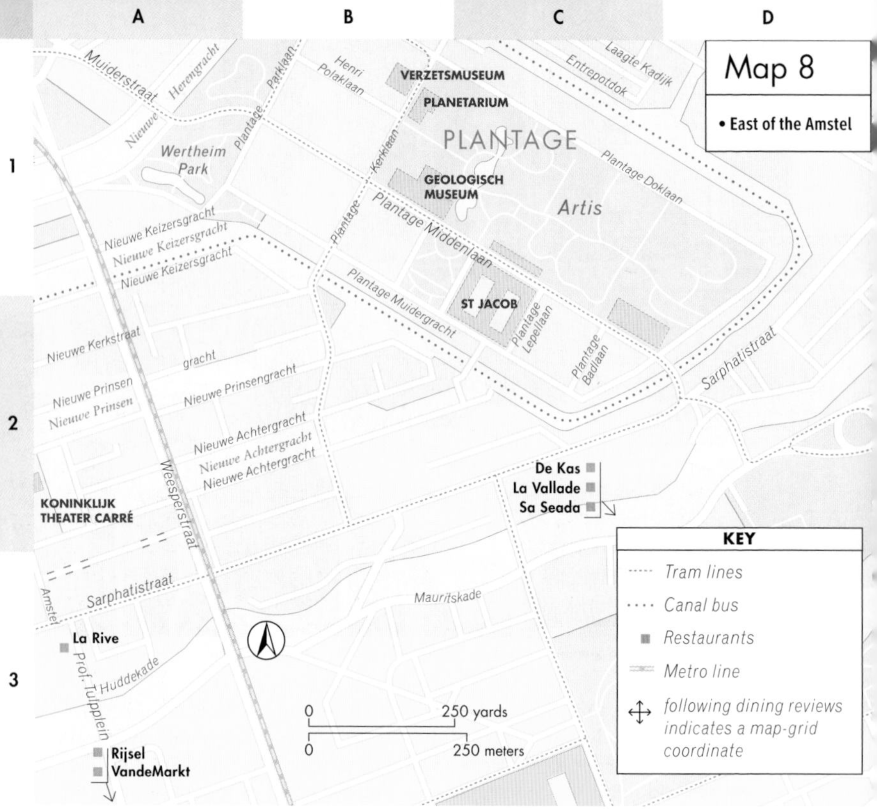
A
B
C
D
1
2
3
Map 8
• East of the Amstel
VERZETSMUSEUM
PLANETARIUM
PLANTAGE
GEOLOGISCH MUSEUM
Artis
ST JACOB
KONINKLIJK THEATER CARRÉ
Muiderstraat
Nieuwe Herengracht
Wertheim Park
Plantage Parklaan
Henri Polaklaan
Laagte Kadijk
Entrepotdok
Plantage Doklaan
Plantage Kerklaan
Plantage Middenlaan
Plantage Muidergracht
Plantage Lepellaan
Plantage Badlaan
Sarphatistraat
Nieuwe Keizersgracht
Nieuwe Kerkstraat
Nieuwe Prinsengracht
Nieuwe Achtergracht
Weesperstraat
Amstel
Mauritskade
Prof. Tulpplein
Huddekade
De Kas
La Vallade
Sa Seada
La Rive
Rijsel
VandeMarkt
0
250 yards
0
250 meters
KEY
Tram lines
Canal bus
Restaurants
Metro line
following dining reviews indicates a map-grid coordinate

bonus, most products on the frequently changing menu are organic—though do keep in mind that dishes (like the smoked mackerel with cucumber coulis or the wontons with mascarpone, ginger, and lemongrass) are small, so order at least two plates per person to avoid walking away hungry. That would be a crime here. [$] *Average main: €30* ✉ *Frans Halsstraat 26, De Pijp* ☎ *020/670–0458* 🌐 *www.witteuyl.com* 🕓 *Closed Sun. and Mon. No lunch* ✥ *7:A2.*

$$ MOROCCAN Fodor's Choice ★

🍴 **Mamouche.** Romantic and posh, this spot has been a hit with locals. This North African restaurant takes delight in the smallest details and prides itself on friendly service—a good thing, then, that all signs of this location's past as a Hell's Angels bar have been erased. Homeruns here include the couscous with saffron-baked pumpkin and the savory lamb tagine. As for desserts, the *Hob El Habiba*—a chocolate-and-date pie—will have chocoholics saying a heartfelt amen. [$] *Average main: €20* ✉ *Quelijnstraat 104, De Pijp* ☎ *020/670–0736* 🌐 *www.restaurantmamouche.nl* 🕓 *No lunch* ✥ *7:B2.*

$ INDONESIAN

🍴 **Warung Spang-Makandra.** The Indonesian-inspired Surinamese food at this often-cramped local favorite includes those long-time favorites, *loempias* (egg rolls of sorts). You can also try Javanese *rames*—a mini-rice-table-style smorgasbord on a plate. The dressed-down interior might remind you of a snack bar, but the staff is friendly, the food is tasty, and the price is right. No wonder the place is always busy.

$ *Average main: €8* ⊠ *Gerard Doustraat 39, De Pijp* ☎ *020/670–5081* ⊕ *www.spangmakandra.nl* ⌕ *Reservations not accepted* ▭ *No credit cards* ✛ *7:B2.*

EAST OF THE AMSTEL

Head away from the historical center, east of the Amstel River, and toward the tranquil neighborhood known as the Plantage for a truly leisurely meal. From extravagant restaurants right along the water to neighborhood joints with truly tasty food, you'll find a range of places to more than satisfy your appetite.

$$$

MEDITERRANEAN

Fodor's Choice

★

✕ **De Kas.** This 1926-built municipal "greenhouse" must be the ultimate workplace for chefs: they can begin the day picking the best and freshest of homegrown produce before building an inspired Mediterranean menu around them. For diners it's equally sumptuous, especially since the setting includes two very un-Dutch commodities—lots of light and a giddy sense of vertical space, thanks to the glass roof. The frequently changing €49.50 prix-fixe menu always consists of a selection of small starters, followed by a main course and a dessert. Don't miss out on their fabulous wine selection—their wine pairings are a real treat. $ *Average main: €49* ⊠ *Kamerlingh Onneslaan 3, East of Amstel* ☎ *020/462–4562* ⊕ *www.restaurantdekas.nl* ⌕ *Reservations essential* ☾ *Closed Sun. No lunch Sat.* ✛ *8:C2.*

$$$$

FRENCH

Fodor's Choice

★

✕ **La Rive.** Located within the InterContinental Amstel Amsterdam Hotel—the lodging of choice for royalty, dignitaries, and rock stars—La Rive is the city's unparalleled purveyor of refined French and Mediterranean cuisines. The setting is chic, with views directly on the river and formal service that is solicitous but not stuffy. If you don't mind emptying your wallet, settle in for the full seven-course menu for €112 (but you might just want to settle for a two-course lunch for €49). Anjou pigeon with apricots, duck liver, and beetroot is a typical starter, and main courses reflect a marked fetish for the ultimate ingredients. For instance, a meatier choice is their Wagyu sirloin with *kailan* (Chinese broccoli), pumpkin, and bay leaf. Even though the economy has made an impact on reservations here, it doesn't hurt to make a booking well ahead of time—after all, this has long been known as one of Amsterdam's haute cuisine showplaces. $ *Average main: €65* ⊠ *InterContinental Amstel Amsterdam Hotel, Professor Tulpplein 1, East of Amstel* ☎ *020/520–3264* ⊕ *www.restaurantlarive.com* ⌕ *Reservations essential* ☾ *Closed Sun. and Mon. Closed last two wks of July, first two wks of Aug., and first wk of Jan. No lunch Sat.* ✛ *8:A3.*

$$

MEDITERRANEAN

✕ **La Vallade.** A candlelit cozy atmosphere and revered country cooking inspire many to take Tram 9 to this outlying restaurant on the Ringdijk, the city's perimeter dike. Every night a new five-course menu is posted, which you can get for just €34, or opt for the plat du jour for €17.50. Monday night's menu is always strictly vegetarian. A lovely terrace that opens in the summer slightly increases the chances of being able to book a table. $ *Average main: €17* ⊠ *Ringdijk 23, East of Amstel* ☎ *020/665–2025* ⊕ *www.lavallade.nl* ▭ *No credit cards* ☾ *No lunch* ✛ *8:C2.*

$$ ✕ **Neva.** If you want a little food with your art, look no further than the
EUROPEAN   restaurant inside Amsterdam's Hermitage museum, the only branch of
the St. Petersburg original. Considering the setting, the food is much
better than it needs to be—entrées may include pickled pigeon with
roasted black carrots or turbot with asparagus—and attracts cultured
patrons lunching on the three-course chef's tasting menu or grabbing
dinner before a show at the nearby Carré or Muziektheater. Watch the
chefs prepare your meal in the theatrical open kitchen and be sure to
choose a wine pairing from the large wine cellar in the middle of the
restaurant. $ *Average main: €20 ⊠ Hermitage Amsterdam, Amstel 51,
East of Amstel ☎ 020/530–7483 ⊕ www.neva.nl ⊘ No dinner Sun. and
Mon. ✛ 3:D5.*

$$ ✕ **Rijsel.** With the feel of a boisterous high school cafeteria—albeit with
BELGIAN   an open kitchen in the back—this new Flemish restaurant in Amster-
Fodor's Choice   dam's emerging Eastern District boasts some of the liveliest diners in
★   town. All the excitement must be over the three-course daily changing
menus; you may find duck sausage with smoked duck slices, green
beans, and roasted hazelnuts; or perfectly roasted chicken with rose-
mary, served with a Belgian-style salad of lettuce, vinegar, and potatoes.
The flavors sound deceptively simple, but the preparations give more
expensive places a run for their money—and, unlike at school, the
casual, friendly service is sure to bring you back for seconds. $ *Aver-
age main: €18 ⊠ Marcusstraat 52, East of Amstel ☎ 020/463–2142
⊕ www.rijsel.com ⌆ Reservations essential ⊘ Closed Sun. and Mon.
No lunch ✛ 8:A3.*

$$ ✕ **Restaurant VandeMarkt.** Newly reopened on the Amstel with expanded
FRENCH   hours and an expansive wine cellar, "From the Market" lives up to its
name: each course of the day's three- (€39), four- (€46), five- (€54),
or six- (€60) course feast is made from the freshest ingredients found
at Amsterdam's food markets that morning. As such, the vegetarian-
friendly menu might include anything from fava beans with pesto,
chickpeas, and asparagus to baked scallops with a green Thai curry to
grilled turbot with artichoke mousseline. (Often, dishes exhibit an Asian
touch.) The new setting is sleek, modern, and very refined. $ *Average
main: €21 ⊠ Weesperzijde 144-147, East of Amstel ☎ 020/468–6958
⊕ www.vandemarkt.nl ✛ 8:A3.*

Where to Stay

WORD OF MOUTH

"I very much enjoyed my stay at the Ambassade Hotel. I walked to almost every tourist and not-so-tourist location, and the hotel, while in a historic building, was in very good condition, and had all the services I needed. I felt I had chosen well."

—elaine

Updated by
Marie-Claire
Melzer

For those who view hotels as an integral part of their travel experience—and not simply as somewhere to spend the night—it can be thrilling to stay in a listed Golden Age 17th-century gabled house, especially one furnished with antique mirrors, down-stuffed duvets, and a general sense of *gezellig*, a term that embodies the very Dutch notions of cozy comfort.

To walk down medieval passages on the way to sleep in a four-poster bed, sit down to dinner before a baronial fireplace, have breakfast on a terrace overlooking a river that has flowed through history—all these flesh out the shadows that a lucky traveler feels in a city as time-burnished as this one. Behind many of the quaint decorative facades, however, are all the modern conveniences and luxuries one could hope for. So, go ahead: revel in the 18th century over morning coffee, then get a head-start on your day by flicking on the Wi-Fi.

Accommodations throughout this city are egalitarian; no matter the budget, from grand hotels to family-run bed-and-breakfasts, easy access to attractions and idyllic canal views are available to all. Naturally, there's more to any hotel stay than the panoramas, which is where Amsterdam's hotels flex their muscles.

Solid standards keep reaching the next level thanks to such upmarket heavyweights as the stately InterContinental Amstel Amsterdam, the Okura, and the Grand, or the old-world Krasnapolsky, or the grande dame American—each offers doorknob-to-bedpost luxe. Although varying dramatically, these top places demonstrate how historic monumental buildings can be modernized and transformed into state-of-the-art facilities, providing rooms fit for royalty, business travelers, and tourists in one impressive swoop.

At the other end of the scale, young backpackers can mingle in the city's hip hostels for as little as €20, while down-to-earth properties such as Museumzicht and Fita set exceptionally clean standards, serving customers with a smile and a personal local touch; chances are your room was scrubbed only hours, or mere minutes, before you arrived. If cleanliness is next to godliness, then Amsterdam's moteless hotels attain heavenly heights.

In the middle of the price range, serene yet unexpected Dutch-flavored experience can be found around Vondelpark, where, at the Roemer and JL no. 76 modern luxury goes hand in hand with an eye for Dutch art and design. Also near Vondelpark is the charming Sandton Hotel de Filosoof, which will make you feel as if you were a 19th-century traveler visiting an old friend in a stately home; locals gathering in the lobby for weekly lectures and meetings give the place a definitive Dutch touch. Or what about the Exchange? It offers a Dutch-flavored experience of a different sort: each room has been uniquely designed by Dutch fashion students and artists.

Of course, the Netherlands continues to make waves at the forefront of European design. Thus it is little wonder that copious ink has been spilt about the gorgeous "new" Conservatorium, which has revitalized a grand old Amsterdam bank building. Inside, cutting-edge interior design and furnishings blend in with traditional elements and luxury is balanced with sustainability (even if you stay elsewhere you should enjoy a drink or meal in the soaring seven-story atrium). And then there is the worldwide buzz around the new Marcel Wanders-designed 122-room Andaz Amsterdam Hyatt, located in a former public library. Not yet quite open by press time, it is already causing a citywide stir thanks to the first photo images (guest room walls plastered with giant goldfish, etc.).

All in all, Amsterdam's span of hotels befits a dowager who is ten centuries old but growing younger every day. Some visitors will choose the latest design hot spot, others will always opt for lodgings in an archetypal canal-house hotel. If you're one of the latter, just remember to keep a steady eye, and hand, out when navigating those traditional Dutch staircases. If you're not nimble-footed, find out in advance if you need to walk stairs at your hotel—how many, what type, and the degree of incline. And watch out for that last step out the door; if not careful, you might end up doing a slow breaststroke.

PLANNING

LODGING STRATEGY

Where should we stay? With hundreds of Amsterdam hotels, it may seem like a daunting question. But fret not—our expert writers and editors have done most of the legwork. The selections here represent the best this city has to offer—from the best budget stays to the sleekest designer hotels. Scan "Best Bets" on the following pages for top recommendations by price and experience. Or find a review quickly in the listings—search by neighborhood, then alphabetically. Happy hunting!

WHERE SHOULD I STAY?

	NEIGHBORHOOD VIBE	PROS	CONS
The Old City Center (Het Centrum)	Historic monuments are in abundance, with hotels surrounded on all sides by sights, bars, restaurants, and shops.	The vibrant beating heart of the city, with all the important attractions within easy walking distance.	With its maze of narrow streets and canals, it's easy to get lost in the seedier parts of the Red Light District. Beware of pickpockets.
The Canal Rings	Independent stores line the narrow streets; Golden Age properties converted into hotels.	The many canals offer a picture-perfect postcard view at every turn. Boat companies have numerous jetties.	The more expensive shops and restaurants are located here. Pickpockets work the streets.
The Jordaan	A lovely neighborhood comprised of 17th-century properties and beautiful churches.	A sense of Old Amsterdam, with its quiet, narrow streets and stretches of water free of tour boats.	Many original Amsterdam residents have moved away, making room for more affluent homeowners and increased prices.
The Leidseplein	The city's central entertainment area bustles with activity from early evening to morning hours.	Bars, restaurants, theaters, concert halls, and nightclubs occupy every possible space.	Noise from bars, trams, and late-night revelers penetrates the windows of many hotels located in the thick of it.
Museum District	All of the city's top museums are found here, as well as Amsterdam's plushest shopping street.	There's enough surrounding culture to last for days, while the renowned Vondelpark is the perfect location to chill out.	Tour buses regularly block roads around the major museums.
De Pijp	A residential area provides a feel for what it's like to live in the city.	Home of the famous Albert Cuypmarkt, local charm, many affordable bars and eateries, and a calming respite from the central tourist traps.	Fewer famous attractions in the neighborhood means you'll spend more time traveling back and forth to your hotel.

SMOKING

Smoking is banned in public spaces within buildings in the Netherlands. As such, smoking within hotel receptions, foyers, bars, and restaurants is illegal. Almost all hotels offer no-smoking rooms, and an increasing number have gone entirely smokeless.

FACILITIES

Most hotels offer TV, phone, and tea and coffeemakers. Due to Amsterdam's temperate climate and age of many hotel buildings, air-conditioning is far from being a standard option, found most commonly in the high-priced accommodations. Internet and Wi-Fi are found in almost all hotels, though some may charge a fee for the services. Some hotels, especially those in the Museum District, sell tickets for museums, which means you can avoid long waiting lines.

DID YOU KNOW?

The Old City Center is home to the Magna Plaza Shopping Centre (pictured here) with stores like Polo Ralph Lauren, Nike, and Guess. Shopaholics may want to consider a stay at the nearby NH Grand Hotel Krasnapolsky or the Singel.

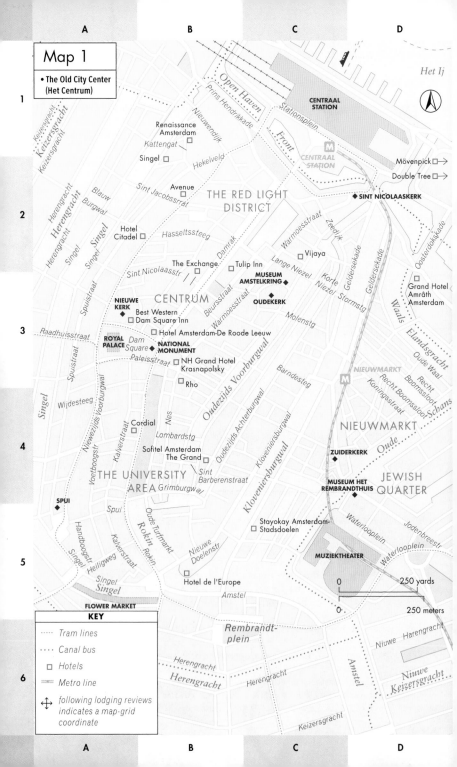

Parking in Amsterdam is restricted, expensive, and often frustrating, especially in the old center and around the canals. Few hotels have private parking garages, instead partnering with nearby facilities and offering discounted street parking or utilizing citywide valet services. Parking fees vary on average from €40to €60 per day.

PRICES

Hotel-room prices in Amsterdam typically include a VAT (value added tax) of 6% and a city tax of 5%. The majority of hotels follow the European Plan (EP) for meals, meaning breakfast is offered at an additional charge. Low-budget hotels often buck this trend by offering a Continental Plan, with a varied hot and cold buffet included in the price. While almost all major credit cards are accepted, a 5% surcharge is not uncommon, particularly in smaller hotels. High season in Amsterdam runs from April through September, but room rates fluctuate not only per season, but also per week, or per day, and sometimes even per hour. Be aware that some discount deals for advance reservations are nonrefundable.

HOTEL REVIEWS

Listed alphabetically within neighborhoods. Use the coordinate (⊕ 1:B2) at the end of each listing to locate a site on the corresponding map.

Prices in the reviews are the lowest cost of a standard double room in high season. For expanded hotel reviews, visit Fodors.com.

THE OLD CITY CENTER (HET CENTRUM)

If you want to stay in the heart of Amsterdam, head for the area surrounding Dam Square. Its bustling crowds mean you'll always have company. The adjacent Red Light District may cast a less-than-rosy glow, but this part of Amsterdam is a must-see area that remains one of the city's most historic neighborhoods. And seedy as it can be, the Red Light District is one of the liveliest parts of Amsterdam, filled with bars and surprisingly good, inexpensive (mostly Asian) eateries.

$$ HOTEL 🏨 **Avenue Hotel.** Small though comfortable rooms, furnished in a bright, cheerful contemporary style, are spread across several historic buildings, including one that used to be a warehouse for the United East India Company. **Pros:** historic building; quiet despite bustling neighborhood. **Cons:** plain rooms. [$] *Rooms from: €160* ✉ *Nieuwezijds Voorburgwal 33, Centrum* ☎ *020/530–9530* 🌐 *www.avenue-hotel.nl* 🛏 *82 rooms* 🍴 *Breakfast* ⊕ *1:B2.*

$$ HOTEL 👶 🏨 **Best Western Dam Square Inn.** A surprisingly quiet oasis just around the corner from the Royal Palace and Dam Square is adorned with storybook-ornate brick-and-stone trim and a gabled roof and offers modern and comfortable guest rooms. **Pros:** good value; on a meandering lane just off Dam Square; children up to 6 stay for free. **Cons:** rooms fill up fast; reception area feels claustrophobic. [$] *Rooms from: €152* ✉ *Gravenstraat 12–16, Centrum* ☎ *020/623–3716* 🌐 *www.*

BEST BETS FOR AMSTERDAM LODGING

Fodor's offers a selective listing of quality lodging experiences in every price range, from the city's best budget options to its most sophisticated luxury hotels. Here, we've compiled our top recommendations by price and experience. The very best properties—in other words, those that provide a particularly remarkable experience in their price range—are designated in the listings with the Fodor's Choice logo.

bestwesterndamsquareinn.com ⇨ *38 rooms, 1 suite* 🍴 *No meals* ✥ *1:A3.*

$ HOTEL **Cordial Hotel.** Easy on the budget, informal, and centrally located, with a terrace in front for people-watching while enjoying a drink, this utilitarian place is popular with young, international travelers. **Pros:** central location; helpful staff. **Cons:** basic rooms; some rooms are noisy; no air-conditioning. [$] *Rooms from: €120* ✉ *Rokin 62–64, Centrum* ☎ *020/626–4411* 🌐 *www.cordialhotel.nl* ⇨ *52 rooms* 🍴 *Breakfast* ✥ *1:A4.*

$$$ HOTEL Fodor's Choice ★ **DoubleTree by Hilton Amsterdam Centraal Station.** The shiny modern tower may look a bit unwelcoming from the outside, but on the plus side are great location, welcoming staff, well-equipped contemporary-style rooms, and some wonderful city views. **Pros:** good location, especially for shopping; helpful staff; pleasant restaurant and rooftop lounge and terrace. **Cons:** businesslike atmosphere; parking and other extras are expensive. [$] *Rooms from: €225* ✉ *Oosterdoksstraat 4, Centrum* ☎ *020/530–0800* 🌐 *doubletree3.hilton.com* ⇨ *553* 🍴 *No meals* ✥ *1:D2.*

$$$ HOTEL **Grand Hotel Amrâth Amsterdam.** The former office of the major Dutch shipping companies is glorious from the outside, with stone and brick decoration, while the public rooms (though not all of the guest quarters) retain the distinctive style of the Amsterdam School, a Dutch version of Art Nouveau. **Pros:** architecturally unique; fantastic location across from the Centraal Station; optional high tea; nice pool and spa. **Cons:** cramped entrance; contemporary guest rooms are a bit gloomy and not in style with the building; breakfast is expensive. [$] *Rooms from: €230* ✉ *Prins Hendrikkade 108, Centrum* ☎ *020/552–0000* 🌐 *www.amrathamsterdam.com* ⇨ *165 rooms, 20 suites* 🍴 *No meals* ✥ *1:D3.*

$$ HOTEL **Hotel Amsterdam–De Roode Leeuw.** An elegant 19th-century landmark on a corner of Dam Square offers some surprisingly stylish guest rooms, oases of calm with contemporary furnishings, subdued lighting, and soundproofed windows overlooking the comings and goings below. **Pros:** central location; easy access to public transport; Dutch flavor. **Cons:** small lobby; noisy surroundings. [$] *Rooms from: €135* ✉ *Damrak 93–94, Centrum* ☎ *020/555–0666* 🌐 *www.hotelamsterdam.nl* ⇨ *79 rooms, 2 suites* 🍴 *No meals* ✥ *1:B3.*

$$ HOTEL **Hotel Citadel.** The crisp, well-kept rooms here feature dramatic, mural-size photographs of city sights, many of which are within easy walking distance, and some provide a photograph-worthy, sweeping view of gabled rooftops. **Pros:** beautiful brick building; near shops, public transport, and the Anne Frank house and other sights. **Cons:** noise from trams; plain rooms lack character and charm. [$] *Rooms from: €150* ✉ *Nieuwezijds Voorburgwal 98–100, Centrum* ☎ *020/627–3882* 🌐 *www.hotelcitadel.nl* ⇨ *38 rooms* 🍴 *Breakfast* ✥ *1:B2.*

$$$$ HOTEL Fodor's Choice ★ **Hotel de l'Europe.** Movie buffs may remember this gracious landmark overlooking the Amstel River and the Muntplein as the setting of Hitchcock's *Foreign Correspondent;* all guests will relish the reproductions of Dutch masters, handsome carpets, and all sorts of other luxuries. **Pros:** wonderful Coco-Mat beds and marble bathrooms; cozy bar; some rooms have balconies with water views. **Cons:** entrance is on a narrow,

4

busy street. $ *Rooms from: €258* ✉ *Nieuwe Doelenstraat 2–14, Centrum* ☎ *20/531–1777* ⊕ *www.leurope.nl* ⤏ *69 rooms, 42 suites* ✛ *1:B5.*

$$$ 🛏 **Hotel The Exchange.** All of the rooms in three adjoining buildings have
HOTEL   been designed by students and alumni from the Amsterdam Fashion
Institute and are unique and funky, with a creative use of specially woven
fabrics. **Pros:** fun atmosphere; central location; nice in-house restaurant.
Cons: design comes before comfort; quirkiness may not suit everyone;
basic bathrooms; street noise in some rooms. $ *Rooms from: €166*
✉ *Damrak 50, Centrum* ☎ *020/523-0080* ⊕ *www.exchangeamsterdam.*
com ⤏ *61 rooms* ✛ *1:B3.*

$$$ 🛏 **Mövenpick.** Most of the businesslike rooms in this striking glass sky-
HOTEL   scraper built on an island within the blossoming docks area offer stun-
Fodor'sChoice   ning views of the Amsterdam skyline and beyond. **Pros:** upper-floor
★   suites offer the best views in town; the terrace is a great waterfront
☾   spot for refreshments; atmosphere is casual and welcoming. **Cons:** lacks
Dutch character; a bit off the beaten path. $ *Rooms from: €229* ✉ *Piet*
Heinkade 11, Eastern Docklands, Station and Docklands ☎ *020/519–*
1200 ⊕ *www.moevenpick-amsterdam.com* ⤏ *408 rooms, 31 suites*
🍴*No meals* ✛ *1:D2.*

$$$ 🛏 **NH Grand Hotel Krasnapolsky.** The monumental Krasnapolsky is one
HOTEL   of the few places in Amsterdam where you can still inhale a true Belle
Epoque atmosphere—though sadly, not in the frustratingly bland
though well-maintained guest rooms. **Pros:** well situated on the Dam
Square; gorgeous Belle Epoque breakfast room and restaurant; near
transportation; choice of in-house dining. **Cons:** impersonal feel; rooms
vary greatly in size and decor so beware of what you get. $ *Rooms*
from: €219 ✉ *Dam 9, Centrum* ☎ *020/554–9111* ⊕ *www.nh-hotels.*
com ⤏ *468 rooms, 7 suites, 35 apartments* 🍴*No meals* ✛ *1:B3.*

$$$$ 🛏 **Renaissance Amsterdam.** It's not every day you find a 17th-century
HOTEL   church that is part of a hotel, especially a stylishly contemporary one
like this, with white and minimalistic public areas and vibrant lounges
and restaurants. **Pros:** a stone's throw from Centraal Station; on a
charming thoroughfare; nice fitness center with steam bath, sauna,
and whirlpool; terrace. **Cons:** rather dull rooms; gloomy corridors;
large and impersonal. $ *Rooms from: €259* ✉ *Kattengat 1, Centrum*
☎ *020/621–2223* ⊕ *www.renaissancehotels.com* ⤏ *402 rooms, 6 suites*
🍴*No meals* ✛ *1:B1.*

$$$ 🛏 **Rho Hotel.** Turn-of-the-20th-century Jugendstil ornamentation, tiles,
HOTEL   and etched glass in the marvelous lobby all conjure up the music-hall
tinkle of the building's origins as a theater, though guest-room furnishings are for the most part standard-issue modern. **Pros:** great location; gorgeous high-ceilinged lobby; near some fabulous restaurants.
Cons: alleylike entrance; basic rooms. $ *Rooms from: €190* ✉ *Nes*
5–23, Centrum ☎ *020/620–7371* ⊕ *www.rhohotel.com* ⤏ *167 rooms*
🍴*Breakfast* ✛ *1:B3.*

$$$ 🛏 **Singel Hotel.** Three quirky, charmingly lopsided 17th-century canal
HOTEL   houses, with cheerful, striped window canopies were once the homes
of merchants and now welcome guests in comfortably modern rooms.
Pros: near many great restaurants and bars; lovely facade; doting ser-
vice; elevator. **Cons:** area is often noisy on weekends; not all rooms

DoubleTree by Hilton Amsterdam Centraal Station

Sofitel Legend The Grand Amsterdam

have canal views. $ *Rooms from: €174* ✉ *Singel 13–17, Centrum* ☎ *020/626–3108* ⊕ *www.singelhotel.nl* ↝ *32 rooms* ❍| *Breakfast* ✛ *1:B2.*

$$$$ ⌂ **Sofitel Legend The Grand Amsterdam.** Beyond the necoclassical court-
HOTEL   yard and carved marble pediments is a haven of style and luxury, a
Fodor's Choice   stunning symphony of color and chic furniture—appropriately deluxe
★   surroundings for a guest list that includes rock stars and heads of
state. **Pros:** sophisticated, chic design throughout; beautiful garden;
gorgeous spa; very luxurious; butler service and all sorts of other ame-
nities. **Cons:** rather noisy location; staff somewhat frosty. $ *Rooms from: €345* ✉ *Oudezijds Voorburgwal 197, Centrum* ☎ *020/555–3111* ⊕ *www.sofitel-legend-thegrand.com* ↝ *177 rooms, 52 suites* ❍| *No meals* ✛ *1:B4.*

$ ⌂ **Stayokay Amsterdam Stadsdoelen.** If you're looking for simple accom-
HOTEL   modation at a bargain-basement price, you can't do better than this
backpacker's Ritz in a canal house at the edge of the Red Light District.
Pros: cheap and cheerful; friendly vibe; in a lively area with many bars,
affordable eateries, and secondhand bookstores. **Cons:** books up fast;
only two private doubles. $ *Rooms from: €69* ✉ *Kloveniersburgwal 97, Centrum* ☎ *020/624–6832* ⊕ *www.stayokay.com* ↝ *10 dormitories, 2 double rooms* ❍| *Breakfast* ✛ *1:C5.*

$ ⌂ **Tulip Inn Amsterdam Centre.** A heart-of-the-city location is the best thing
HOTEL   going for these 11 connected 18th-century town houses overlooking the
Oudekerk (Old Church), where the modern rooms can be noisy and
often feel cramped. **Pros:** central location; pleasant and helpful staff.
Cons: no-frills accommodations; nearby streets attract late-night revel-
ers; Wi-Fi (fee) only in the lobby. $ *Rooms from: €115* ✉ *Beursstraat 11–19, Centrum* ☎ *020/622–0535* ⊕ *www.tulipinnamsterdamcentre. com* ↝ *109 rooms* ❍| *No meals* ✛ *1:B2.*

$ ⌂ **Vijaya.** Front rooms in this modest but eye-catching 18th-century
HOTEL   canal house have a nice view of the waterway below and some sleep up
☾   to five, so are perfect for families. **Pros:** good value; near plenty of res-
taurants; rooms for families. **Cons:** no frills; in a noisy area. $ *Rooms from: €120* ✉ *Oudezijds Voorburgwal 44, Centrum* ☎ *020/638–0102* ⊕ *www.hotelvijaya.com* ↝ *30 rooms* ❍| *Breakfast* ✛ *1:C2.*

THE CANAL RINGS

Most Grachtengordel (Canal Ring) lodgings are in older buildings with
all the Golden Age trimmings and scenic views that take you back to
the 17th-century. These canalside lodgings are mostly in the Western
Canal Ring, northwest of the Golden Bend area, or the Eastern Canal
Ring, to its southeast.

WESTERN CANAL RING

The Western Canal Ring is separated from its eastern counterpart by
the Leidsestraat, a narrow street running from the Leidseplein in the
south to the Koningsplein in the north. The Nine Streets shopping area
is just west of the Leidsestraat.

$$$ ⌂ **Ambassade.** Friday's book market on nearby Spui Square lends a
HOTEL   literary ambience to these 10 connected, stylishly decorated 17th- and
Fodor's Choice
★

18th-century houses, where Howard Norman set part of his novel *The Museum Guard* and many well-known writers are regulars. **Pros:** great atmosphere; some guest rooms overlook a picturesque canal; hub for literati; massage salon on premises. **Cons:** somewhat worn; rooms at rear can be small and dark. $ *Rooms from: €225* ✉ *Herengracht 341, Western Canal Ring* ☎ *020/555–0222* ⊕ *www.ambassade-hotel.nl* ⤳ *58 rooms, 5 suites* ¶⊙¶ *No meals* ✛ *2:A4.*

$$
B&B/INN

🏠 **Chic&Basic.** Clean simple design, with white walls, little in the way of decorative trimmings, and accents of bright bursts of color, dominate here—at least in the public areas and the nicest of the rooms. **Pros:** central yet quiet location within walking distance of Centraal Station; pleasant and helpful staff; free coffee and tea all day; boat-rental service. **Cons:** rooms are rather basic, some have not been modernized, and some are without windows; appeals most to guests with a taste for austerity. $ *Rooms from: €135* ✉ *Herengracht 13–19, Western Canal Ring* ☎ *020/522–2345* ⊕ *www.chicandbasic.com* ⤳ *35 rooms* ¶⊙¶ *Breakfast* ✛ *2:B1.*

$$$$
HOTEL

🏠 **Dylan Amsterdam.** Lacquered trunks, mahogany screens, modernist hardwood tables, and luxurious upholstery all lend design flair to these lovely quarters on the site of the historic Municipal Theater, which burned down in the 17th century (an arched entryway remains). **Pros:** a taste of old Amsterdam; good for celebrity spotting; updated business facilities. **Cons:** some parts of the hotel feel overdesigned; few rooms have canal views. $ *Rooms from: €275* ✉ *Keizersgracht 384, Western Canal Ring* ☎ *020/530–2010* ⊕ *www.dylanamsterdam.com* ⤳ *40 rooms, 8 suites* ¶⊙¶ *No meals* ✛ *2:A4.*

$$$
HOTEL
Fodor's Choice
★

🏠 **Estheréa.** Flowery wallpaper, boldly upholstered furniture, antiques, and screaming crystal chandeliers are all put together harmoniously at this gorgeously designed and cozy, family-owned hotel on a picturesque canal. **Pros:** friendly, enthusiastic staff; very comfy public areas; near restaurants; free use of iPads; nice 17th-century details remain. **Cons:** low ceilings; some rooms are small, though stylish. $ *Rooms from: €180* ✉ *Singel 303–309, Western Canal Ring* ☎ *020/624–5146* ⊕ *www. estherea.nl* ⤳ *92 rooms* ¶⊙¶ *No meals* ✛ *2:A3.*

$
HOTEL

🏠 **Hampshire Inn Prinsengracht.** Rooms in these two 18th-century connected town houses are more functional than stylish, but those in front overlook the houseboat-graced Prinsengracht Canal through huge windows. **Pros:** great location; nice views; garden terrace. **Cons:** some rooms are uncomfortably small; tends to book up fast. $ *Rooms from: €110* ✉ *Prinsengracht 1015, Western Canal Ring* ☎ *020/623–7779* ⊕ *www.prinsengrachthotel.nl* ⤳ *34 rooms* ¶⊙¶ *No meals* ✛ *2:B5.*

$$
HOTEL

🏠 **Hegra.** Here you'll find what the Dutch call *klein maar fijn* (small but good)—unpretentious, comfortable surroundings and lots of friendly service with a gentle price tag. **Pros:** central yet quiet location; historic 17th-century building; bicycle and boat rental available; nice staff. **Cons:** basic furnishings; some rooms have shared bathrooms. $ *Rooms from: €155* ✉ *Herengracht 269, Western Canal Ring* ☎ *020/623–7877* ⊕ *www.hotelhegra.nl* ⤳ *9 rooms* ✛ *2:A3.*

$$$$
HOTEL

🏠 **Hotel Pulitzer, Amsterdam.** A labyrinth of narrow halls and steep stairs leads to surprisingly large and modern guest rooms, with beamed

4

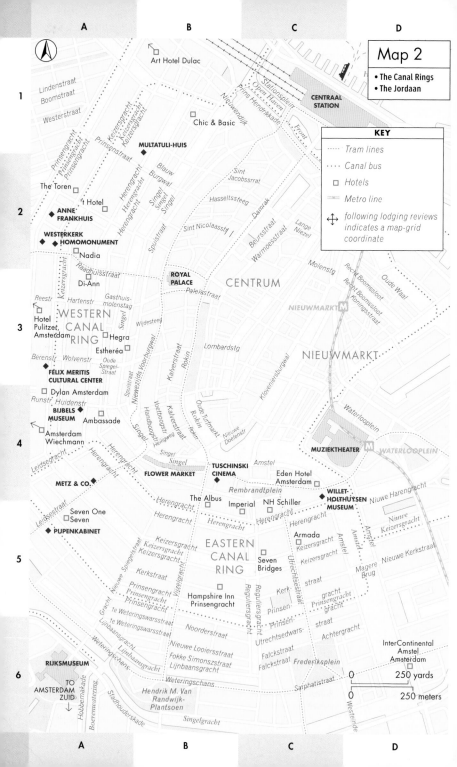

ceilings and stylish contemporary decor, that overlook the Prinsengracht and the Keizersgracht canals or nicely landscaped courtyards. **Pros:** friendly vibe; beautiful gardens; many services; nice Dutch flavor. **Cons:** clanging of church bells; rooms vary in size and quality. $ *Rooms from: €309* ✉ *Prinsengracht 315–331, Western Canal Ring* ☎ *020/523–5235* ⊕ *www.pulitzeramsterdam.com* ⤵ *230 rooms, 3 suites* ⦿ *No meals* ✛ *2:A3.*

$$$$
B&B/INN
Seven One Seven. Guest rooms in this intimate 19th-century house are each named for a different composer or writer and reflect the eye of a discerning designer, filled with nicely framed art, flowers, and antiques. **Pros:** wonderful atmosphere; free refreshments throughout the day. **Cons:** no restaurant; staff is not big on smiles; expensive. $ *Rooms from: €400* ✉ *Prinsengracht 717, Western Canal Ring* ☎ *020/427–0717* ⊕ *www.717hotel.nl* ⤵ *9 suites* ⦿ *Breakfast* ✛ *2:A5.*

$$$
B&B/INN
't Hotel. Modern functional furniture fills the larger-than-average guest rooms of this 17th-century canalside house; those in the front overlook the canal and quais, while those in the rear are blessedly quiet. **Pros:** some water views; close to dining options; friendly staff. **Cons:** uninspired basic decor; no restaurant or communal area; no elevator (chairlift for mobility-impaired guests). $ *Rooms from: €169* ✉ *Leliegracht 18, Western Canal Ring* ☎ *020/422–2741* ⊕ *www.thotel.nl* ⤵ *8 rooms* ⦿ *Breakfast* ✛ *2:A2.*

$$$
HOTEL
The Toren. A baroque vibe prevails in these two 17th-century canalside buildings, with red, purple, and gold color schemes; lots of velvety fabrics and chandeliers; and lights that can be changed to different colors for different moods. **Pros:** wonderful cozy bar/lounge; very helpful staff; whirlpool baths in some rooms; marble fireplaces and other architectural touches. **Cons:** lobby gets busy; slightly overwhelming decoration. $ *Rooms from: €200* ✉ *Keizersgracht 164, Western Canal Ring* ☎ *020/622–6352* ⊕ *www.hoteltoren.nl* ⤵ *40 rooms, 3 suites* ⦿ *No meals* ✛ *2:A2.*

EASTERN CANAL RING AND REMBRANDTPLEIN

Rembrandtplein may be a glaring tribute to neon and nightclubs, but the area east of the square offers a peaceful respite. Here you'll find such kid-friendly attractions as Artis Zoo, the Hortus Botanicus, and the Tropenmuseum.

$$$
HOTEL
The Albus. Behind a re-creation of a vintage Amsterdam exterior are seven floors of smart modern design, enhanced with wooden floors, nice views of the flower market from some rooms, contemporary art, and double-paned windows that ensure blessed quiet. **Pros:** pleasant modern atmosphere; great in-room storage and coffee; child-care facilities. **Cons:** smallish rooms; no air-conditioning. $ *Rooms from: €124* ✉ *Vijzelstraat 49, Eastern Canal Ring and Rembrandtplein*

☎ *020/530–6200* 🌐 *www.albushotel.com* 🛏 *74 rooms, 3 apartments* 🍴 *No meals* ✥ *2:B5.*

$$ HOTEL 🏨 **Armada Hotel.** A lack of charm—rooms are plain and functional—is offset by a canalside location near excellent shopping and dining in the heart of old Amsterdam and extremely reasonable prices. **Pros:** near Rembrandtplein and flower market. **Cons:** functional furnishings and decor; front rooms can be noisy; some rooms share bathrooms. [$] *Rooms from: €125* ✉ *Keizersgracht 713, Eastern Canal Ring and Rembrandtplein* ☎ *020/623–2980* 🌐 *www.amsterdamfinehotels.com* 🛏 *26 rooms* 🍴 *Breakfast* ✥ *2:C5.*

$$ HOTEL 🏨 **Eden Hotel Amsterdam—Hampshire Eden.** Clean and comfortable, this large and rather anonymous hotel overlooking the Amstel River is perfectly situated for those who want to enjoy the nearby club scene. **Pros:** views of the Amstel; close to Rembrandtplein; cheerful lobby; free Wi-Fi in lobby. **Cons:** on a run-down street; lots of noise in front rooms. [$] *Rooms from: €165* ✉ *Amstel 144, Eastern Canal Ring and Rembrandtplein* ☎ *020/530–7878* 🌐 *www.hampshire-hotels.com* 🛏 *210 rooms, 8 apartments* 🍴 *No meals* ✥ *2:C4.*

$$ HOTEL 🏨 **Imperial.** Individually decorated rooms, the cobblestone street, and a pretty adjoining square all lend a Parisian flair to this attractive little getaway close to Rembrandtplein. **Pros:** efficient, pleasant staff; cheerful, personalized surroundings. **Cons:** room decor varies, from sedate to bold, and may not appeal to all tastes; noise spills out from local bars. [$] *Rooms from: €121* ✉ *Thorbeckeplein 9, Eastern Canal Ring and Rembrandtplein* ☎ *020/622–0051* 🌐 *www.imperial-hotel.com* 🛏 *14 rooms* 🍴 *No meals* ✥ *2:B5.*

$$$$ HOTEL Fodor's Choice ★ 🏨 **InterContinental Amstel Amsterdam.** Elegant enough to please a queen, extroverted enough to welcome pop stars, this grand hotel with its palatial facade and regal guest quarters has wowed just about everyone since it opened its doors in 1867. **Pros:** palatial; you can do cartwheels in many of the spacious rooms and suites; very attentive staff. **Cons:** slightly old-fashioned decoration. [$] *Rooms from: €383* ✉ *Professor Tulpplein 1, Amsterdam East* ☎ *020/622–6060* 🌐 *www.amsterdam.intercontinental.com* 🛏 *79 rooms, 24 suites* 🍴 *No meals* ✥ *2:D6.*

$$ HOTEL 🏨 **NH Schiller.** Though this 1912 landmark is now in the hands of a large chain, a lot of Art Nouveau style still distinguishes the premises, packed with stained glass, paneling, and wrought-iron; even the blandly modernized guest rooms are enlivened with colorful paintings by founder Fritz Schiller. **Pros:** friendly staff; historical building; Wi-Fi in lobby. **Cons:** somewhat anonymous atmosphere; noise from nearby nightclubs and bars. [$] *Rooms from: €139* ✉ *Rembrandtplein 26–36, Eastern Canal Ring and Rembrandtplein* ☎ *020/554–0700* 🌐 *www.nh-hotels.com* 🛏 *92 rooms* 🍴 *No meals* ✥ *2:C5.*

$$$ HOTEL 🏨 **Seven Bridges.** These uniquely styled guest rooms, meticulously decorated with dark woods, Oriental rugs, and handcrafted Art Deco furnishings, overlook one of Amsterdam's famous sights, a lineup of seven consecutive bridges across the Reguliersgracht. **Pros:** friendly owners; optional breakfast delivered to your room; wonderful views; spacious well-decorated rooms. **Cons:** no public areas; must reserve well in advance. [$] *Rooms from: €200* ✉ *Reguliersgracht 31, Eastern Canal*

Ring and Rembrandtplein ☎ *020/623–1329* 🌐 *www.sevenbridgeshotel.nl* 🛏 *6 rooms* 🍴 *No meals* ✥ *2:C5.*

THE JORDAAN AND LEIDSEPLEIN

THE JORDAAN

While wandering this most singular of neighborhoods, you may decide it's your favorite in the city. The bells from the Westertoren take you back in time; sleepy little canals and narrow cobblestone streets with lopsided 17th-century houses give the area a special charm. On the surface, the neighborhood still looks very much as it did about a century ago, although this former workers' quarter has been upgraded and many quaint little houses have a big price-tag now. Behind the yesteryear exteriors are fascinating boutiques and antiques shops, as well as hip coffee shops, restaurants, and, of course, hotels.

4

$$ HOTEL 🏨 **Amsterdam Wiechmann.** Popularity with musicians—of both the punk (Sex Pistols) and country (Emmylou Harris) persuasions—is announced by a Gold "Top Sales" Record displayed in the lobby, one of many delightful personal touches here. **Pros:** smiling staff; spic-and-span rooms; picturesque location; canal views from some rooms. **Cons:** rooms are plain and some are small; no elevator. [$] *Rooms from: €150* ✉ *Prinsengracht 328–332, Jordaan* ☎ *020/626–3321* 🌐 *www.hotelwiechmann.nl* 🛏 *37 rooms, 1 suite* 🍴 *Breakfast* ✥ *2:A4.*

$$ HOTEL 🏨 **Art Hotel Dulac.** A severe early-20th-century building on a popular shopping street offers airy and spacious, white and bright guest rooms, with light wood furniture, comfortable beds made out of natural materials, and wonderful marble bathrooms. **Pros:** central, but not touristy location; beautiful bathrooms; nice views from rooms over Jordaan neighborhood. **Cons:** some street noise; staff is friendly but not always attentive. [$] *Rooms from: €130* ✉ *Haarlemmerstraat 120, Jordaan* ☎ *020/320–0020* 🌐 *www.arthoteldulac.nl* 🛏 *23, 6 suites* 🍴 *No meals* ✥ *2:B1.*

$ HOTEL 🏨 **Di-Ann.** Guest rooms in this gorgeous historic building with gable roofs, Romanesque balconies, and half-moon windows are surprisingly though attractively modern. **Pros:** good views; some rooms have balconies; attractive breakfast room; gift shop. **Cons:** steep staircases; central but noisy location. [$] *Rooms from: €119* ✉ *Raadhuisstraat 27, Jordaan* ☎ *020/623–1137* 🌐 *www.hoteldiann.com* 🛏 *42 rooms* 🍴 *Breakfast* ✥ *2:A3.*

$ HOTEL 🏨 **Nadia.** The 19th-century building is an architectural extravaganza with Art Nouveau portals and redbrick trimmings, but inside the rooms are white, modern, casual, and a good value for what you get. **Pros:** helpful staff; lovely breakfast room; free drink upon arrival and other nice touches. **Cons:** no elevator and steep stairs (though staff will cart your luggage); noise from church bells. [$] *Rooms from: €108* ✉ *Raadhuisstraat 51, Jordaan* ☎ *020/620–1550* 🌐 *www.nadia.nl* 🛏 *52 rooms* 🍴 *Breakfast* ✥ *2:A2.*

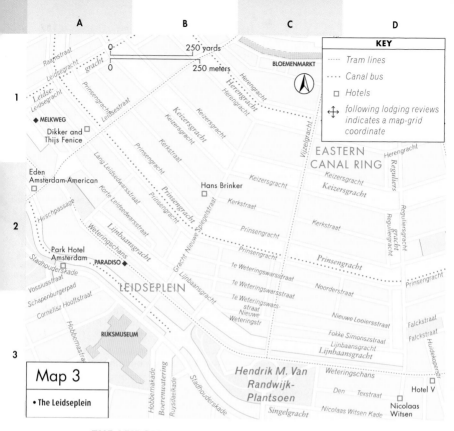

THE LEIDSEPLEIN

It can be noisy around Leidseplein, but then again sometimes it pays to be so centrally located. The square itself is surrounded by bars and offers leafy shade during summer and an ice-skating rink in winter. The Vondelpark is a stone's throw away.

$$$ **Amsterdam American Hotel—Hampshire Eden.** Calling this 1902
HOTEL assemblage of turrets, gables, stained-glass, and a clock tower home for even a day or two is a pleasure, and guest rooms are sizable, bright, and furnished in a modern Art Deco style. **Pros:** alluring history; great happening location; inspired decoration throughout the building; free Wi-Fi; fitness center and other good amenities. **Cons:** some rooms are a bit cramped; service can be a bit cold. $ *Rooms from: €220* ⊠ *Leidsekade 97, Leidseplein* ☎ *020/556–3000* ⊕ *www. edenamsterdamamericanhotel.com* ↪ *175 rooms, 16 suites* ⊕ *3:A2.*

$$ **Dikker and Thijs Fenice.** "Lavish," "classical," and "cozy" all describe
HOTEL this 1895 landmark with a regal address on the Prinsengracht Canal and its fully modernized, spacious, and gracious Art Deco rooms that retain gables, beams, skylights, and other stunning details. **Pros:** water views; babysitting service; central location. **Cons:** small lobby gets crowded; rooms book up fast. $ *Rooms from: €149* ⊠ *Prinsengracht*

444, Leidseplein ☎ *020/620–1212* 🌐 *www.dtfh.nl* 🛏 *42 rooms* 🍴 *No meals* ✣ *3:A1.*

> **WORD OF MOUTH**
>
> "Leidseplein, in my opinion, is the area with the most vibrant nightlife with loads of restaurants, bars, and coffee houses. It is a major gathering sight for many young tourists, and has wide range of hotel options." —Roce48

$ HOTEL 🏨 **Hans Brinker.** Many of the no-frills but sparkling clean rooms, with white walls and blue floors, are dorm style with bunks, but those who don't fancy waking up with strangers can also book one of the private doubles or triples. **Pros:** international crowd; fun atmosphere; the Ritz among hostels. **Cons:** best for the young; staff can be brusque; checking in seems to take forever. [$] *Rooms from: €107* ✉ *Kerkstraat 136, Leidseplein* ☎ *020/622–0687* 🌐 *www.hans-brinker.com* 🛏 *124 rooms* 🍴 *Breakfast* ✣ *3:B2.*

$$$ HOTEL Fodor's Choice ★ 🏨 **Hotel V.** These exquisitely designed lounges and guest rooms are a pleasure to experience, a hip showcase of contemporary furnishings and textiles that lend a spacious, luxurious, and welcoming atmosphere to the center of the old city. **Pros:** free coffee and tea; good value; really helpful staff. **Cons:** slightly off-center location; best rates are nonrefundable. [$] *Rooms from: €169* ✉ *Weteringschans 136, Leidseplein* ☎ *020/662–3233* 🌐 *www.hotelv.nl* 🛏 *48 rooms, 6 apartments* 🍴 *Breakfast* ✣ *3:D3.*

$$ HOTEL 🏨 **Nicolaas Witsen.** If you're just looking for a place to hang your hat and get a quiet night's sleep, these standard-issue, tidily kept guest rooms with white walls punctuated by lots of windows are a good choice. **Pros:** quiet location; cheery breakfast room and freshly baked croissants; valet parking. **Cons:** no-frills interior; smallish rooms. [$] *Rooms from: €121* ✉ *Nicolaas Witsenstraat 4, Leidseplein* ☎ *020/626–6546* 🌐 *www.hotelnicolaaswitsen.nl* 🛏 *28 rooms* 🍴 *Breakfast* ✣ *3:D3.*

$$$ HOTEL Fodor's Choice ★ 👶 🏨 **Park Hotel Amsterdam.** Though this stately 18th-century Amsterdam fixture has one foot in history, the other is firmly entrenched in the here and now, with modern-luxe decor, cosmopolitan ambience, and all sorts of high-tech amenities. **Pros:** stylishly appointed rooms; excellent service; convenient location. **Cons:** no particular Dutch flavor. [$] *Rooms from: €189* ✉ *Stadhouderskade 25, Leidseplein* ☎ *020/671–1222* 🌐 *www.parkhotel.nl* 🛏 *189 rooms, 21 suites* 🍴 *No meals* ✣ *3:A2.*

MUSEUM DISTRICT

If you've come to Amsterdam to enjoy the arts, then you should book a room in this quarter, home to all the city's top museums. Also here is the city's most exclusive shopping strip while the lovely green Vondelpark is just to the west. Little wonder that this area has been colonized by fine hotels.

$$ HOTEL 🏨 **Aalders.** With large windows overlooking a quiet street and within striking distance of the Vondelpark, this cozy and charming house provides a nice retreat from city life. **Pros:** friendly staff; close to museums. **Cons:** books up fast; some bathrooms are cramped. [$] *Rooms from: €149* ✉ *Jan Luykenstraat 13–15, Museum District and Environs*

Hotel V

Park Hotel Amsterdam

☎ *020/662–0116* 🌐 *www.hotelaalders.nl* 🛏 *28 rooms* ⏲ *Closed 2 wks in mid-Dec.* 🍴 *Breakfast* ✥ *4:C2.*

$$ HOTEL

🏨 **Atlas.** Guests feel right at home in this Art Nouveau mansion, where spacious guest rooms are furnished with a nice smattering of old and new pieces and contemporary art work hangs on the walls. **Pros:** friendly staff and genuinely welcoming atmosphere; well-used public areas; relaxing atmosphere; close to the Vondelpark. **Cons:** mostly residential area; some room furnishings feel randomly assembled. [$] *Rooms from: €129* ✉ *Van Eeghenstraat 64, Museum District and Environs* ☎ *020/676–6336* 🌐 *www.hotelatlas.nl* 🛏 *23 rooms* ✥ *4:A2.*

$$ HOTEL

🏨 **Bilderberg Jan Luyken.** This stylish trio of quaint 19th-century town houses offers a peaceful sanctuary, complete with a serene garden and restrained *Wallpaper*-worthy design—tripod lamps, steel ashtrays, Knoll-ish chairs, and hint of Art Nouveau. **Pros:** leafy environs; modern rooms; nice architectural details. **Cons:** some rooms are snug; slightly unwelcoming entrance; service and housekeeping leave a bit to be desired. [$] *Rooms from: €129* ✉ *Jan Luykenstraat 58, Museum District and Environs* ☎ *020/573–0730* 🌐 *www.bilderberg.nl* 🛏 *62 rooms* 🍴 *No meals* ✥ *4:B2.*

$$$ HOTEL

🏨 **The College Hotel.** This 1895 landmark is a training ground for students of the country's top hotel management schools, which accounts for the fresh-faced staff and eager service in the contemporarily styled, high-ceilinged guest rooms and acclaimed restaurant. **Pros:** trendy bar; air-conditioned rooms; in-room massages; spacious bathrooms; carpets you can sink into and other touches of luxury. **Cons:** located slightly off center; expensive parking. [$] *Rooms from: €200* ✉ *Roelof Hartstraat 1, Museum District and Environs* ☎ *020/571–1511* 🌐 *www.thecollegehotel.com* 🛏 *40 rooms, 1 suite* 🍴 *No meals* ✥ *4:B3.*

$ B&B/INN Fodor's Choice ★

🏨 **The Concert Hotel.** The spotless, sparsely contemporary, good-value bedrooms in this early-20th-century house opposite the Concertgebouw are decked out in soothing neutral tones and decorated with photographs of famous jazz and pop musicians. **Pros:** elevator; garden; convenient to museums. **Cons:** surrounded by expensive shops and restaurants. [$] *Rooms from: €100* ✉ *De Lairessestraat 11, Museum District and Environs* ☎ *020/364–0504* 🌐 *www.theconcerthotel.com* 🛏 *26* 🍴 *Breakfast* ✥ *4:B3.*

$$ HOTEL

🏨 **Conscious Hotel Museum Square.** From cleaning products to breakfast cereals, everything in this refined little outpost of design is organic—even the hip room furnishings are made out of sustainable or recycled materials. **Pros:** light and airy rooms; designer vibe. **Cons:** overburdened staff can get snappy; breakfast (additional) is very basic. [$] *Rooms from: €140* ✉ *De Lairessestraat 7, Museum District and Environs* ☎ *020/671–9596* 🌐 *www.conscioushotels.com* 🛏 *36 rooms* 🍴 *No meals* ✥ *4:B3.*

$$$$ HOTEL Fodor's Choice ★

🏨 **Conservatorium Hotel.** An impressive early 20th-century bank-turned-music-school is a visual feast, with a glass-roofed, tree-filled courtyard lobby and dramatically modern guest rooms, many of them duplexes, with huge windows, muted tones, and splashes of color. **Pros:** stunning contemporary surroundings; spacious and beautiful accommodations; spa with lap pool; near museums. **Cons:** quite expensive; a bit removed from city center. [$] *Rooms from: €325* ✉ *Van Baerlestraat 27, Museum*

District and Environs ☎ *020/570 0000* 🌐 *www.conservatoriumhotel.com* 🛏 *129 rooms, 42 suites* 🍴 *No meals* ⊕ *4:B2.*

$$ HOTEL 🏨 **EMB Memphis.** The ivy-clad, mansard-roofed former residence of beer tycoon Freddy Heineken is fresh, airy, and exceptionally spacious, with large, comfortably contemporary guest rooms and nice lounges. **Pros:** quiet location near the Concertgebouw; pleasant lobby/bar area; elegant yet relaxed; children under 12 stay for free. **Cons:** rather bland decoration; a bit far from the sites. [$] *Rooms from: €149* ✉ *De Lairessestraat 87, Museum District and Environs* ☎ *020/673–3141* 🌐 *www.memphishotel.nl* 🛏 *78 rooms* 🍴 *No meals* ⊕ *4:A3.*

$ HOTEL 🏨 **Europa 92.** Low-key charm prevails in this tidy little house where the nicest of the modest-but-nattily furnished rooms face a lovely garden that doubles as a breakfast room and lounge in good weather. **Pros:** friendly staff; specials (check the website) are often a very good deal. **Cons:** off-center location; no parking (but street parking is easy). [$] *Rooms from: €105* ✉ *1e Constantijn Huygenstraat 103–107, Museum District and Environs* ☎ *020/618–8808* 🌐 *www.europa92.nl* 🛏 *47 rooms, 2 suites* 🍴 *No meals* ⊕ *4:A1.*

$ HOTEL Fodor's Choice ★ 🏨 **Flying Pig Uptown Hostel.** For backpackers who like to chill out and meet lots of gezellige people, the Flying Pig is the place to be—and the few doubles are some of the best-value accommodations in town. **Pros:** fun vibe; tons of activities; smoking room; good value. **Cons:** located in a residential area. [$] *Rooms from: €70* ✉ *Vossiusstraat 46, Museum District and Environs* ☎ *020/400–4187* 🌐 *www.flyingpig.nl* 🛏 *6 double rooms, 23 dormitories* 🍴 *Breakfast* ⊕ *4:B2.*

$ B&B/INN 🏨 **Hestia.** With a helpful and courteous staff and basic, light, and simply modern rooms tucked into a lovely red-brick, mansard-roofed house, this is the kind of place that reinforces the image of the Dutch as being nice and orderly. **Pros:** friendly staff; close to museums. **Cons:** some rooms are on the small side (and priced accordingly); rooms book up fast. [$] *Rooms from: €120* ✉ *Roemer Visscherstraat 7, Museum District and Environs* ☎ *020/618–0801* 🌐 *www.hotel-hestia.nl* 🛏 *18 rooms* 🍴 *Breakfast* ⊕ *4:B1.*

WORD OF MOUTH

"We enjoyed our stay at the Hestia. It is within two blocks of canals, and the Van Gogh and Rijks Museums. It also has a nice little garden area that the kids would enjoy."—avalon

$$ B&B/INN Fodor's Choice ★ 👶 🏨 **Hotel Fita.** A favorite with travelers for years is friendly and cozy and getting better all the time—nice improvements like an honor bar enhance such longtime perks as a great breakfast and in-room espresso machines. **Pros:** Dutch flavor; spacious rooms in pleasing contemporary style; beautiful location; family-friendly. **Cons:** no real public areas; no air-conditioning (but ceiling fans). [$] *Rooms from: €134* ✉ *Jan Luykenstraat 37, Museum District and Environs* ☎ *020/679–0976* 🌐 *www.fita.nl* 🛏 *15 rooms* 🍴 *Breakfast* ⊕ *4:B2.*

$$$ HOTEL 🏨 **Hotel JL no. 76.** These two 18th-century buildings on leafy Jan Luykenstraat may look traditional, but in the lounges and guest rooms everything is stylishly contemporary, with Dutch art on the walls, colorful wallpaper, natural fabrics, and all sorts of high-tech gadgets. **Pros:**

Conservatorium Hotel

Sandton Hotel de Filosoof

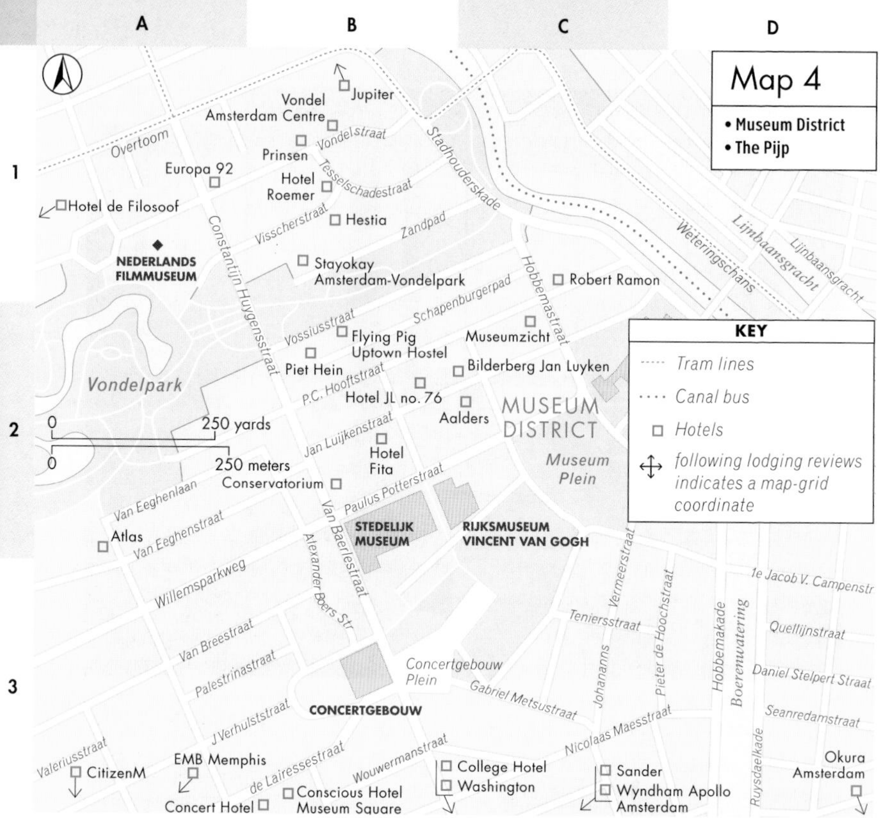
A
B
C
D
1
2
3
Map 4
• Museum District
• The Pijp
KEY
Tram lines
Canal bus
Hotels
following lodging reviews indicates a map-grid coordinate
Jupiter
Vondel Amsterdam Centre
Overtoom
Vondelstraat
Prinsen
Europa 92
Hotel Roemer
Tesselschadestraat
Stadhouderskade
Hotel de Filosoof
Visscherstraat
Hestia
Zandpad
NEDERLANDS FILMMUSEUM
Constantijn Huygensstraat
Stayokay Amsterdam-Vondelpark
Hobbemastraat
Robert Ramon
Weteringschans
Lijnbaansgracht
Schapenburgerpad
Vossiusstraat
Flying Pig Uptown Hostel
Museumzicht
Piet Hein
P.C. Hooftstraat
Bilderberg Jan Luyken
Vondelpark
Hotel JL no. 76
Aalders
MUSEUM DISTRICT
0
250 yards
250 meters
Jan Luijkenstraat
Hotel Fita
Museum Plein
Conservatorium
Van Eeghenlaan
Paulus Potterstraat
Atlas
Van Eeghenstraat
STEDELIJK MUSEUM
RIJKSMUSEUM
VINCENT VAN GOGH
Alexander Boers Str
Van Baerlestraat
Vermeerstraat
Pieter de Hoochstraat
1e Jacob V. Campenstr
Willemsparkweg
Teniersstraat
Hobbemakade
Boerenwetering
Quellijnstraat
Van Breestraat
Concertgebouw Plein
Johannes
Daniel Stelpert Straat
Palestrinastraat
Gabriel Metsustraat
CONCERTGEBOUW
Seanredamstraat
J Verhulststraat
Nicolaas Maesstraat
Ruysdaelkade
Valeriusstraat
CitizenM
EMB Memphis
de Lairessestraat
Wouwermanstraat
College Hotel
Washington
Sander
Wyndham Apollo Amsterdam
Okura Amsterdam
Concert Hotel
Conscious Hotel Museum Square

stylish surroundings; air-conditioning; within easy walking distance of main museums; nice family room. **Cons:** small garden; off the beaten track; some complaints about service. [$] *Rooms from: €180* ✉ *Jan Luykenstraat 76, Museum District and Environ* ☎ *020/348–5555* 🌐 *www.vondelhotels.com* 🛏 *39* 🍴 *No meals* ✥ *4:B2.*

$$$ 🏨 **Hotel Roemer.** A zest for modern art and design and a sense of travelers' comfort shows up everywhere, from the cozy lounge opening onto a beautiful garden to the stylish, well-equipped guest rooms, where even the bathrooms have flat-screen TVs. **Pros:** elegant and very comfy rooms; extra-long beds; breakfast and drinks included in some rates. **Cons:**a bit expensive; fee for Wi-Fi. [$] *Rooms from: €199* ✉ *Roemer Visscherstraat 10, Museum District and Environ* ☎ *020/589–0800* 🌐 *www.vondelhotels.com* 🛏 *23* 🍴 *Breakfast* ✥ *4:B1.*

HOTEL
Fodor's Choice ★

$$$ 🏨 **Hotel Vondel.** The generously sized guest rooms are so soothingly done that you're almost ensured a good night's sleep—actually, everything about this hip hostelry instills calm, from the light-and-flower-filled lounges with their sumptuous couches to the garden. **Pros:** artsy vibe; refined and comfy guest rooms; art-filled restaurant. **Cons:** rooms book up fast. [$] *Rooms from: €199* ✉ *Vondelstraat 26, Museum District and Environs* ☎ *020/612–0120* 🌐 *www.vondelhotels.com* 🛏 *87 rooms, 3 suites* 🍴 *No meals* ✥ *4:B1.*

HOTEL

$ ⛶ **Jupiter.** Convenient, no-nonsense, and with a few amenities—includ-

B&B/INN   ing an elevator and free Wi-Fi—this well-known budget choice has a great thing going for it: low rates. **Pros:** quiet yet convenient area near the Rijksmuseum and the Concertgebouw; decent bathrooms. **Cons:** no particular Dutch flavor; uninspiring surroundings. $ *Rooms from: €108* ⊠ *2e Helmersstraat 14, Museum District and Environs* ☎ *020/618–7132* ⊕ *www.jupiterhotel.nl* ↴ *20 rooms* ▬ *No credit cards* ⓧ *Breakfast* ✛ *4:B1.*

$ ⛶ **Museumzicht.** Most guest rooms have shared bathrooms, but the sur-

B&B/INN   roundings may compensate for any inconvenience: etchings hang on the

Fodor'sChoice   walls, much of the furniture is antique, and the Rijksmuseum looms just

★   outside the windows. **Pros:** quirky decoration with a personal touch; panoramic views; Dutch flavor; many nearby attractions. **Cons:** steep staircase; shared bathrooms are cramped. $ *Rooms from: €95* ⊠ *Jan Luykenstraat 22, Museum District and Environs* ☎ *020/671–2954* ⊕ *www.hotelmuseumzicht.com* ↴ *14 rooms, 11 with shared bath* ⓧ *Breakfast* ✛ *4:C2.*

$ ⛶ **Prinsen.** The storybook charm of the 1870 exterior—all dormers,

HOTEL   bay windows, jigsaw trim, neoclassical columns, and sculpted reliefs of cats—ends as soon as you step into the cheerful but banally reno-vated interior. **Pros:** good value; gay-friendly vibe; close to the Vondel-park. **Cons:** rather bland interior. $ *Rooms from: €120* ⊠ *Vondelstraat 36–38, Museum District and Environs* ☎ *020/616–2323* ⊕ *www.prinsenhotel.nl* ↴ *45 rooms, 1 suite* ⓧ *Breakfast* ✛ *4:B1.*

$$ ⛶ **RobertRamon.** A nice design vibe shows up throughout these unpre-

HOTEL   tentious but comfortable rooms—which range from snug singles to spacious family units—at the foot of the P. C. Hooftstraat, one of Amsterdam's most exclusive streets. **Pros:** friendly staff; close to shops and museums; spacious bathrooms; good breakfast (extra). **Cons:** rooms facing the tramlines are a bit noisy; some rooms are cramped. $ *Rooms from: €139* ⊠ *P. C. Hooftstraat 24, Museum District and Environs* ☎ *020/671–4785* ⊕ *www.robertramon.com* ↴ *51 rooms* ✛ *4:C1.*

$$ ⛶ **Sander.** With guest rooms that are best described as typically Dutch—

HOTEL   clean and comfortable—the Sander is known for being welcoming to everyone. Seating areas in window bays give some rooms additional charm. The breakfast room opens out onto a garden. **Pros:** gay-friendly vibe; close to museums; inexpensive. **Cons:** simple furnishings; rooms book up fast. $ *Rooms from: €160* ⊠ *Jacob Obrechtstraat 69, Museum District and Environs* ☎ *020/662–7574* ⊕ *www.hotel-sander.nl* ↴ *20 rooms* ⓧ *Breakfast* ✛ *4:C3.*

$$ ⛶ **Sandton Hotel de Filosoof.** The quirky Edwardian lobby with its comfy

HOTEL   armchairs will capture your heart, as will the guest rooms decorated in

Fodor'sChoice   philosophical themes—Greek style in the Aristotle room, Faustian texts

★   in the Goethe room. **Pros:** off-the-wall interior; cozy and comfortable public areas; lovely garden; quiet location. **Cons:** the hotel can be hard to find; some newer rooms lack the charm of others. $ *Rooms from: €125* ⊠ *Anna van den Vondelstraat 6, Museum District and Environs* ☎ *020/683–3013* ⊕ *www.sandton.eu* ↴ *43 rooms, 5 suites* ⓧ *Break-fast* ✛ *4:A1.*

4

Okura Amsterdam

Lloyd Hotel

$ **Stayokay Amsterdam Vondelpark.** More than 75,000 backpackers stay
HOTEL   in this hostel hidden on a small side path within the Vondelpark every year, in accommodations that range from doubles to dormitories for 20. **Pros:** like staying in a secret forest; probably the cleanest hostel anywhere; sheets included. **Cons:** no particular Dutch flavor; harried staff. $ *Rooms from: €86 ⊠ Zandpad 5, Museum District and Environs ☎ 020/589–8996 ⊕ www.stayokay.com ⤳ 100 rooms ❙❍❙ Breakfast ♦ 4:B1.*

$ **Washington.** A stay at this cozy favorite with musicians across from
HOTEL   the Concetgebouw is almost like staying with an old friend: the lounges are filled with antiques, the light-filled guest rooms are simply and charmingly decorated in white and pastel shades, and the friendly staff is on hand with advice. **Pros:** laid-back aura; friendly staff; everything is polished and sparkling clean; good value. **Cons:** no elevator; a few rooms share bathrooms; books up fast. $ *Rooms from: €110 ⊠ Frans van Mierisstraat 10, Museum District and Environs ☎ 020/679–7453 ⊕ www.hotelwashington.nl ⤳ 22 rooms, 1 suite, 2 apartments ❙❍❙ Breakfast ♦ 4:B3.*

DE PIJP

Both budget and posh, homey and businesslike, accommodations come together in the more quiet residential neighborhoods of de Pijp and the high-toned Oud Zuid (Old South). They are set a mere 15-minute tram ride away from Centraal Station, but far enough removed from center-city crowds. De Pijp is lively, with an exotic food market and plenty of bars and affordable eateries. Old South is leafy and tranquil, with upscale shops and restaurants.

$$ **CitizenM.** Trendy travelers on a budget will enjoy the cosmopolitan
HOTEL   vibe, lavish public spaces, and airy guest rooms with their high-tech
Fodor'sChoice   gadgetry—but maybe not the sci-fi-like see-through glass tubes that
★   contain the toilet and shower. **Pros:** luxurious furnishings surpass the price tag; king-size beds and nice ambient lighting; sandwiches and salads available 24/7. **Cons:** guest rooms resemble hospital rooms; out-of-the-way location. $ *Rooms from: €158 ⊠ Prinses Irenestraat 30, De Pijp and Environs ☎ 020/811–7090 ⊕ www.citizenm.com ⤳ 215 rooms ❙❍❙ No meals ♦ 4:A3.*

$$$ **Okura Amsterdam.** Although the guest rooms are plushly done in tra-
HOTEL   ditional dark-wood Western style, you'll bask in an Asian sense of
Fodor'sChoice   luxury and service from the moment you enter the spacious lobby with
★   its marble floors and elegant furnishings. **Pros:** city and water views; nice top-floor bar; great dining options; waterfront terrace; guest services helps you with almost anything. **Cons:** a bit far from the center; international, not Dutch, flavor. $ *Rooms from: €210 ⊠ Ferdinand Bolstraat 333, De Pijp and Environs ☎ 020/678–7111 ⊕ www.okura.nl ⤳ 300 rooms, 34 suites ❙❍❙ No meals ♦ 4:D3.*

$$ HOTEL 👶 Fodor's Choice ★ **Lloyd Hotel.** A former holding-area home for immigrants, this bohemian hotel is well suited to its current quirky incarnation as an offbeat design showcase, where some rooms have log walls, beds sleep up to seven, and bathtubs stand in the middle of living rooms. Guest quarters in the Art Deco landmark structure come in varying sizes and suit various budgets, from snug alcoves with shared baths to enormous penthouse harbor-view suites, but everyone enjoys the soaring, white-walled, sun-drenched lobby and fittingly unusual restaurants. **Pros:** historic Art Deco building; rooms priced for all budgets; interesting crowd. **Cons:** slightly out-of-the-way location. [$] *Rooms from: €140* ✉ *Oostelijke Handelskade 34, Amsterdam East* ☎ *020/561–3636* 🌐 *www.lloydhotel.com* 🛏 *117 rooms, 9 suites* 🍴 *No meals.*

Nightlife and the Arts

WORD OF MOUTH

"De Jaren has a lovely outside terrace. The café is very light, airy and spacious. There's a bar, a restaurant and, a very customer friendly international reading table, with daily newspapers from around the world."

—bellini

Updated by
Marie-Claire
Melzer

Everybody knows that *The Night Watch* is the name of Rembrandt's most famous painting but not everyone remembers that, back in the early 2000s, it was also the nickname of a bunch of "Night Mayors." This group of cultural leaders saw their role as fighters against the frumpiness that had cast a shadow over Amsterdam's night scene, thanks to the fact that the city fathers had cleared away the "squats"—the deserted buildings that were the settings for city's wildest nighttime events and raves. Now, ten years later, Amsterdam is happily experiencing a renaissance in its reputation as a true nightlife capital.

The city is still rich with inspired folk who are willing to organize a video arts festival in a cruise ship terminal, a gentle Bach recital in an ancient church, an arts festival in an abandoned factory, a house party in a football stadium, or some heart-stopping spectacle in a park. So get ready to savor Amsterdam's giant cultural wallop through its numerous venues—from former churches and industrial monuments to the acoustical supremacy of the legendary hall of the Concertgebouw. And the beautiful thing about the Netherlands is that if by the smallest—and we do mean smallest—of chances Amsterdam is slow one night, a short train trip to Rotterdam or the Hague will undoubtedly have you at the center of some cultural storm.

PLANNING

HOURS

Bars and cafés that open during the day normally close at 1 or 2 am weekdays and at 2 or 3 am weekends. Establishments that open around 9 in the evening stay open until 3 am on weekdays and 5 am on weekends. Clubs stay open until 4 am on weekdays and 5 am on weekends.

Live gigs start as early as 8 or 9 pm or as late as midnight. Theater shows usually kick off earlier. Always check the official websites for updates or call ahead.

WHERE TO GET TICKETS

Amsterdams Uitburo (AUB) Ticketshop. *The* official selling-point for theater shows and concerts in Amsterdam also sells tickets for museums—without extra charge—as well as passes for public transport. AUB is a safer bit than the many unofficial ticket-sales websites, many of which are rip-offs, and some venues, such as the Paradiso, don't sell tickets at their own box offices but only through AUB. If you call, don't hang up when you hear Dutch—an English speaker will soon come on the line. ⊠ *Leidseplein 26, Leidseplein* ☎ *020/6211311 (corporate office only)* ⊕ *www.aub.nl* ☉ *Mon.–Fri. 10–7; Sat 10–6; Sun. noon–6.*

Sometimes tickets can also be purchased at theater box offices or ⊕ *www.ticketmaster.nl*, although some theaters only sell tickets just before a performance. To be sure to get into a dance club, just arrive early (around 10 pm) and pick up tickets at the register or buy tickets early through the venue's website.

LATE-NIGHT TRANSPORTATION

If you're heading out late, know that regular public transportation ends at midnight. Grabbing a cab is your best option for getting home. They can sometimes be flagged down on the streets, but it's better to wait in line at a designated taxi stand; most venue employees can direct you to the closest one, or they can call a taxi for you. Alternatively, you can use the cumbersome night buses, but the routes are difficult to determine and trips can be time-consuming.

GANJACAKES AND OTHER SMOKEABLES

Headlines were made around the world in 2011 when it was announced that Amsterdam was cutting back on "vice tourism" and that tourists were no longer going to be permitted to light up their marijuana and hashish joints in the city's freewheeling "coffee shops." In point of fact, this legislation—while passed in parts of the Netherlands—has not been passed as of Fall 2012 (press time), and, as you'll read in our "Lighting Up in Amsterdam" section, may *never* come to pass. Be sure to read all the fascinating details below.

WHERE TO GET INFO

For the latest on what's happening, you'd do well to browse through the many fliers, pamphlets, booklets, and magazines that can be picked up at cafés such as De Balie, Café De Jaren, and Dantzig.

Lastminute Ticketshop. Every morning the website ⊕ *www.lastminuteticketshop.nl* lists a choice of half-price tickets for shows and concerts that day. Sale starts at noon. You can purchase the tickets on the website or at one of three venues: AUB Ticketshop, Leidseplein 26; the VVV Amsterdam Tourist Office (NZH Koffiehuis), Stationsplein 10, and the OBA (the public library) at Oosterdokskade 143. ⊠ *Leidseplein 26, Leidseplein* ⊕ *www.lastminuteticketshop.nl.*

I amsterdam is the city's official site (⊕ *www.iamsterdam.com*) and an excellent source of information. There are several good English-language

5

Weather permitting, Cafe t' Smalle sets up a great canalside seating area that overlooks a bridge—lovely!

publications. Pick up the monthly *Time Out Amsterdam* (⊕ *www.timeoutamsterdam.nl*) at most tourist offices, bookshops, and newsstands. The free magazine *Subbacultcha!* (⊕ *www.subbacultcha.nl*) keeps you updated about the underground music scene, as well as alternative cultural events and exhibitions. *Vice* magazine (⊕ *www.viceland.nl*) is published in both Dutch and English.

NIGHTLIFE

Amsterdam's nightlife can have you careening between smoky coffee shops, chic wine bars, mellow jazz joints, laid-back lounges, and clubs either intimate or raucous. The Dutch are extremely sociable people who enjoy going out, so don't hesitate to join the revelry. It will definitely make for a memorable trip.

The bona fide local flavor can perhaps best be tasted in one of the city's ubiquitous brown café-bars—called "brown" because of their woody walls and nicotine-stained ceilings. Here, both young and old, the mohawked and the merely balding, come to relax, rave, and revel in every variety of coffee and alcohol.

Thankfully, the city's club scene has been picking up after a long lull that began in the '90s, when some of the most established venues closed their doors for good.

New clubs such as Trouw, Studio 80, and Club Up and Air are programming cutting-edge acts and DJs, and old standbys like Paradiso, Melkweg, and Bitterzoet still pull in big names on a weekly basis. Amsterdam

A Jenever Primer

The indigenous liquor of the Netherlands is *jenever*, a potent spirit that was invented in the mid-1600s, when an alchemist in Leiden discovered a way to distill juniper berries. It was first sold as medicine, but by the late 17th century people liked it so much that they soon started drinking it for fun. Soon the English got in on the jenever game. They bumped up the alcohol content, smoothed over the rough-edged flavor, and called it gin.

There are two basic kinds of jenever—*oude* (old) and *jonge* (young). The names aren't a matter of aging but of distilling techniques. Young jenever uses a newer (post-WWII) distilling technique that produces a lighter, less outspoken spirit. Old jenever has a much more pronounced flavor. If you want to drink jenever like a true Lowlander, find yourself a *proeflokaal*, an old-fashioned "tasting house." We recommend the legendary **Wynand Fockink**, which has been hydrating Amsterdammers since 1679. Once you have made your choice from the milder jonge saps or the more sophisticated oude spirits, let the fun begin. The bartender fills a sherrylike glass until it is so precariously full that you must lean over the bar, hands behind your back, and take your first sip without touching the glass. Only then are you free to lift the glass by its dainty stem. When jenever is served with a beer it is called a *kopstoot*, literally meaning "headbang." This should be taken as a warning to the uninitiated.

is also home to several important electronic music festivals: the Amsterdam Dance Event (⊕ *www.amsterdam-dance-event.nl*) and 5 Days Off (⊕ *www.5daysoff.nl*) are the biggest.

BROWN CAFÉS

Along with French's *ennui* and Portuguese's *saudade,* a Dutch word often makes linguists' list of culturally untranslatable terms. *Gezelligheid*, however, is a positive one, referring to a state of total coziness created by warm social circumstances. People, places, and things are all contributing factors, though if you want to experience gezelligheid like a true Lowlander, learn this equation: drink + conversation with friends = gezellig! The best place for these pleasures is a traditional brown café, or *bruine kroeg.* Wood paneling, wooden floors, comfortably worn furniture, and walls and ceilings stained with eons' worth of tobacco smoke are responsible for their name—though today a little artfully stippled paint achieves the same effect. Customarily, there is no background music, just the hum of *kletsen* (chitchat) and the housecat meowing. There will also be a beer or two, and perhaps a jenever as the evening wears on.

BARS, CAFÉS, AND LOUNGES

Perhaps like the diners of New Jersey, brown cafés will remain an institution as much for the sake of wood-paneled nostalgia as for practical reasons: affordability and coziness. In recent years, though, brown has given way to black, as some of Amsterdam's watering holes take on a sleeker intercontinental vibe. If a Berlin DJ hasn't popped in for the evening, a digital jukebox pulsates lounge-y, deep house beats. Diners go gaga over Asian-fusion menus. Frosted walls shed mood lighting onto the latest Droog furniture. And even the Jack Russell faces a threat as favorite purse pooch from hip rivals like the French bulldog.

> ## KOEKJE BIJ?
>
> The Dutch have a reputation for being frugal, but one act of their generosity is the phenomenon of *een koekje erbij*: a cookie (or sometimes a piece of chocolate) is always served perched on the saucer of a hot beverage.

COFFEE SHOPS

Coffee shops (that really sell weed) tend to be dim, noxious places, with an interior decor rivaling that of your local deli. However, in our listings below, you'll find the best of the cleaner and more sophisticated establishments in the city. Still, the vibe is really different (almost the antithesis) to the gezelligheid of Amsterdam's precious brown cafés.

DANCE CLUBS

If you feel the need to get up off the bar stool and shake your groove thing, Amsterdam has a full array of venues where you can do just that; see our By Neighborhood listings below.

GAY, LESBIAN, AND MIXED BARS

GAY

Whether or not Amsterdam is the "Gay Capital of the World," as proclaimed by some admirers of the Netherlands' long-standing acceptance of gays and their right to marry, the city undoubtedly has a très gay nightlife. While every nook and cranny is fair game to experience the whole gamut of Amsterdam's sexual orientations and gender-based identities, the gay scene divides into something of a three-ring circus throughout the city center.

Reguliersdwarsstraat has been the center of gay nightlife for decades, but lately its glory has somewhat faded. Hotspots such as ARC, April, and Soho have closed down, which made things a lot more quiet around here. The trend is towards bars that emphasize *gezelligheid* (good vibes) rather than sex, attracting a more mixed crowd, such as you'll find crowding Prik on Spuistraat, or Getto on Warmoesstraat. Things still can get steamy at the Thermos Saunas *(see below)*, not too far away on Kerkstraat. Of the three districts, the one that has evolved along **Warmoestraat** is considerably the least egalitarian. One of the main streets that borders the Red Light District, it feels a little too cut off from the rest of the city. There are a few bars that do welcome all walks of life (including straight folks), but the majority of the clubs here are men-only, leather-heavy, and dungeon-prone. Your surest bet at all-encompassing *homo-gezelligheid* is **Amstel**, located right off Rembrandtplein. These coordinates make it likely you'll have to dodge some drunken Rembrandtplein tourists or their speeding taxis, but it's well worth it. With kitschy gay pubs, lively lesbian clubs, and drag bars, Amstel is a haven of pansexual hospitality.

Cheers to Dutch Beers

If you think Dutch beer begins and ends with Heineken, think again! The Netherlands has a thriving little industry of microbrews and produces some top-notch stuff. While most of the beer can be roughly broken down into three mouthwatering categories (*pils*, *wit bier*, and *bokbier*), *pils* (pilsner) is by far the most popular and commonly consumed. A refreshing light golden lager, it is served in smaller glasses and with more foam (two fingers' worth) than you're probably used to.

In summer, Amsterdammers find refreshment in *wit bier*, a white zesty brew served with a slice of lemon. *Bokbier*, a stronger variety of *pils*, is made with warming spices. The Dutch also love Belgian brews, so you'll have no problem finding Trappist beers, Lambics, fruit beers, wheat beers, and dark brown ales.

OUR FAVORITE WATERING HOLES

Brouwerij 't IJ. Perched under a windmill on the eastern outskirts of the city is an evocative, if out-of-the-way, microbrewery where Kasper Peterson offers Natte, Zatte, Struis, Columbus, and other home brews, enjoyed on the large terrace, weather permitting. ⊠ *Funenkade 7, East of Amstel* ☎ *020/320–1786* ⊕ *www.brouwerijhetij.nl* ⊗ *Daily 2–8.*

Café Belgique. As the name suggests, this welcoming little café, located right behind Nieuwe Kerk, has an excellent selection of Belgian ales. ⊠ *Gravenstraat 2, The Old City Center (Het Centrum)* ☎ *020/625–1974* ⊕ *www.cafe-belgique.nl.*

De Zotte. The name of this little pub off the Leidseplein translates as "the

drunk" in Flamish, and with around 100 Belgian beers available, the place is aptly named. ⊠ *Raamstraat 29, Leidseplein* ☎ *020/626–8694* ⊕ *www.dezotte.nl.*

Het Elfde Gebod. Right in the heart of the Red Light District, this cozy bar has seven Belgian beers on tap and more than 60 bottled. ⊠ *Zeedijk 5, The Old City Center (Het Centrum)* ⊕ *www.hetelfdegebod.com.*

In de Wildeman. A wide range of beers and ales from around the globe and jolly surroundings attract all types and ages. There are 250 bottled brews to chose from, 17 beers on tap, and a featured beer of the month. ⊠ *Kolksteeg 3, The Old City Center (Het Centrum)* ☎ *020/638–2348* ⊕ *www.indewildeman.nl.*

BEST BEER STORE

Bierkoning. Located behind Dam Square, Bierkoning is the best beer store in Amsterdam, and possibly even the Netherlands, with more than 1,100 international brews in stock and tons of glassware and other accessories. The friendly, knowledgeable staff can tell you everything you ever wanted or needed to know about beer. ⊠ *Paleisstraat 125, The Old City Center (Het Centrum)* ☎ *020/625–2336* ⊕ *www.bierkoning.nl.*

Wonderful canal views make Café de Jaren a great place to grab a drink.

LESBIAN

Compared to many other coordinates on the globe, Amsterdam has had women's rights and gay rights down pat for several decades. What can still use a little more loving, however, is society's accommodation of gay women, particularly when it comes to nightlife. Yet the scene is steadily expanding its repertoire with an increasing number of lesbian bars and nightclubs.

MIXED

With a population of just 750,000 inhabiting what are essentially a series of canal-determined concentric circles, it's hard for Amsterdam residents not to bump into one another. Some confluences are less felicitous than others, but you can always count on the ones at "mixed" bars to be merry and gay, with gay men usually outnumbering lesbians and straight folk.

JAZZ CLUBS

Amsterdam has provided a happy home-away-from-home for jazz musicians since the early '50s, when such legends as Chet Baker and Gerry Mulligan would wind down after their official show at the Concertgebouw by jamming at one or another of the many bohemian bars around the Zeedijk. For the last quarter century, the world-statured but intimate Bimhuis has taken over duties as the city's major jazz venue with an excellent programming policy that welcomes both the legendary jazz performer and the latest avant-garde up-and-comer. New on the scene is the North Sea Jazz Club at the Westergasfabiek, where you can wine and dine while enjoying performances by international stars and up-and-coming artists.

ROCK MUSIC VENUES

Quaint yet cosmopolitan, Amsterdam has been the place where many of the world's musicians dream of playing one day. The Melkweg and Paradiso have savvily kept their fingers on the pulse of every major musical trend since the late '60s. Today both legendary venues and a whole new-millennial phalanx of other clubs manage to keep the music real. The long-clichéd unholy trinity of sex, drugs, and rock and roll may not define Amsterdam as well as it used to, but the city remains one of the defining places for musicians worldwide to indulge in dreams of excess. And this makes for a rocking dance floor. In recent years quite a few alternative music clubs have come up, such as De Nieuwe Anita at Hugo de Grootplein and Bitterzoet on Spuistraat. Here drinks are cheap and the music is often exciting.

AMSTERDAM SOUTHEAST

ROCK MUSIC VENUES

Heineken Music Hall. This relatively new and rather out-of-the-way concert hall with a capacity for 5,500 has a sterile but acoustic-rich environment. It's usually for touring bands that have outgrown (and most likely sold out) the Melkweg and Paradiso. ⊠ *Arena Boulevard 590* ☎ *0900/687-4242 (charge for info)* ⊕ *www.heineken-music-hall.nl.*

BARS, CAFÉS, AND LOUNGES

Roest. A former gas building now houses a café hosting tons of activities and events: on Mondays you can have your hair cut while enjoying a drink, and on other nights there are DJs, film screenings, music performances, and much more. Or, you can just sit back and relax on the terrace. ⊠ *Czaar Peterstraat 213, Amsterdam East* ☎ *020/308–0283* ⊕ *www.amsterdamroest.nl.*

AMSTERDAM WEST

BROWN CAFÉS

Cafe Cook. Overlooking a beautiful square in the up-and-coming De Baarsjes neighborhood, this is a nice place for a drink or lunch or dinner, especially on the terrace in good weather. ⊠ *James Cookstraat 2, Amsterdam West* ☎ *06/219–66916* ⊕ *www.cafecook.nl.*

Club 8. Eclectic offerings here range from dance nights to German beer fests to burlesque shows, and on some afternoons, even to children's parties. You can also play pool. ⊠ *Admiraal de Ruyterweg 56B, Amsterdam West* ☎ *020/685–1703* ⊕ *www.club-8.nl.*

Proeflokaal Gollem. Live jazz on Saturday evenings is one of many attractions at this long-standing institution that features Belgian beers. ⊠ *Overtoom 160–162, Amsterdam West* ☎ *020/612–9444* ⊕ *www.cafegollem.nl.*

Zaal 100. *"Podium voor onge-hoord geluid"* ("a stage for unheard sounds") is how this former squat describes itself. It's one of the few places in Amsterdam where you can hear live impro-jazz; every Tuesday they feature local and international musicians, and on Thursdays any-one with an instrument can join in with the Oktopedians, a workshop orchestra playing jazz, blues, and world music. The restaurant serves a three-course vegetarian meal some nights. ⊠ *De Wittenstraat 100, Amsterdam West* ☎ *020/688–6127* ⊕ *www.zaal100.nl.*

> **READY, SET, TOKE!**
>
> During November, a conspicuous number of tourists with glazed-over eyes and smiles that stretch from dreadlock to dreadlock can be spotted around Amsterdam. No, Phish isn't in town—it's **Can-nabis Cup**, the weeklong contest sponsored by *High Times* maga-zine. The premise of this event is to provide a friendly competition among the city's pot purveyors to see who has the best stuff. Win-ners are selected by public judges who have all-access to the pot at stake, though at the cost of a €250 judges' pass.

GAY AND LESBIAN (MIXED)

De Trut. Every Sunday night, the basement of an old squat in an unmarked building opens its doors to *potten en flikkers* (dykes and fags). All the workers are volunteers, and all proceeds from the evening go to vari-ous gay-rights nonprofit organizations. The beer and the entrance fee are cheap, and despite a few strict rules—no straight friends, no mobile phones, and certainly no cameras—it is still as popular as ever, so be sure to arrive on time (before 11) to get in. ⊠ *Bilderdijkstraat 165* ⊕ *www.trutfonds.nl.*

JAZZ CLUBS

North Sea Jazz Club. Finally Amsterdam has an American-style jazz club where you can wine and dine while enjoying live jazz. The diverse pro-gram features big names as well as up-and-coming artists. ⊠ *Pazzanis-traat 1, Amsterdam West* ☎ *020/722–0980 info/tickets, 020/722–0981 restaurant* ⊕ *www.northseajazzclub.nl.*

ROCK MUSIC VENUES

De Nieuwe Anita. The quirky Nieuwe Anita, much loved by the alterna-tive crowd, is home to screenings of cult classics, spoken word nights, and live gigs put up by underground magazine *Subbacultcha!*. They also do cocktails and club nights. ⊠ *Frederik Hendrikstraat 111* ⊕ *www. denieuweanita.nl.*

OT301. This legalized squat, housed in the former film academy, offers fun alternative nights with live bands and DJs. The music featured cov-ers anything from hardcore to free jazz, just so long as some noise is involved. Also on the premises are a movie theater, an art gallery, and an organic restaurant. ⊠ *Overtoom 301* ⊕ *www.ot301.nl.*

Okura Hotel's super-swank champagne bar, Twenty Third, is named after the floor it's located on.

ENTERTAINMENT CENTERS

Westergasfabriek. A former gas factory founded in 1883 is now an arts and cultural center comprising 13 monumental buildings of various sizes and shapes that play host to film and theater companies, fashion shows, art exhibitions, operas, techno parties, and assorted festivals. There are also bars, nightclubs, restaurants, and a cinema. ✉ *Polonceaukade 27* ☎ *020/586–0710* ⊕ *www.westergasfabriek.nl.*

EAST OF AMSTEL

BARS, CAFÉS, AND LOUNGES

Canvas. Housed in a former newspaper building, just like its neighboring club Trouw, Canvas offers splendid views over the city from its seventh-floor perch. The restaurant and cocktail bar are satisfying, and the music is as diverse as it comes: live jazz, experimental house, hip-hop, indie, and so forth. Besides a place for cocktails and clubbing, this is also an art gallery. ✉ *Wibautstraat 150* ☎ *020/716–3817* ⊕ *www.canvas7.nl.*

DANCE CLUBS

Hotel Arena. From tabernacles to turntables, yet another of Amsterdam's churches has been refurbished to accommodate the city's nightlife. Part of Hotel Arena complex, this club is popular for its weekend dance nights (mostly acid, house, and techno). ✉ *'s-Gravesandestraat 51* ☎ *020/850–2400* ⊕ *www.hotelarena.nl* ☾ *Closed weekdays.*

CLOSE UP

Lighting Up in Amsterdam

Unless you're a regular user, checking out one of those euphemistically named venues where marijuana is sold is hard to justify from a "when in Rome" rationale. The coffee-shop industry caters mostly to travelers, and the Dutch are reported to smoke less pot than most other European populations. That said, if you do decide to indulge in Amsterdam's infamous weed scene, there are a few things you should know, especially concerning the new legislation that will allow only native Hollanders to "lite up." In point of fact, as of October 2012, this ban was voted down by Amsterdam's new Labor/Liberal government, so tourists and locals alike can continue to light up.

THE SELECTION

Most coffee shops sell a robust selection of weed and hash, sold anywhere from €5 to €20 per gram. Don't hesitate to describe your dream high to the dealer, and he (or, rarely, she) will try to accommodate you.

HANDLING YOUR HIGH

Be wary. Dutch-sold marijuana is potent and blows the socks off the most hardcore potheads. If cannabis is not your usual drug of choice, don't feel you have to play cool: ask questions of the staff and use caution whatever your medium—joint, bong, or brownie. If you do overindulge, try not to panic. Find a quiet place, take deep breaths, and remember that the discomfort will pass. Sometimes consuming something sweet will help to soften the high.

THE DEAL ON DEALING

Amsterdam is home to an estimated 240 coffee shops, but statistics are looking grim for those who go gaga for ganja. An April 2007 law that prohibits the side-by-side sale of marijuana and alcohol has forced proprietors to dry out their bars to retain coffee shop licenses. What's more, since July 1, 2008, Amsterdam, like many other cities, has become smoke free. Smoking tobacco is banned from interior public spaces, including coffee shops, and is only allowed in designated smoking areas. Confusingly for visitors and locals alike, it is legal to smoke a pure joint (rolled with just weed or hash) in a coffee shop, but not in bars, restaurants, and clubs. Currently, it's acceptable to sell small amounts of marijuana via the "front door" of a coffee shop where the customer enters. However, the "back door" through which the product arrives is linked to the illegal world of the mysterious wholesale supplier. Technically, selling marijuana is officially prohibited, but the government has barely bothered to enforce this legislation—the buzzword here is "decriminalized." Thanks to the Dutch Opium Act of 1976, an important distinction is made between hard drugs and soft drugs—weed being soft.

STAYING LEGAL

Throughout 2011 and 2012, a movement was afoot to require a membership card, or *"wietpas,"* for tourists wishing to partake of the offerings of Amsterdam's famed coffee shops—anything and everything from marijuana to hashish ang ganga cookies—that law was voted down in 2012. Happily, things will stay as they are and tourists will keep the same rights as the Dutch when it comes to lighting up.

The old laws on the book currently allows up to 5 grams of marijuana and several other cannabis-laden comestibles (pot brownies, space cakes, ganja cookies) to be dispensed at a licensed venue to anyone over 18. It also allows possession of up to 30 grams by individuals, solely for personal use. Marijuana must be purchased on regulated premises (coffee shops), and used on the spot (since 2008 most coffee shops have created a designated "smoking room" where you can enjoy your spliff, or joint), or you can take it home. It is also legal to smoke it in the street or in the park.

Where Dutch drug policy differs from the rest of the world is that Dutch law makes a distinction between hard drugs and soft drugs. Hard drugs such as heroin and cocaine are considered as highly addictive and a dangerous threat for people's health and so it is illegal to sell them. Drug addicts, however, are not seen as criminals, but as patients, so they don't risk imprisonment simply for possession of hard drugs. Cannabis may be psychologically addictive but not physically; thus, soft drugs are tolerated in Dutch society.

MEMBERSHIP CARDS

Being the only country in Europe with a rather laid-back attitude to soft drugs, however, means that Holland now gets a lot of "pot tourists" from other countries. This has led, disastrously in the border towns (near Amsterdam), to coffee shops the size of supermarkets (catering mostly for foreigners) and streets jammed with traffic. Locals started to complain. To end these problems the government came up with a brilliant plan, or so they thought: a membership card, or "*wietpas*" for coffee shops. This card,

which would exclude tourists from coffee shops, was introduced in the border towns in 2012 as an experiment; the plan was that the rest of Holland would follow in 2013. But that is now history.

First of all, the experiment has not proved to be a success, as the wietpas seems to only increase illegal trade on the streets (which also involves hard drugs). Secondly, most other cities in Holland, such as Amsterdam, Utrecht, and Rotterdam, have always been against the plan. (In Amsterdam, the only things that have changed is that the area around schools has to be coffee shop–free—coffee shops within a 1,000 feet of a school have closed down—plus some coffee shops on the Wallen have closed only because they were in criminal hands.) And last but not least, in the meantime the Netherlands have gotten a new, and liberal, government, one that doesn't believe in the wietpas.

. . . OR NOT?

A spokeswoman of the mayor clearly stated to Fodor's: "Amsterdam will not introduce the wietpas." She went on to say that even if the government will go through with the new cannabis law (only time can tell), Amsterdam will fight it. And, in fact, it did. Thus things will stay as they are in Amsterdam (and the other major cities) and tourists will keep on having the same rights as the Dutch when it comes to lighting up. To check the latest on this amazing saga log onto Amsterdam's official website ⊕ www.iamsterdam.com.

LESBIAN

Garbo. This women-only dance night for lesbians and bisexuals takes place every third Saturday of the month at the popular bar-restaurant Strand West. If you like, you can also have a bite to eat beforehand. ⊠ *Strand West, Stavangerweg 900, Amsterdam West* ☎ *06/1864–7954* ⊕ *www.garboforwomen.nl.*

ROCK MUSIC VENUES

Trouw. This cutting-edge club housed in a former newspaper building comprises two main halls and an excellent restaurant where you can refuel. The music leans towards underground techno, dubstep, and experimental electronica, which suits the industrial décor splendidly. A monthly program called De Verdieping offers films screenings, lectures, and other cultural events. ⊠ *Wibaustraat 127* ☎ *020/463–7788* ⊕ *www. trouwamsterdam.nl.*

EASTERN DOCKLANDS

BARS, CAFÉS, AND LOUNGES

Zouthaven. Whether or not you have the musical motivation to visit the Muziekgebouw aan 't IJ, the building's bar-restaurant is worth the hike alone. Stop by for a drink or a meal of fresh fish and take in the panoramic views of the harbor and docklands. ⊠ *Muziekgebouw aan't IJ, Piet Heinkade 1* ☎ *020/788–2090* ⊕ *www.zouthaven.nl.*

BROWN CAFÉS

Cafe Pakhuis Wilhelmina. A former warehouse is the scene of fun musical events such as "zap nights," when local artists perform, and Hard Rock Karaoke, where you can unleash your inner rock star. A basement is used for live jazz performances. ⊠ *Veemkade 576, Eastern Docklands* ☎ *020/419–3368* ⊕ *www.cafepakhuiswilhelmina.nl.*

Café Restaurant Barco. One of the owners of hot spot ⇨ *De Nieuwe Anita* has started this lovely bar and restaurant on a boat opposite the public library (OBA). The staff is friendly, the food tasty, the atmosphere very laid-back, and there's live music Thursday to Saturday. ⊠ *Oosterdokskade 10, Eastern Docklands* ☎ *020/626–9383* ⊕ *www.cafebarco.nl.*

Hannekes Boom. A hot spot for laid-back creatives offers a waterfront terrace and live music some nights. ⊠ *Dijksgracht 4, Eastern Docklands* ☎ *020/419–9820* ⊕ *www. hannekesboom.nl.*

DANCE CLUBS

Panama. The plush and gold interior is the scene of dance nights, as well as live-band performances and a bit of theater. In-house restaurant

---

SOWING WEEDS

Those with a green thumb (who do not live in a country where growing of pot is punishable with jail time) may want to consider getting to the root of their high. Marijuana seeds can be purchased from seed shops, coffee shops, and smart shops. A 10-pack can cost somewhere between €30 and €100. Amsterdam's legendary seed shops include **Dutch Passion** (⊠ *Utrechtsestraat 26* ☎ *020/625–1100* ⊕ *www.dutch-passion.nl*) and **The Flying Dutchman** (⊠ *Oudezijds Achterburgwal 131* ☎ *020/428–4110*).

Psilocybin—uh, can you spell that?

Only two decades after the Dutch government condoned the sale of marijuana and hash under the Opium Act of 1976, another "soft drug" came onto the scene: psilocybin. More commonly known as magic mushrooms, or paddos, psilocybin was legal until December 2008. The stuff was banned after some fatal accidents with visitors (even though paddo consumption was never proven). The ban still stands and smart shops can no longer sell the mushrooms, either fresh or dried. Smart shops are still allowed to sell a veritable salad of other "natural" high-producing substances—peyote, aphrodisiacal herbs and oils, and herbal XTC.

If you choose to take any of these products, use your own innate smarts: not only are many of them illegal if carried outside the Netherlands, they can produce strong—and not necessarily pleasant—judgment-impairing hallucinations.

Kokopelli. Dating from 1994, the city's first smart shop promotes "mind-body awareness." Besides the usual suspects of "natural" drugs," you'll find a selection of "harm reduction kits" said to speed up the recovery process after a hyperconscious weekend. In the back of the shop you can experiment under the safe guidance of the knowledgeable staff, accompanied by loungy beats. ✉ *Warmoestraat 12, The Old City Center (Het Centrum)* ☎ *020/421–7000* ⊕ *www. consciousdreams.nl.*

Inner Space. "The only legal coke alternative" and liquid drops to produce "that real MDMA feeling" are among the products sold here. So are mushroom grow kits, marijuana seeds, and some good ol' vitamin C. ✉ *Spuistraat 108, The Old City Center (Het Centrum)* ☎ *020/624–3338* ⊕ *www.innerspace.nl*

5

Mercat takes its name and dishes from the markets of Barcelona. ✉ *Oostelijke Handelskade 4* ☎ *020/311–8686* ⊕ *www.panama.nl.*

JAZZ CLUBS

Fodor's Choice ★ **Bimhuis.** The best-known jazz place in town occupies the utterly awesome Muziekgebouw aan 't IJ. Everyone, fans of the old legends to those of the latest avant-gardists, agrees: the space is close to perfect. Views of the city are breathtaking, the acoustics great, the chairs comfy, and the house rules laid-back; all drinks ordered at the bar, even full wine bottles, can be carried inside. ✉ *Piet Heinkade 3* ☎ *020/788–2188 box office* ⊕ *www.bimhuis.nl.*

LESBIAN

Flirtation. This highly successful women-only dance event for young lesbians and bi-curious girls takes over club Panama four times a year, with a bevy of female DJs, special acts, and live performances. ✉ *Panama, Oostelijke Handelskade 4* ☎ *020/311-8686 Panama* ⊕ *www. flirtation.nl.*

If you're into throbbing music and strobe lights, then the Escape club might be just the thing.

JEWISH QUARTER AND PLANTAGE

BROWN CAFÉS

Café Sluyswacht. Beware: the slant of this oldie-but-goodie can lead to nausea after one too many beers on the patio. A quintessential Amsterdam view of the Oudeschans, however, has been bringing relief since 1695. ⊠ *Jodenbreestraat 1* ☎ *020/625–7611* ⊕ *www.sluyswacht.nl.*

JORDAAN

BARS, CAFÉS, AND LOUNGES

Nol. Just getting started at 9, Nol resonates with lusty-lunged native Jordaaners having the time of their lives. ⊠ *Westerstraat 109* ☎ *020/624–5380* ⊙ *Mon. and Tues.*

Rooie Nelis. Despite the area's tendency toward trendiness, this café has kept its traditional Jordaan vibe. ⊠ *Laurierstraat 101* ☎ *020/624–4167* ⊕ *www.caferooienelis.com.*

Winkel 43. This corner café's famous *appeltaart* (apple pie) beckons locals and travelers alike. Those without a sweet tooth will most probably find something else to satisfy them on the extensive lunch menu. The large, sunny terrace is a popular hangout in all seasons. ⊠ *Noordermarkt 43* ☎ *020/623–0223* ⊕ *www.winkel43.nl.*

BROWN CAFÉS

Café Chris. This venue has been pouring beverages since 1624, which makes it the oldest bar in the Jordaan. The tiny washrooms remind you how small people used to be. ✉ *Bloemstraat 42* ☎ *020/624–5942* ⊕ *www.cafechris. nl.*

Fodor's Choice ★ **Café Tabac.** One of the best modern cafés in the Jordaan commands a charming corner between Brouwersgracht and Prinsengracht. The staff is friendly and has a funky taste in music. At night the place is packed, but this is also a perfect place to enjoy an afternoon drink on the canalside terrace. ✉ *Brouwersgracht 101, Jordaan* ☎ *020/622–4413* ⊕ *www.cafetabac.eu.*

De Prins. This mainstay on the Prinsengracht is blessed with a canalside patio. A brown-café atmosphere prevails, while a modern kitchen sends out well-priced, simple meals. ✉ *Prinsengracht 124* ☎ *020/624–9382* ⊕ *www.deprins.nl.*

De Twee Zwaantjes. If you want to hear the locals sing folk music, stop by this classic canal-side café. ✉ *Prinsengracht 114* ☎ *020/625–2729* ⊕ *www.cafedetweezwaantjes.nl.*

Fodor's Choice ★ **'t Smalle.** Set with Golden Age chandeliers, leaded-glass windows, and the patina of centuries, this charmer is one of Amsterdam's most glorious spots. The after-work crowd always jams the waterside terrace, though you are just as well to opt for the historic interior, once home to one of the city's first jenever distilleries. They serve breakfast and lunch. ✉ *Egelantiersgracht 12* ☎ *020/623-9617* ⊕ *www.t-smalle.nl.*

COFFEE SHOPS

Siberie. Slightly off the beaten track, at the beginning of the Brouwersgracht, Siberie is one of the best coffee shops in town, selling high-quality goodies (try the organic weeds). Once legislation is passed to allow tourists to indulge (final laws were pending at press time), visitors can also enjoy Siberie's friendly staff and the changing art on its walls. ✉ *Brouwersgracht 11, Jordaan.*

DANCE CLUBS

Club Roses. What used to be the plain old Club More and then Club More Amor now makes a nod to its location on Rozengracht, a.k.a. the Roses Canal. Latin-flavored tunes prevail with DJs playing salsa, Caribbean, and other Hispanophilic beats. ✉ *Rozengracht 133* ☎ *020/416–2211* ⊕ *www.clubroses.nl.*

FOR LAVENDER LADIES

Xantippe Unlimited. Lesbians on the lookout for parties should stop by Xantippe Unlimited, a bookstore that specializes in women's literature. ✉ *Prinsengracht 290, The Canal Ring* ☎ *020/623-5854* ⊕ *www.xantippe.nl.*

Boekhandel Vrolijk. Another fine resource for seeing what's down with dames is the gay and lesbian bookstore Boekhandel Vrolijk. ✉ *Paleisstraat 135, The Old City Center (Het Centrum)* ☎ *020/623-5142* ⊕ *www.vrolijk.nu.*

Women should consider consulting **COC Amsterdam** (⇨ *listed below*) for their list of highly recommended reverie.

5

Check out the Bimhuis theater on the water—perfect in every sense.

Werck. This former coach house to the Westerkerk is now a watering hole for yuppies, Jordaanites, and the loungey house DJs who serve them smooth late-night beats. During the day, tourists from the nearby Anne Frank House enjoy the bi-level interior and spacious patio. ⊠ *Prinsengracht 277* ☎ *020/627–4079* ⊕ *www.werck.nl.*

GAY
COC. Founded in 1946, this center of the Dutch Association for the Integration of Homosexuality is the oldest organization of its kind in the world. ⊠ *Rozenstraat 14* ☎ *020/626-3087* ⊕ *www.cocamsterdam.nl.*

LESBIAN
Saarein. Amsterdam's best lesbian bar, as it's been labeled, started out in the 1920s as a brown café in the Jordaan and has since been modernized; a "mixed" policy prevails. ⊠ *Elandsstraat 119* ☎ *020/623–4901* ⊕ *www.saarein.com* ☾ *Closed Mon.*

ROCK MUSIC VENUES
Korsakoff. Since the 1980s this has been a dark but friendly magnet for pierced and tattooed rockers who like their music rough and ready (there's a bit of trance, techno, and dubstep thrown in too). And somehow the club feels cozy, albeit in a scruffy way. ⊠ *Lijnbaansgrach 161* ☎ *020/625–7854.*

★ **Maloe Melo.** What could be nicer than a friendly hangout dive and place for rock, blues, and roots musicians? Sometimes said musicians are joined on stage by bigger celebrities, fresh from their gigs at more reputable venues. ⊠ *Lijnbaansgracht 163* ☎ *020/420–4592* ⊕ *www. maloemelo.com.*

LEIDSEPLEIN

BARS, CAFÉS, AND LOUNGES

Café de Koe. Hardly bovine, the "Cow's Café" is a fine place to chew the cud or graze a little, and is especially favored by local musicians and students. There's an extensive beer menu and downstairs a no-nonsense restaurant where on Sundays you can watch the football on a big screen with a plate on your lap. ⊠ *Marnixstraat 381* ☎ *020/625–4482* ⊕ *www. cafedekoe.nl.*

De Balie. Eyeglasses peek over books and tablets as a well-read and socially conscious crowd fills the café-bar of this center for culture and politics. This is the ideal spot to pick up local-event flyers or, for that matter, a date. On weekend nights things loosen up with live DJs. ⊠ *Kleine Gartmanplantsoen 10* ☎ *020/553–5131* ⊕ *www.balie.nl.*

BROWN CAFÉS

Café de Spuyt. One of the few authentic pubs around Leidseplein has a genuinely friendly staff, an extensive beer list, and acoustic music sessions, all of which provide an oasis of civilized authenticity among the noisy tourist traps in the area. ⊠ *Korte Leidsedwarsstraat 86, Leidseplein* ☎ *020/624–8901* ⊕ *www.despuyt.nl.*

COFFEE SHOPS

Fodor's Choice ★ **De Rokerij.** For over a decade, this coffee shop has managed to maintain a magical-grotto aura that, ironically enough, requires no extra indulgences to induce a state of giddy transcendence. Dim lights, Indian-inspired murals, and low-to-the-ground seating keep the vibe chill regardless of how busy the Leidseplein headquarters can get. De Rokerij's other branches may inspire smaller-scale out-of-body experiences. ⊠ *Lange Leidsedwarsstraat 41, Leidseplein.* ⊠ *Singel 8, The Canal Ring.*

DANCE CLUBS

Club Up. An intimate little shoebox of a venue shares some of its amenities with members-only artists' society De Kring. As a result, arty house parties and banging electro nights attract a hip crowd that's sometimes sprinkled with puzzled tourists in search of a dive bar. ⊠ *Korte Leidsedwarsstraat 26–1* ☎ *020/623–6985* ⊕ *www.clubup.nl* ☽ *Open Thurs.–Sat.*

Sugar Factory. Self-stylized as a "night theater," the Factory takes Amsterdam clubbing into the 21st century and beyond. An average evening may involve DJs, as well as bands, theater, dance, spoken word, and slam poetry. ⊠ *Lijnbaansgracht 238* ⊕ *www.sugarfactory.nl.*

Jimmy Woo's. Thursday through Sunday, this is probably the hottest club in town for the rich and famous and their wannabes. The urban grooves

---

HERE AND QUEER?

For more information about gay life in Amsterdam, visit the gay-and-lesbian information kiosk Pink Point (⊕ www.pinkpoint.org) located at the Homomonument on the corner of Keizersgracht and Westermarkt; it's open daily from 10 to 6. For details on gay nightlife, consult the listings at ⊕ www.amsterdam4gays.com.

5

are funky and the sound system, not too shabby. ⊠ *Korte Leidsedwarsstraat 18* ☎ *020/626–3150* ⊕ *www.jimmywoo.com.*

ENTERTAINMENT CENTERS

Melkweg. The legendary "Milk Way" features live bands and DJ's covering everything from punk to dance to world music. A former milk factory, this space began as a hippie squat in the '60s. Today it's a slickly operated multimedia center equipped with two concert halls, a theater, cinema, gallery, and café-restaurant. ⊠ *Lijnbaansgracht 234–A* ☎ *020/531–8181* ⊕ *www.melkweg.nl.*

★ **Paradiso.** This former church, intact with vaulted ceilings and stained glass, is the country's most famous "pop temple," an epic venue for pop legends as well as exciting new bands. Paradiso also hosts live gigs in some smaller venues around Amsterdam. ⊠ *Weteringschans 6–8* ☎ *020/626–4521* ⊕ *www.paradiso.nl.*

GAY AND LESBIAN

Club Church. Three floors of play-and-dance space offer changing theme nights six times a week. If you're looking to cruise, this is a good bet. ⊠ *Kerkstraat 52* ☎ *No phone* ⊕ *www.clubchurch.nl* ☾ *Closed Mon.*

Habibi Ana. Meaning "my sweetheart" in Arabic, Habibi Ana is a one-of-a-kind experience in Amsterdam and, quite possibly, the world over. Founded by the same-titled foundation, this bar caters to gay, bisexual, and transsexual men and women of Arab descent. ⊠ *Lange Leidsedwarsstraat 93* ⊕ *www.habibiana.nl* ☾ *Closed Mon.*

Thermos Sauna. Men interested in more than just a little dip into the city's gay scene might consider taking the plunge at Amsterdam's most luxurious sauna for men, which provides ample opportunity for fraternizing in the Finnish sauna, Turkish steam bath, swimming pool, whirlpool, "rest cabins," or bar. Amenities extend to a beauty salon, rooftop terrace, and restaurant. ⊠ *Raamstraat 33, Leidseplein* ☎ *020/623–9158* ⊕ *www.thermos.nl* ☾ *Daily noon–8 am.*

JAZZ CLUBS

Alto. Hear the top picks of local ensembles and some well-respected locals in the jam-packed environment of one of Amsterdam's oldest jazz joints. A little latin can be enjoyed here as well. ⊠ *Korte Leidsedwarsstraat 115* ☎ *020/626–3249* ⊕ *www.jazz-cafe-alto.nl.*

Bourbon Street Jazz & Blues Club. Mainstream blues and jazz are served up to a largely out-of-town clientele, but it does the job—and a late one at that, open until 5 in the morning on Fridays and Saturdays and until 4 all other days. ⊠ *Leidsekruisstraat 6–8* ☎ *020/623–3440* ⊕ *www.bourbonstreet.nl.*

MUSEUM DISTRICT

BARS, CAFÉS, AND LOUNGES

Fodor'sChoice   **College Hotel.** Looking for a little New Amsterdam in Old Amsterdam?
★   Stop by the lounge-bar of this hotel, where dark oak floors, fireplace, sleek black tables, low lights, and sequestered seating arrangements evoke an old boys' club in midtown Manhattan—minus the elitism.

CLOSE UP

Dutch-Style Theater

Over het IJ Festival. Such internationally statured companies as Dogtroep (⊕ *www.dogtroep.nl*), PIPS:lab (⊕ *www.pipslab.nl*), and Vis-à-Vis (⊕ *www.visavis.nl*) are specialists in the typically Dutch school of spectacle theater, which is hardly bound by language and goes in search of unique locations—and other dimensions—to strut its stuff. Groups like this usually participate, along with many others of like mind from around the world, in the amazing annual Over het IJ Festival. This festival is held every July at the abandoned shipyard-turned-postmodern-culture-center NDSM in Amsterdam North (see above), gathering together dozens of dance and theater troupes dedicated to the more wild and physical aspects of the arts. ⊠ *NDSM-werf, Neveritaweg 15* ☎ *020/820-2625* ⊕ *www.overhetij.nl.*

Parade. If you happen to be in town for the first two, and sometimes the third, weeks of August, don't miss Parade, a traveling tent city that specializes in quirky performances and a social and carnivalesque ambience. ⊠ *Martin Luther Kingpark, Amsterdam South* ☎ *033/465-4555* ⊕ *www.deparade.nl.*

There's live jazz some Sundays. ⊠ *The College Hotel, Roelof Hartstraat 1* ☎ *020/571–1511* ⊕ *www.thecollegehotel.com.*

Wildschut. This 1920s Amsterdam School edifice is a delightful place for a pre- or postrecital stop, with the Concertgebouw just down the road. The large sunny terrace has great views for architecture enthusiasts. ⊠ *Roelof Hartplein 1–3* ☎ *020/676–8220* ⊕ *www.goodfoodgroup.nl.*

ENTERTAINMENT CENTERS

Het Blauwe Theehuis. The Vondelpark's quietly pulsating epicenter is a blue flying saucer–shape "teahouse" dating back to 1937. In step with the style of *Nieuwe Bouwen* (the Dutch version of Bauhaus), the building was erected from concrete, glass, and steel, and with its minimalist forms it still looks strikingly modern. ⊠ *Vondelpark 5, Vondelpark* ☎ *020/662–0254* ⊕ *www.blauwetheehuis.nl.*

ROCK MUSIC VENUES

OCCII. The former squat and slightly out of the way hole-in-the-wall, just beyond the gates of the Vondelpark's western exit, has stayed true to its punky vibe over the years. ⊠ *Amstelveenseweg 134* ☎ *020/671–7778* ⊕ *www.occii.org.*

REMBRANDTPLEIN

BARS, CAFÉS, AND LOUNGES

Fodor'sChoice ★ **Café Schiller.** Next to the same-named hotel, this classy place has an authentic Art Deco interior, all cozy wood paneling. This landmark is especially inviting when it's cold and wet outside. ⊠ *Rembrandtplein 24a* ☎ *020/624–9846* ⊕ *www.cafeschiller.nl.*

De Kroon. This grand café dating back to 1898 is popular for both its intimate seating arrangements and a U-shape bar surrounding old-style wooden museum cases filled with zoological specimens. In the evenings, the clientele sits pretty, high above the noisy, street-level clubs on Rembrandtplein. On weekends there are dance nights with live DJs. ⊠ *Rembrandtplein 17, 1st Floor* ☎ *020/625–2011* ⊕ *www.dekroon.nl.*

Le Montmartre. This kitschy corner pub attracts an outgoing, all-ages crowd stopping in for a drink and perhaps a sing-along before heading out clubbing. ⊠ *Halvemaansteeg 17* ☎ *020/620–7622* ⊕ *www. cafemontmartre.nl.*

DANCE CLUBS

Escape. Thursdays through Sundays, this megaclub opens its doors to some 2,500 people. The great Escape is meant for those who take "dress to impress" literally and are keen to dance under laser lights as DJs spin techno and all its new-millennial derivatives. ⊠ *Rembrandtplein 11* ☎ *020/622–1111* ⊕ *www.escape.nl.*

GAY AND LESBIAN

Amstel Fifty Four. Formerly known as Amstel Taveerne, this is still a gay-friendly bruine kroeg. Tankards and brass pots hanging from the ceiling reflect the cozy crowd of locals around the bar. Go just for the raucous sing-alongs that erupt whenever an old favorite is played. ⊠ *Amstel 54, East of Amstel* ☎ *020/623–4254* ⊕ *www.amstelfiftyfour.nl.*

LESBIAN

Vive-la-Vie. For more than three decades pretty women have been vying for space in these petite quarters on the edge of Rembrandtplein. Today this cozy late-night bar is as popular as ever, and is also straight-friendly and open to men—as long as they behave. ⊠ *Amstelstraat 7* ☎ *020/624–0114* ⊕ *www.vivelavie.net.*

THE CANAL RING

BARS, CAFÉS, AND LOUNGES

Bar With No Name. Too popular to be incognito, this Nine Streets mainstay is now often referred to by its address. An excellent selection of wines, generous cocktails, and a dim-sum-y menu is served in the '70s-style interior. ⊠ *Wolvenstraat 23* ☎ *020/320–0843.*

De Admiraal. The tasting house of the only remaining traditional distillery in Amsterdam serves potent liqueurs, including Dutch jenever. ⊠ *Herengracht 319* ☎ *020/625–4334* ⊕ *www.de-ooievaar.nl.*

BROWN CAFÉS

Cafe Kobalt. Occupying a 17th-century canalside warehouse, this beam-ceilinged bar with a large terrace serves beers, cocktails, and meals from morning until the wee hours. ⊠ *Singel 2A, Western Canal Ring* ☎ *020/320–1559* ⊕ *www.cafekobalt.nl.*

DANCE CLUBS

Studio 80. With its dim lighting and alternative programming, Studio 80 is unlikely to share its clientele with the neighboring mainstream clubs. On any given night you'll find underground DJs from all over the globe, or unapologetic indie bands that cater to a smart young crowd. ⊠ *Rembrandtplein 17, Rembrandtplein* ☎ *020/521–8333* ⊕ *www.studio-80.nl.*

GAY AND LESBIAN

Lellebel. This decade-old drag-show bar is renowned for its extravagant weekend performances. Recent additions to the weekday program include karaoke, salsa, and a Wednesday night Transgender Café. ⊠ *Utrechtsestraat 4, Rembrandtplein* ☏ *020/427–5139* ⊕ *www.lellebel.nl.*

THE OLD CITY CENTER (HET CENTRUM)

BARS, CAFÉS, AND LOUNGES

Amstelhoeck. Jutting out of the music theater Stopera, this grand café is the perfect point for a pre- or postperformance drink or meal. The staff is as *allegro* as you'll get in this city, and the lovely terrace overlooks the Amstel. ⊠ *Amstel 1* ☏ *020/620–9039* ⊕ *www.amstelhoeck.nl.*

Café Cuba. The always lively Nieuwmarkt mainstay serves relatively cheap cocktails and offers a jazzy electronic sound track. On sunny days you can enjoy your drink on the terrace overlooking the square. ⊠ *Nieuwmarkt 3* ☏ *020/627–4919* ⊕ *www.cafecuba-amsterdam.com.*

Café de Jaren. This light and airy multilevel café with a lovely terrace overlooking the Amstel is popular with a big cross-section of the population, from students and hipster knitting circles to artists and businesspeople. Food and drinks are reasonably priced. ⊠ *Nieuwe Doelenstraat 20-22* ☏ *020/625–5771* ⊕ *www.cafedejaren.nl.*

★ **Café Luxembourg.** The original Art Deco interior has been brought back to its full glory and the glassed-in terrace is perfect for people watching. Those with less interest in urban sociology can entertain themselves at the communal table with an assortment of international newspapers and magazines. ⊠ *Spui 24* ☏ *020/620–6264* ⊕ *www.luxembourg.nl.*

De Dokter. Wine and whiskey are just what patrons of De Dokter ("the doctor") have been ordering for centuries. Founded in 1789 to serve the doctors and medical students from the nearby university, the place is still run by the same family. ⊠ *Rozenboomsteeg 4* ☏ *020/626–4427* ⊕ *www.cafe-de-dokter.nl* ☉ *Sun.–Mon.*

Kapitein Zeppos. Nestled on an easy-to-miss alley is this atmospheric bar and restaurant named after a Flemish TV hero from the 1960s. The food, the furniture, and the French chansons playing transfer you to Paris in the 1950s. A glass of wine or a simple meal here can be memorable, especially when accompanied by live music on some Wednesdays and Sundays. ⊠ *Gebed Zonder End 5* ☏ *020/624–2057* ⊕ *www.zeppos.nl.*

Lime. This unpretentious minimalist bar sandwiched between the Red Light District and Chinatown offers great cocktails at reasonable prices. ⊠ *Zeedijk 104* ☏ *020/639–3020.*

Lokaal 't Loosje. Artists, students, and businesspeople unite in this popular café installed in a building from 1900 that used to be a waiting room for the horse-drawn trams. Much of the turn-of-the-century interior, including the tile-covered walls, has remained. ⊠ *Nieuwmarkt 32–34* ☏ *020/627–2635.*

Lux. A fantastic 1960s look and an attractive young crowd keeps it lively at this Marnixstraat club. ⊠ *Marnixstraat 403* ☎ *020/422–1412* ⊕ *www.weberlux.nl* ⊠ *Marnixstraat 397* ☎ *020/422–1412* ⊕ *www. weberlux.nl.*

The Tara. This labyrinth of an Irish pub is large enough to host live music and large-screen football matches. Yet, there are still plenty of cozy nooks for a quiet meal, Wi-Fi web surfing, or cuddling with ye olde sweetheart. ⊠ *Rokin 85–89 and Nes 100* ☎ *020/421–2654* ⊕ *www. thetara.com.*

Winston. Deep in the 1990s this was kind of a rough late-night bar where artists, students, and prostitutes mingled. Things have cleaned up since then, and now it's a happy preppy club offering a bit of everything—from punk bands to DJs, from neo-Christian to the easiest of easy tunes. ⊠ *Warmoesstraat 131* ☎ *020/623–1380* ⊕ *www.winston.nl.*

Fodor's Choice ★ **Wynand Fockink.** This is Amsterdam's most famous—and miraculously least hyped—*proeflokaal* (tasting room). Opened in 1679, this dim-lit, blithely cramped little bar just behind the Hotel Krasnapolsky has a menu of more than 60 Dutch spirits that reads like poetry: *Bruidstranen* (bride's tears) and *Boswandeling* (a walk in the woods) are just two favorites. Call ahead for a guided tour of the distillery. ⊠ *Pijlsteeg 31 and 43* ☎ *020/639–2695* ⊕ *www.wynand-fockink.nl.*

BROWN CAFÉS

De Engelse Reet. Also referred to as "The Pilsner Club," this decidedly ancient and unmistakably brown venue belongs to some lost age when beer was the safest alternative to drinking water. ⊠ *Begijnensteeg 4* ☎ *020/623–1777* ⊗ *Closed Sun.*

Dwaze Zaken. Just before you set out to some serious sinning in the Red Light District, stop at this friendly café for a drink or simple meal. An excellent selection of beers is on tap, and the food is tasty and cheap. The place has a Christian identity, but if you're not looking for it, you probably won't see it. ⊠ *Prins Hendrikkade 50, The Old City Center (Het Centrum)* ☎ *020/612–4175* ⊕ *www.dwazezaken.nl.*

Skek. Run by students, this bar on the Zeedijk attracts a slightly younger, more alternative crowd. They serve tasty, well-priced food, and on some nights there is live music. ⊠ *Zeedijk 4–8, The Old City Center (Het Centrum)* ☎ *020/427–0551* ⊕ *www.skek.nl.*

COFFEE SHOPS

Abraxas. Down a small alley, just a stone's throw from the Dam, you'll come upon what would seem to be the multilevel home of a family of hip hobbits. You'll think better once you make out the poor-postured travelers smoking joints or nibbling on ganja cakes. At No. 6 is the souvenir shop, and a second coffee shop, Abraxas Too, can be found at Spuistraat 51. ⊠ *Jonge Roelensteeg 12–14* ☎ *020/625–5763.*

Dampkring. One of the best coffee shops in town became even more popular after its use as a set for *Ocean's Twelve*. The weed menu is exceptional and the smoothie selection remarkable. Other coffeeshops have opened under the same name, but this is the one and only real Dampkring. ⊠ *Handboogstraat 29* ☎ *020/638–0705.*

Green House. Another Cannabis Cup darling, and a not uncommon docking station for celebrities staying at the Grand Hotel up the block, this chain is renowned for quality weeds and seeds. Artful mosaics provide a trippy background, and storefront tables let patrons take in a breath of fresh air. ⊠ *Oudezijds Voorburgwal 191, The Old City Center (Het Centrum)* ☎ *020/627–1739* ⊠ *Tolstraat 91, Amsterdam South* ☎ *020/673–7430* ⊠ *Waterlooplein 345, The Old City Center (Het Centrum)* ☎ *020/622–5499.*

DANCE CLUBS

Air. Although spacious, Air aims for an intimate vibe, with loads of dimly lit nooks and multiple bars. If you're traveling with a crowd, know that table service for up to eight people can be booked in advance. House, club, techno, and urban sounds prevail on the dance floor. ⊠ *Amstelstraat 16* ☎ *020/820–0670* ⊕ *www.air.nl.*

Bitterzoet. An adventurous and diverse program of entertainment includes DJs, live bands, and even theater. When it comes to music, hip-hop, funk, and soul are top dog. ⊠ *Spuistraat 2, Centrum* ☎ *020/421–2318* ⊕ *www.bitterzoet.com.*

Cafe Casablanca. On the edge of the Red Light District sits this neighborhood's classic club, dating back to the 1940s. For better or for worse, cracks are appearing in its jazzy foundation as the programming gets diluted with DJ sets and karaoke. ⊠ *Zeedijk 26* ⊕ *www.cafecasablanca.nl.*

Odeon. If you feel like some weekend dancing in a gracious old canal house, head for this 17th-century brewery turned 19th-century concert hall. Many of the rooms retain their spectacular painted and stucco ceilings. ⊠ *Singel 460* ☎ *020/521–8555* ⊕ *www.odeonamsterdam.nl* ⊙ *Closed weekdays.*

GAY

Club Fuxxx. This strictly men-only venue, formerly known as the Cockring, is almost an institution in the leather scene. Besides a lotta meat, there is music, and it stays open until the wee hours of the morning. ⊠ *Warmoestraat 96* ☎ *020/623–9604* ⊕ *www.clubfuxxx.com.*

Cuckoo's Nest. Back in 1984, this bar was so leather-lined it put San Francisco's Folsom Street to shame. Today it attracts a more diverse crowd, many of whom find their way to what's rumored to be one of the biggest dark rooms in Europe. ⊠ *Nieuwezijds Kolk 6* ⊕ *www.cuckoosnest.nl.*

Dirty Dick's. Founded in 1974, this must be the oldest leather cruise bar in Amsterdam. On Thursdays all local beers and soft drinks are €2. ⊠ *Warmoestraat 86* ⊕ *www.dirtydicksamsterdam.com.*

Getto. Founded in 1996, this truly mellow place welcomes everyone: gay, lesbian, bi, queer, or straight. They have an appetizing cocktail menu and offer food at reasonable prices. The "Gettoburger" is a hit. ⊠ *Warmoesstraat 51* ☎ *020/421–5151* ⊕ *www.getto.nl.*

Fodor's Choice ★ **PRIK.** This highly popular bar is situated rather off-the-beaten-*queer*-path, which was exactly the intention of its founding gay couple as they aim to be as all-inclusive as possible. No matter their intentions, they keep winning "best gay bar" awards. The staff and clientele are as cheerful as the venue's name— *prik* means bubbles in Dutch and (among other things) refers to the Prosecco on tap. They serve great cocktails and finger food, too. ✉ *Spuistraat 109* ☎ *020/320–0002* ⊕ *www.prikamsterdam.nl.*

Queen's Head. You won't find Her Majesty the Queen here, but a mainstream crowd of well-built and fun-loving princes enjoying DJ beats and parties that pour out onto the sidewalk. ✉ *Zeedijk 20* ☎ *020/420–2475* ⊕ *www. queenshead.nl.*

The Web. Leather, piercing, and tattoos predominate, but meeting one's soul mate at this cruise bar is not out of the question. On Sunday evenings they serve free hotdogs and homemade soup. ✉ *Sint Jacobstraat 6* ☎ *020/623–6758* ⊕ *www. thewebamsterdam.nl.*

> ### MIDNIGHT MUSEUM CRAWL
>
> For one night in early November, all the city's major museums stay open until the wee hours to host a variety of themed parties. If you only have a very short period of time to visit Amsterdam, elasticize those euros by arriving for **Museum Nacht**. At this fantastic party, you'll find activities such as tangos under Rembrandt's *Night Watch*, house beats at the Jewish Historical Museum, bossa nova in the Stedelijk, master classes on how to paint like Bob Ross, and ghost stories for kids in the Bible Museum. For annual details see ⊕ *www.n8.nl.*

JAZZ CLUBS

Cotton Club. Fans of more traditional jazz should check out this legendary venue, named for Surinamese trumpet player Teddy Cotton, who started the place in the 1940s. Every Saturday afternoon the club hosts live jazz, with a line-up that quite often features big names from the local scene. ✉ *Nieuwmarkt 5* ⊕ *www.cottonclubmusic.nl.*

Kadinsky. This chain serves mellow jazz alongside scrumptious chocolate-chip cookies, providing a refreshingly understated approach to getting high. ✉ *Rosmarijnsteeg 9, The Old City Center (Het Centrum)* ☎ *020/624–7023* ✉ *Zoutsteeg 14, The Old City Center (Het Centrum)* ☎ *020/620–4715.*

ROCK MUSIC VENUES

De Buurvrouw. In this small sawdusted and kitsch-strewn haven, students and alternative types don't mind yelling over the latest in loud guitars and funky beats. They also enjoy a pool tournament every now and then. ✉ *St. Pieterspoortsteeg 29* ☎ *020/625–9654* ⊕ *www. debuurvrouw.nl.*

DE PIJP

COFFEE SHOPS

Yo-Yo. This quintessential friendly neighborhood coffee shop is in the heart of the multicultural Pijp. They have a patio where you can freely smoke their high-quality, all-organic products. ✉ *2e Jan van der Heijdenstraat 79, De Pijp* ☎ *020/664–7173* ⊗ *Closed Sun.*

BARS, CAFÉS, AND LOUNGES

Kingfisher. For a flavor of the neighborhood's regentrified café culture, check out this favorite corner bar that fills up most nights with parched Pijpers. They also serve snacks and light meals. ⊠ *Ferdinand Bolstraat 24* ☎ *020/671–2395* ⊕ *www.kingfishercafe.nl.*

Fodor's Choice ★ **Twenty Third.** This champagne bar, named after the top floor on which it perches, provides an eagle's-eye view of Amsterdam South, along with 17 different kinds of champagne, various cocktails, and snacks (if caviar could be so categorized). ⊠ *Hotel Okura, Ferdinand Bolstraat 333* ☎ *020/678–7111* ⊕ *www.okura.nl.*

THE ARTS

Although a relatively small city, Amsterdam packs a giant cultural wallop and its residents are a culturally inclined people that supports a milieu whose spectrum ranges from the austerely classical to the outrageously avant-garde. Many festivals invariably highlight both homegrown and international talent. So book that ticket fast! Amsterdam's theater and music season begins in September and runs through June, when the Holland Festival of Performing Arts is held.

CABARETS

September marks the official start of the cultural season, as the greater majority of Amsterdam's performing arts do not give shows during the summer. But don't fret: June, July, and August are jam-packed with festivals (both in the city and its environs), outdoor concerts and movie screenings, and appearances by many foreign artists stopping through Amsterdam on their summer tours.

FILM

Have you ever wondered how the Dutch came to speak such impeccable English? History's answer to this is that a small nation with few resources had no choice but to speak the language of the people with whom they traded. Pop culture's answer to this is much simpler: Hollywood! All films and TV are subtitled, not dubbed, so viewers are constantly exposed to English. What's more, in a nation whose last half-century would generally be characterized by political peace and social harmony, it's no wonder local folks yearn for a bit of good old-fashioned American cussing and carnage. Conversely, a number of Dutch directors—alienated by the long lackluster local scene—have manifested their blockbuster destinies in Hollywood. Creator of *Basic Instinct* and

FILM FESTIVALS

If you're a film lover with a flexible schedule, plan your trip around Holland's big film events. The International Film Festival Rotterdam (⊕ www.filmfestivalrotterdam. com) is in late January/early February; the International Documentary Film Festival Amsterdam (⊕ www.idfa.nl) and the smaller-budget documentary sideshow the Shadow Festival (⊕ www. shadowfestival.nl) are in November; the Imagine Amsterdam Fantastic Film Festival (⊕ www. imaginefilmfestival.nl) is in April.

RoboCop, the notorious Paul Verhoeven, is the nation's most famous cinematic export.

MUSIC

Some of Amsterdam's most esteemed music venues also happen to be in the city's most beautiful structures. Enjoy a night of music in a breathtaking, and acoustically stellar, setting.

DANCE AND THEATER

Although many associate the Dutch dance scene with two names—Het Nationale Ballet and Nederlands Dans Theater—there are many more innovative local companies. Certainly the Hungarian ex-pat Krisztina de Châtel, now teamed up with Itzik Galili under the umbrella of Dansgroep Amsterdam (⊕ *www.dansgroepamsterdam.nl*), has turned Amsterdam into a jumping-off point for international acclaim, thanks to her physical approach that also often employs the latest technologies in the visual arts. One annual not-to-be-missed event—that mixes both local and international names of a cutting-edge nature—is the month-long Julidans (⊕ *www. julidans.nl*), which is centered around the Stadsschouwburg.

> **NES TIX**
>
> Amsterdam's Off Broadway–type theaters are centered along the Nes, an alley leading off the Dam. One-stop ticket shopping for the Brakke Grond, De Engelenbak, and Frascati can be done at the central ticket office (⊕ *www. indenes.nl*).
>
> **Vlaams Cultuurhuis de Brakke Grond.** This theater is the main venue for Flemish culture in the city. ⊠ *Nes 45, The Old City Center (Het Centrum)* ☎ *020/626–6866* ⊕ *www.debrakkegrond.nl.*

AMSTERDAM SOUTH

CABARETS

Toomler. Borrowing its name from the Yiddish word for "noisemaker," this is the podium for the acclaimed Dutch stand-up group Comedytrain. Many members of this group have grown into national celebrities. The programming is often English-friendly, with regular appearances by international guests. ⊠ *Breitnerstraat 2* ☎ *020/670–7400* ⊕ *www. toomler.nl.*

AMSTERDAM WEST

FILM

Filmhuis Cavia. This is one of several repertory cinemas that show a savvy blend of classics and modern world cinema, with programming that is decidedly edgy and politically alternative. The location is alternative, too—the first floor of a boxing school. ⊠ *Van Hallstraat 52-I, First floor* ☎ *020/681–1419* ⊕ *www.filmhuiscavia.nl.*

DID YOU KNOW?

First described as the "Prune Cake" when opened in 1921, the interior of Tuschinski is a dizzying and dense mixture of Baroque, Art Nouveau, Amsterdam School, Jugendstil, and Asian influences. It began as a variety theater welcoming such stars as Marlene Dietrich but soon became a cinema, and to this day watching movies from one of the extravagant private balconies remains an unforgettable experience—especially if you order champagne.

EAST OF THE AMSTEL

CABARET

De Kleine Komedie. For many years, this riverside theater has been the city's most vibrant venue for cabaret and comedy, mostly in Dutch. ⊠ *Amstel 56–58, Eastern Canal Ring and Rembrandtplein* ☎ *020/624–0534 for tickets, 020/626-5917* ⊕ *www.dekleinekomedie.nl* ⊗ *Box office daily 4–7:30.*

DANCE AND THEATER

Koninklijk Theater Carré. Although more focused on commercial and large-scale musicals, this former circus theater also schedules acclaimed Eastern European ballet and opera companies. International pop stars can be seen, too; Tom Waits and Juliette Greco are among those who have performed here. ⊠ *Amstel 115–125* ☎ *0900/252–5255 for tickets* ⊕ *www.carre.nl.*

> **OPEN-AIR ENTERTAINMENT**
>
> Theatrical events in the Vondelpark have a long and glorious history. Nowadays, during the **Openluchttheater** season, there's a lunchtime concert and a midafternoon children's show on Wednesdays, Thursday night shows are in the bandstand, and there's theater every Friday night. Various activities take place on Saturdays, and theater events and pop concerts are held on Sunday afternoons. It's a full agenda!

Muiderpoorttheater. Although not within the Nes zone, this theater also follows an off-Broadway path by presenting new faces of the international drama and dance scene in an intimate setting. ⊠ *2e Van Swindenstraat 26, Amsterdam East* ☎ *020/668–1313 for reservations, 020/692-5421 for info* ⊕ *www.muiderpoorttheater.nl.*

FILM

Kriterion. This cinema is run by students and reflects their world-embracing tastes (especially during the late showings of cult films). The adjoining café is always buzzing with chatty humanities types, but that's not to say that the long-graduated among us are unwelcome. ⊠ *Roetersstraat 170, Amsterdam East* ☎ *020/623–1708* ⊕ *www.kriterion.nl.*

Studio K. The Amsterdam foundation Kriterion, which has been promoting student-run business ventures since World War II, has added yet another venue to its résumé. This two-screen movie house shows not only art and foreign films, but with a theater, an open stage, and a restaurant-bar, it's a multidisciplinarian's dream come true. ⊠ *Timorplein 62, Amsterdam East* ☎ *020/692–0422* ⊕ *www.studio-k.nu.*

EASTERN DOCKLANDS

ENTERTAINMENT CENTERS

NDSM. What were once industrial shipyards have been reinvented as, quite possibly, the city's largest *broedplaats*, or "breeding ground" for the arts, where regular theater performances and festivals take place. And with a ferry departing from behind Centraal Station, getting there could not be easier. ⊠ *Neveritaweg 61* ☎ *020/493-1070* ⊕ *www.ndsm.nl.*

Catch any number of outstanding shows at the Muziektheater.

JORDAAN

FILM

Fodor's Choice ★ **The Movies.** A full-swing 1920s ambience sets the stage for artsy and indie flicks, and the ambiance is enhanced with an excellent restaurant, lively bar, and smiling staff. On weekdays you can opt for a film-and-dinner deal. ⊠ *Haarlemmerdijk 161–163, Centrum* ☎ *020/638-6016* ⊕ *www.themovies.nl.*

LEIDSEPLEIN

CABARETS

Boom Chicago. This is what happens when a bunch of zany expat Americans open their own restaurant-theater to present improvised comedy inspired by life in Amsterdam and the rest of the world. Dinner and seating begin at 6, with show time at 8:15; on weekends there are also late shows and DJs. ⊠ *Leidseplein 12* ☎ *020/423-0101* ⊕ *www. boomchicago.nl.*

Comedy Café Amsterdam. For some(often English)stand-up, check the schedule of this club on the Max Euweplein. Mondays and Tuesdays are open stage nights; the rest of the week you get the pros. ⊠ *Max Euweplein 43–45* ☎ *020/638-3971* ⊕ *www.comedycafe.nl.*

ENTERTAINMENT CENTERS

Fodor's Choice ★ **Stadsschouwburg.** The red-and-gold plushness of the city theater is the setting for plays with top-notch Dutch actors and modern dance by international companies. The plays are usually in Dutch but there are occasional stagings in English. ⊠ *Leidseplein 26* ☎ *020/624–2311 Box-office* ⊕ *www.ssba.nl.*

FILM

Cinecenter. Sleek modern decor fills the lounge of this theater opposite the Melkweg, while four screens downstairs play arty, internationally acclaimed films. ⊠ *Lijnbaansgracht 236* ☎ *020/623–6615* ⊕ *www.cinecenter.nl.*

De Uitkijk. Opened in 1913, this small canal-side "lookout," as its name means in Dutch, ranks as the city's oldest cinema. In recent years the theater fell into decline but was taken over by a group of students and now presents a rather diverse program of documentaries, kid flicks, Hollywood classics, and the odd mainstream film. ⊠ *Prinsengracht 452* ☎ *020/223–2416* ⊕ *www.uitkijk.nl.*

SPECTACLE SPECIALISTS

Alternative forms of theater are very Amsterdam. Not unlike the stampot—a traditional Dutch peasant's stew made of mashed potatoes and pretty much any other vegetable and scrap of meat you can find in your pantry—anything goes. Multimedia, multidimensional, and multicultural are the three basic components to such pieces. Be warned: some performers are not shy about trying to convert the uninitiated. If you decide to attend a show, therefore, keep in mind that your position as a spectator can quickly transmogrify into participant.

MUSEUM DISTRICT

FILM

Fodor'sChoice
★
EYE Film Institute Netherlands. Now housed in an eye-popping, protofuturistic waterfront structure designed by Viennese architects Delugan Meissl, the former Filmmuseum at Vondelpark not only relocated in the Spring of 2012 to their ambitious brand-new building but also changed its name in the process. While this cutting-edge museum moved to north Amsterdam and its cutting-edge neighborhood of Overhoeks, they have also made access easier then ever, thanks to a free ferry that now connects in a two-minute ride with Amsterdam Central Station. Along with restoring thousands of films (Martin Scorsese used footage from Georges Méliès films restored here in his film *Hugo*), the institute has finally brushed off its somewhat dusty image with this state-of-the-art film center. The EYE contains four massive screening rooms (showing a fine mix of classic and contemporary films), a large exhibition space, and a library open to the public. There is also a restaurant with a waterfront terrace. ⊠ *IJpromenade 1* ☎ *020/589–1400 for info and tickets, 020/589–1402 for restaurant* ⊕ *www.eyefilm.nl* ☉ *Box office, Sun.– Thur. 10–10, Fri.–Sat. 10 am–11 pm. Exhibition space, daily 11–6. Bar-restaurant, Sun.–Thur. 10–1, Fri.–Sat. 10–2.*

REMBRANDTPLEIN

FILM

Pathé De Munt. The largest cinema in the city center has 13 screens showing the latest mainstream films. It's a typical blockbuster venue, so don't expect any charm, but there will be plenty of legroom, state-of-the-art sound systems, and huge screens. ⊠ *Vijzelstraat 15* ☎ *0900/1458* for *reservations* ⊕ *www.pathe.nl.*

★ **Tuschinski.** Since 1921, this eclectic Art Deco reverie has been the most dazzling place for moviegoers to escape from reality. Owned by the country's main movie distributor, the theater has six screens showing the latest Hollywood blockbusters and the occasional art-house number. Before the lights go out, enjoy the beautiful interior of the main room. ⊠ *Reguliersbreestraat 26–34* ☎ *0900/1458* ⊕ *www.pathe.nl.*

THE OLD CITY CENTER (HET CENTRUM)

CABARETS

Comedy Theater in de Nes. This intimate venue is home to up-and-coming Dutch and international comedians. Inspired by American comedy clubs, it has a fully fledged bar that stays open during shows. In short, it's the Paradiso of comedy. ⊠ *Nes 110* ☎ *020/422–2777* ⊕ *www. comedytheater.nl.*

DANCE AND THEATER

Frascati. This renowned lab for innovative and experimental theatre has three venues where it puts on plays. ⊠ *Nes 63* ☎ *020/626-8666 Box-office* ⊕ *www.theaterfrascati.nl.*

de Theaterschool. This institution unites students and teachers from all over the world to share their experiences in the fields of dance and theater. Performances are occasionally put on. ⊠ *Jodenbreestraat 3* ☎ *020/527–7763* for *reservations* ⊕ *www.ahk.nl/theaterschool.*

ENTERTAINMENT CENTERS

Fodor's Choice ★ **Muziektheater.** This theater's huge and flexible stage acts as a magnet for directors with a penchant for grand-scale décor, such as Robert Wilson, Willy Decker, and Peter Sellars. ⊠ *Waterlooplein 22* ☎ *020/625–5455* for *tickets* ⊕ *www.muziektheater.nl.*

MUSIC

Bethanienklooster. Many of the city's churches are being used these days by music lovers and players (see also Nieuwe Kerk, Noorder Kerk, Nicolaas Kerk, and Oude Kerk in Exploring Amsterdam). This former monastery dating from the 15th century still provides a calm and holy setting for regular chamber music concerts. ⊠ *Barndesteeg 6B* ☎ *020/625–0078* ⊕ *www.bethanienklooster.nl.*

Beurs van Berlage. The architectural landmark and progenitor of the Amsterdam School was built in the early 20th century as the Stock Exchange and now functions as a cultural center featuring classical concerts and art exhibitions. The indoor cafe (entrance opposite the Bijenkorf) is worth a visit in itself with the Amsterdam School interior. ⊠ *Damrak 243* ☎ *020/530–4141* ⊕ *www.beursvanberlage.nl.*

DE PIJP

FILM

Rialto. Away from the maddening crowd, this little theater is noted for showing world cinema and more highbrow film classics. ✉ *Ceintuurbaan 338* ☎ *020/676-8700* ⊕ *www.rialtofilm.nl.*

Shopping

WORD OF MOUTH

"Diamond Factory Tour: some people hate it, we went to The Gassan and found it very educational, and they were candid and diplomatic when provoking questions (i.e. blood diamonds) were asked; no pressure to purchase."

— Shanghainese

HOT, NEW, AND DUTCH

Dutch fashion? Yes! Ever since Viktor & Rolf woke the fashion world up to the new, edgy, and inventive lines of fashion in the Netherlands a decade ago, many other Dutch designers are now making the scene.

(Above) Shopping on the Leidsestraat. (Top right) Ilja Visser's Ready to Fish. (Bottom right) One of the seven racks at Open Shop.

Following in their wake—and making it less stuffy and more democratic in the process—are Bas Kosters, Claes Iversen, Iris van Herpen, and Ilja Visser, all of whom have garnered *Idol*-level acclaim across the country for conflating their individual perspectives with ready-to-wear sensibility. Though note: the Dutch clean-lined approach has long been characterized as, at best, Calvinism dressed in Calvin Klein. Send that old generalization to Good Will. The turn of the millennium prompted another turning—of sartorial asceticism on its own shaven head. Welcome to new Dutch fashion. Decades know no boundaries, inseams and necklines cross-dress, and sociocultural references are as irreverent as they are irrelevant. Another new development is the mixing of vintage clothes with new design and customized goods, as seen by Jutka & Riska.

NINE STREETS PLUS ONE

The Nine Streets has a distinctly old-world feel. This cluster of quaint canal crossings between the Rozengracht and the Leidsegracht dates back to the 17th century, then inhabited by artisans whose leather trade is commemorated in the street names. Today, the neighborhood offers one-of-a-kind retail. And in fall 2009, Hazenstraat joined in, becoming the district's 10th street.

Ready to Fish. Unlike many of her creative compatriots, Ilja Visser is less concerned with appearing edgy than outfitting women in clothes with, like the sea, their own natural ebb and flow (apropos of her surname, meaning "fisher"). After years of consistently well-received catwalk shows, this is the designer's first boutique, bringing the public a ready-to-wear collection that holds onto Visser's signature scalloped sleeves and low-inseamed trousers in nature-at-sunset palettes. Despite being housed in a 17th-century tobacco and coffee warehouse, Ready to Fish provides a timely antidote of tranquility for an overstimulated industry. ⊠ *Prinsengracht 581, The Canal Ring* ☏ *020/330–9332* ⊕ *www.www.readytofish.nl.*

Open Shop. Seven days a week, seven racks here showcase eye-striking, one-of-a-kind handmade clothes, shoes, and accessories. A dashiki made of sports jersey material, or feather-tasseled clogs, or eco-fabric T-shirts reading "100% Halal," or psychedelic harem pants: like their young creators, each collection preaches its own distinct style of streetwear. So what holds the collective together? Affordability, super-affable staff, and successfully channeling Punky Brewster's *joie de vivre.* ⊠ *Nieuwezijds Voorburgwal 291, The Old City Center (Het Centrum)* ☏ *020/528–6963* ⊕ *www.openshopamsterdam.com.*

Francesco Van Benthum. Now a darling of the fashion avant-garde, Van Benthum has spent more than a decade earning his stripes by redefining menswear. While many pieces look traditional, he made his mark with his shirt-over-shirt looks, transparent lace netting, and *blousson* effects that went into his more headline-making outfits. It comes as no surprise that he started out designing for both men and women in Paris. Now he's opened his first store and it's a jewel: half art gallery, half gentlemen's closet. Look for amazing sophistication in the details, ranging from pre-revolutionary Russian touches and choirboy and cardinal vibes to all those layered silhouettes. ⊠ *Herenstraat 13, Canal Ring* ☏ *020/820–8208* ⊕ *www.franciscovanbenthum.com.*

6

Updated by
Marie-Claire
Melzer

What will be your perfect gift? A folkloric *koekeplank* (cookie mould)? A Makkum ceramic herring platter? A box of those delicious hard candies called Haagse Hopjes? A cutting-edge vest styled by Viktor & Rolf? A psychedelically hued ski cap from Oilily? Or one of those other delights that have made contemporary Dutch design the darling of high-style fans the world over?

Whether you go for Baroque antiques or for post-millennium fashion, the variety of goods available in Amsterdam energizes a continuous parade of boutiques, street markets, and department stores. Be it for the millionaire trade or economy-minded nabobs, hunting in Amsterdam for that special purchase is akin to grand entertainment.

Where do shop-till-you-droppers love to melt their credit cards? Amsterdam's priciest street: the P. C. Hooftstraat, located in the Museum District and affectionately called the P. C. (pronounced "Pay Say"). Here, staff members treat customers like visiting royalty, BMWs are parked along the street, and many shop interiors mimic stately Dutch mansions, replete with marble floors, crystal chandeliers and antique furnishings arrayed for your comfort. Even if shopping the P. C. is beyond your budget, you might indulge voyeuristic tendencies and drink an over-priced glass of wine at one of the chic outdoor terraces while watching the Beautiful People parade by. Don't neglect the Van Baerlestraat and the Willemsparkweg, (just steps away from the P. C. Hooftstraat), where you're likely to discover a stunning lamp or home accessory.

At the other end of the scale, tackle the more youthful crowds on the Damrak and Nieuwendijk, where shops blasting deafening music stand shoulder to shoulder, selling inexpensive fashions and club/street wear for the young and trendy, along with cheesy souvenirs. If it all gets too noisy and crowded, but you're not shopped out yet, traverse the Rokin, where it's more refined, spacious and quiet, with proportionately escalated prices.

Amsterdam is an antique-lover's paradise. Collectors, museum curators, and antique dealers routinely shop here for old Delft and Makkum treasures. The Spiegel Quarter is home to elegant antiques shops whose beautiful displays include a variety of antique art, maps, furnishings, jewelry and clocks. If you enjoy the thrill of the chase, explore the short, maze-like streets of the Jordaan, where you'll stumble upon a surprising number of tiny specialist antique businesses. The perfect Dutch "antique" is a piece of authentic Delftware. The key word is "authentic." A variety of blue and white "delft" is available in a range of brands and prices, and you can pick up attractive souvenir-quality "delft" pieces at any giftware shop. But the real McCoy is known as Royal Delft and it can be found in the better giftware shops, such as those on the Rokin and the P. C. Hooftstraat, and bear the worthy name of De Porceleyne Fles. Blue is no longer the only official color; today, you can find "New Delft," a range of green, gold, and black hues, whose exquisite miniscule figures are drawn to resemble an old Persian tapestry; the Pynacker Delft, borrowing Japanese motifs in rich oranges and golds, and the brighter Polychrome Delft, which can strike a brilliant sunflower-yellow effect.

Another great gift is chocolates, as Holland is a chocoholic's mecca. Everyone knows the mmmmmmm-boy flavors crafted by Droste and Van Houten but, droolingly, we recommend one of the city's noted "chocolateries," such as Puccini Bomboni.

If you have enough time during your stay, shop at one of the outdoor markets for a "total immersion" experience and a sense of how old this city is. At the Albert Cuypmarkt, while bombarded by vendors hawking their wares, the multi-lingual hubbub and ethnic diversity of the crowd, and the exciting selection of goods, keep in mind that the scene before you is pretty much unchanged from centuries ago. Go to it, and how we envy you!

PLANNING

TAX-FREE SHOPPING

Nearly all the price tags you see will already include Value-Added Tax (V.A.T.), or what the Dutch call B.T.W. (*belasting over de toegevoegde waarde*). Most consumer goods and luxury items (including alcohol) are taxed 21%; basic goods and service, 6%. If you're a non–European Union (EU) resident, you can claim this back.

When spending €50 or more at a store, ask for a V.A.T. refund form to be completed on your behalf and attach it to your receipt. Repeat this ritual wherever you shop. Before leaving the EU, have your forms stamped by an airport customs official—be ready to show your forms and receipts and all the new, unused goods you've purchased (thus keeping them separate from checked-in luggage). Afterwards, get remunerated at a refund-service counter or mail in your request. According to Dutch law the form is only valid when stamped within three months after the purchase.

Global Blue is a European-wide service with more than 240,000 affiliated stores and hundreds of refund counters. Its Tax Free Check remunerates shoppers via cash, check, or credit-card adjustment. Global Blue also offers Currency Choice, allowing you to pay with your own currency. For more information ⊕ *www.global-blue.com* or ☎ *866/706–6090* within the United States or ☎ *00800/32–111–111* within the EU.

GETTING ORIENTED

Getting your shop on in Amsterdam won't require GPS. Just down the road from Centraal Station is **Nieuwendijk**, the city's oldest shopping street, today a pedestrians' paradise for chain-store-hopping and basics at a bargain. The Dam forms the delta of **Kalverstraat**, the city's other roaring river of international retailers and favorite Dutch franchises open seven days a week. Nearby **Leidsestraat** is a scaled-down version equipped with an escape route of canalside cafés. Just east is the **Spiegelkwartier,** one of Europe's most fabled agglomerations of antiques shops.

Peek around the Rijksmuseum and you'll find **P. C. Hooftstraat.** The "*Pay-Say,*" as locals refer to it, is Amsterdam's own little Madison Avenue, bustling with global luxury brands and their new-moneyed fannies. For those less loco about their labels, head to the adjoining **Van Baerlestraat**, offering concessions to match the area's well-heeled cultural consumers. Get back to Amsterdam's more egalitarian enterprises in **The Pijp,** where shops appealing to young and old, tried and trendy, native and newcomer offset the market-frenzied Albert Cuypstraat. Continue farther south, through to the other side of the Vondelpark, and you'll come upon **Cornelis Schuytstraat.** Footballers' wives and fashionistas love "*De Schuyt,*" an undeniably cozy cluster of chichi clothing and shoe boutiques, sleek homeware, and fancy delis.

If price tags listed in more than one currency leave you cold, get off the tourist trek. Chic boutiques, vintage stores, and quirky gift shops dot the **Nine Streets,** a sweet li'l hair comb of a neighborhood tucked behind the right ear of the Dam. From there, head northward through the **Jordaan,** where trendy and traditional cross-fertilize to produce quintessential Amsterdam charm. Don't miss the gamut of high-end specialty stores on **Haarlemmerstraat,** which goes over into **Haarlemmerdijk.** Here you'll find the finest chocolate, fantastic gelato, Spanish ham, Portuguese pastries, and the best hummus in town. And besides all that, there are also many non-food specialty shops and funky boutiques. Still haven't found what you seek? Take a foray into classic Amsterdam shopping on **Utrechtsestraat.** This beloved neighborhood main street is so close to Rembrandtplein you can hear the clubs' bass lines pumping yet so civilized you would think you were invited to a private sale, eight blocks long.

As for art, modern to contemporary, many of the best galleries that deal in modern and contemporary art are centered on the **Keizersgracht** and **Spiegelkwartier,** others are found around the Western Canal Ring, and the Jordaanartists have traditionally gravitated to low-rent areas. **De Baarsjes,** a neighborhood in Amsterdam West, is increasingly attracting small galleries that showcase exciting works of art. With a rough

Hawking oranges at the Monday flea market at the Noordermarkt.

charm reminiscent of the early days of New York's SoHo, it's worth a detour for adventurous art lovers. The tourist office website ⊕ *www. iamsterdam.com* is a reasonable source of information on current exhibitions. Also helpful is the bilingual art zine *PRESENTeert*, available at select galleries and online at ⊕ *presenteert.wordpress.com*.

SHOPPING NEIGHBORHOODS

AMSTERDAM SOUTH

ART AND ANTIQUES

Christie's Amsterdam. Founded in London in 1766 by James Christie, this internationally known auction house hosts glamorous sales of art, furniture, wines, jewelry, and porcelain. Even if you leave empty-handed, the surrounding neighborhood is well worth the journey. ✉ *Cornelis Schuytstraat 57* ☎ *020/575–5255* ⊕ *www.christies.com*.

CHILDREN

De Winkel van Nijntje. Most department stores and toy shops in the Netherlands carry the classic children's brand, but here, at one of only three shops in the country, you'll find every imaginable Nijntje product—clothes, books, night-lights, tooth-fairy boxes, car seats, and more. ✉ *Scheldestraat 61* ☎ *020/664–8054* ⊕ *www.dewinkelvannijntje.nl*.

CLOTHING

Fodor'sChoice ★ **Ennu.** Haute couture gets Gothic à la the likes of Rick Owens and Comme des Garçons at this exclusive boutique. The shop's name is a blending of the Dutch words *en nu*—for "and now"—aptly intimating that once you've shopped here, what could possibly be next? ✉ *Cornelis Schuytstraat 15* ☎ *020/673–5265* ⊕ *www.ennu.nl.*

CHOCOLATE

Arti Choc. Chocoholics, take note, this Amsterdam South secret not only sells handmade bonbons, but will also custom-design just about anything you can imagine made from chocolate. The staff is lovely, and serves a very generous scoop of *gelato,* ideal to take along on a walk through the nearby Vondelpark. ✉ *Koninginneweg 141* ☎ *020/470–9805* ⊕ *www.artichoc.nl.*

> ## THANK GOD IT'S THURSDAY
>
> Most shops close between 5 and 6 except on Thursday, famously known as the *koopavond* ("shopping night"), when the retail riots end around 9. Many shops have delayed openings on Mondays, and most shops situated outside the city center are closed on Sundays. Also note that many shopowners go home a little earlier on Saturdays, usually around 5. Some of the smaller shops and boutiques tend to be open only a few days a week, or only in the afternoon. To avoid disappointment, call ahead or check the website.

CRYSTAL AND GLASS

& klevering Zuid. You'll find yourself in a rainbow world at this quiet corner, thanks to its wide range of tints in porcelain and glass tableware, colorful household accessories, and bright table linens. Women's Wear Top European design brands are all here, including stainless steel cookware from Iittala, Peugeot pepper mills, lush towels and bathrobes from Van Dijck Sanger, and artistic storage boxes from Galerie Sentou. There is another store at Haarlemmerstraat 8 in the Jordaan district. ✉ *Jacob Obrechtstraat 19a* ☎ *020/670–3623* ⊕ *www.klevering.nl.*

BUITENVELDERT

ART AND ANTIQUES

Sotheby's. Many antiques dealers buy from the fabled auctions held at the Amsterdam branch of this auction house. The Dutch are some of the savviest businesspeople in the world, but you can try to beat them to the bid. ✉ *Emmalaan 23, Amsterdam Zuid* ☎ *020/550–2200* ⊕ *www. sothebys.com.*

EAST OF THE AMSTEL

MARKETS

Dappermarkt. Its length running along the eponymous street between Mauritskade and Wijttenbachstraat, this market has, since 1910, been a consumer crossroads for what is today known as Amsterdam Oost ("East"). A couple hundred stalls, set up Monday through Saturday (10–4:30), sell everything from discount clothing and cosmetics to flowers and food. Successful juxtaposition of 100% pure lamb-meat kebabs

CLOSE UP

Antiquing on a Budget

For more gently priced collections, you might opt to tiptoe past the 18th-century tulipwood armoires and explore an increasingly popular neighborhood for adventurous collectors—the Jordaan. In stark contrast to the elegant stores in the Spiegelkwartier with their beautiful displays, the tiny unprepossessing shops dotted along the Elandsgracht and connecting streets, such as the 1e Looiersdwarsstraat, offer equally wonderful treasures. Those who take the time to carefully examine the backroom shelves, nooks, and crannies of a small shop may be rewarded with a big find. Prices here are also more in keeping with a downtowner's budget for interior decor. Indeed, this is one of the best-kept secrets of New York's antiques shop dealers, who often scour the Jordaan for their imported wares. You can also enjoy happy hunting in the shops on Rozengracht and Prinsengracht, near the Westerkerk, which offer Dutch country furniture and household items; take a look at the antiques and curio shops along the side streets in that part of the city. Many of the antiques shops in the Spiegelkwartier and the Jordaan keep irregular hours and some are open only by appointment, so it's wise to call first.

6

with Indonesian *lumpia* is surely just one reason *National Geographic Traveler* has included the market in its top-10 list of markets worldwide. ✉ *Amsterdam East* ⊕ *www.dappermarkt.nl.*

SHOES

United Nude. Entering UN feels more like walking into an art gallery than a shoe shop. No wonder, the man behind this brand's flagship store—and the various models of the signature floating-heeled pump contained therein—is Rem D. Koolhaas (yes, indeed, nephew of celebrity architect Rem Koolhaas, who designed the Prada store in New York City's SoHo, among many other high-style triumphs). ✉ *Spuistraat 125A, Centrum* ☎ *020/626–0010* ⊕ *www.unitednude.com.*

JORDAAN

ANTIQUES

Antiekcentrum Amsterdam. Formerly known as "De Looier," Antiekcentrum Amsterdam is a cooperative, housing more than 80 dealers, that is the largest covered art and antiques market in the Netherlands. You may have to browse through a lot of junk, but you wouldn't be the first to end up with a buy on an antique doll, a first-edition book, military memorabilia, or even a jeweled trinket. The place is open on weekdays from 11 to 6, Saturday and Sunday from 11 to 5. ✉ *Elandsgracht 109* ☎ *020/624–9038* ⊕ *www.antiekcentrumamsterdam.nl.*

Bruno de Vries. A large collection of orginal—all still functioning—Art Deco and Jugendstil lamps, as well as items from the 19th-century Amsterdam School, are on display in this unique shop. It's open on Saturdays only. ✉ *Elandsgracht 67* ☎ *06/2027–2947* ⊕ *www. brunodevries.com.*

Anton Heyboer Winkel has a little something for everyone.

Wildschut Antiquiteiten. Once you squeeze past the marvelous wooden wardrobes that fill this store, chances are you'll encounter owner Michael Wildschut at the back, restoring his latest acquisition. A tribute to European craftsmanship, the chests and armoires come mainly from northern France and are made of fine woods such as mahogany. These pieces have been restored with loving care, and can be fit with shelves or drawers as you so desire, and then shipped to your home address. ⊠ *1e Looiersdwarsstraat 8hs* ☎ *06/2187–6724* ⊕ *www.wildschut-antiek.nl.*

BOOKS

Architectura en Natura. Rarely does anyone leave the shop empty-handed—not with its stock of beautiful oversized art and photography books spanning architecture, landscape design, and natural history. ⊠ *Leliegracht 22* ☎ *020/623–6186* ⊕ *www.architectura.nl.*

The English Bookshop. Get served tea in a cozy little shop while the staff recommend reading according to your personal tastes. Secondhand books, Dutch authors translated into English, children's books, and lots of fine literature is at your fingertips. ⊠ *Lauriergracht 71* ☎ *020/626–4230* ⊕ *www.englishbookshop.nl.*

GIFTS

Baobab. Founded in 1967, this shop is like Ali Baba's cave of treasures. You'll find a rich trove of jewelry, buddhas, fabrics, and furniture, both old and newly-made, from Asia, Africa and the Middle East. ⊠ *Elandsgracht 105* ☎ *020/626–8398* ⊕ *www.baobab-aziatica.nl.*

★ **La Savonnerie.** For 10 years, this sweet little shop has been hand-making its own brand of palm oil soap. There are more than 70 different scents, colorfully ranging from Aqua to Winterberry, and, best of all, bars can be custom engraved. ✉ *Prinsengracht 294* ☎ *020/428–1139* ⊕ *www.savonnerie.nl.*

The Otherist. As they put it on their website, "The Otherist offers its own version of a Cabinet of Curiosities." This friendly gift shop has a great collection of contemporary, often cheeky, jewelry, stationery, toys, and housewares. The goods come from around the globe, spanning Denmark to Uruguay. ✉ *Leliegracht 6* ☎ *020/320–0420* ⊕ *www.otherist.com.*

CLOTHING

Cherry Sue. Sexy 1950s-style gear made by Dutch designer Cherry Sue can be found in this cute little Jordaan shop. You can also bring your own piece of fabric and let the owner transform it into a fabulous dress. ✉ *1e Leliedwarsstraat 6, Jordaan* ⊕ *www.cherrysue.com.*

MARKETS

★ **Lapjesmarkt.** Fabric lovers will think they've taken a magic carpet to heaven when they visit the so-called rag market, which takes place on Mondays from 9 to 1, adjacent to Noordermarkt. Down along Westerstraat, you'll find stalls with every possible kind of fabric—beautiful rainbow-colored Asian silks embedded with mirrors and embroidery, batiks from Indonesia, Surinam, and Africa, fabulous faux furs, lace curtains, velvet drapery materials, calicos, and vinyl coverings, all being admired and stroked by eager shoppers. Couturiers rub elbows with housewives, vendors measure out meters, and the crowds keep getting denser. ✉ *Westerstraat, Jordaan.*

Lindenmarkt. On Saturday from 9 to 5 check out the Noordermarkt's less yuppified sister, which winds around Noorderkerk and runs down the length of Lindengracht. All the basics are here, though you'll find exceptionally tasty food stalls. ✉ *Lindengracht, Jordaan.*

★ **Noordermarkt.** The Noordermarkt is probably most cherished by Amsterdammers for its weekly *boerenmarkt,* the organic farmers' market held every Saturday from 9 to 6 around the perimeter of the Noorderkerk. With comestibles such as free-range meats, cruelty-free honey, homemade pestos, and vegan cakes on offer, it's an orgasm for the organic-loving. Just be prepared to open your wallet. On Mondays, from 9 to 1, the Noordermarkt shape-shifts into what is locally known as the *maandagmarkt* (Monday Market). Evocative of the Old World, it's a sprawling affair, mostly of used clothing, books, and toys, but careful collectors can find a range of good stuff, from antique silverware

THE GLOBE-HOPPING BUNNY

Created by Utrecht native Dick Bruna in 1955, Nijntje is to the Netherlands what Mickey Mouse is to the United States. Rarely does a Dutch child today go without at least one Bruna book or toy. The beloved storybook bunny is named after the Dutch word for "little rabbit," *konijntje,* though you may know her by her less diphthongy international handle, Miffy. Experts in cuteness, the Japanese are especially fond of Miffy, as well as her diverse animal friends, whose simple lines and expressionless features have no doubt inspired Hello Kitty.

6

Diamonds are an Amsterdammer's best friend.

and pottery to wartime and advertising memorabilia. ⊠ *Noordermarkt, Jordaan.*

TOYS

A Space Oddity. This little shop combs a big world for robots, toys, and memorabilia from TV and film classics. ⊠ *Prinsengracht 204, The Canal Ring* ☏ *020/427–4036* ⊕ *www.spaceoddity.nl.*

Fodor's Choice ★ **Kleine Eland.** If your toddler back home simply must have a dollhouse version of a four-story gabled canal house, head to this Jordaanese gem. Also available here are kiddie carts in the shape of jumbo jets and fire engines, collectible medieval-style castles, figurines, and unusual wooden rockers in the form of bears, ducks, and motorcycles. Heaven for kiddies! ⊠ *Elandsgracht 58* ☏ *020/620–9001* ⊕ *www.kleineeland.nl.*

LEIDSEPLEIN

COMPUTERS

Apple Store–Amsterdam. Apple never does things by half measures, so when they opened (in March 2012) their Amsterdam flagship store they made sure it was in a suitably grand building—in this case, an early 20th-century building on the Leidseplein that once housed a famed fashion house. One step past the classic European exterior and you blast off into the future: a minimalist, high-tech decor where the wow factor is a shimmering glass staircase. ⊠ *Hirschgebouw, Leidseplein 25, Leidseplein* ☏ *020/530–2200* ⊕ *www.apple.com.*

MUSEUM DISTRICT

BOOKS

Boekhandel Robert Premsela. Tempting window displays allure browsers into this specialty shop for art books. They also have a selection of novels, non-fiction and other genres. ⊠ *Van Baerlestraat 78* ☎ *020/662–4266* ⊕ *www.premsela.nl.*

JEWELRY

Tiffany & Co. Has your *beau* still not popped the question? A quick glance at the gorgeous diamond engagement rings on display here at this world-famed jewelers just might do the trick. ⊠ *P. C. Hooftstraat 86–88* ☎ *020/305–0920* ⊕ *www.tiffany.com.*

PARALLAXE

Whether you're a pro photographer, amateur porn-maker, or just a collector of lenses, this place will fulfill all your filmic needs: Super 8 cameras, Polaroids, projector lamps, ad infinitum. Owner Johan Parallaxe combs flea markets, antique fairs, and estate sales looking to grow his shop and, in the process, feed his own personal obsession. ⊠ *Pieter Langendijkstraat 64, Amsterdam West* ☎ *020/412–2082* ⊕ *www.parallaxe.nl.*

MEN'S CLOTHING

Fodor's Choice ★ **McGregor Menswear.** Originating in New York in 1921, McGregor made a name with casual chic fashion that could best be described as the "Great Gatsby" meets the Kennedys. Since the late 1980s, the international chain has been owned by two Dutchmen who are nicely keeping McGregor's American-born classic casuals alive on the European continent. ⊠ *P. C. Hooftstraat 114* ☎ *020/675–3125* ⊕ *www.mcgregor-fashion.com* ⊠ *P. C. Hooftstraat 113* ☎ *020/662–7425* ⊕ *www.mcgregor-fashion.com.*

★ **Oger.** Gossips say that wives accompany their corporate husbands to this Dutch purveyor of Italian custom-tailored suits so they can ogle the shop clerks (who look like moonlighting male runway models). This store takes "dressed to the nines" to a 10 in its self-proclaimed goal to "Latinize" its clients' sense of style. ⊠ *P. C. Hooftstraat 75–81* ☎ *020/676–8695* ⊕ *www.oger.nl.*

The Society Shop. This mainstay of the Museum District is noted for all the clothing classics that businessmen and politicians aspire to. ⊠ *Van Baerlestraat 20* ☎ *020/664–9281* ⊕ *www.thesocietyshop.com.*

MUSIC STORES

Broekmans & Van Poppel. Apropos of the neighboring Concertgebouw, this store specializes in recordings, sheet music, and accessories for classical and antiquarian music. ⊠ *Van Baerlestraat 92–94* ☎ *020/675–1653* ⊕ *www.broekmans.com.*

SHOES

Shoebaloo. One might mistake the interior of this store for that of a spaceship. Some of the shoe styles are just as wild (the Day-Glo tiger-striped stilettos, for example), though many are simply high-end leather heels for vampy fashionistas. ⊠ *P. C. Hooftstraat 80* ☎ *020/671–2210* ⊠ *Leidsestraat 8, Leidseplein* ☎ *020/330–9147* ⊠ *Koningsplein 7, The*

6

Canal Ring ☎ 020/626–7993 ✉ Cornelis Schuytstraat 9, Amsterdam
South ☎ 020/662–5779 ⊕ www.shoebaloo.nl.

WOMEN'S CLOTHING

Pauw. Madeleine Pauw's elegant pieces are particularly suited for the
sophisticated (and perhaps equestrian-inspired) type of woman, be she
a professional or society dame. ✉ Van Baerlestraat 72 ☎ 020/671–7322
✉ Leidsestraat 16, Centrum ☎ 020/626–5698 ✉ Beethovenstraat 68,
Museum District and Environs ☎ 020/679–0331 ⊕ www.pauw.com.

THE CANAL RING

ANTIQUES

Fodor'sChoice
★
Anouk Beerents. The Hall of Mirrors at the Palace of Versailles may
be evoked should you have the opportunity to visit the dazzling, skylighted quarters of this Jordaan atelier-cum-store. For 20 years, the
ever-gracious Anouk Beerents has been buying 18th- and 19th-century
antique mirrors from France and Italy, and then restoring them for local
and international clients (including, for example, Ralph Lauren shops
in the United States). Replete with ornate gold- or silver-gilded frames,
some 400 museum-quality mirrors (some actually from the Palace of
Versailles) hang upon the walls of this space, which is so large that customers are invited to park their cars inside. Visits are by appointment
only and shipping can be arranged to other countries. ✉ Prinsengracht
467 ☎ 020/622–8598 ⊕ www.anoukbeerents.nl.

Jan Beekhuizen Kunst en Antiekhandel. For antique European pewter from the 15th through the 19th centuries, Jan Beekhuizen is *the*
authority. His store also carries antique furniture, Delftware, metal-
ware, and other collectible trea-
sures. ✉ Nieuwe Spiegelstraat 49,
Spiegelkwartier ☎ 020/626–3912
⊕ www.janbeekhuizen.nl.

★ **Prinsheerlijk Antiek.** Spanning 1,800
square feet, this emporium sells a
princely assortment of furniture,
bric-a-brac, and chandeliers dating
from the early 18th century, as well
as unique clock cases, and Dutch
handpainted folk pieces (some even
come from royal palaces and warehouses). The shop also includes
a renowned work studio, where
antique furniture is upholstered
and refurbished. Check the website
for new arrivals. ✉ Prinsengracht
579 ☎ 020/638–6623 ⊕ www.
prinsheerlijkantiek.nl.

Fodor'sChoice
★
Spiegelkwartier. A William-and-
Mary-era harpsichord? One of the
printed maps that figured prominently in Vermeer's *Lutenist*? An

A TWOFER THAT TURNS HEADS

**Poppendokter Kramer/Pontifex
kaarsen.** On the off chance you're
looking for a potion that will promote inner peace and harmony,
and you also happen to have
an antique porcelain doll that
needs a tune-up, you have only
one place to go. On one side of
this Nine Streets shop, you'll find
candles, incense, and nearly 200
types of ethereal and spiritual oils.
On the other side, shopkeeper
Kramer carries on a 40-year-
old tradition of doll repair and
recapitation (there are shelves of
bodyless heads to choose from).
✉ Reestraat 18–20, The Canal
Ring ☎ 020/626–5274.

CLOSE UP

Cutting-Edge Dutch Design

Ever since Gerrit Rietveld produced his "Red and Blue Chair," the Dutch have been in the international limelight, famous for graphic design, fashion (clothing, jewelry, accessories), industrial design, interior design, furniture design, advertising, and architecture. Rietveld has been followed by the likes of Bruno Ninaber van Eyben (inventor of the pendant watch and the Dutch euro), Trude Hooykaas (architect), Viktor & Rolf (fashion), Jan Jansen (shoes), Ted Noten (jewelry), KesselsKramer (advertising), and Marcel Wanders (industrial designer best known for his Knitted Chair). These and other equally acclaimed designers have works displayed in commercial galleries and modern art museums alike. Since 45,000 Dutch designers produce more than 2.5 billion euros' worth of new stuff per year, you'd think somebody could tell you exactly what "Dutch Design" is. But it's too diverse to pin down, and ranges from modern, conceptual, kitsch, functional, sober, innovative, ironic, experimental, intelligent, and alternative to everything in between. A steady stream of

Marcel Wanders' famous egg vase

new talent, graduating from one of the numerous national institutes dedicated to design, make Dutch Design a perennially hot topic that takes center stage no matter what time of year you visit. The Utrecht School for the Arts (HKU), Design Academy Eindhoven (dubbed the "School of Cool" by *Time* magazine), the Industrial Design department at TU Delft, and the Rietveld Academy in Amsterdam are talent pools feeding into the trend mecca that the Netherlands has become.

The Frozen Fountain. For the very best in Dutch design, head to the Frozen Fountain, which pools the Benelux's most edgy of designers in home goods, furniture, and jewelry. ⇨ *See Shopping for more design stores.* ✉ *Prinsengracht 645, The Canal Ring* ☎ *020/622–9375* ⊕ *www. frozenfountain.nl.*

A Droog table and chair, produced and designed by Richard Hutton

18th-century bed-curtain tie-up? Or a pewter nautilus cup redolent of a Golden Age still life? All these and more may be available in Amsterdam's famous array of antiques stores in the city's "Mirror Quarter," centered around Nieuwe Spiegelstraat and its continuation, Spiegelgracht. If perusing fine art is more your scene, the Quarter also houses around 20 contemporary art galleries and 10 tribal and oriental art specialists. But—with five double-sided blocks' worth of shops and galleries, from the Golden Bend of the Herengracht nearly to the Rijksmuseum—this section of town often requires a royal House of Orange budget. ✉ *Nieuwe Spiegelstraat.*

ART

Kunsthandel M.L. De Boer. Founded in 1945, this gallery is renowned for showing contemporary figurative and abstract works by Dutch, French, and Belgian artists, as well as by Dutch and French masters from the 19th century and early 20th century. ✉ *Keizersgracht 542* ☎ *020/623–4060* ⊕ *www.kunsthandeldeboer.com.*

Peter Donkersloot Galerie. This is a top stop for contemporary art—mostly modern figurative painting done with a lush brush (as if Rembrandt were painting now)—along the Spiegelkwartier. There is also a venue at Herengracht 435. ✉ *Spiegelgracht 14–16* ☎ *020/623–6538* ⊕ *www.peterdonkerslootgalerie.nl.*

BOOKS

★ **Selexyz Scheltema.** With five floors of books on every imaginable subject, plus an international spread of newspapers and magazines, and a Bagels & Beans café on the first floor, this is one of Amsterdam's busiest and best-stocked international bookstores. It'll come close to satisfying Americans jonesing for a Barnes & Noble. ✉ *Koningsplein 20* ☎ *020/523–1411* ⊕ *www.selexyz.nl.*

CERAMICS AND GLASS

Breekbaar. Here you'll find a top-brand selection of zany glassware and unique china, including a splendid menagerie of Ritzenhoff stems and saucers. The owner is a jovial, cigar-smoking gent who seems to have sprung from the pages of Lewis Carroll. ✉ *Weteringschans 209* ☎ *020/626–1260* ⊕ *www.breekbaar.com.*

CHILDREN

Fodor'sChoice
★ **Anton Heyboer Winkel.** Art dealer Couzijn Simon sells work by Dutch painter Anton Heyboer, hence the name. But besides Heyboer's works the shop is crammed with an assortment of wonders—an 18th-century

---

THE TUMBLE MAN

Duikelman Kookboeken & Porselein. Duikelman is named in honor of the original "Tumble Man." In the 1940s, Joop van Hal, grandfather to David Appelboom, the business's current owner, had invented a flashlight that automatically shut off when flipped over in a downward tumbling—"*duikelen*"—motion. This timely device was a crucial invention, helping to keep the Dutch army strategically obscured from enemy sight. It also began the Appelboom family's tradition of selling simple yet well-designed tools, now in more tranquil times. ✉ *Gerard Doustraat 54, De Pijp and Environs* ⊕ *www.duikelman.nl.*

rocking horse, a 4-foot-long wooden ice skate sign, antique trains, collector teddy bears, and porcelain dolls bedecked for a costume ball—that might catch the eye of a doting millionaire grandfather. ✉ *Prinsengracht 578* ☎ *020/624–7691* ⊕ *www.antonheyboerwinkel.nl.*

CHOCOLATE

★ **Chocolaterie Pompadour.** In 2013 this beloved chocolaterie/patisserie celebrates its 50th anniversary. The civilized still sit here for afternoon tea and tart. The front of the store attends to a steady stream of chocoholics—no less cultivated, just on the go. The Florentines are an éclat in their own right. ✉ *Huidenstraat 12, Negen Straatjes* ☎ *020/623–9554* ✉ *Kerkstraat 148, Spiegelkwartier* ☎ *020/330–0981* ⊕ *www.patisseriepompadour.com.*

De Kaaskamer. This store stinks—of a smell testifying to its terrific selection of high-quality cheeses. In addition to the usual Dutch suspects (Edam, Gouda, Old Amsterdam, and the smoked curds), this family business also sells rare choices from farms in France, Greece, Italy, England, and Switzerland. ✉ *Runstraat 7, Negen Straatjes* ☎ *020/623–3483* ⊕ *www.kaaskamer.nl.*

FOOD

★ **Patisserie Holtkamp.** From Sachertorte to sabayon, Holtkamp has mastered all the European pastry classics. However, this 120-year-old local business is just as beloved for savory Dutch specialties like the stuffed *kroket* crispy roll. Their 33,000-piece weekly production of the deep-fried ragout roll has made them famous. Beware Saturday morning lines out the door. ✉ *Vijzelgracht 15* ☎ *020/624–8757* ⊕ *www.patisserieholtkamp.nl.*

GIFTS

Fodors Choice ★ **Brilmuseum.** A must-visit when you're strolling the Nine Streets, this boutique displays a collection of eyeglasses from antique to contemporary in a setting that evokes the atmosphere of the 17th century (the upstairs galleries actually have museum status). It's open only Wednesday through Saturday. ✉ *Gasthuismolensteeg 7, Negen Straatjes* ☎ *020/421–2414* ⊕ *www.brilmuseumamsterdam.nl.*

Cortina Papier. Poet or paper-pusher, you'll find a luscious array of notebooks, albums, stationery, gift wrap, and 26 colors of writing ink here. And if even for five minutes, you'll forget all about the invention of the computer. ✉ *Reestraat 22, Negen Straatjes* ☎ *020/623–6676* ⊕ *www.cortinapapier.nl.*

CO-OPTING THE CLOG

So you love your Crocs. But you may well forget about those riddled pieces of galactic resin once you try on a pair of *klompen*. Though you'll find a fantastic selection of stylish modern offshoots, the classic wooden Dutch clog is still used by some farmers and fishermen. Traditionally worn over a thick pair of *geitenwollen sokken* (socks made from goat's wool), *klompen* help keep toes warm while providing durable soles to stomp through wet and muddy surfaces. Some creative residents have co-opted the clog, using it as a wall-mounted flowerpot on their terraces.

6

A wedge of gourmet cheese, bread, and fruit make a satisfying lunch.

HOUSEHOLD ITEMS

★ **The Frozen Fountain.** This gallery-cum-store carries contemporary furniture and innovative home accessories from such top Dutch designers as Hutten and Wanders en Jongerius as well as by such international names as Arad, Newson, and Starck. You can find custom-made scrapwood cabinets by Piet Hein Eek, as well as artistic perfume dispensers, jewelry, and carpets. The look? Minimalism juxtaposed with paper-cut chandeliers and rococo seats. ⊠ *Prinsengracht 645* ☎ *020/622–9375* ⊕ *www.frozenfountain.nl.*

MARKETS

Fodor's Choice
★ **Bloemenmarkt.** Hands down, this is one of Amsterdam's must-see shopping delights. Along the Singel canal, between Koningsplein and Muntplein, the renowned Flower Market is where blooming wonders are purveyed from permanently moored barges. Besides bouquets of freshly cut flowers, you'll find plants, small trees, bulbs, seeds, and a colorful array of souvenir trinkets. The market is open Monday–Saturday 9:30–5:30, Sunday 11–5:30. ⊠ *Koningsplein, Centrum.*

MEN'S CLOTHING

Jojo Outfitters. Discounted luxury one-offs from Italy and France are sold at this haberdasher frequented by old-world gents and dandified hipsters. The collection of hats, suits, and shoes is not the only impressive thing here: also worth a visit is the shop's nostalgic interior, delightfully adorned with vintage furniture, bibelots, and dolls. ⊠ *Huidenstraat 23* ☎ *020/623–3476* ⊕ *www.de9straatjes.nl.*

MUSIC STORES

★ **Concerto.** With a staff channeling vintage issues of *High Fidelity* as well as recent *Opera Now*s, this bilevel, multidoored music mecca is stocked with new and used records and CDs covering all imaginable genres—and it is open seven days a week. ⊠ *Utrechtsestraat 52–60* ☎ *020/623–5228* ⊕ *www.platomania.nl.*

SHOES

Hester van Eeghen. Since 2000, cool, contemporary Dutch design has been available for ladies' feet—that is, after being manufactured from fine leather in Italy. And if you like Van Eeghen's shoes, walk west to her eponymous handbag boutique at Hartenstraat 37. Geometry never before seemed so colorful or portable. ⊠ *Hartenstraat 1* ☎ *020/626–9211* ⊕ *www.hestervaneeghen.com.*

Onitsuka Tiger. With just a few flagships stores scattered throughout the world, Amsterdam provides some uppity canal-side real estate for this trendy Japanese line of Asics sneakers. There seems to be a style for every breed of tulip. ⊠ *Herengracht 365* ☎ *020/528–6183* ⊕ *www.onitsukatiger.nl.*

VINTAGE

Episode. It's Grandma's attic meets the Salvation Army at this stylists' playground that originally opened on Waterlooplein and now has branches in Antwerp, London, and Paris. ⊠ *Berenstraat 1, Negen Straatjes* ☎ *020/626–4679* ⊠ *Waterlooplein 1, The Old City Center (Het Centrum)* ☎ *020/320–3000* ⊕ *www.episode.eu.*

Fodor'sChoice **I Love Vintage.** In 2010 this online store got its hands on some vintage ★ digs: a canal-side building replete with sewing atelier, lounge, and photo studio. Most items are, in fact, newly-made, yet in vintage style. You can even shop here—wow!—by decade: just pick a dress from the '20s, '30s, '40s, '50s or '60s. ⊠ *Prinsengracht 201* ☎ *020/330–1950* ⊕ *www.ilovevintage.nl.*

Fodor'sChoice **Zipper.** Their website says it best: "You can style-surf through time, ★ from posh to punk . . . re-freshing . . . re-designing . . . re-cycling . . . re-inventing . . . re-creating . . . re-producing . . . one-of-a-kind clothing." Obviously, a place for vintage fashion hounds. The '80s are highly regarded here, though amid Wrangler corduroys and trucker hats, you'll find plenty more quality fashion pieces from decades past. ⊠ *Huidenstraat 7, Negen Straatjes* ☎ *020/623–7302* ⊠ *Nieuwe Hoogstraat 8, Negen Straatjes* ☎ *020/627–0353* ⊕ *www.zipperstore.nl.*

WOMEN'S CLOTHING

Cora Kemperman. This Dutch minichain appeals to a set of self-labeled modern women with a penchant for architectural cuts and monochrome colors. Think a futuristic Eileen Fisher. ⊠ *Leidsestraat 72, Centrum* ☎ *020/625–1284* ⊕ *www.corakemperman.nl.*

Fodor'sChoice **Rika.** Swedish stylist-turned-designer Ulrika Lundgren's boutique may ★ be smaller than your walk-in closet but her designs are shipped all over the world, reaching the likes of Kate Moss (who's been spotted carrying one of her famous tote bags). Her style—ideal for posturing to look like a rock star trying not to look like a rock star—is so popular Ulrika recently opened the Maison Rika guesthouse—very hip, of

No child can resist Christmas time on the Kalverstraat.

course—at Spiegelgracht 12. ⊠ *Oude Spiegelstraat 9* ☎ *020/330–1112* ⊕ *www.rikaint.com.*

★ **Van Ravenstein.** This chic boutique carries top Belgian labels such as Walter van Beirendonck, Martin Margiela, Dries van Noten, and Ann Demeulemeester, many now rated among the most fashion-forward designers in the world. On Saturdays they open the bargain basement and the deals are outrageously well priced. ⊠ *Keizersgracht 359* ☎ *020/639–0067* ⊕ *www.van-ravenstein.nl.*

Young Designers United. Since 2003, this collective has been giving 10 locally schooled, up-and-coming designers a rack to call their own (for half-year stints at a time, anyway). These couturiers produce new women's wear and accessories on a weekly basis. Working toward establishing a label or shop of their own, many take cues from customer feedback—meaning you could have a hand in shaping the next big trend. ⊠ *Keizersgracht 447, The Canal Ring* ☎ *020/626–9191* ⊕ *www. ydu.nl.*

THE OLD CITY CENTER (HET CENTRUM)

ANTIQUES

Antiquariaat Kok. This antiquarian's heaven has, for the last 60 years, offered readers oodles of treasures on Amsterdam history. It also takes pride in housing the city's largest secondhand Dutch-language book collection and a fair share of other literature nicely shelved according to subject. ⊠ *Oude Hoogstraat 14–18* ☎ *020/623–1191* ⊕ *www.nvva. nl/kok.*

ANTIQUES

★ **Salomon Stodel.** When hunting for a piece of Royal Dutch Delftware, a Meissen candelabra, or some Italian Renaissance majolica, museum curators and collectors often do their shopping here at this nearly 150-year-old antiques landmark. ⊠ *Rokin 70* ☎ *020/623–1692* ⊕ *www. salomonstodel.com.*

BOOKS

★ **ABC Treehouse.** For the past decade, the American Book Center has been hosting bookshop-related events and exhibitions in this venue, just across from their new headquarters on the Spui. The Treehouse has also built a solid reputation for all kinds of Anglophonic activities, such as English-language readings, open-mike nights, and its annual Thanksgiving potluck dinner. ⊠ *Voetboogstraat 11* ☎ *020/423–0967* ⊕ *www.treehouse.abc.nl.*

★ **American Book Center.** What began in the early '70s as an erotic magazine outlet has grown into reputedly the largest English-language book emporium on the continent. True to its name, the stock is strongly oriented toward American tastes and expectations, with its vast selection spread over seven stories. (Students, senior citizens, and teachers receive a 10% discount.) ⊠ *Spui 12* ☎ *020/625–5537* ⊕ *www.abc.nl.*

Athenaeum Boekhandel. Since the late '60s, this mainstay on the Spui has been one of the Netherlands's largest independent bookshops. Celebrity authors sometimes pop in, and scholars and university students often rely on the stock for academic literature. ⊠ *Spui 14–16* ☎ *020/514–1460* ⊕ *www.athenaeum.nl.*

★ **Athenaeum Nieuwscentrum.** For the city's best selection of international periodicals and newspapers, as well as a smattering of cool local zines, follow your way to the unmissable red-and-white awning on the Spui. ⊠ *Spui 14–16* ☎ *020/514–1470* ⊕ *www.athenaeum.nl.*

Boekenmarkt. The city has a number of book markets, though its most famous takes place every Friday on Spui Square, from 10 to 6. Under the little white tents, it's an antiquarian and used book–browsing paradise. ⊠ *Spui, Centrum.*

Book Exchange. Redolent of a bygone era in a rural New England town, this browse-worthy shop sells used English-language books on all subjects and many a secondhand paperback. ⊠ *Kloveniersburgwal 58* ☎ *020/626–6266* ⊕ *www.bookexchange.nl.*

★ **De Slegte.** Possibly the largest bookstore in Amsterdam, this is a true haven for book hunters. Every floor stocks tomes in various languages, across all genres, and covering many subjects. The shop is known for its large nonfiction collection of popular titles at bargain prices, and upstairs floors have a humongous antiquarian book section. ⊠ *Kalverstraat 48–52* ☎ *020/622–5933* ⊕ *www.deslegte.com.*

Evenaar Literaire Reisboekhandel. Armchair travelers and ground-stomping wayfarers visit this store for publications on travel, anthropology, and literary essays. What you need to know about foreign cultures you'll discover here. ⊠ *Singel 348, The Canal Ring* ☎ *020/624–6289* ⊕ *www. evenaar.net.*

6

Oudemanhuis Book Market. This tiny, venerable, covered book market is snuggled in the heart of the University of Amsterdam's meandering edifices. Booksellers in this alleyway have been hawking used and antiquarian books, prints, and sheet music for more than a century. ✉ *Oudemanhuispoort 4.*

CHOCOLATE

Puccini Bomboni. Seemingly dreamed up by Roald Dahl, this chocolatier sells knockout bonbons: one is quite enough to satiate the most gluttonous among us. Only natural ingredients are used, some being rather unusual, such as prune, pepper, and tamarind. ✉ *Singel 184, The Canal Ring* ☎ *020/427–8341* ✉ *Staalstraat 17* ☎ *020/626–5474* ⊕ *www.puccinibomboni.com.*

CLOTHING

Concrete. Along with esoteric urban labels and vintage Levi's and Nikes, you'll find a stock of high-tops, hoodies, and plastic Japanese toys in this fun and trendy store. ✉ *Spuistraat 250, Centrum* ☎ *020/625–2225* ⊕ *www.concrete.nl.*

Vezjun. A group of young fashion designers started this charming little boutique in 2004, and each item of clothing is unique and handmade. Among the bags and sweaters, you'll find "Rat" (head) T-shirts, Buddha armbands, and dramtically simple black-on-white blouses. This is "young Amsterdam" at its liveliest. ✉ *Rozengracht 110, Centrum* ⊕ *www.vezjun.nl.*

DEPARTMENT STORES

De Bijenkorf. Akin to, say, Macy's is "The Beehive," the nation's best-known department store and the swarming ground of its moneyed middle classes. Top international designer lines of clothing, shoes, and cosmetics are well stocked, along with a decent repertoire of furniture, appliances, and one of the best stationery selections in town. The in-house eateries are upscale with a ground-floor café corner that successfully channels a retail refueling post à la Paris. ✉ *Dam 1* ☎ *020/800–0818* ⊕ *www.bijenkorf.nl.*

★ **Maison de Bonneterie.** With its over-a-century-old skylighted cupola, chandeliers, and majestic staircases, this is Amsterdam's loving homage to the *grand magasin* department store. The prices aren't always right, but the ambience is appreciated by many types of shoppers, from fashion plates in need of a last-minute designer frock to proper ladies who dutifully match handbag with shoes. ✉ *Rokin 140–142* ☎ *020/531–3400* ⊕ *www.debonneterie.nl.*

Vroom & Dreesmann. If Dutch department store behemoth De Bijenkorf is Macy's, V & D, as it's called, is a much smaller version of New York's landmark. From ties to towels, the selections are more than decent, though none will make much of an impression nor, when it comes to your wallet, a depression. That noted, in recent years the women's clothes have become quite trendy. Check out the children's section as well as in-house eatery La Place, whose bakery practically spills into the department store, scenting the accessories department with a dash of sugar. ✉ *Kalverstraat 203* ☎ *0900/235–8363* ⊕ *www.vd.nl.*

FOOD

Fodor's Choice ★ **Geels & Co.** Still run by the family Geels, this Warmoesstraat store has been selling tea, coffee, and brewing utensils since 1866. It's a great place to find gifts like replica antique spice necklaces and traditional Dutch candy (not easy to find elsewhere). ⊠ *Warmoesstraat 155* ☎ *020/624–0683* ⊕ *www.geels.nl.*

★ **Jacob Hooy & Co.** Filled with teakwood canisters and jars bearing Latin inscriptions, fragrant with the perfume of seeds, flowers, and medicinal potions, this health-and-wellness store has been in operation on Nieuwmarkt since 1743. Gold-lettered wooden drawers, barrels, and bins contain not just spices and herbs, but also a daunting array of *dropjes* (hard candies and medicinal drops) and teas. ⊠ *Kloveniersburgwal 12* ☎ *020/624–3041* ⊕ *www.jacob-hooy.nl.*

GIFTS

De Condomerie. A discreet, well-informed staff promote healthful sexual practices at this condom emporium (with an equally handy online store). It's also strategically located on one of the city's boulevards for gay nightlife. ⊠ *Warmoesstraat 141* ☎ *020/627–4174* ⊕ *www.condomerie.com.*

De Klompenboer/Knuffels. Located in a former metro station, Knuffels is the upstairs venue that sells toys, including a fun-loving selection of *knuffels* (the word for hugs and, by extension, cuddle toys). Downstairs is the *klompen* shop, where you can order wooden shoes in all sizes and colors, as well as request handpainted or wood-burned designs. ⊠ *Sint Antoniesbreestraat 39–51* ☎ *020/427–3862* ⊕ *www.woodenshoefactory.com.*

Fodor's Choice ★ **Sukha.** If you're looking for that special something that really says "Modern Dutch," head here. A combined love for for fashion, furniture, books, and travel resulted in this stylish and diverse shop, which offers everything from casual shifts to modernistic stuffed animals to Balinese "jewel-rock" bracelets. Father and daughter Mertens run it, together with a bunch of other family members and friends, providing a Woodstock-y vibe (hey, sign up for one of the workshops). ⊠ *Haarlemmerstraat 110, Centrum* ☎ *020/330–4001* ⊕ *www.sukha-amsterdam.nl.*

HATS

★ **De Hoed van Tijn.** You're forgiven for thinking you've time traveled into the Roaring '20s when entering this hat shop. Dutch royalty among their clientele, De Hoed van Tijn is most sought out for its Flapper-style cloches and bespoke hairpieces. ⊠ *Nieuwe Hoogstraat 15* ☎ *020/623–2759* ⊕ *www.dehoedvantijn.nl.*

The English Hatter. In 1935 this shop started out to provide the Dutch with English hats and caps. In later years they added pullovers, tweed jackets, deerstalkers, and many other trappings of the English gentleman to their business. The cozy shop is small, but the inventory is large, and they still sell hats, too. ⊠ *Heiligeweg 40* ☎ *020/623–4781* ⊕ *www.english-hatter.nl.*

HOUSEHOLD ITEMS

Fodor's Choice ★ **Droog.** Besides exhibiting highlights of its collection, this design collective also sells a number of its edgy, often industrial, furniture and home accessories. What began as a decidedly Dutch group now comprises designers from all over the globe, who have together cultivated an international reputation for groundbreaking interior design. ⊠ *Staalstraat 7B* ☎ *020/523–5059* ⊕ *www.droog.com.*

> **DIAMOND DRILL**
>
> Even if you're not in the market for new rocks, a visit to a diamond factory is worth one of its free, guided tours. You'll learn all about the industry's "four Cs"—carat, color, clarity, and cut—and get to watch workers plying their trade. There's also a replica of the factory's most famous cut—the Koh-I-Noor diamond, one of the prize gems of the British crown jewels.

HEMA. Even the Dutch equivalent of Sears has high-style household items at reasonable prices (along with some low-style traditional goodies that every Dutchman cherishes, such as its smoked sausages and pink-cream custard cakes), along with a cool minimalist shop design, to boot. ⊠ *Nieuwendijk 174–176* ☎ *020/623–4176* ⊕ *www.hema.nl.*

Fodor's Choice ★ **Options!.** Located on the Damrak, this fantastic store is filled with cool, cute, and convenient designer objects, all with a Dutch touch—just the place when you don't want to return home empty-handed but don't particularly want to load up on kitschy wooden shoes. They have something for every budget, from bike bells and placemats to precious tulip vases. For fancy, how about a Heath Nash "art from rubbish" lamp made from pink and orange plastic detergent bottles? Or, for cheap, a "Relax Mama" nail polish. Truly delightful, quirky, and designed for those who appreciate a tongue-in-chic wink, this is a must-do. Payment with plastic only. ⊠ *Damrak 49, The Old City Center (Het Centrum)* ☎ *020/620–1400* ⊕ *www.optionsamsterdam.com.*

JEWELRY

★ **Bonebakker.** In business since 1792, this is one of the city's oldest and finest jewelers. Founder Adrian Bonebakker was commissioned by King Willem II to design and make the royal crown for the House of Orange. Today you'll find watches by Piaget, Corum, Chaumet, Cartier, and Jaeger-LeCoultre, and beautiful silver and gold tableware. ⊠ *Conservatorium Hotel, Van Baerlestraat 27, Museum District* ☎ *020/673–7577.*

Gassan Dam Square. One of the world's largest processors of diamonds, Gassan is now mostly known for tours through its humongous factory (inquire here; the factory is located elsewhere). A family business since 1945, Gassan has perhaps rightly claimed a perch on people-packed Dam Square, but this is hardly the most alluring surrounds to purchase your precious bauble. Besides diamonds, one can shop for other jewelry, watches, and silver gifts. ⊠ *Rokin 1–5* ☎ *020/624–5787* ⊕ *www. gassan.com.*

Grimm Sieraden. Small but savvy, this boutique is known for unearthing the latest in jewelry by young Dutch designers. Pieces here are mostly in silver but also use such unusual materials such as rubber, wood, and fabrics. ⊠ *Grimburgwal 9* ☎ *020/622–0501* ⊕ *www.grimmsieraden.nl.*

Hans Appenzeller. Situated on a tiny street near the university is one of the international leaders in contemporary jewelry design. ⊠ *Grimburgwal 1* ☎ *020/626–8218* ⊕ *www.appenzeller.nl.*

Premsela & Hamburger. Fine antique silver and jewelry have been purveyed here since 1823. ⊠ *Rokin 98* ☎ *020/627–5454* ⊕ *www.premsela. com.*

MARKETS

Nieuwmarkt. At the northern end of Kloverniersburgwal, the square known as Nieuwmarkt hosts a small-scale *boerenmarkt,* or farmers' market, on Monday through Saturday from 9 to 5. You'll find essential oils, fresh soaps, and other New Age needs alongside flowers, cheese, organic breads, and fresh-pressed juices. On Sundays from 9 to 5, delightful curiosa, art, and books appear when the *antiekmarkt* (antique market) throws the shrouds off its stalls. ⊠ *Nieuwmarkt, Nieuwmarkt.*

Postzegelmarkt. Philatelists, dust off your tweezers. During good weather, you'll find the city's stamp market set up near the Spui along Nieuwezijds Voorburgwal, held on Wednesdays and Saturdays from 1 to 4. And there are some coins for you numismatists, too. ⊠ *Nieuwezijds Voorburgwal, in front of Number 280, The Old City Center (Het Centrum).*

Waterlooplein. This lopen-air market is a descendant of the haphazard pushcart trade that gave this part of the city its distinct lively character in the early part of the 20th century. It's amusing to see the old telephones, typewriters, and other arcana all haphazardly displayed—as well as the shoppers scrambling and vying with each other to reacquire such items. Professional dealers sell secondhand and vintage clothing, hats, and purses. New fashions are mostly for generic alterna-types who will enjoy a wide selection of slogan T-shirts, hippie bags, and jewelry for every type of piercing. The flea market is open Monday–Saturday 9–6. ⊠ *Waterlooplein, East of Amstel.*

SHOES

Fodor's Choice ★ **Fred de La Bretoniere.** This is *the* shop to find a classic style that still lets you walk with your own unique verve. Fred de la Bretonire has been selling men's and women's leather footwear since 1970, and it's no surprise that his shoes have been entered into the permanent collections of several Dutch design museums. ⊠ *Sint Luciënsteeg 20* ☎ *020/623–4152* ⊠ *Utrechtsestraat 77, The Canal Ring* ☎ *020/626–9627* ⊠ *Van Baerlestraat 34, Amsterdam South* ☎ *020/470–9320* ⊕ *www.bretoniere.nl.*

Fodor's Choice ★ **Jan Jansen.** Forget fairy godmothers: this is where today's urban Cinderella finds her glass slippers. Since the '60s, the Nijmegen-born artist and craftsman Jan Jansen has made footwear beloved for its conceptual design, outrageous color, and uncompromised wearability. ⊠ *Rokin 42* ☎ *020/810–0523* ⊕ *www.janjansen.com.*

Betsy Palmer. Tucked away on a quiet part of the Rokin, this is a shoe store to scream about. Betsy Palmer offers a colorful selection of high-heeled shoes that are elegant *and* walkable. The friendly, non-obtrusive staff is another reason to come back here. ⊠ *Rokin 9-15, The Old City Center (Het Centrum)* ☎ *020/422–1040* ⊕ *www.betsypalmer.com.*

TOYS

Gone with the Wind. Specializing in mobiles from around the world, this mecca of mirth also sells unusual handcrafted wooden flowers and toys and spring-operated jumping toys. ☒ *Vijzelstraat 22* ☎ *020/423–0230* ⊕ *www.gonewiththewind.nl.*

VINTAGE

Joosje. A mix of funky vintage clothing and cheerful young designers' wear, all neatly arranged by color, make this shop a must for fashionistas. The smiling, helpful staff, along with Elvis singing in the background, certainly makes you want to come back here to shop again. Other similarly stocked stores that belong to this mini-chain are Marbles at Nieuwe Hoogstraat 12 and Rumors at Haarlemmerstraat 99A. ☒ *Spuistraat 62, Centrum* ☎ *No phone.*

WOMEN'S CLOTHING

★ **Jutka & Riska.** An interesting mix of vintage, new design, and customized goodies are on display at this quirky store, one of the first places to shop if you're interested in seeing the latest looks from this year's Antwerp and Amsterdam's Fashion Weeks, often kitted out with biker jackets, skull rings, crosses, and peace signs. There is also a Jutka & Riska at Bilderdijkstraat 194. ☒ *Haarlemmerdijk 143, Centrum* ☎ *062/466–8593* ☒ *Bilderdijkstraat 194, Amsterdam West* ☎ *020/618–8021* ⊕ *www. jutkaenriska.nl.*

DE PIJP

MARKETS

★ **Albert Cuypmarkt.** This century-old market, found on Albert Cuypstraat between Ferdinand Bolstraat and Van Woustraat, is the heart of The Pijp. It's open Monday through Saturday from 9–5, rain or shine, and you're likely to hear the vendors barking out their bargain deals over the pleasant sound track of a street musician. Interspersed among the crowds, stalls sell food, clothing, fabrics, plants, and household goods from all over the world. Just about every ethnic culture is represented here by purveyors, their goods, and their buyers. Be sure to try some of the exotic nibbles, or just order the Dutchman's favorite fast food— *patat,* piping-hot French fries served with mayonnaise, ketchup, curry sauce, or peanut satay dip. ☒ *Albert Cuypstraat, De Pijp and Environs* ⊕ *www.albertcuypmarkt.com.*

SPORTING GOODS

★ **Skatezone.** The dike-plugging Dutch boy Hans Brinker would have loved this modern skating outlet, which stocks well over 150 models of ice skates in all styles: from those made for wintertime canal gliding to hockey skates. The shop carries top brands such as Viking, Raps, Bauer, CCM, Zandstra, Graf, with a large variety of *noren,* the most popular style of speed skates for adults, as well as traditional Dutch wooden training skates for children (the double blades make for easier balance). Skatezone is also the place to rent in-line skates manufactured by all the bigwigs in extreme sports, including Rollerblade, K2, and Powerslide. ☒ *Ceintuurbaan 59* ☎ *020/662–2822* ⊕ *www.skatezone.nl.*

Day Trips from Amsterdam

WORD OF MOUTH

"Keukenhof in bloom is sheer magic! Don't miss it! The countryside around it is endless tulip bulb fields, flat as a pancake, and beautiful when in bloom."

—USNR

Updated by Floris Dogterom

The Netherlands is such a manageably small country that there's practically no excuse not to explore a little farther afield. And the payoff is immense, for just a short excursion can bring you to the Holland of your dreams: castles, harbor resorts, folkloric villages framed in lace, "the cleanest town in all the Netherlands," and, of course, the postcard-perfect tulip fields of the Keukenhof. Thanks to Amsterdam's great transport connections, many of these day trips are very accessible.

Indeed, most are under an hour away. Whether you are driving or cycling, the routes are well maintained and clearly signposted. Trains and regional buses are frequent and punctual, with a range of passes for discount travel. Pick up the Amsterdam Metropolitan Map at the VVV tourist office, with concise information on these delightful day trips, along with extra tips on getting around using public transport.

GUIDED TOURS

Entrepreneurs in the Netherlands offer a smorgasbord of excursions for individuals and groups.

Bus tours of the Holland-in-a-hurry variety, whether half- or full-day excursions, can be booked directly with the operator or via:

Joy Ride Bike Tours. This outfittter has an enthusiastic approach to private trips covering "anywhere you can ride a bike to from Amsterdam." Suggestions include longer (but leisurely) visits to villages such as Durgerdam and Ouderkerk aan de Amstel, with a swimming stop, and the possibility of tulips (or whatever is in bloom) in the spring. ☎ 06/4361–1798 ⊕ www.joyridetours.nl.

MacBike. Known as "the red ones," MacBike offers both guided and self-guided tours for architectural and historical interests. ☎ 020/624–8391 ⊕ www.macbike.nl.

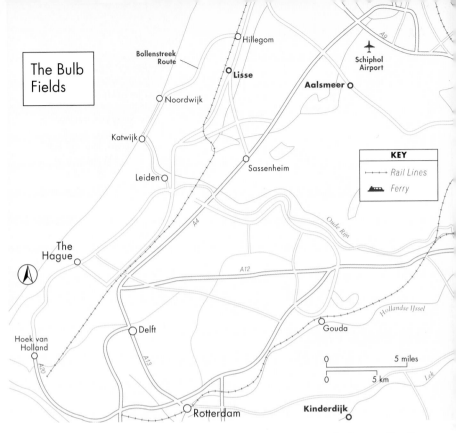

The Bulb Fields

Bollenstreek Route

Hillegom

Lisse

Aalsmeer

Schiphol Airport

Noordwijk

Katwijk

Sassenheim

Leiden

The Hague

A4

A12

Oude Rijn

KEY

Rail Lines

Ferry

Hoek van Holland

Delft

A13

A20

Gouda

Hollandse IJssel

0   5 miles

0   5 km

Lek

Rotterdam

Kinderdijk

Museum De Paviljoens. For a hip and contemporary look at Holland's landscape, consider joining one of Museum De Paviljoens's tours of "land art" in Flevoland (given on Sundays). They are based in Almere, a 25-minute train ride from Amsterdam. ☎ *036/545–0400* ⊕ *www.depaviljoens.nl.*

Orangebike. Offering both guided and self-guided options, this outfit caters to architectural and culinary interests. ☎ *020/528–9990* ⊕ *www.orangebike.nl.*

Pampus Island. Boat excursions from Amsterdam include Pampus Island, with its fort that is part of the Amsterdam Defence Line. It can be reached from IJburg (☎ *020/427–8888* ⊕ *www.amsterdamboatexcursion.com*) and Muiden. Guided or self-guided tours of the island are available. Note that the 13th-century Muiderslot castle in Muiden is worth a visit in itself. ☎ *020/427–8888* ⊕ *www.pampus.nl.*

Rebus Varende Evenementen. The highlight of this outfitter is their three-hour trip from Rotterdam along the river Lek to Kinderdijk, available from April to the first week of October. Boats leave most days at 10:45 am and 2:15 pm from Boompjeskade (where there is a ticket office) or you can buy tickets from any VVV tourist office in the Netherlands. ☎ *06/5582–6463* ⊕ *www.rebus-info.nl* 🚢 *€14.*

VVV. Bus tours of the Holland-in-a-hurry variety, whether half or full-day excursions, can be booked directly with most operators or via the VVV (meaning the Netherlands Board of Tourism offices, found throughout Holland). ⊠ *In front of Centraal Station, Amsterdam* ☎ *020/551–2525* ⊕ *www.iamsterdam.com.*

EXCLUSIVE BLOOM

In the 17th-century floral futures market, fortunes were made and lost in a day with reckless gambling on the price of tulip bulbs. One Semper Augustus bulb clocked in at 5,500 guilders—at that time the cost of a fancy house in Amsterdam.

Wetlands Safari. For watery options, Wetlands Safari runs canoe trips through a 17th-century landscape of reedlands and quake-moors. Guided tours last five and a half hours and the €43 fee covers transport from Amsterdam and back, drinks, and lunch. Be sure to wear rain boots or old footwear. ☎ *06/5355–2669* ⊕ *www.wetlandssafari.nl.*

Yellowbike. This popular firm runs guided tours not only of Amsterdam but its surrounding countryside. ☎ *020/620–6940* ⊕ *www.yellowbike.nl.*

THE BULB FIELDS

In the spring (late March until mid-May) the bulb fields of the province of South Holland are transformed into a vivid series of Mondriaan paintings through the colors of millions of tulips and other flowers. The bulb fields extend from just north of Leiden to the southern limits of Haarlem, with the greatest concentration beginning at Sassenheim and ending between Hillegom and Bennebroek. Floral HQ is the town of Lisse and the fields and glasshouses of the Keukenhof Gardens. The bulb, rather than the bloom, is the prize, and to promote growth and subdivision tulips are decapitated in the field by specialized machines designed by fanatical breeders. Timing can be volatile, but there's a general progression from croci in the middle of March, daffodils and narcissi from the end of March to the middle of April, early tulips and hyacinths from the second week of April to the end of the month, and late tulips immediately afterward. An early or late spring can shift these approximate dates by as much as two weeks.

Fodor's Choice   **Bollenstreekroute** (*Bulb District Route*). The Bulb District Route—more
★   popularly known as the Bloemenroute (Flower Route)—is a series of roads that meander through the bulb-growing region. Marked by small blue-and-white signs that say "Bollenstreek," this route was originally designed by Dutch motoring organization ANWB (which began life as a cycling association). Driving from Amsterdam, take the A4 towards Leiden then the N207 signposted Lisse. By train, head for Haarlem and take the No. 50 or No. 51 bus, which allows you to embark and disembark along the route. Tour companies and the local VVVs (tourist information offices) also organize walking and bicycle tours along this route which usually include a visit to Keukenhof. A round-trip tour from Lisse through Hillegom, Noorderwijkerhout, Sassenheim, De

The flower auction in Aalsmeer is put together by a cooperative of 5,000 flower farmers in the Netherlands.

Zilk, and Voorhout is approximately 25 km (15 miles). For information about this route consult the VVV in your chosen area.

Some of the towns along the Bollenstreek (particularly if you are in a car) are worth a little detour. The dunes of **Noordwijk** make it a popular seaside resort with a vast, sandy nature reserve almost as big as the bulb district itself. It is also the home of **Space Expo,** Europe's first permanent space exhibition for those with budding astronauts in the party. Part of the historic white church in **Noordwijkerhout** dates back to the 1400s. In **Sassenheim,** there is an imposing 13th-century ruined castle.

LISSE

27 km (17 miles) southwest of Amsterdam.

On arrival in Lisse in springtime, you will be in no doubt that this is the center of the Netherlands' biggest tourist attraction, with bumper-to-bumper tour buses and weaving cyclists overwhelming this provincial town. In the 17th century, like its neighbors Sassenheim and Hillegom, it was surrounded by country estates, of which just one remains (the rest were dug over for bulbs). The estate's former garden is the main attraction, but Kasteel Keukenhof (☎ *0252/750–690* ⊕ *www.kasteelkeukenhof.nl*) is also open to the public. If you want to include this in your visit, ring first to check opening times; you can see inside only by guided tour, for which you need a reservation. Another escape from the crowds is the tower directly south of the gardens. Built by a knight-cum-forester (an important position back then), 't Huys

DID YOU KNOW?

The Keukenhof is one of the most popular attractions in Holland, having thus far clocked more than 45 million visitors in the past 62 years. Covering 32 hectares and with 100 varieties of its 4.5 million tulips, it's the largest bulb park in the world.

Dever (☎ 0252/411–430 ⊕ www. kasteeldever.nl) is an atmospheric 14th-century keep.

GETTING HERE AND AROUND

By car from Amsterdam take the A4 in the direction of Schiphol and Den Haag, then take exit 4. Continue on the N207 to Lisse and follow the signs for the Keukenhof. Parking costs €6. You can buy a ticket in advance from the website (⊕ www.keukenhof.nl). The most convenient route from central Amsterdam is via Schiphol Airport, where you take the No. 58 bus. Buses are available from Leiden Centraal (No. 54) or Haarlem (No. 50 or No. 51) or The Hague (No. 89). For bus departure times, call ☎ 0900/9292. Bicycles can be rented at a number of places, including Haarlem railway station and Van Dam in Lisse outside the gardens, or you can hire a bike in Amsterdam and either push those pedals yourself or take the bike on the train (€6 surcharge).

> ## THE FLOWER PARADE
>
> **Bulb District Flower Parade.** If you're visiting the Netherlands in late April, don't miss the annual Bulb District Flower Parade—known locally as the *Bloemencorso*. A series of extravagantly designed floats constructed from millions of blooms, and accompanied by marching bands, parade along a 40-km (20-mi) route that extends from Noordwijk and on to Sassenheim, Lisse, Hillegom, Bennebroek, Heemstede, and finally ends in Haarlem (check the websites for these towns for further information).

ORIENTATION

Lisse is a village with all sights close at hand, though you will want to arm yourself with a map for bicycle touring. There are few snacking opportunities out in the fields, so bear this in mind if you're cycling.

TIMING

Many visitors spend all day at the Keukenhof—but try not to spend any of it queuing. Booking your ticket, or a combination bus/entrance ticket, online can save you wasted time at the front desk.

ESSENTIALS

Bicycle Rentals Rent-a-bike van Dam ⊠ Parkeerterrein De Keukenhof, Stationsweg 166a ☎ 06/1208–9858 ⊕ www.rent-a-bikevandam.nl.

Taxis Taxi Direct ZH ☎ 0172/740–909 ⊕ www.markt.nl/en/Boskoop/Taxi-Direct-ZH.

Visitor Information VVV Lisse ⊠ Grachtweg 53 ☎ 0252/414–262 ⊕ www.vvvlisse.nl.

EXPLORING

Fodor'sChoice ★ **Keukenhof.** This famed 17-acre park and greenhouse complex was founded in 1950 by Tom van Waveren and other leading bulb growers. It's one of the largest open-air flower exhibitions in the world, and draws huge crowds between the end of March and the end of May. As many as 7 million tulip bulbs bloom here every spring, either in hothouses or flower beds along the sides of a lake. In the last weeks of April (peak season) you can catch tulips, daffodils, hyacinths, and narcissi all flowering simultaneously. In addition there are blooms on show in the pavilions along with floral demonstrations and exhibitions about the history of tulips. Leading Dutch bulb-growing exporters use it as a showcase for their latest hybrids, which unfortunately means that commercial, not creative, forces are at play here. Some of the planting is of the rather gaudy tulip varieties, and there's no holding back on the bulb-buying opportunities. It's a lovely—if squashed at times—wander around meandering streams, placid pools, and paved paths. The avenues were designed by Zocher, designer of the Vondelpark in Amsterdam. Keukenhof's roots extend back to the 15th century, when it was the herb farm (Keukenhof means "kitchen courtyard") of one of Holland's richest ladies. Any sense of history has almost been obliterated, though there is a historical garden recreating the oldest botanical garden in the Netherlands in Leiden and at least a nod to contemporary trends in the "Inspiration" section. Head for the windmill for some calm and a vista over the surrounding fields, or view the crowds from a distance with an hour-long boat tour (book this near the windmill, €7.50). This is the Netherlands' most popular springtime attraction, and it's easy to reach from all points of the country. Traveling independently rather than in an organized group should present no problem—just follow the crowds. ☎ 0252/465–555 ⊕ www.keukenhof.nl ✉ €15 ⊗ Late Mar.–late May, daily 8–7:30 (ticket office closes at 6).

WORD OF MOUTH

"Biking in Amsterdam was AWESOME. We rented great bikes from the Marriott for 12 euros a day. The first day we went to a market then got a bike map from MacBike and took the ferry behind the train station and headed through the countryside for a 20-mile ride to Marken." —Jeff

AALSMEER

13 km (8 miles) southwest of Amsterdam.

A small town just north of Schiphol Airport, on the edge of the Westeinder Plassen, it's no exaggeration to say this is one of the flower capitals of the world, thanks to the auction that sells 12.5 billion cut-flowers and plants a year.

GETTING HERE AND AROUND

By car from Amsterdam from the A10 (ring) take the A4 in the direction of Den Haag, then exit 3, signposted Aalsmeer (N201). Follow signs for Bloemenveiling, and once inside the complex follow the route to the visitors' car park. For public transport, take the No. 172 bus from Amsterdam Centraal (which also stops in Leidseplein) or the No. 198 bus from Schiphol Airport.

ESSENTIALS

Taxis TCA Taxi Centrale Amsterdam ☎ 020/777-7777.

Visitor Information VVV Aalsmeer ✉ Zijdstraat 12 ☎ 020/201-8800 ⊕ www.beleefaalsmeer.nl.

EXPLORING

Bloemenveiling FloraHolland. Five days a week from the predawn hours until midmorning, the largest flower auction in the world takes place in the biggest commercial building in the world—it's the size of 120 soccer fields. You can watch the proceedings from the catwalk above as carts laden with flowers and plants zip about at warp speed. The buying system is what's called a Dutch auction—the price goes down, not up, on a large "clock" on the wall (though there are also Internet buyers these days). The buyers sit lecture-style with buzzers on their desks; the first to register a bid gets the bunch, and they work their way through 50 million purchases of flowers and plants daily! ⊠ *Legmeerdijk 313* ☎ *0297/390–697* ⊕ *www.floraholland.com* ✉ *€5* ⊙ *Mon.–Wed. and Fri. 7–11 am, Thurs. 7–9.*

STORYBOOK HOLLAND

If you want your postcards to come to life, head here. Tulips, castles, windy beaches, epic engineering feats that hold back the waters—you won't have to travel far to experience authentic landscapes and sights. For the heritage-inclined, the folkloric villages of the former Zuiderzee (now IJsselmeer) have an interesting story to tell. Volendam and Marken are traditional little fishing ports lost in time, where on high days you may still see residents stroll around in Hans Brinker dress. Most of the canal vistas that once looked like ink sketches by Salomon van Ruisdael have disappeared, but if you look hard enough (mostly when the tour buses stop running) you might still spot some Rembrandtesqueness in the quiet corners and cul-de-sacs of these time-warp towns.

BROEK-IN-WATERLAND

14 km (9 miles) northeast of Amsterdam.

With a centuries-old reputation of being "the cleanest town in all the Netherlands," Broek-in-Waterland is still mostly immaculate—so much so that visitors are tempted to walk barefoot on the roads. It's hard to imagine, but the picture-perfect 17th-century wooden houses are said to be even tidier inside. Note the color differences: gray houses belonged to "commoners," whereas the wealthy class distinguished theirs with a purplish tint. There are opportunities for lunch or picnics around the town's big lake that freezes in the winter, making it an excellent spot for watching (or participating in) a Dutch obsession: ice-skating.

GETTING HERE AND AROUND

By car from Amsterdam start on the S116, take the N247 (Nieuwe Leeuwarderweg), and follow the signs to Broek-in-Waterland. There is no train station in Broek-in-Waterland, so from Amsterdam public transportation is by bus. The Nos. 110, 118, 311, 312, 314, 315, 316, and 317 buses all go through

BOAT RENTALS

Kano & Electroboot Waterland. When exploring various villages, go native and rent a canoe or a kayak from this popular outfitter. ⊠ *Drs. J. van Disweg 4, Broek-in-Waterland* ☎ *020/403–3209* ⊕ *www.fluisterbootvaren.nl.*

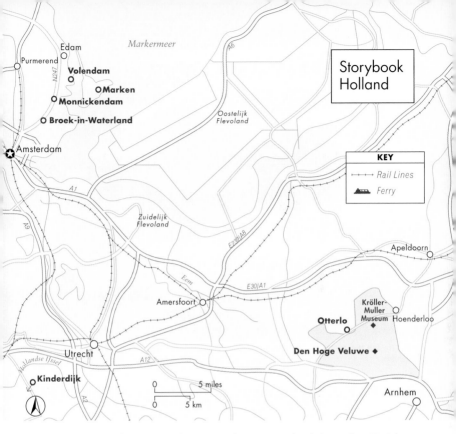

Amsterdam Centraal. You can buy a Waterland day ticket (EBS bus company) for €10 and combine visits to several villages in this region in one day. This is a popular cycling trip suitable for enthusiastic eight-year-olds upward. Take one of the free ferries behind Centraal Station that cross the IJ, and follow the signs.

ORIENTATION

There are new and old bits, and when you cycle from Amsterdam, you need to go *through* the foot tunnel to reach the nicest part of the *dorp* (village), where many of the cafés line the central lake. On weekends in the summer, look for the ferry crossing from Holysloot, where, close-by, you can take an entertaining walk amid the cows along the Wittebruggetjesroute ("White Bridges Route") while wheeling your bike.

TIMING

Broek-in-Waterland is less than a half hour by bus from Amsterdam Centraal, so if you have time only for a quick trip, this is a very accessible and authentic option.

ESSENTIALS

Bicycle Rentals Wim Rijwiel- en Bromfietshandel ⊠ *Laan 44* ☏ *020/403–1462.*

Taxis Matthaei Taxi Nr 55 ☏ *06/4186–1824.*

In the 17th and 18th century, Broek-in-Waterland was a popular residence for merchants and seafarers from Amsterdam.

EXPLORING

★ No 18th-century visitor on the Dutch leg of a grand tour would miss this picturesque, wealthy Waterland village where even the local grocer is called *Posch*. The village is full of pretty 17th- and 18th-century wooden houses built for merchants and farmers (83 of the houses have national historic status). Back in the day, the residents here amassed legendary fortunes. The 16th-century church is the burial place for Dutch East India Company businesswoman Neeltje Pater, who left the enormous sum of 7 million guilders when she died in 1789. Today's inhabitants include media moguls and finance types. (Check out the super-chic houseboats, with matching speedboats, on the dike leading into the village.) It's a charming step-back-in-time stroll around the village, where you can admire **De Kralentuinen**, the fine houses with hedges clipped into baroque patterns and elaborate garden mosaics studded with antique blue glass beads. Hundreds of years ago, Dutch sea merchants used these beads to trade with primitive cultures for spices and other goods; the beads that were left over and brought back to Holland were used to decorate such gardens. There's an old-fashioned pancake house and a slightly funkier café for a spot of lunch, or, if you prefer, bring a picnic. It's a lovely area to explore by boat, canoe, or kayak, and you can rent all of them here. Potter round the **Havenrak**, the large lake that is popular with ice skaters in the winter, or go for a more extensive Waterland tour.

CLOSE UP

Holding the Waters at Bay

There's a good reason the Dutch countryside looks as it does, crisscrossed by canals and dikes, and dotted with more than 1,000 windmills. Those picturesque mills used to serve a vital role in keeping everybody's feet dry. About a quarter of the land, including most of the Randstad, lies below sea level, and without major human intervention, large swathes of the Netherlands would either be underwater, or uninhabitable swamps. Just imagine, when you land at Schiphol—the name, "ship's hole," is a clue—you should be about 20 feet below the surf.

The west coast has always been protected by high dunes, but the rest of the land had to take its chances for centuries. The first to begin the fight against the sea were early settlers who built mounds in the north of the country around 500 BC, and the battle has continued ever since. Real progress was made around AD 1200 when dikes began appearing. In the 14th century, canals were dug, and the first windmills were built to pump the water off the land (a job now done by electric pumps). This transformed the fertile alluvial landscape, turning it into a farmer's paradise.

War on nature has waged ever since, as Holland gradually clawed back territory, by closing off the Zuiderzee inland sea in 1932 to form the IJsselmeer (IJssel Lake), and by a century-long land reclamation program of polder building. The sea bit back with a vengeance one wintry night in 1953. On January 31 that year, a combination of exceptionally high tides and strong winds sent a storm surge pouring up the Rhine delta, killing around 2,000 and inundating 1,000 square miles of land.

Dutch engineers vowed this disaster would never be repeated. They responded by constructing an extensive network by building the Delta Works, one of the great engineering feats of the 20th century.

7

MONNICKENDAM

4.7 km (3 miles) north from Broek-in-Waterland, 16 km (10 miles) northeast of Amsterdam. Take Route N247.

This is a bustling little town without the full-on folkloric ex-fishing-village effect of its neighbors Marken and Volendam, but no less charming for that. Now a yachting base with an interesting mix of old and new and swanky vessels in the harbor, there are some good restaurants, a boutique hotel, and (not only tourist-kitsch) shopping opportunities. Its landmark is the Speeltoren with its famed carillon sporting (on the hour) galloping knights.

GETTING HERE AND AROUND

If you're driving from Amsterdam, take the S116, then the N247 (Nieuwe Leeuwarderweg), and follow signs to Monnickendam. It's a 10- to 15-minute trip. By bus it's a few minutes farther from Broek-in-Waterland on the No. 311 or No. 315 from Amsterdam Centraal.

ORIENTATION

Get your bearings with a drink at the old weigh house, which is on the central canal, before heading for a stroll round the harbor. A camping and recreation zone (Hemmeland) with all kinds of water sports juts out into the Gouwzee.

TIMING

You can explore Monnickendam in a couple of hours, or a little longer if you're looking to do some sailing or boating. In July and August you can travel to Marken on the oldest passenger ship (1887) in the Netherlands.

ESSENTIALS

Bicycle Rentals Ber Koning Tweewielers ⊠ *Noordeinde 12* ☎ *0299/651–267* ⊕ *www.berkoning.nl.*

Taxis Taxi Jado ☎ *0299/650–864* ⊕ *www.taxi-jado.com.*

EXPLORING

One possible explanation for the name of the historic town of Monnick-endam has to do with the monks of a nearby monastery, who were calling the shots here in the 13th century. Granted city rights in 1355 and a prominent port by the 1660s, Monnickendam still has a large yacht harbor where swanky, spanking-new 125-foot trophy vessels (some of which are constructed here) bob alongside old Dutch sailing barges. The center of town is well preserved with narrow canals and bridges, cobbled streets, and pretty gabled houses. If you need a time-out, take a table under the portico of the 17th-century Weigh House, which is now an elegant café and restaurant. Even if you get lost as you stroll about, you won't lose track of time. Every quarter of an hour, the mellifluous bells of the Speeltoren ring out, on the hour accompanied by knights on horseback galloping round the clockwork under the watchful gaze of a female angel. The bells are part of the oldest (1597) carillon in the world, and on Saturdays (at 11 am) a carillonneur climbs the ladders inside the narrow tower to give a recital.

★ **Waterlandsmuseum de Speeltoren.** To the left and right of the town's famed 16th-century bell tower, the Waterlandsmuseum de Speeltoren has found a new home in two charming historic buildings. You can see exhibitions on the history of Monnickendam (and neighboring villages), on the Waterland landscape, shows of contemporary art, plus a display of a noted collection of decorative blue-and-white tiles and majolica. And, for the first time, it is possible to see how the carillon of the Speeltoren—the oldest one in the world—works, from the inside. You can also inquire here about walking tours, as almost every building in town has an interesting history (one is hallowed as a hiding place for Jews during World War II). ⊠ *Noordeinde 4* ☎ *0299/652–203* ⊕ *www.despeeltoren.nl* 🎫*€4.50* ☉ *Apr.–Oct., Tues.–Sun. 11–5; Nov.–Mar., Sat.–Sun. 11–5.*

MARKEN

8.9 km (6 miles) east of Monnickendam, 16 km (10 miles) northeast of Amsterdam. Take Route N518.

The former island of Marken was once an isolated fishing village, but today it's filled with sightseers riding over the causeway to view the characteristic green-and-white wooden houses built on piles.

GETTING HERE

From Amsterdam by car and on the S116, go through the IJ tunnel and take the N247 (Nieuwe Leeuwarderweg) and follow signs to Marken. You can also take the No. 311 bus from Amsterdam Centraal Station. The Marken Express ferry travels between Marken and Volendam. You can board it at either harbor. It's also possible to arrange a boat tour or charter from Volendam. Visit the local VVV tourist office for further details.

ORIENTATION

This little triangular peninsula is well signposted. The lighthouse facing the sea that marks the furthest point was built in 1839.

TIMING

An hour or so may be enough in high season if you are not fond of crowds. During off-season, Marken's secludedness is impressive.

ESSENTIALS

Bicycle Rentals **Fietsverhuur Marken** ☎ *06/4230–5828* ⊕ *www.dagjemarken. com.*

EXPLORING

The tidal wave that hit the Netherlands in 1916 was a defining factor in the decision to drain the Zuiderzee, but with the construction of the enclosing dam (the Afsluitdijk), traditional Dutch fishing villages like Marken lost their livelihood. Heritage tourism has now taken over on this former island (a causeway to the mainland was built in 1957) that, despite the busloads of visitors, retains its charm. Many of the green-and-white gabled homes are built on timber piles, dating from when the Zuiderzee used to flood, and a maritime past is revealed in the sober Calvinist church (1904) with its hanging herring boats and lugger. There is a *klompen* (clog) maker, and *kleding* (dress) shop that includes designs dating from the 1300s, some of which are still worn today. The floral chintzes are inspired by the Dutch East Indies, and the caps, in particular, are incredibly intricate. The full folkloric effect can be viewed in the film showing at the local museum.

Marker Museum. The intimate Marker Museum consists of six former smokehouses (where the smoke left in a hole in the ceiling rather than a chimney) with exhibits showcasing the past life of Marken. You can see how a fisherman's family lived until about 1932. ⊠ *Kerkbuurt 44–47* ☎ *0299/601–904* ⊕ *www.markermuseum.nl* 🎫 *€2.50* ☉ *Apr.–Sept., daily 10–5; Oct., Mon.–Sat. 11–4, Sun. noon–4.*

Volendam is built on a patch of reclaimed land that used to be the harbor of nearby Edam. The original spelling of the name Vollendam literally meant something like "filled dam."

VOLENDAM

6.7 km (4 miles) northwest of Marken, 18 km (11½ miles) northeast of Amsterdam. Take Routes N247–N517.

Assuming that other visitors don't block your view, you can stare to your heart's content at the residents of Volendam still wearing traditional costumes immortalized in Dutch dolls the world over. Yes, indeed, they dress this way for real (even cosmopolitan Amsterdammers stop in their tracks when someone from Volendam or Marken visits the city in full gear). The men wear dark baggy pantaloons fastened with silver guilders instead of buttons, striped vests, and dark jackets with caps. Women wear long dark skirts covered with striped aprons and blouses with elaborately hand-embroidered floral panels. Their coral necklaces and famous winged lace caps complete the picture. Of course, everyone wears klompen. You'll have the most fun in Volendam if you have your photo taken in traditional costume (a real hoot for the folks back home), enjoy a stroll on the dike (or maybe even a swim on one side of it), and explore the narrow streets with their small nostalgic fishermen's cottages. Don't let the many tacky touristy businesses—a room wallpapered with cigar bands?—throughout the main area selling souvenirs put you off; once you head off the beaten track and see the way the native Volendammers live, you'll get to see the "real" unspoiled Volendam. Be sure to sample the region's renowned smoked eels; they're truly delicious.

GETTING HERE AND AROUND

Drive through the IJ tunnel on S116 and take N247 to Marken and Monnickendam. The Nos. 110, 118, 312, 314, 316, and 317 buses leave from Amsterdam Centraal Station. Once here, you'll be hard-pressed to find rental bikes.

ORIENTATION

The harbor front where the Marken Express docks is very crowded, but there are some quieter streets for wandering off the trinket-packed main drag—the *dijk* (dike). The tourist office is tucked behind here on Zeestraat next to the museum.

> WORD OF MOUTH
>
> "We rented bikes for about 2 hours and rode about 10 miles and the tulip fields were outstanding. We are not experienced 'bikers'—and you don't need to be to do this trip—they give you a route and it is very safe." —illnative

TIMING

After eating some smoked eel, enjoying a photo-op in traditional costume, and visiting the museum, you'll probably be ready to head back in a couple of hours.

ESSENTIALS

Taxis **TCV Taxi Centrale Volendam** ☎ *06/1431–0622.*

Visitor information **VVV Volendam** ⊠ *Zeestraat 37* ☎ *0299/363–747* ⊕ *www.vvv-volendam.nl.*

EXPLORING

★ **Kaasboerderij Alida Hoeve.** A fascinating working cheese farm, Kaasboerderij Alida Hoeve lets you discover how how cheeses are made, and, needless to say, purchases are greatly welcomed. ⊠ *Zeddeweg 1* ☎ *0299/365–830* ⊕ *www.cheesefarms.com* ⊡ *Free* ☉ *Daily 8:30–6.*

Volendams Museum. You can learn about Volendam's history at this museum, located next to the VVV tourist information center. A highlight are the reconstructed period rooms, such as a school filled with mannequins adorned with folkloric costumes. For a real change of pace, there's a photograph of chanteuse Josephine Baker clad in traditional folkloric Dutch garb! ⊠ *Zeestraat 41* ☎ *0299/369–258* ⊕ *www.volendamsmuseum.nl* ⊡ *€3* ☉ *Mar.–Dec., daily 10–5.*

KINDERDIJK

55 km (34 miles) southwest of Amsterdam.

The camera doesn't lie when it comes to Kinderdijk, and the virtual tour on the website gives you a clear idea of exactly what to expect. Touristy, but unquestionably romantic.

GETTING HERE AND AROUND

It is a bit of a trek (2½ hours) from Amsterdam, and there are a number of ways to go. The most straightforward route is to head for Rotterdam Zuid on the train. From there, take the metro to Rotterdam Zuidplein, then the No. 190 bus to Alblasserdam. By car, Kinderdijk is 20 km (12½ miles) from Rotterdam. Follow directions to Rotterdam, then take the A15 to exit 22. There are (small) car parks by the mills. Waterbus

(⊕ *www.waterbus.nl)* runs a fast ferry service from the Erasmusbrug in Rotterdam to Ridderkerk, and then you change onto another ferry to pop across to Kinderdijk. Ferries are every half hour and the trip takes about half an hour. Other tour boats are available from Rotterdam, and there is also (a pricey) water taxi.

TIMING

If the weather is fine, take a picnic along and make a day of it.

EXPLORING

Fodor's Choice
★
Kinderdijk. The sight of the 19 windmills at Kinderdijk under sail is magnificently and romantically impressive. Not surprisingly, this landmark sight (so valued it is found on the UNESCO World Heritage list) is one of the most visited places in the Netherlands These are water-pumping mills whose job was to drain water from the Alblasserwaard polder enclosed by the rivers Noord and Lek—a function now performed by the 1950 pumping station with its humongously sized water screws, which you pass on the way to the site. The somewhat chocolate-boxy name (which means "child's dyke") comes from a legend involving a baby who washed up here in a cradle after the great floods of 1421, with a cat sitting on its tummy to keep them both from tumbling out.

Rarer than ever, these windmills date all the way back to 1740. Just 150 years ago 10,000 windmills were in operation across the country, but today only 1,000 remain. These have been saved from the wrecking ball thanks to the help of heritage organizations. The windmills are open in rotation, so there is always one interior to visit. A walk through a working windmill gives fascinating insight into how the millers and their families lived. The mills can be seen in full action (wind permitting) from 1 to 5 pm on Saturdays in July and August, as well as on National Windmill Day (second Saturday of May) and National Monument Day (second weekend of September). Throughout the first week following the first Monday of September the mills are illuminated at night, really pulling out the tourist stops. You can walk around the mills area whenever you like, so it's a great way to spend a leisurely afternoon. There are a couple of cafés for snacks, but if the weather is good bring a picnic. ⊠ *Molenkade* ☎ *078/691–2830* ⊕ *www.molenskinderdijk.nl* ☞ *Interior of mill: €6.00 (incl. film at visitor's center)* ☉ *Interior of mill: Apr.–Oct., daily 9:30–5:30.*

The Randstad

HAARLEM, THE HAGUE, DELFT, AND ROTTERDAM

WORD OF MOUTH

"I love, love Delft!! It is just big enough that you can wander around (especially in late afternoon after the day-trippers leave) without fear of getting lost. I love its quaintness, its peacefulness, its picturesque canals! We are going back in October!"

—JoyC

WELCOME TO THE RANDSTAD

TOP REASONS TO GO

★ **Paintings, paintings, paintings:** Take in the old masters in Haarlem's Frans Hals Museum. Marvel at Vermeer's *View of Delft* at The Hague's Gemeentemuseum. Visit Vermeer's hometown of Delft to see where he found his muse. Or make yourself bug-eyed deciphering the graphic puzzles in The Hague's Escher in Het Paleis Museum.

★ **The views:** Climb Utrecht's Domtoren—the Netherlands' tallest church tower. Or take the elevator up Rotterdam's Euromast, the country's highest observation deck, for a bird's-eye view of Europe's busiest harbor.

★ **Old-world charm:** Wander Delft's canal-lined medieval streets—time-travel at its best. And step into history in The Hague, inside the 13th-century Knights' Hall.

★ **Holland in half an hour:** Visit the miniature world of the Madurodam in The Hague, and teach kids all about the Netherlands in 30 minutes.

North Sea

IJmuiden ○
1
Haarlem ○

Leiden ○

Den Haag
(The Hague) ✪ **2**

○ Alphen

Hoek van
Holland ○
Delft ○ **3**

○ Gouda

4
○ Rotterdam

Voorne

Dordrecht ○

Schouwen
Overflakkee
Beijerland

Duiveland

1 Haarlem. Just 20 minutes from Amsterdam, this city drips as much history as its illustrious neighbor. Dominated by the imposing hulk of the Great Church, many of its quiet cobbled streets have changed little since painter Frans Hals held court here.

2 The Hague. The center of Dutch government is more elegant and restrained than Amsterdam, with fewer canals but more tree-lined boulevards. The astonishing collection of museums is reason enough to visit, with Gemeentemuseum an especially rewarding stop, with works by Vermeer and other masters usually hanging in the Mauritshuis (under renovation) on view now.

GETTING ORIENTED

The towns and cities of the Randstad are all within easy reach of Amsterdam, and can be visited on day trips, for overnight stays, or incorporated into a circular tour. Rotterdam lies farthest from Amsterdam, yet is still only 73 km (45 miles) to the south, and little more than an hour away by train or car.

8

3 Delft. With long canal-lined streets and medieval houses, Delft is like a scaled-down version of Amsterdam, without the hectic pace of capital city life. It's easy to understand how Johannes Vermeer found such inspiration here.

4 Rotterdam. Rebuilt almost from scratch following the devastation of World War II, Europe's biggest port has worked hard to transform itself into a showpiece of modern architecture. By contrast, the historic area of Delfshaven—from where the Pilgrim Fathers set sail for their New England—escaped intact.

Updated by
Tim Skelton

If beauty, venerable history, sylvan gardens, majestic cathedrals, and great art are at the top of your list, it can be hard choosing between the towns of the Randstad, that horseshoe arc of urban centers which dot the heartland of Holland. So visit them all.

The towns and cities of Zuid-Holland (South Holland) cluster around Amsterdam like filings round the end of a magnet. Each has prospered and grown independently, and today their borders virtually overlap one another to such an extent that the region is now dubbed the *Randstad* (Border City), because locals consider it one mammoth megalopolis. Randstad also means Edge City, another term the Dutch use to describe the circle formed by the cities of Amsterdam, The Hague, and Rotterdam, since the cities lie on the same geologic ridge at the northwestern edge of the country. Whatever the terminology, this entire region is considered "The West" by young Randstad wanna-bes waiting for their opportunity to hit the big time.

In this fascinating area, you can leapfrog from past to future by journeying from Haarlem—earliest center of Dutch art—to Rotterdam, colossus of the waterways and now home to Europe's most daringly modern architecture; travel through an open-air old-master painting by visiting Vermeer's blue-hued Delft. Chief among these peripheral cities, The Hague is often seen as a little aloof—it *is*, after all, Holland's seat of government and home to the Dutch royal family and the International Court of Justice. A quarter of Holland's 16 million residents live within 80 km (50 miles) of the capital: welcome to "Holland in a nutshell."

Rotterdam is not only the industrial center of Holland but also the world's largest port. The city's quaint statue of Erasmus was long ago overshadowed by some of the most forward-looking architecture to dazzle any European city. When Rotterdam's city center and harbor were completely destroyed in World War II, the authorities decided to start afresh rather than try to reconstruct its former maze of canals. The imposing, futuristic skyline along the banks of the River Maas has been developing since then. Today, say architectural pundits, we have seen the future, and it is Manhattan-on-the-Maas (as locals call it), thanks in large part to the efforts of major figures such as Rem Koolhaas, Eric van Egeraat, and UN Studio. But if Rotterdam is now one of the most vibrant centers of architecture in the world, it is also many other things: a skate city, a harbor city, an artists' haven, a design inspiration, a historical museum center, a jazz lover's dream.

Clearly, Rotterdam is a city that has to be remain firmly focused on the present and future—the Nazi bombs of May 1940 took care of its past—but surrounding it is an area that is sublimely history-soaked. Within the span of a single day, you can roll the centuries back from Rotterdam's modern glitter to pursue the ghost of Frans Hals through the Golden Age streets of Haarlem and also wander through the open-air museum of Delft, which once colored the world with its unique blue. Then there's The Hague. Behind the pomp and stuffiness of this world-famed town is a lively metropolis that is both elegant and quirky, filled with grand 17th-century mansions and more than 25 public parks. The Hague's official name *'s-Gravenhage* (literally "the Count's Hedge"), harks back to the 13th century when the Count of Holland had a hunting lodge here. But to the Dutch it is always known simply as Den Haag, and that's what you'll hear on the streets.

All in all, although the Randstad area is small enough to drive through in an afternoon, it would take you weeks to explore fully. Even better: whereas Amsterdam tends to pander to the demands of tourists, this is the beating heart of the Netherlands where the "real" people live. And it's all the more fascinating for that.

PLANNING

WHEN TO GO

This part of Holland is at its best in late spring or early autumn. High summer means too many visitors, and touring in winter often puts you at the mercy of the weather (bring your umbrella year-round). For flora lovers, mid- to late April is ideal for a trip around Haarlem, as the fields are bright with spring bulbs. Many restaurants are closed Sunday (also Monday); museums tend to close Monday.

If you're into the arts, you might prefer to schedule your trip to catch the world-renowned International Film Festival Rotterdam, where 300 noncommercial films are screened in late January and early February or, if a jazz lover, time your arrival in Rotterdam to coincide with the North Sea Jazz Festival, which takes place over three days in mid-July.

GETTING AROUND

Unless you want to make a detailed exploration of the Dutch countryside, you may find it more convenient and less stressful to leave your car behind when touring the Randstad. The region is crossed by a dense network of freeways, but these are frequently clogged with commuter traffic and often grind to a halt at peak times. Avoid the jams by hopping on a train, which is the cheap, convenient, and usually reliable way to get around. *Every city in this chapter is connected to Amsterdam (and most to each other) by direct services that run at least twice each hour throughout the day.* Rotterdam, The Hague, and Delft have hourly train service to Amsterdam all night.

Taxis are available at the railway stations. Alternatively, to get one to collect you from your location, try one of the taxi firms recommended *in this chapter or* by the tourism bureau. You can't hail cabs in the street.

BY BIKE

In this flat land, a bicycle is an ideal means of getting around, and cities have safe cycle lanes on busy roads. Bikes are best rented at outlets near all major railway stations, usually called a **Rijwiel** shop or a **Fietspoint**. These shops are generally open long hours every day, and the bikes are invariably new and well maintained. Rates are around €7.50 a day, and you must show ID and pay a deposit of €50–€100. Cheaper bikes have back-pedal brakes and no gears. Other local rental centers can be found in the regional *Gouden Gids* (Yellow Pages), under *Fietsen en Bromfietsen.*

ABOUT THE RESTAURANTS

Although this area of Holland is home to some of the country's most worldly restaurants, keep in mind that most bars also offer house specials whose prices are usually cheap enough to keep students and young people sated (keep an eye out for the *kleine kaart,* or lighter meal menu, usually offered in the bar area and available throughout the day). Perennially popular dishes such as satay and pepper steak never come off the menu.

ABOUT THE HOTELS

Hotels in the Randstad range from elegant canal houses to cross-country chains with anonymous décor. Most large towns have one or more deluxe hotels that exceed all expectations. Accommodation in Rotterdam and The Hague—big convention and business cities—is at a premium, so book well in advance, although the situation is usually not as tight as it is in Amsterdam. Finding somewhere to stay in the other cities is generally less of a problem. The VVVs (tourist offices) in the region have extensive accommodation listings, and can book your reservations. Assume all rooms have air-conditioning, TV, telephones, and private bath, unless otherwise noted. Assume hotels operate on the EP meal plan (with no meals) unless stated otherwise.

VISITOR INFORMATION

Each VVV tourist board across the country has information principally on its own town and region. Contact the VVV of the area you plan to travel to directly and ask for information, as there is no central office.

HAARLEM

A breath of fresh air just a short train ride, but a million miles, from throbbing downtown Amsterdam, Haarlem was the very first center of Dutch art. Walking past the charming *hofjes* (historic almshouse courtyards), and between the redbrick gabled facades lining Haarlem's historic streets, it is easy to feel you have been transported back to the Netherlands' Golden Age of the 17th century.

This is especially true around the central market square, where the vast hulking form of Sint Bavo's (the Great Church) dominates the city skyline and evokes a bygone era. In fact, the intrusive motorized transport aside, much of Frans Hals' hometown has appeared unchanged for centuries. Indeed, many of the often-narrow ancient streets of the old center have remained residential and are quiet even through the middle of the day. Yet despite its many picturesque monuments and rich supply of fascinating museums, Haarlem isn't a city rooted in the past. It is home to a lively population of students—often the overspill who can't find lodgings in Amsterdam or Leiden—who bring with them a youthful vibrancy, especially at night. With hotel accommodation generally a better value and easier to come by than in nearby Amsterdam, and the city being on a compact and manageable scale, many travelers also end up staying here and using the city as a base from which to explore the surrounding region. In spring it is an easy hop from here to the Keukenhof gardens and the flower fields of the Bollenstreek Route. And with its close proximity to the dunes and the seaside resort of Zandvoort, Haarlem also attracts hordes of beach-going Amsterdammers and Germans every summer. The result is an intoxicating mix of old and new that makes the town well worth checking out.

GETTING HERE AND AROUND

20 km (12 miles) west of Amsterdam, 41 km (26 miles) north of The Hague.

Getting to Haarlem by rail is a simple matter. Around six trains make the 15-minute trip from Amsterdam's Centraal Station every hour during the day. Seat reservations aren't permitted. Driving will take around 20–25 minutes—you'll need to head west out of Amsterdam on the N200/A200. If you have the energy, you can bike.

WHICH WAY TO GO?

If you arrive by train, take a good look around before you leave the railway station—it's a fabulous Art Nouveau building dating from 1908. Next, head down Jansweg (to the left of the station as you exit) for several blocks, over the Nieuwe Gracht canal and into the city center. It will take you right to the Grote Markt.

The center of Haarlem is compact and easy to navigate on foot, but there are plentiful buses if you need them. Use an **OV-chipkaart** (public transport chip card)—a new electronic payment system that will eventually replace all paper transport tickets, including train tickets. These credit card–size tickets can be loaded up with credit from machines in railway and metro stations, and are debited as you board and leave trains, trams, metros, and buses. There are information and sales points in the station. Or visit ⊕ *www.ov-chipkaart.nl* for more information.

Public Transportation Information ☎ *0900/9292* ⊕ *www.9292ov.nl.*

TOURS

City walking tours of Haarlem are often sold as part of a combined package by Amsterdam tour operators, and include visits to the bulb fields when these are in season (spring). Self-guided city walks are easy to arrange—pick up a leaflet with a map from the VVV in Haarlem. Themed city walks are also organized throughout each summer by the VVV in Haarlem. They cost €7.50 per person, but are usually conducted in Dutch. Go to ⊕ *www.haarlemmarketing.nl* for departure dates and times.

TIMING

If you push it, you could cover the main sights of Haarlem in half a day, but take a full day to do everything justice and to enjoy a relaxing break on the Grand Market square (*Grote Markt*).

ESSENTIALS

Bicycle Rentals Fietspoint Pieters ⊠ *Haarlem Station* ☎ *023/531-7066.*

Emergency Services National Emergency Alarm Number ☎ *112 for police, fire, and ambulance.*

Hospitals Spaarne Ziekenhuis ⊠ *Spaarnepoort 1, Hoofddorp* ☎ *023/890-8900* ⊕ *www.spaarneziekenhuis.nl.*

Taxis Taxi Centrale ☎ *023/540-0600* ⊕ *www.taxicentralehaarlem.nl.*

Tourism Information VVV Haarlem ⊠ *Verwulft 11* ☎ *0900/616-1600* ⊕ *www.haarlemmarketing.nl.*

EXPLORING

Haarlem is a compact city and easy to cover on foot. From the main railway station it is about five minutes' walk south to the Grote Markt. The Frans Hals Museum is another five minutes beyond that.

TOP ATTRACTIONS

De Hallen (*The Halls*). A branch of the Frans Hals Museum, De Hallen has an extensive collection of Dutch Impressionists and Expressionists, including sculpture, textiles, and ceramics, as well as paintings and graphics. The complex consists of two buildings—the Vleeshal and the Verweyhal House.

The **Vleeshal** (Meat Market) building is one of the most interesting cultural legacies of the Dutch Renaissance, with a fine sweep of stepped gables that seems to pierce the scudding clouds. It was built in 1602–03 by Lieven de Key, Haarlem's master builder. The ox heads that look down from the facade are reminders of the building's original function: it was the only place in Haarlem where meat could be sold, and the building was used for that sole purpose until 1840. Today it is used for exhibitions—generally works of modern and contemporary art, usually by local artists. Note the early landscape work by Piet Mondriaan, *Farms in Duivendrecht*, so different from his later De Stijl shapes.

The **Verweyhal Gallery of Modern Art** was built in 1879 as a gentlemen's club, originally named *Trou moet Blijcken* (Loyalty Must Be Proven), and now bears the name of native Haarlem artist Kees Verwey, who died in 1995. It is used as an exhibition space for selections from the Frans Hals Museum's enormous collection of modern and contemporary art. In addition to the works of Kees Verwey, the exhibition covers such artists as Jacobus van Looy, Jan Sluijters, Leo Gestel, Herman Kruyder, and Karel Appel. Note, too, a fine collection of contemporary ceramics. ⊠ *Grote Markt 16* ☎ *023/511–5775* ⊕ *www. dehallenhaarlem.nl* ⊡ €6 ☾ *Tues.–Sat. 11–5, Sun. noon–5.*

Fodor'sChoice ★ **Frans Hals Museum.** Named after the celebrated man himself, this not-to-be-missed museum holds a collection of amazingly virile and lively group portraits by the Golden Age painter, depicting the merrymaking civic guards and congregating regents for which he became world famous. The building itself is one of the town's smarter hofjes: an entire block of almshouses grouped around an attractive courtyard. In the 17th century this was a home for elderly men, an *oudemannenhuis*, so it is only fitting that their cottages now form a sequence of galleries for

> ### HAARLEM'S HIDDEN COURTYARDS
>
> Throughout the old city center are the many historic hofjes (almshouse courtyards)—hidden little courtyards that make Haarlem an incredibly pleasant place to explore. Look for the Zuider Hofje, the Hofje van Loo, the Wijnbergs Hofje, and the Brouwershofje (they are all signposted). Closer to the Grote Markt are the Remonstrants Hofje, the Luthershofje, and the Frans Loenen Hofje. These secluded gardens are filled with flowers and birdsong, and offer peace and respite away from the city streets.

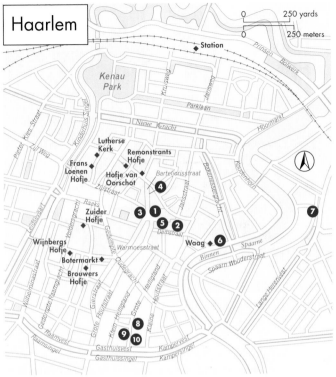

the paintings of Hals and other 17th-century masters of the Haarlem
School, along with period furniture, antique silver, and ceramics.

Many of the works on display represent Hals at his jovial best—for
instance, the *Banquet of the Officers of the Civic Guard of St. Adrian*
(1624–27) or the *Banquet of the Officers of the St. George Militia*
(1616), where the artist cunningly allows for the niceties of rank (cap-
tains are more prominent than sergeants, and so on down the line)
as well as emotional interaction: he was also the first painter to have
people gaze and laugh at each other in these grand portraits.

As respite from nearly 250 canvases, step into the museum's courtyard—lovely, and planted with formal-garden baby hedges, of which
you get only fleeting glimpses as you work your way through the galleries (most of the blinds are shut against the sunlight to protect the paintings). In one room, with curtains drawn for extra protection, is **Sara
Rothé's Dolls' House;** nearby is an exquisitely crafted miniature version
of a merchant's canal house. On leaving, *View of Haarlem* (1655) by
Nicolaes Hals, Frans's son, bids you good-bye. ⊠ *Groot Heiligland 62*
☏ *023/511–5775* ⊕ *www.franshalsmuseum.com* ⊠ *€10* ⊗ *Tues.–Sat.
11–5, Sun. noon–5.*

Gasthuis-huisjes (*Guesthouse–little houses*). Don't miss this series of
houses with their identical step gables at the southern end of Groot

Teylers Museum is the first and oldest museum in the Netherlands.

Heiligland, across the street from the entrance to the Frans Hals Museum. They originally formed part of the St. Elizabeth hospital and were built in 1610.

Grote Kerk (*Great Church*). Late Gothic Sint Bavo's, more commonly called the Great Church, dominates the main market square. It was built in the 14th century, but severe fire damage in 1370 led to a further 150 years of rebuilding and expansion. This is the burial place of Frans Hals—a lamp marks his tombstone behind the brass choir screen. Laurens Coster is buried here, too. It is rumored that he was the first European to use movable type in 1423 (sorry, Gutenberg), which he discovered while carving letters for his children; he was inspired when one of the bark letters fell into the sand and made an imprint. The church is the home of the Müller organ, on which both Handel and Mozart played. Installed in 1738, and for centuries considered the finest in the world, it has been meticulously restored to protect the sound planned by its creator, Christian Müller. Between May and October organists perform free concerts every Tuesday at 8:15 pm, and occasionally on Thursday at 3 pm. Bach fugues have never sounded so magisterial. ✉ *Grote Markt* ☎ *023/533–2040* ⊕ *www.bavo.nl* 🎫 *€2.50* ☉ *Sept.– June, Mon.–Sat. 10–4; July–Aug., Mon.–Sat. 10–5.*

Grote Markt. Around this great market square the whole of Dutch architecture can be traced in a chain of majestic buildings ranging from the 14th to the 19th century (with a smile and a little bravado, you can enter most of them for a quick look). Yet it is the imposing mass of Sint Bavo's that catches the eye and towers over everything.

QUICK
BITES

Grand Café Brinkmann. The spacious Grand Café Brinkmann, adorned with cherubic ceiling paintings, offers baguettes, pancakes, and other light snacks. Windows edged with Art Deco stained glass overlook the Grote Markt and Sint Bavo's church across the square. ✉ *Brinkmannpassage 41* ☎ *023/532-3111* ⊕ *www.grandcafebrinkmann.nl.*

Teylers Museum. Just north of the **Waag** (the Weigh House, built entirely of stone in 1598 and now a plesasant little café), Teylers is housed in a grand 18th-century building with mosaic floors and is the best sort of small museum. It is based on the eclectic whims of an eccentric private collector, in this case the 18th-century merchant Pieter Teyler van der Hulst. Founded in 1784, it's the country's oldest museum and has a mixture of exhibits—fossils and minerals sit alongside antique scientific instruments, such as a battery of 25 Leiden jars, dating from 1789 and used to store an electric charge. The major artistic attraction is a legendary collection of drawings and prints by Michelangelo, Rembrandt, Raphael, and other old masters that once belonged to Queen Christina of Sweden. ✉ *Spaarne 16* ☎ *023/516–0960* ⊕ *www.teylersmuseum.nl* 🎟 *€10* ⊙ *Tues.–Sat. 10–5, Sun. noon–5.*

WORTH NOTING

Amsterdamse Poort (*Amsterdam Gate*). Built around 1400, this is Haarlem's only remaining city gate; remains of the city wall can be seen at its base. It's slightly to the east of the current center, just to the east of the Spaarne River.

Corrie ten Boomhuis (*Corrie ten Boom House*). Just off the Grote Markt, and tucked into a small gabled building above a shop, this house honors a family of World War II resistance fighters who successfully hid a number of Jewish families before being captured by the Germans in 1944. Most of the Ten Boom family died in the concentration camps, but Corrie survived and returned to Haarlem to tell the story in her book *The Hiding Place*. The family clock shop is preserved on the street floor, and their living quarters now contain displays, documents, photographs, and memorabilia. Visitors can also see the hiding closet, which the Gestapo never found, even though they lived six days in the house hoping to starve out anyone who might be concealed here. The upstairs living quarters are not accessible through the shop, but via the side door of No. 19, down a narrow alley beside the shop. Meeting instructions giving the time of the next guided tour are posted on the door. Note that the last tour begins 30 minutes before the posted closing times. ✉ *Barteljorisstraat 19* ☎ *023/531–0823* ⊕ *www.corrietenboom. com* 🎟 *Donations accepted* ⊙ *Apr.–Oct., Tues.–Sat. 10–4; Nov.–Mar., Tues.–Sat. 11–3.*

OFF THE
BEATEN
PATH

Zandvoort. Zandvoort is only 9 km (5½ miles) from Haarlem and has the area's biggest and best beach around—it's a favorite of sun-starved Amsterdammers. It can get crowded but if you wander south for 10 minutes or so, you can find isolated spots among the dunes; after about 20 minutes, you come to the nude, in places gay, sunbathing beach.

Historisch Museum Haarlem. Located near the Frans Hals Museum, the town's history museum makes the most of its limited resources to mount two or three small temporary exhibitions a year, offering insight into the history of the city and the surrounding area. Among the permanent exhibits are video screenings (in English), models of the city, and touch-screen computers relating stories that take you back in history. There are fascinating old prints and maps, along with some apparently random exhibits, including one of the earliest printing presses, dating from the 17th century. Also on view here is an incisive exhibition on modern Dutch architecture, **ABC Architectuur Centrum Haarlem,** with plans and photographs from city projects already finished and still in the planning stages (De Bruijn's Woonhuis is particularly ingenious). ✉ *Groot Heiligland 47* ☎ *023/542–2427* 🌐 *www.historischmuseumhaarlem.nl* 🎟 *€5* 🕒 *Tues.–Sat. noon–5, Sun. 1–5.*

SHOP 'TIL YOU DROP

The pedestrianized Barteljorisstraat has lots of top fashion chains, such as Vanilia, Esprit, and MEXX, as well as a number of streetwear shops for men. The top end of Kruisstraat has furniture shops, from antiques to designer. Flowers can be found on Krocht, on the corner of Kruisstraat and Barteljorisstraat—the sumptuous displays echo the nearby tulip fields between Haarlem and the Keukenhof.

Stadhuis (*Town Hall*). This former hunting lodge on the market square,belonged to the Count of Holland, who permitted it to be transformed into Haarlem's Town Hall in the 14th century. The large main **Gravenzaal** (Count's Hall) is worth a visit—if you can sneak in between bouts of confetti throwing, as there are a good number of bridal parties ascending its steps on a regular basis—to study its collection of 16th-century paintings amassed by the Count of Holland. If you wish to tour the premises, call in advance to get permission. ✉ *Grote Markt 2* ☎ *023/511–5115* 🎟 *Free* 🕒 *Weekdays 10–4 (when not closed for civic functions).*

WHERE TO EAT

$ INDONESIAN 🍴 **De Lachende Javaan.** Stepping into "The Laughing Javanese," off an old Haarlem street that hasn't changed in centuries, you are hit with a flash of color and pungent smells. You can sit upstairs at one of the window tables and look out over the sober gabled houses while eating *kambing saté* (skewers of lamb in soy sauce) and *kipkarbonaade met sambal djeroek* (grilled chicken with a fiery Indonesian sauce). The menu's choices are vast, so you can mix and match, choosing a meal of 12 small dishes if you want. [$] *Average main: €10* ✉ *Frankestraat 27* ☎ *023/532–8792* 🕒 *Closed Mon. No lunch.*

$ CAFÉ 🍴 **Jacobus Pieck.** One of Haarlem's best *eetlokaals* (dining spots) attracts locals with its long bar, cozy tables, and lovely sun trap of a garden. The menu offers standards but with a twist: try the Popeye Blues Salad—a wild spinach, blue cheese, and bacon number, with creamy mustard dressing for a lighter option—or, for dinner, lamb with ratatouille and rosemary jus. As you'll see, the food makes this restaurant-café very popular, so get here early or book ahead to snag a table. [$] *Average*

Haarlem's City Hall as seen from the Grote Markt square.

main: €13 ⊠ *Warmoestraat 18* ☎ *023/532–6144* ⊕ *www.jacobuspieck. nl* ▭ *No credit cards* ☉ *Closed Sun. and Mon.*

$$
CONTEMPORARY
★

✕ **Jopenkerk.** The café/restaruant/brewery tap of the Jopen brewery enjoys a magnificent setting in the lovingly restored interior of the former Jacobskerk. The ecclesiastical feel has been maintained by retaining the high ceilings and stained-glass windows, but elsewhere the style is more contemporary, with the gleaming brewery equipment dominating one side of the room. The restaurant on the mezzanine (open evenings only) serves weekly changing stews and a variety of other meat and fish mains; a simpler lunch menu is available in the grand café below. The menu suggests a house beer to match each of the main dishes—we recommend all of them. Ⓢ *Average main: €15* ⊠ *Gedempte Voldersgracht 2* ☎ *023/533–4114* ⊕ *www.jopenkerk.nl.*

$$$$
DUTCH

✕ **ml.** This new restaurant in a 17th-century mansion that was once a bank has become a showpiece for the creative talents of chefs Mark and Liane Gratema. The small gracious dining room is traditional, with white-painted wooden beams, brightened crisp linens, and light filtering through the mullioned windows. Ask for a table with a view of the enclosed garden (open in summer), or better yet, a table outside, and try the monkfish with shrimp, calf's cheek, spinach, and sherry. The restaurant is convenient to both the Frans Hals and the Teylers museums. Ⓢ *Average main: €34* ⊠ *Kleine Houtstraat 70* ☎ *023/534–5343* ⊕ *www.restaurant-ml.nl* ✎ *Reservations essential* ☉ *Closed Sun. and Mon. No lunch Tues. and Sat.*

$
CONTEMPORARY
★

✕ **XO.** A very funky restaurant-bar, XO has chunky silver graphics, purple-and-gray walls, and oversize but softly lighted lamps. Throw in some fun touches—"king" chairs, complete with claw feet and red

Don't forget to dream an afternoon away at one of Haarlem's many outdoor cafés.

cushions; nifty recesses at the bar for extra intimacy; big stone candlesticks—and you've got an alluring setting for lunch and evening edibles. The dinner menu changes regularly but always contains mouthwatering and exquisitely presented dishes, such as cod fillet baked in a sun-dried-tomato-and-truffle crust, with black pasta, spinach, and a white-wine cream sauce. For a lunchtime snack try the imaginative bread rolls stuffed with marinated salmon and horseradish cream, or a cucumber salad; a fine range of tapas is served all day. $ *Average main: €14* ⊠ *Grote Markt 8* ☎ *023/551–1350* ⊕ *www.xo-haarlem.nl.*

WHERE TO STAY

For expanded hotel reviews, visit Fodors.com.

$ **Carillon.** This is an old-fashioned place with a friendly staff, set in
HOTEL the shadow of Sint Bavo's across the Grote Markt, with small rooms that are spartan but fresh and comfortable. **Pros:** good value; friendly; great location; top spot for a day of exploring and a night out. **Cons:** steep stairs; no elevator; front rooms can be noisy, especially from neighboring bars on weekends. $ *Rooms from: €80* ⊠ *Grote Markt 27* ☎ *023/531–0591* ⊕ *www.hotelcarillon.com* ⤵ *21 rooms, 15 with bath* ⦿| *Breakfast.*

$$ **Golden Tulip Lion d'Or.** Rooms in this pretty 18th-century building near
HOTEL the railway station and within walking distance of major downtown sights are spacious with good lighting and upscale chain-hotel-style furnishings. **Pros:** friendly; attractive; free Wi-Fi and lots of other amenities. **Cons:** not central; not terribly Dutch in flavor. $ *Rooms from: €160*

✉ *Kruisweg 34–36* ☎ *023/532–1750* 🌐 *www.goldentulipliondor.nl* 🛏 *30 rooms, 4 suites* 🍴 *Breakfast.*

$$ HOTEL 🏨 **Stempels.** These sumptuous guest quarters, stylishly contemporary and painted in sleek, modern slates and creams, are the work of Martijn Franzen and Frans van Cappelle, who transformed what was once a mint where Dutch banknotes were printed into an elegant hotel. **Pros:** great location; front rooms face St. Bavo's; historic building; luxury at a reasonable price. **Cons:** lots of stairs. [$] *Rooms from: €113* ✉ *Klokhuisplein 9* ☎ *023/512–3910* 🌐 *www.stempelsinhaarlem.nl* 🛏 *15 rooms, 2 suites* 🍴 *Breakfast.*

ORGAN IMPROV

International Organ Improvisation Competition. Haarlem hosts an International Organ Improvisation Competition in even-numbered years for two weeks in mid-July, giving people ample opportunity to hear the renowned Müller organ in Sint Bavo's church at full throttle. Entry is free. For more information, call ☎ 020/488–0481, or visit 🌐 *www.organfestival.nl.*

NIGHTLIFE AND THE ARTS

Patronaat. Haarlem is more than a city of Old Dutch nostalgia. The Patronaat is an excellent rock music venue, Haarlem's answer to the Melkweg in Amsterdam, only without the really big bands. ✉ *Zijlsingel 2* ☎ *023/517–5858* 🌐 *www.patronaat.nl.*

If you feel like bar hopping but don't want to wear a hole in your shoe, head to Lange Veerstraat or the Botermarkt square, where you'll find a lot of bars and cafés.

Café de Linde. This mellow place is a fine spot for a drink or a light meal. ✉ *Botermarkt 21* ☎ *023/531–9688* 🌐 *www.cafedelinde.nl.*

CaféStudio. Located in a converted Art Deco cinema on the Grote Markt, CaféStudio has an exceptional range of Belgian beers. A mellow café by day, by midevening at weekends it can turn into a rowdy club (free entry) with a DJ, serious lighting, and enormous speakers to ensure the ambience is just right. ✉ *Grote Markt 25* ☎ *023/531–0033* 🌐 *www.cafestudio.nl.*

Gay Café Wilsons. A nighttime landmark, this is the "in" gathering place for gays in Haarlem. ✉ *Gedempte Raamgraacht 78* ☎ *023/532–5854* 🌐 *www.wilsons.nl* ⏲ *Closed Tues.*

Jopenkerk. As well as being a great place to dine, the Jopenkerk brewpub has also become one of *the* places to be seen in Haarlem. ✉ *Gedempte Voldersgracht 2* ☎ *023/533–4114* 🌐 *www.jopenkerk.nl.*

8

THE HAGUE

It's easy to see The Hague as nothing more than Amsterdam's prissy maiden aunt—it's the Netherlands' seat of government, home to the Dutch royal family, and site of the International Court of Justice. Most foreign embassies are located here, too.

Yet The Hague doesn't have the honor of being the national capital, a fact that delights Amsterdammers and confounds quiz teams globally. While it seems at first that the city has been handed all the serious tasks to get on with whilst Amsterdam has all the fun, those who experience the city up close will find a lively metropolis that is both elegant and quirky. Take the time to explore a little and you'll encounter more than 25 public parks, plus a maze of narrow winding streets where contemporary architecture sits comfortably and unabashed beside grand 17th-century mansions. For a time out, relax at sidewalk cafés and watch as they fill with a stream of civil servants and diplomats spilling out from the offices all around the 13th-century Ridderzaal (Knights' Hall), the centerpiece of the parliament. Visit the galleries and museums and you'll find no end of masterpieces by the likes of Rembrandt and Johannes Vermeer, or the dazzling optical conundrums of Dutch graphic artist M.C. Escher, whose logic-defying creations appear to bend the laws of physics.

If you should find yourself tiring of The Hague's grace and charm, seek out its brasher Siamese twin, neighboring Scheveningen, once a fishing port, now a tacky beach resort par excellence. Here you can lose your shirt in the city's casino—or else lose your dignity by taking a dip in the stupendously icy waters of the North Sea.

The Hague's official name is 's-Gravenhage (literally "the Count's Hedge"). It harks back to the 13th century when the Count of Holland's hunting lodge was based here, in a village then called Die Haghe. To the Dutch the city is known simply as Den Haag, and that's the name you'll always hear used on the street.

GETTING HERE AND AROUND

There are two railway stations in The Hague:

Centraal Station. Centraal Station is in the residential area. ⊠ *Koningin Julianaplein.*

Station Hollands Spoor. Station Hollands Spoor is in the central business district. ⊠ *Stationsplein.*

Trains from Amsterdam run directly to both the Centraal and Hollands Spoor stations, but the Centraal stop is an end stop, whereas Hollands Spoor is a through destination and is used as a stop for trains to and from Amsterdam, Delft, and Rotterdam. All international and intercity trains from Brussels and Paris to Amsterdam also stop in The Hague HS (Hollands Spoor). By car from Amsterdam, take E19 via Amsterdam Schiphol Airport. To reach the city from Utrecht, take the A12. Once you're approaching the city, follow the signs for the central parking route. This is an extremely helpful ring road that covers the many inexpensive parking lots within the city center.

On buses trams and trains you can use an **OV-chipkaart** (public transport chip card). These credit card–size tickets can be loaded up with credit from machines in the railway stations, and are debited as you board and leave trains, trams, metros, and buses. There are information and sales points in the stations. Or visit ⊕ *www.ov-chipkaart.nl* for more information.

Taxis are available at railway stations, at major hotels, and at taxi stands in key locations. You can also order a taxi by phone, but they cannot be hailed in the street.

Contacts HTM ⊠ *Grote Marktstraat 43* ☎ *0900/486–4636 €0.10 per min.* ⊕ *www.htm.net.* **Public Transportation Information** ☎ *0900/9292* ⊕ *www.9292ov.nl.*

ORIENTATION

For a city that sees so much political, legal, and diplomatic action, The Hague can seem surprisingly quiet, and a pleasure to those who want to escape the crowds. It's a flat compact city, and most of the sights in the town center are within a 15-minute walk from either of the city's train stations. Tramline Nos. 3 and 17 cover many of the sights in town. Tram No. 17 will also get you to the outlying Statenkwartier museums. Tram No. 9 goes to Madurodam. For information on specific lines, ask at the HTM offices in The Hague's stations, *or at offices listed here.* For information on public transport (trains, buses, trams, and ferries), call the national information line (☎ *0900/9292*).

TOURS

The VVV arranges a variety of tours covering everything from royalty to architecture. Or you can purchase booklets that will allow you to follow a walking tour at your own pace. The VVV does tours and has brochures for them, as well as tickets, at the VVV offices.

From April to October, De Ooievaart runs boat tours around The Hague's canals. The boats depart from Bierkade and offer a peaceful and relaxing way to see the city. Trips last one and a half hours, cost €10, and tickets can be bought from the VVV.

Contacts Day Trips Department, Den Haag Marketing ☎ *070/338–5800* ⊕ *www.denhaag.com/tours.* **De Ooievaart** ☎ *070/445–1869* ⊕ *www.ooievaart. nl.*

TIMING

Done at a pace that will allow you to soak up The Hague's historical atmosphere, a minimal tour around the city center should take about three or four hours. If you stop to visit the main sights en route, you're looking at a very full day. At the very least, allow 30 minutes for each site you visit.

Before you start out, bear a couple of things in mind. First, as in all other Dutch cities, both walking surfaces and the weather can change at short notice; if you're going to be on your feet all day, make sure you're equipped with an umbrella and sturdy walking shoes. Second, most museums and galleries close at 5 and many sites are also closed Monday, so plan accordingly.

ESSENTIALS

Bicycle rentals Fietsverhuur Den Haag. Fietsverhuur Den Haag Bikes cost €10 per day to rent; ID and a €60 deposit are required. ⊠ *Noordeinde 59* ☎ *070/326–5790.*

Emergency Services National Emergency Alarm Number ☎ *112 for police, fire, and ambulance.*

Hospitals Bronovo Hospital ⊠ *Bronovolaan 5* ☎ *070/312–4141* ⊕ *www. bronovo.nl.*

Pharmacies Late-Night Pharmacy Information ☎ *070/345–1000.*

Taxis Taxi Centrale Haaglanden ☎ *070/390–6262* ⊕ *tch.nl.*

Tourism Information VVV The Hague ⊠ *Spui 68* ☎ *070/361–8860* ⊕ *www. denhaag.nl* ⊗ *Mon. noon–8, Tues.–Fri. 10–8, Sat. 10–5, Sun. noon–5.*

EXPLORING

The Hague's center is crammed with the best the city has to offer in terms of art, history, and architecture. An exploration of a relatively small area will take you to the Binnenhof, home to the famous Ridderzaal or along the leafy Lange Voorhout for a stroll through what in the 19th century was the place to see and be seen. Venture a little farther afield and you'll come upon the Gemeentemuseum Den Haag, where works by Vermeer and other masters usually hanging in the Mauritshuis (under renovation) are on view.

TOP ATTRACTIONS

Fodor'sChoice   **Binnenhof and the Ridderzaal** (*Inner Court and the Knights' Hall*). The
★   governmental heart of the Netherlands, the Binnenhofcomplex is in the very center of town yet tranquilly set apart, thanks to the charming Hofvijver (court lake). The setting creates a poetic contrast to the endlessly dull debates that go on within its walls—the basis of everyday Dutch politics. Pomp and decorum are in full fig every third Tuesday of September, when Queen Beatrix arrives at the 13th-century Ridderzaal in a golden coach to open the new session of Parliament.

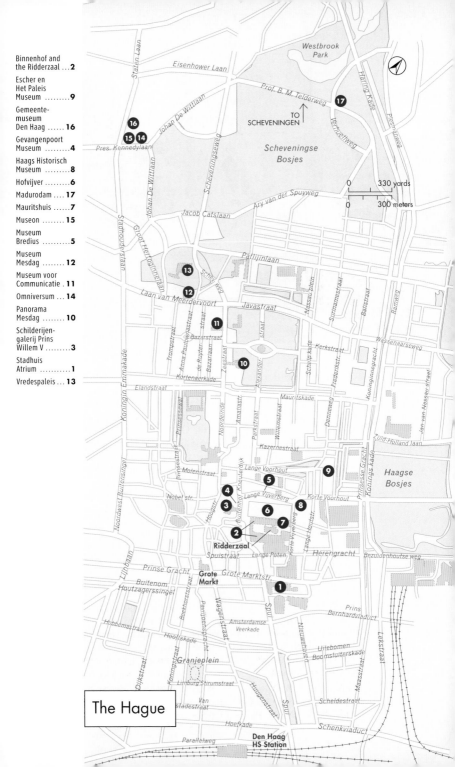

The Hague

The square in front of the Binnenhof is a great place to relax and people-watch.

For many centuries the Binnenhof was the court for the Counts of Holland; it is now a complex of buildings from several eras. As you enter, the twin-turreted former castle of the Earls of Holland dominates the scene. The castle was originally built by Count Floris V and became a meeting hall for the Knights of the Order of the Golden Fleece (one of the most regal societies of the Middle Ages). Their Great Hall simply drips with history: there are vast wooden beams, flags of the Dutch provinces, and a massive rose window bearing coats of arms. In 1900 the hall was restored to its original 13th-century glory; it is still called Knights' Hall, and you can almost feel the feasts and revelries that took place there. The room still plays a key role in Dutch legislative life.

The Binnenhof also incorporates the halls used by the First and Second Chambers of Parliament (equivalent to the U.S. Senate and House of Representatives, respectively). You can wander freely around the open outer courtyard, but entrance to the Ridderzaal and other interior rooms is by guided tour only. The vaulted reception area below the Knights' Hall contains a free exhibition detailing the political history of the Low Countries.

Buy tickets for guided visits at the Pro Demos visitor center at Hofweg 1, across the road from

AM I BEING WATCHED?

As you wander around the Ridderzaal, check out the carved heads by the wooden beams—the ones that seem to be looking down on you judgmentally. And indeed they are. When the hall previously served as a court, judges would tell the accused to fess up, otherwise these "eavesdroppers" would have words with the heavenly powers.

the west entrance to the Binnenhof. ⊠ *Binnenhof 8a* ☎ *070/364–6144* ⊕ *www.prodemos.nl* 🎫 *€6* ⊘ *Mon.–Sat. 10–4 (some areas may be closed when government meetings are taking place).*

Fodor's Choice ★ ℭ **Escher in Het Paleis Museum** (*Escher Museum*). First known as the Lange Voorhout Palace, this lovely building was originally the residence of Caroline of Nassau, daughter of Prince Willem IV—in 1765 Mozart performed for her here. In 2001 the palace was transformed into a museum devoted to Dutch graphic artist M. C. Escher (1892–1972), whose prints and engravings of unforgettable images—roofs becoming floors, water flowing upward, fish transforming into birds—became world famous in the 1960s and '70s. Replete with ever-repeating Baroque pillars, Palladian portals, and parallel horizons, Maurits Cornelis Escher's visual trickery presages the "virtual reality" worlds of today. Fittingly, the museum features an Escher Experience where you don a helmet and take a 360-degree digital trip through his unique world. Concave and convex, radical metamorphoses, and dazzling optical illusions are on view in the impressive selection of his prints (including the famed *Day and Night* and *Ascending and Descending*); distorted rooms and video cameras make children big and adults small; and there are rooms that are Escher prints blown up to the nth power. Don't forget to look up as you walk around—dangling glitteringly from the ceiling is a series of custom-designed chandeliers by Dutch sculptor Hans van Bentem that are inspired by Escher's work. These delightfully playful creations include umbrellas, sea horses, birds, and even a giant skull and crossbones. A family ticket for €23 makes this museum even more attractive for kids. ⊠ *Lange Voorhout 74* ☎ *070/427–7730* ⊕ *www.escherinhetpaleis.nl* 🎫 *€8.50* ⊘ *Tues.–Sun. 11–5.*

> **WHO'S THAT GIRL?**
>
> Johannes Vermeer's immortal *Girl with a Pearl Earring* (to return to the Mauritshuis when its renovations end in 2014) is one of the few paintings ever to have its own spinoff novel and movie. The enigma surrounding the work remains to this day—historians have never been able to determine who this sphinxlike lady actually is. Some think she is Maria, the eldest of Vermeer's 11 children. The novel claims she is Vermeer's maid. Considering the complete lack of ostentatious dress and iconographic symbols, the latter could be a real possibility.

QUICK BITES

Le Café Hathor. Down a quiet side street, off Vos in Tuinstraat and very near the Escher in Het Paleis Museum, the friendly Le Café Hathor is a great spot for a snack, a full lunch, or just a quiet drink. Wood-paneled walls and flickering candles create an intimately cozy atmosphere, while in good weather, tables on a raft overlook a gently flowing canal. Closed on Sundays. ⊠ *Maliestraat 22* ☎ *070/346–4081* ⊕ *www.hathor.nl.*

Fodor's Choice ★ **Gemeentemuseum Den Haag** (*Hague Municipal Museum*). One of the finest examples of 20th-century museum architecture was designed by H. P. Berlage (the grand old master of modern Dutch architecture) and completed in 1935. Although the collection ranges from A to Z—Golden Age silver, Greek and Chinese pottery, historic musical instruments, and paintings by Claude Monet and Vincent van Gogh—the museum is best known for the world's largest collection of works by Piet Mondriaan (1872–1944), the greatest artist of the Dutch De Stijl movement. The crowning masterpiece, and widely considered one of the landmarks of modern art, is Mondriaan's *Victory Boogie Woogie*—an iconic work, begun in 1942 but left unfinished at the artist's death. The painting's signature black-and-white grid interspersed with blocks of primary color arrived only in 1998, when the Netherlands Institute for Cultural Heritage controversially paid 80 million guilders for the (then American-owned) work. Also be sure to see the dollhouse with real doll-size Delft Blue chinaware. Elsewhere, the museum's Costume Gallery contains no fewer than 55,000 items (not all are on display at one time!), providing endless inspiration for dedicated students of fashion.

As a bonus to visitors, the museum is also playing genial if temporary host to 100 or so works normally on show in the ⇨ *Mauritshuis*. Masterpieces by Rembrandt, Jan Steen, and Vermeer (including the latter's immortal *View of Delft*) will be displayed here until renovation work at the latter is completed in mid-2014. ⊠ *Stadhouderslaan 41* ☎ *070/338–1111* ⊕ *www.gemeentemuseum.nl* ▦ *€13.50* ⊙ *Tues.–Sun. 11–5.*

Hofvijver (*Court Lake*). Beside the Binnenhof, this long, rectangular reflecting pool—the venerable remains of a medieval moat—comes complete with tall fountains and a row of pink-blossomed horse-chestnut trees. Today, the lake is spectacularly surrounded by some of The Hague's most elegant historic buildings and museums.

Fodor's Choice
★
☺

Madurodam. Statistically, the Dutch are the tallest people in Europe, and never must they be more aware of their size than when they visit this miniature version of their own land, reopened in April 2012 after a mammoth refurbishment. Set in a sprawling "village" with pathways, tram tracks, and a railway station, every important building of the Netherlands is reproduced here, on a scale of 1:25. Many aspects of Dutch life ancient and modern are also on view: medieval knights joust in the courtyard of Gouda's magnificent Town Hall; windmills turn; the famous cheese-weighing ritual is carried out in Alkmaar; and a harbor fire is extinguished.

Thirty interactive points enable visitors to operate the awe-inspiring Delta Works storm surge barrier (constructed after the disastrous flooding of 1953), closing it to hold the ocean at bay and save villages from drowning. Or you can make a plane take off at Schiphol Airport, or load and unload container ships in the Port of Rotterdam.

Madurodam has two restaurants, a picnic area, and a playground, and the entire exhibit is surrounded by gardens. It is located in the woods that separate The Hague from the port of Scheveningen to the north. To get here take Tram No. 9 from either railway station in the city center. ⊠ *George Maduroplein* ☎ *070/416–2400* ⊕ *www.madurodam. nl* ▦ *€14.50* ⊙ *Nov.–Mar., daily 9–5; Apr.–June, daily 9–8; July and Aug., daily 9–9; Sept. and Oct., daily 9–7.*

Fodor's Choice
★

Mauritshuis. One of Europe's greatest museums, the Mauritshuis is currently closed for essential renovation work until mid-2014. During

H. P. Berlage's Gemeentemuseum Den Haag is considered to be one of the finest examples of 20th-century museum architecture.

this time, thankfully, one hundred of its most important works are on temporary display at the ⇨ *Gemeentemuseum*, including some fabled paintings as Vermeer's *View of Delft*.

8

When the museum reopens, it will have double the floor area, thanks to the creation of a new modern underground lobby (linking the structure with the neighboring Plein 26 building) and a new wing for a café, museum shop, education area, library, and auditorium. To quote the website: "The Mauritshuis of the future will be a cultural meeting place where visitors will not just look at art, but truly experience it." In point of fact, the old Mauritshuis was magnificent enough, thanks to its incomparable feast of art, including no less than 14 Rembrandts, 10 Jan Steens, and 3 Vermeers. The latter's remarkable *View of Delft* takes pride of place; its rediscovery in the late 19th century assured the artist's eternal fame. In the same room is Vermeer's (1632-75) most haunting work, *Girl with a Pearl Earring*, which inspired Tracy Chevalier's 1999 best-selling novel as well as the 2003 filmed version. For something completely different, look to Jan Steen (1626-79), who portrayed the daily life of ordinary people in the Netherlands of the 17th century. His painting *The Way You Hear It Is the Way You Sing It* is particularly telling. Don't miss local boy Paulus Potter's vast canvas *The Bull*, complete with steaming cow dung; the 7-foot-by-11-foot painting leaves nothing to be said on the subject of beef on the hoof.

As an added treat, the original building itself is worthy of a 17th-century master's brush: a cream-colored mansion tucked into a corner behind the Parliament complex and overlooking the Hofvijver river. It was built around 1640 for one Johan Maurits, Count of Nassau-Siegen and governor-general of Dutch Brazil. The pair behind its creation, Jacob van Campen and Pieter Post, were the two most important Dutch architects of their era. Soon to be brought beautifully into the 21st century, this will truly be one of the finest museums in Europe. ⊠ *Korte Vijverberg 8* ☎ *070/302–3456 for info* ⊕ *www.mauritshuis.nl.*

★ **Panorama Mesdag.** Long before TV was capable of reproducing reality, painted panoramas gave viewers the chance to immerse themselves in another world. The *Panorama Mesdag,* painted in 1880 by the renowned marine artist Hendrik Willem Mesdag and a team including his wife, Sientje Mesdag-van Houtenback, is one of the largest and finest surviving examples of the genre. The cinematic vision is a sweeping view of the sea, the dunes, and the picturesque fishing village of Scheveningen. To enhance the effect of the painting, you are first led through a narrow, dark passage, then up a spiral staircase, and out onto a "sand dune" viewing platform. To the southeast is The Hague, detailed so perfectly that old-time residents can identify particular houses. So lifelike is the 45-foot-high panorama with a 400-foot circumference that it's hard to resist the temptation to step across the guardrail onto the dune and stride down to the water's edge. ⊠ *Zeestraat 65* ☎ *070/364–4544* ⊕ *panorama-mesdag.nl* 🖾 *€7; combined ticket with De Mesdag Collection €10* ☉ *Mon.–Sat. 10–5, Sun. noon–5.*

★ **Vredespaleis** (*Peace Palace*). Facing the world across a broad lawn, this building houses the International Court of Justice plus a 500,000-volume law library. The court was initiated in 1899 by Czar Nicolas II of Russia, who invited 26 nations to meet in The Hague to set up a permanent world court of arbitration. The current building was constructed in 1903 with a $1.5 million gift from Scottish-American industrialist Andrew Carnegie. Built in Flemish style, its red-and-gray granite-and-brick pile has become a local landmark. Gifts from the participating nations embellish the interior and include statuary, stained-glass windows, doors, and clocks. Comparatively few litigations are heard here these days, although some still make headlines, such as the famous trial of Slobodan Milošević.

A visitor center at the entrance gate provides a brief introduction to the workings of the palace and its exhibits. Free audioguides in English are provided. ⊠ *Carnegieplein 2* ☎ *070/302–4242* ⊕ *www.vredespaleis.nl* 🖾 *Visitor center free, tours €8.50* ☉ *Visitor center: Mar.–Oct., daily 10–5; Nov.–Feb., daily 10–4. Hours for guided tours vary when court is not in session.*

STREET MARKETS

Grote Kerk. The main traditional street market (and an organic farmers' market) in The Hague is held outside the Grote Kerk Wednesday from 11 to 6.

Lange Voorhout. From early May until late October on Thursday and Sunday, an antiques market takes over Lange Voorhout. Wandering through the stalls on a fine day, perhaps to the accompaniment of a street musician, is a lovely experience. An alfresco café supplies that all-important coffee and apple cake.

WORTH NOTING

De Mesdag Collectie (*The Mesdag Collection*). Literally wallpapered with grand paintings and exquisite fabrics and tapestries, this oft-overlooked treasure-house is the former residence of noted 19th-century Dutch painter H. W. Mesdag. Famed for his vast *Panorama Mesdag,* he left this house as a repository for his collection of works from The Hague School, which often featured seascapes and the life of fisherfolk in nearby Scheveningen. ⌧ *Laan van Meerdervoort 7f* ☎ *070/364–6940* ⊕ *www.museummesdag.nl* ✆ *€7.50, combined ticket with Panorama Mesdag €10* ☉ *Wed.–Sun. noon–5.*

BY BIKE

With plenty of cycle lanes, The Hague is as safe for cyclists as anywhere else in the Netherlands. Be wary of bikes with back-pedal brakes, which can be alarming if you're not used to them. Most railway station shops will rent you a model with handlebar brakes for a slightly higher rate.

Galerij Prins Willem V (*Prince William V Painting Gallery*). One of the last remaining Dutch art *kabinets,* this princely gallery is packed with Old Masters hung in 18th-century *touche-touche* fashion (with barely an inch between paintings). Opened in 1773, the gallery became the Netherlands' first public museum (until then most collections were seen only by special appointment). The cream of the collection was later moved to the Mauritshuis, but many fine works remain. The long narrow room has grand Louis XVI stucco ceilings, but nevertheless exudes an intimate homey atmosphere, as if a friend who just happened to own a collection that included works by Jan Steen and Rembrandt had asked you over to see them. ⌧ *Buitenhof 35* ☎ *070/302–3435* ⊕ *www.galerijprinswillemv. nl* ✆ *€5; combined ticket with Gevangenpoort Museum €10* ☉ *Tues.– Sun. noon–5.*

Gevangenpoort Museum (*Prison's Gate Museum*). Originally a gatehouse to the local duke's castle, Gevangenpoort was converted to a prison around 1420. In 1882, it opened in its current incarnation as both a monument to its own past and a museum to apparatuses of punishment. After a slide presentation, the guided tour will take you through the torture chamber, the women's section, and the area where the rich were once imprisoned. If you're drawn to the macabre, the Gevangenpoort Museum offers a fascinating, if chilling, experience, showcasing enough instruments of inhumanity to satisfy any criminologist. But it's not recommended for smaller children. ⌧ *Buitenhof 33* ☎ *070/346–0861* ⊕ *www.gevangenpoort.nl* ✆ *€7.50; combined ticket with Galerij Prins Willem V €10* ☉ *Tues.–Fri. 10–5, weekends noon–5. Guided tours only, every hr at 15 mins to the hr (first tour at 10:45; last at 3:45).*

Haags Historisch Museum (*Hague Historical Museum*). One of the series of museums that encircle the Hofvijver lake, the Historical Museum is in the Sebastiaansdoelen, a magnificent Classical-Baroque mansion dating from 1636. Worthy of a visit in itself, the mansion houses collections that offer an in-depth look at The Hague's past. Treasures include Jan van Goyen's enormous 17th-century panoramic painting of the city, a collection of medieval church silver, and a dollhouse from 1910. The idyllic views out the windows over the Hofvijver lake and

Check out mini-Holland at Madurodam.

the greensward of the Lange Voorhout are good for the soul. ⊠ *Korte Vijverberg 7* ☎ *070/364–6940* ⊕ *www.haagshistorischmuseum.nl* ⊡ *€7.50* ⊙ *Tues.–Fri. 10–5, weekends noon–5.*

Museon. Museon claims to be "the most fun-packed popular science museum in the Netherlands," and perhaps they're right. Permanent exhibitions center on the origins of the universe and evolution, with hands-on, interactive displays, frequent special exhibitions, and children's workshops on Wednesday and Sunday afternoons (book in advance). The Museon is right next door to the Gemeentemuseum, so you can easily combine a visit to both. ⊠ *Stadhouderslaan 37* ☎ *070/338–1338* ⊕ *www.museon.nl* ⊡ *€10* ⊙ *Tues.–Sun. 11–5.*

Museum Bredius. Housed in an 18th-century patrician mansion, the collection of traveler and art connoisseur Abraham Bredius (1855–1946) supports the argument that the private collections are often the best. It includes works by Jan Steen, as well as nearly 200 paintings by Dutch "little masters"—whose art Bredius trumpeted. Once curator of the Mauritshuis, Bredius was the first art historian to question the authenticity of Rembrandt canvases (there were zillions of them in the 19th century), setting into motion a seismic quake that reduced the master's oeuvre to fewer than 1,000 works. The house, overlooking the Hofvijver, makes a fittingly elegant setting for the art. ⊠ *Lange Vijverberg 14* ☎ *070/362–0729* ⊕ *www.museumbredius.nl* ⊡ *€6* ⊙ *Tues.–Sun. 11–5.*

Museum voor Communicatie (*Communication Museum*). Ultramodern and with lots of space, light, and activities, the Communication Museum looks at the ways in which people have gotten in touch with one another over the years, from carrier pigeon to e-mail. Some exhibits are specifically designed for young children, allowing them to play with old telex machines or design their own cell-phone ringtones. Much of the signage is in Dutch, although English-speaking audio guides are available. ✉ *Zeestraat 82* ☎ *070/330–7500* 🌐 *www.muscom.nl* 🎟 *€8.50* 🕒 *Weekdays 10–5, weekends noon–5.*

Omniversum. The IMAX theater shows a rotating program of film spectaculars, including several with nature-based and futuristic themes, on a screen six stories high. It's one of the few Hague sights open in the evenings. ✉ *Pres. Kennedylaan 5* ☎ *0900/666–4837 €0.35/min.* 🌐 *www.omniversum.nl* 🎟 *€10.*

Stadhuis Atrium (*Town Hall*). Richard Meier's Neo-Modernist 1995 complex, comprising the Town Hall, Central Library, and Municipal Record Office, is an awe-inspiring creation in aluminum, glass, and white epoxy resin. Take the elevator to the 11th floor (weekdays only) to get the full effect of the building's light and space. The architect's attention to mathematical relationships—every aspect of the design is based on measurements that are multiples of 17.73 inches—makes for mesmerizing effect. Meier has endeavored to show the building, both literally and metaphorically, in its best light—the quality of light in the vast central lobby belies the fact you are actually indoors. ✉ *Spui 70* ☎ *070/353–3629* 🌐 *www.atriumdenhaag.nl* 🎟 *Free* 🕒 *Mon.–Wed. and Fri. 7–7, Thurs. 7–9:30, Sat. 9:30–5.*

WHERE TO EAT

$ ECLECTIC ★ 🍴 **Dudok Brasserie.** These days, Dudok is *the* in place in The Hague. It's ideal for people-of-every-stripe-watching, from politicians debating over a beer to the fashionistas toying with their salads to pensioners tucking into an afternoon tea of cream cakes and salmon sandwiches. The vast granite-and-metal interior looks like a cross between a 1930s railway station and an ultracontemporary factory, and besides the countless small tables and roomy bar area, there's a communal central table and a packed magazine rack to keep solo diners busy. The menu combines international dishes—carpaccio of beef, steaks, and grilled chicken—with traditional Dutch fare such as mustard soup (surprisingly mild and flavorful) and sausage with cabbage. Additional pluses include a terrace for outdoor dining and a post-midnight closing on Thursday, Friday, and Saturday. [$] *Average main: €9* ✉ *Hofweg 1a* ☎ *070/890–0100* 🌐 *www.dudok.nl.*

$$ INDONESIAN ★ 🍴 **Garoeda.** Named after a golden eagle in Indonesian mythology, a symbol of happiness and friendship, Garoeda is something of an institution among locals, many of whom consider it the best Indonesian spot in town. Established in 1949 and spread over five floors, the restaurant is decorated with Eastern art, and filled with wicker chairs and lush plants to give it a unique "colonial" atmosphere. Waiters are dressed in traditional costume and are more than happy to advise patrons new to the Indonesian dining experience. In addition to a choice of no less than seven different *rijsttafels* (an exotic smorgasbord of Indonesian dishes), there is also an extensive à la carte menu, featuring some unusual finds, such as spicy mussels and crispy roasted chicken in soy sauce.

8

$ *Average main: €15* ✉ *Kneuterdijk 18a* ☎ *070/346–5319* ⊕ *www.garoeda.com.*

$$$ ✗ **It Rains Fishes.** Crown Prince Willem Alexander has been known to pop in here, so you know it must be good. A gleaming eggshell, ivory, and mirrored jewel box, It Rains Fishes is run by a team of international chefs, whose predominantly aquatic specialties combine Thai, Malaysian, Indonesian, and French flavors. Its name, taken from a Thai folktale of fishes jumping from the river after a heavy rainfall, finds a few echoes in the restaurant's décor, with the occasional painted fish leaping around on the ceiling and walls. Specialties include sea bass with lemon and tarragon oil, and king crab in the shell with Malay black pepper sauce. For an unorthodox but totally winning dessert, choose the Thai-basil-and-chocolate sorbet. Outdoor dining is available in good weather. $ *Average main: €26* ✉ *Noordeinde 123* ☎ *070/365–2598* ⊕ *www.itrainsfishes.nl* ☾ *Closed Sun. No lunch Sat.*

ECLECTIC
Fodor'sChoice
★

> **BAR FOOD**
>
> When sitting down to a glass of beer, there's little the Dutch like more than a portion of hot *bitterballen*: half a dozen or so deep-fried, breadcrumb-coated "balls," with a side of mustard for dipping. When you bite into one you'll encounter finely ground meat-based goo with negligible nutritional value. What this is exactly, no one seems to know for sure. The meat part may have once belonged to a cow, but you can bet your life it wasn't finest rump. We love them!

$$ ✗ **Lokanta.** A well-priced menu and funky colorful decorations, like floral oilcloths on the tables and gilded tissue holders, make this eatery popular with trendy young locals, who flock in to enjoy a delicious combination of Greek, Turkish, and Moroccan dishes. Try the *imam beyildi* (Turkish for "the imam fainted"), the name for a dish of eggplant stuffed with a spicy meat mixture. Because Lokanta is less expensive than some other places on this central street, it fills up fast, so get there early or reserve ahead. $ *Average main: €15* ✉ *Buitenhof 4* ☎ *070/392–0870* ⊕ *www.lokanta.nl* ☾ *Closed Sun. and Mon. No lunch.*

ECLECTIC
★

$$ ✗ **'t Goude Hooft.** Magnificently dating from 1423 but rebuilt in 1660, the oldest restaurant in The Hague has a well-preserved interior redolent of the Dutch Golden Age, complete with wood-beamed ceilings. A 2012 makeover removed the former antique furniture and replaced most of it with something altogether more contemporary, but it remains impressive nonetheless. In warm weather, the large terrace overlooking the market square makes a pleasant spot in which to enjoy a drink and a platter of bitterballen. For something more substantial, try the wine-enriched beef stew. $ *Average main: €15* ✉ *Dagelijkse Groenmarkt 13* ☎ *070/744–8830* ⊕ *www.tgoudehooft.nl.*

DUTCH

$$$ ✗ **The Penthouse.** One of The Hague's top dining spots in every sense of the word sits on the 42nd floor of the Hague Tower, close to Den Haag HS railway station. Better still, the prices are far less than sky high, and sumptuous dishes such as skate wing in almond butter or roasted guinea fowl can be enjoyed without the need to extend your credit line. The views over the city are simply stunning, particularly from the sheltered outdoor terrace some 400 feet above street level. $ *Average main: €22*

DUTCH

✉ The Hague Tower, Rijswijkseplein 786, Centrum ☎ 070/305–1003 🌐 www.thepenthouse.nl ✍ Reservations essential.

WHERE TO STAY

For expanded hotel reviews, visit Fodors.com.

$$ HOTEL 🏨 **Best Western Hotel Petit.** Two large houses that date from 1895, fronted by a pretty garden, are tastefully furnished in warm shades of red and gold, with the occasional period stained-glass accent. **Pros:** quiet; friendly; family-run. **Cons:** a little way from the center. [$] *Rooms from: €125 ✉ Groothertoginnelaan 42 ☎ 070/346–5500 🌐 www.hotelpetit.nl 🛏 20 rooms 🍴 Breakfast.*

$$$$ HOTEL Fodor's Choice ★ 🏨 **Hotel Des Indes.** What was once a 19th-century mansion is one of the world's premier hotels, with a harmonious blend of marble fluted columns, brocaded walls, and gilding, as well as ample bedrooms with all the best facilities. **Pros:** sumptuous; elegant; centrally located. **Cons:** such luxury doesn't come cheap. [$] *Rooms from: €240 ✉ Lange Voorhout 54–56 ☎ 070/361–2345 🌐 www.hoteldesindesthehague.com 🛏 79 rooms, 13 suites.*

$ 🏨 **Hotel Mozaic.** Modern décor and furnishings, color schemes in shades of white and gray, and spacious surroundings lend guest rooms and lounges a light, airy feel. **Pros:** very friendly; a short walk north of the main sights. **Cons:** some rooms face a busy junction and can be a bit noisy. [$] *Rooms from: €119 ✉ Laan Copes van Cattenburch 38, Centrum ☎ 070/352–2335 🌐 www.mozaic.nl 🛏 25 rooms 🍴 Breakfast.*

$ HOTEL 🏨 **Novotel Den Haag City Centre.** These standard-issue guest rooms decorated in shades of peach and blue are housed in what was once a cinema, although you'll need a bit of imagination to visualize this past life. **Pros:** central; friendly. **Cons:** not for those with an aversion to chain hotels. [$] *Rooms from: €99 ✉ Hofweg 5–7 ☎ 070/203–9003 🌐 www.accorhotels.nl 🛏 104 rooms, 2 suites.*

$$ HOTEL ★ 🏨 **Parkhotel Den Haag.** A beautiful secluded sculpture garden and light, airy rooms with wooden floorboards and all the modern conveniences add to the charms of a 1912 building that still exults in plenty of Art Nouveau detailing. **Pros:** friendly; grand; snazzy bathrooms. **Cons:** expensive parking. [$] *Rooms from: €135 ✉ Molenstraat 53 ☎ 070/362–4371 🌐 www.parkhoteldenhaag.nl 🛏 120 rooms 🍴 Breakfast.*

$$$ B&B/INN 🏨 **Residenz Stadslogement.** In the stylish Duinoord neighborhood, this luxurious and friendly bed and breakfast occupies an elegant 1895 townhouse that was once the residence of the Spanish Consul. **Pros:** feels like a private home; a short tram ride from the central sights and a few minutes' walk from the Gemeentemuseum and the Omniversum. **Cons:** fills up quickly, so book well in advance if possible. [$] *Rooms from: €175 ✉ Sweelinckplein 35, Duinoord ☎ 070/364–6190 🌐 www.residenz.nl/ 🛏 6 rooms 🍴 Breakfast.*

$ HOTEL 🏨 **Sebel.** Tidy and comfortable guest rooms here are sparsely furnished but large, and have high ceilings and tall windows for lots of light and air. **Pros:** historic surroundings; friendly staff. **Cons:** a little way from the action between the city center and the Peace Palace; fairly basic.

[$] *Rooms from: €79* ✉ *Prins Hendrikplein 20* ☎ *070/345–9200* 🌐 *www.hotelsebel.nl* 🛏 *33 rooms* 🍴 *Breakfast.*

$ HOTEL **Stayokay.** An outlet of one of the leading hostel chains in Holland enjoys a location close to Holland's Spoor train station and offers 12 double rooms, along with dorms that sleep up to nine people each. **Pros:** nice canalside deck; good value. **Cons:** like any hostel, can be noisy and you can't always choose your roommates. [$] *Rooms from: €60* ✉ *Scheepmakersstraat 27* ☎ *070/315–7888* 🌐 *www.stayokay.com* 🛏 *49 rooms* 🍴 *Breakfast.*

NIGHTLIFE AND THE ARTS

THE ARTS

The Hague has a thriving cultural life—look no further than the gleaming Spui theater complex for proof. The resident orchestra and ballet company are so popular that advance reservations are essential. If you do catch a show, you'll note an unusual phenomenon from the otherwise normally reserved Dutch: the compulsory standing ovation. For some mysterious reason, this response seems to be given with far greater frequency here than in other countries.

Haags Uitburo. For information on cultural events, call the Haags Uitburo or visit their website. ✉ *Spui 68* ☎ *070/361–8860* 🌐 *www.haagsuitburo.nl.*

MUSIC, THEATER AND DANCE

Kooman's Poppentheater. For an outing with children, visit Kooman's Poppentheater, which performs musical shows with puppets every Wednesday and some Saturdays. Advance booking is recommended. ✉ *Frankenstraat 66* ☎ *070/355–9305* 🌐 *www.koomanspoppentheater.nl.*

Nederlands Danstheater. The Nederlands Danstheater is the national modern dance company and makes its home at the Lucent Dance Theatre, built exclusively for dance performances. The company has an international reputation for groundbreaking productions, some of which cause a run on tickets. ✉ *Spuiplein 150* ☎ *070/880–0333* 🌐 *www.ldt.nl.*

Residentie Orkest. The Hague's Residentie Orkest has an excellent worldwide reputation and performs at the Dr. Anton Philipszaal concert hall. ✉ *Spuiplein 150* ☎ *070/880–0200* 🌐 *www.residentieorkest.nl.*

NIGHTLIFE

Though The Hague seems fairly quiet at night, don't be fooled. Behind the reserved facade are plenty of clubs and bars tucked away, often discreetly hidden down tiny backstreets. However, if you like your nightlife of the pumpingly loud variety, you'd best hop on a train to Amsterdam.

BARS

Bodega de Posthoorn. To enjoy an aperitif in an upscale setting while surrounded by The Hague's bold and beautiful, a trip to Bodega de Posthoorn is a must. You can have light meals here and the leafy terrace is particularly appealing. ✉ *Lange Voorhout 39a* ☎ *070/360–4906* 🌐 *www.bodegadeposthoorn.nl.*

Boterwaag. A local favorite, this is located in a 17th-century weigh house with high, vaulted brick ceilings that make this magnificent bar feel open and airy even when packed. It draws a trendy young crowd. ⊠ *Grote Markt 8a* ☎ *070/365–9686* ⊕ *www.gmdh.nl.*

Café Van Delden. This spot has a delightful old-world ambience, with lots of wood, tiles, and a magnificent fireplace. ⊠ *Noordeinde 137* ☎ *070/364–2394.*

De Paap. Head here to enjoy live music most nights and a cozy welcoming aura. The beer's cheap, too. ⊠ *Papestraat 32* ☎ *070/365–2002* ⊕ *www.depaap.nl.*

> ## DISTINGUISHED COMPANY
>
> The Café Schlemmer's convenient location right in the heart of the city, just around the corner from the Parliament building, makes it a meeting point for some pretty high-fliers. You could find yourself rubbing shoulders with anyone from local politicians to Dutch movie stars. If you hear a gasp followed by awed chatter when someone you don't recognize walks in, it probably means they're big in Holland.

Paas. This popular place sits beside a picturesque canal between Hollands Spoor Station and the city center. A haven for beer connoisseurs, it offers 180 brews, by far the best selection in town. Dunne Bierkade is also home to many other bars and restaurants, and has been dubbed the city's "Avenue Culinaire." ⊠ *Dunne Bierkade 16a* ☎ *070/360–0019* ⊕ *www.depaas.nl.*

Schlemmer. This comfortable brown-style bar is one of Den Haag's top places to see and be seen. ⊠ *Lange Houtstraat 17* ☎ *070/360–9000* ⊕ *www.schlemmer.nl.*

Stairs. The friendly and relaxed Stairs is gay-oriented, but women are welcome here, too. ⊠ *Nieuwe Schoolstraat 11* ☎ *070/364–8191.*

MUSIC CLUBS

Het Paard van Troje. The latest local and international bands can be heard at Het Paard van Troje, where you can also dance and watch movies and multimedia shows. ⊠ *Prinsegracht 12* ☎ *070/750–3434* ⊕ *www.paard.nl.*

SHOPPING

There is a plethora of intimate, idiosyncratic specialty boutiques to explore in The Hague, and in the larger department stores you can kid yourself that you're there only to admire the architecture—several are housed in period gems. With its historic and artistic connections, the city's art and antiques trade has naturally developed a strong reputation, and you can certainly find treasures here. Despite the Dutch reputation for thrift, haggling for antiques isn't "done." That said, you can almost always secure some kind of discount if you offer to pay in cash. Late-night shopping in The Hague is on Thursday until 9. Increasingly in the center of town, you'll find larger stores open on Sunday. Many shops take a half day or don't open at all on Monday.

DID YOU KNOW?

More than 125 years old, the Hague's Passage is the oldest shopping arcade in the Netherlands. Three covered streets—Spuistraat, Buitenhof, and Hofweg—converge in a neo-Renaissance and expressionist–style rotunda that is flooded with natural light thanks to the massive skylights. Along with the shopping arcades in Milan, Moscow, and Brussels, The Passage is one of the finest remaining historical arcades in Europe.

DEPARTMENT STORES

De Bijenkorf. De Bijenkorf is Holland's premier department-store chain. It has a reputation for combining class with accessibility and is excellent for cutting-edge housewares, fashion accessories, and clothing basics. Do look, too, at the building's period detailing: stained-glass windows, carvings, and original flooring adorn the sweeping stairway on the left of the store. ⊠ *Wagenstraat 32, entrance on Grote Markstraat* ☎ *0800/0818* ⊕ *www.debijenkorf.nl.*

Maison de Bonneterie. The Maison de Bonneterie is The Hague's most exclusive department store—and it's got the "By Royal Appointment" labels to prove it. Built in 1913 and with an enormous central atrium, the landmark is a glittering mixture of glass and light. On four floors you'll find everything from Ralph Lauren shirts to wax candles. ⊠ *Gravenstraat 2* ☎ *070/330–5300* ⊕ *www.debonneterie.nl.*

WHERE TO SHOP

Denneweg, Frederikstraat, and Noordeinde are best for antiques shops, galleries, and boutiques. For quirky, one-of-a-kind gift shops, try Molenstraat and Papestraat. You'll find chain stores in the pretty, light-filled Hague Passage (⊠ Spuistraat 26), which dates from the 1880s and is the Netherlands' last remaining period mall. In the little streets behind the Passage are more fashion and house-ware boutiques. Between the Venestraat and Nieuwstraat is the charmingly named Haagsche Bluf (the name is akin to the "hot air" coming out of Washington, D.C.) pedestrian mall, featuring mainly clothing chain stores.

SPECIALTY STORES

ANTIQUES AND FINE ART

There are so many reputable antiques and art specialists on Noordeinde and Denneweg that a trip down either street is sure to prove fruitful.

Smelik & Stokking. Specializing in contemporary art, Smelik & Stokking welcomes browsers, and has a pretty sculpture garden full of unusual pieces. ⊠ *Noordeinde 150* ☎ *070/364–0768* ⊕ *www.smelik-stokking.nl.*

BOOKS AND PRINTS

Selexys Verwijs. You can buy English-language newspapers at the city's train stations, and the centrally located Selexys Verwijs, one of a franchise chain of bookstores, also sells a good range of English-language magazines and books. ⊠ *De Passage 39* ☎ *070/311–4848* ⊕ *www. selexyz.nl.*

CLOTHING

FG Van den Heuvel. For handmade men's shirts, visit the diplomats' favorite supplier, FG Van den Heuvel, in business since 1882. ⊠ *Hoge Nieuwstraat 36* ☎ *070/346–0887* ⊕ *www.fgvandenheuvel.com.*

Hoogeweegen Rouwers. Both men and women can find classics with a twist in natural linens, cottons, and wools at Hoogeweegen Rouwers. The service is as timeless as the clothes—it's the sort of place where purchases are carefully wrapped in tissue paper. ⊠ *Noordeinde 23* ☎ *070/365–7473* ⊕ *www.hoogeweegenrouwers.nl.*

CRYSTAL, CHINA AND HOUSEWARES

Rivièra Maison. Head here for household goods, chinaware, and furnishings with—their words—a "New England resort" theme. There's plenty of room to look around without fear of breaking anything. ⊠ *Hoogstraat 5* ☎ *070/356–9986.*

GIFTS, SOUVENIRS AND JEWELRY

Emma Plate & Strass. Tucked away from the crowds is Emma Plate & Strass, a tiny, very feminine store complete with whitewashed walls and a wooden floor. The owner specializes in silver plate and costume jewelry, much imported from Paris and Berlin. She also stocks a small range of fabulous chandeliers, sometimes in unusual colors, such as purple. ⊠ *Molenstraat 22* ☎ *070/345–7027.*

Backers & Zoon. Customers at Backers & Zoon receive the sort of personal attentive service one would expect from an old-fashioned family jeweler. There's a sophisticated stock of pieces, including signet rings, diamond rings, and Fabergé-style accessories. Prices are not for the fainthearted. ⊠ *Noordeinde 58* ☎ *070/346–6422* ⊕ *www.zegelring. com.*

Damen/Papier Royaal. This is a delightfully old-fashioned store that sells exquisite handmade papers and gift wrap, as well as covered notebooks. Damen/Papier Royaal doesn't appear to have changed a great deal since it first opened in 1895. ⊠ *Noordeinde 186* ☎ *070/360–0166* ⊕ *www. papier-royaal.nl.*

DELFT

For many travelers, few spots in Holland are as intimate and attractive as this charming little town. With time-burnished canals and cobblestone streets, Delft possesses a calm that recalls the quieter pace of the 17th-century Golden Age, back when Johannes Vermeer was counted among its citizens.

Fodor's Choice
★

Imagine a tiny Amsterdam, but with smaller canals, narrower bridges, and fewer people, and you have the essence of Old Delft. But even though the city reveres its favorite son, and folks have one foot rooted in the past, another is planted firmly in the present. In fact, today's Delft teems with hip cafés, and—being a college town—revelers can be seen piling in and out of bars almost every day of the week. It's quaint, but it's no museum piece swaddled in cotton wool to keep it safe for future generations. Nonetheless, if living it up isn't your thing, the revelry is easy to escape, and there are plenty of quiet residential corners where you could imagine Vermeer strolling the streets looking for his next subject.

If you are arriving by train in the coming years, your first impression, however, may be somewhat different. Major construction work in and around the railway station is underway. It will eventually see the train tracks moved underground, and thus the city's approaches will be greatly beautified. But that work is scheduled to last until at least 2016, and some skeptics who see the slow progress of the north-south line in Amsterdam believe it may cause disruption as far into the future as 2020. The biggest victim of all this is the Rose Windmill (*Molen de Roos*), which sits directly over the proposed underground route. For safety reasons it is closed to visitors, and the bakery that operated within has been rehoused.

Rest assured, however, that once you pick your way through the chaos, the old center is—apart from a couple of sites *mentioned below*—largely

8

unaffected and every bit as beautiful as it ever was. Well, almost: sad to say, virtually nothing is left standing that Vermeer immortalized in his *View of Delft*—once proclaimed "the most beautiful painting in the world" by Marcel Proust—other than the soaring Gothic spire of the town's Oude Kerk. To find "Vermeer's View," head from the train station along Zuiderstraat or hew instead to the canal bank over to the Zuidwal avenue, which leads to the site of Rotterdamse Poort: it was on the far side of this big canal that Vermeer stood when painting his famous cityscape.

GETTING HERE AND AROUND

14 km (9 miles) southeast of The Hague, 71 km (44 miles) southwest of Amsterdam.

Direct trains leave Amsterdam Central Station for Delft every half hour throughout the day—the journey time is a little under one hour. If driving, take the A10, then the A4 south from Amsterdam. The drive will take between 45 minutes and one hour, depending on traffic.

Trams also run between Delft and The Hague. On buses, trams, and trains, you can use an **OV-chipkaart** (public transport chip card). These credit card–size tickets can be loaded up with credit from machines in the railway stations, and are debited as you board and leave trains, trams, metros, and buses.

Public Transportation Information ☎ *0900/9292* ⊕ *www.9292ov.nl.*

TOURS

The Delft City tour is a two-hour combined walking and canal boat tour, which provides the ideal way to capture the essence of the town in a nutshell if time is short. It leaves from the tourist office daily at 11:30, April through September. Tours cost €12.50 per person—sign up at least 30 minutes beforehand. Canal boat tours cost €6.75 per person, and leave hourly on the hour from Koornmarkt 113 between 11 and 5 daily, April through October.

Rondvaart Delft ✉ *Koornmarkt 113* ☎ *015/212-6385* ⊕ *rondvaartdelft.nl.*

TIMING

Delft is the kind of place you'll want to linger. Allow at least a day to enjoy it all, two if you take in all the museums.

ESSENTIALS

Bicycle Rentals Rijwiel Shop ✉ *Delft train station (at rear)* ☎ *015/214-3033* 🖃 *From €7.50 per day and a security deposit of €50–€100 with ID* ☾ *Weekdays 5:45–midnight, weekends 6:30–midnight.*

Emergency Services National Emergency Alarm Number ☎ *112 for police, fire, and ambulance.*

Hospitals Reinier de Graaf Gasthuis ✉ *Reinier De Graafweg 3–11* ☎ *015/260-3060* ⊕ *www.rdgg.nl.*

Taxis Delftse Taxicentrale Deltax ☎ *015/219-1919* ⊕ *www.dtdeltax.nl.*

Visitor Information Toeristen Informatie Punt Delft (Delft Tourist Information Point) ✉ *Hippolytusbuurt 4* ☎ *0900/515-1555 €0.40 per min.* ⊕ *www. delft.nl.*

A Brief History of Delft

Delft has more than painterly charm—many great men lived and died here. Toward the end of the 16th century, Prince William of Orange (known as William the Silent) settled in Delft to wage his war against Spanish rule. He never left: the nation's founder was assassinated in his mansion in 1584 by a spy of the Spanish Duke of Alva and buried in the Nieuwe Kerk (New Church). Also buried here is Grotius, the humanist and father of international law. And Delft was home to Anthonie van Leeuwenhoek, who mastered the fledging invention of the microscope and was born the same year as Vermeer, in 1632. Vermeer was just one of many artists who set up shop in the city—which had grown rich with the trade in butter, cloth, beer, and pottery.

Delft's history was often turbulent. In the 17th century, the canal water became tainted, forcing 180 of the 200 resident breweries to close. In 1654, the "Thunderclap," an accidental gunpowder explosion, leveled half the town and killed hundreds. But Delft rebounded thanks to riches it had amassed as the headquarters of the Dutch East India Company. The porcelains their traders brought back from the Far East proved irresistible, and in 1645 De Porceleyne Fles started making and exporting the famous blue-and-white earthenware that soon became known the world over as Delft Blue.

EXPLORING

Compact and easy to traverse despite its web of canals, Delft is best explored on foot, although water taxis are available in summer to give you an armchair ride through the heart of town. Everything you might want to see is in the old center, with the exception of the two Delft-ware factories, which are an additional 15 minutes' walk or a short taxi ride away.

TOP ATTRACTIONS

Bagijnhof (*Bagijn courtyard*). The city sided with the (Protestant) Dutch rebels during the Eighty Years' War, and when the (Catholic) Spanish were driven out in 1572, the city reverted to Protestantism, leaving many Catholic communities in dire straits. One group of women was permitted to stay and practice their religion, but according to a new law, their place of worship had to be very modest: a drab exterior in the Bagijnhof, a weather-beaten 13th-century Gothic gate on the Oude Delft, just north of the Lambert van Meerten Museum, hides their sumptuously Baroque church.

Gemeenlandshuis. The pretty, tree-lined Oude Delft canal has numerous historic gabled houses along its banks and takes the honors for being the first canal in the city, and possibly the first city canal anywhere in the Netherlands. One of the finest buildings along its length, the "Common Land house," is a spectacular example of 16th-century Gothic architecture and is adorned with brightly painted shields and a coat of arms. A few yards east of here, across the canal on the corner of Hippolytusbuurt and Cameretten, is a row of *visbanken* (fish stalls), built

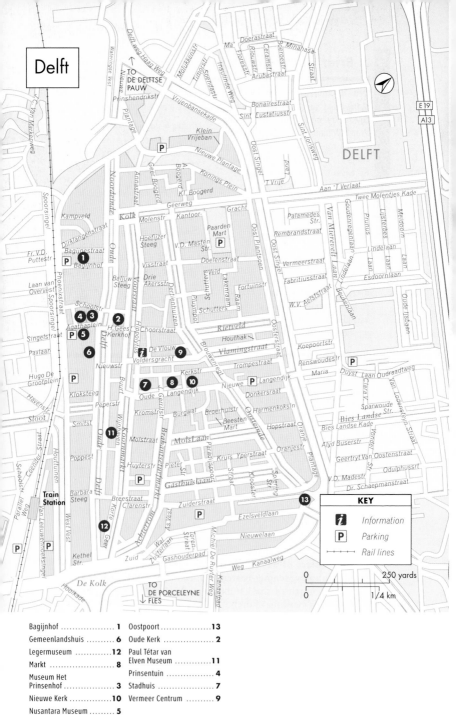

Delft

TO DE DELFTSE PAUW

DELFT

KEY

_i_ Information

P Parking

Rail lines

0 — 250 yards

0 — 1/4 km

TO DE PORCELEYNE FLES

Be sure to climb the 380-odd steps of the church tower for spectacular views of Delft and the surrounding countryside.

along the canal in 1650. Fish has been sold over the counter here pretty much ever since. ⊠ *Oude Delft 167.*

QUICK BITES

Kleyweg's Stads-Koffiehuis. Kleyweg's Stads-Koffiehuis looks out over the oldest and one of the most beautiful canals in Delft. Inside, you'll find a *stamtafel,* a large table laid out with newspapers and magazines, where anyone may sit and chat. There are also smaller individual tables where you can enjoy good coffee, delicious pancakes, and terrific apple pie. In fine weather, the tables on the barge moored on the canal are very popular. The café is closed Sunday. ⊠ *Oude Delft 133* ☎ *015/212–4625* ⊕ *www. stads-koffyhuis.nl.*

★ **Lambert van Meerten Museum.** Within the shadow of the Oude Kerk, this Renaissance-era, canalside mansion has gloriously paneled rooms that provide a noble setting for antique tiles, tin-glazed earthenware, paintings, and an extensive collection of ebony-veneer furniture. Note especially the great collection of tiles, whose subjects range from foodstuffs to warships. The gardens here are alluring, with a spherical sundial, two busts, and a stone gateway leading the eye through to the tangled woods beyond. The museum is closed for structural and internal renovations, and it is not yet known how long these will take. ⊠ *Oude Delft 199* ☎ *015/260–2358* ⊕ *www.lambertvanmeerten-delft.nl* 🎫*€3.50, combined ticket with Het Prinsenhof and Nusantara museums €10* ☯ *Tues.–Sun. 11–5.*

Markt. Delft's main square is bracketed by two town landmarks, the Stadhuis (Town Hall) and the Nieuwe Kerk. Here, too, are cafés, restaurants, and souvenir shops (most selling imitation Delftware) and, on Thursday, a busy general market. Markt 52 is the site of Johannes Vermeer's house, where the 17th-century painter spent much of his youth. Not far away is a statue of Grotius, or Hugo de Groot, born in Delft in 1583 and one of Holland's most famous humanists and lawyers.

Fodor's Choice ★ **Museum Het Prinsenhof.** A former dignitary-hosting convent of St. Agatha, the Prinsenhof Museum is celebrated as the residence of Prince William the Silent, beloved as *Vader des Vaderlands* (Father of the Nation) for his role in the Spanish Revolt and a hero whose tragic end here gave this structure the sobriquet "cradle of Dutch liberty." The complex of buildings was taken over by the government of the new Dutch Republic in 1572 and given to William of Orange for his use as a residence. On July 10, 1584, fevered by monies offered by Philip II of Spain, Bathasar Gerard, a Catholic fanatic, gained admittance to the mansion and succeeded in shooting the prince on the staircase hall, since known as Moordhal (Murder Hall). The fatal bullet holes—the *teykenen der koogelen*—are still visible in the stairwell. Today, the imposing structure is a museum, with a 15th-century chapel, a quaint courtyard, and a bevy of elegantly furnished 17th-century rooms filled with antique pottery, silver, tapestries, and House of Orange portraits, along with exhibits on Dutch history. ⊠ *Sint Agathaplein 1* ☎ *015/260–2358* ⊕ *www. prinsenhof-delft.nl* ☜ *€7.50; combined ticket for Lambert van Meerten and Nusantara museums €10* ⊙ *Tues.–Sun. 11–5.*

Nieuwe Kerk (*New Church*). Presiding over the Markt, this Late Gothic edifice was built between 1483 and 1510. It represents more than a century's worth of Dutch craftsmanship—it's as though its founders knew it would one day be the last resting place of the man who built the nation, William the Silent, and his descendants of the House of Orange. In 1872 the noted architect P. J. H. Cuypers raised the tower to its current height. There are 22 columns surrounding the ornate black-marble-and-alabaster tomb of William of Orange, which was designed by Hendrick de Keyser and his son. The small dog you see at the prince's feet is rumored to have starved to death after refusing to eat following his owner's death. Throughout the church are paintings, stained-glass windows, and memorabilia associated with the Dutch royal family. There are other mausoleums, most notably that of lawyer-philosopher Hugo de Groot, or Grotius. In summer it is possible to climb the 380-odd steps of the church tower for an unparalleled view that stretches as far as Scheveningen to the north and Rotterdam to the south. ⊠ *Markt 2* ☎ *015/212–3025* ☜ *Combined ticket with Oude Kerk €3.50, tower €3.50* ⊙ *Apr.–Oct., Mon.–Sat. 9–6; Nov.–Jan., weekdays 11–4, Sat. 10–5; Feb.–Mar., Mon.–Sat. 10–5.*

Oude Kerk (*Old Church*). At the very heart of historic Delft, the Gothic Oude Kerk, with its tower 6 feet off-kilter, is the last resting place of Vermeer. This is the oldest church in Delft, having been founded in 1200. Building went on until the 15th century, which accounts for the combination of architectural styles, and much of the austere interior dates from the latter part of the work. The tower, dating to 1350, started leaning in the Middle Ages, and today the tilt to the east is somewhat stabilized by the 3-foot tilt to the north but sill prevents ascension

CLOSE UP

Buying Delftware

De Porceleyne Fles. It's corny, even sometimes a little tacky (miniature clogs, anyone?), but no visit to Delft would be complete without stopping at a Delft porcelain factory to see plates and tulip vases being painted by hand and perhaps picking up a souvenir or two. De Porceleyne Fles is the original and most famous home to the popular blue-and-white pottery. Regular demonstrations of molding and painting pottery are given by the artisans. On the bottom of each object is a triple signature: a plump vase topped by a straight line, the stylized letter "F" below it, and the word "Delft." Blue is no longer the only official color. In 1948, a rich red cracked glaze was premiered depicting profuse flowers, graceful birds, and leaping gazelles. There is New Delft, a range of green, gold, and black hues, whose exquisite minuscule figures are drawn to resemble an old Persian tapestry; the Pynacker Delft, borrowing Japanese motifs in rich

oranges and golds; and the brighter Polychrome Delft, which can strike a brilliant sunflower-yellow effect. ⊠ *Royal Delftware Factory, Rotterdamseweg 196* ☎ *015/251–2030* ⊕ *www. royaldelft.com* ☎ *Museum €12* ⊗ *Mid-Mar.–Oct., daily 9–5; Nov.–mid-Mar., Mon.–Sat. 9–5.*

De Delftse Pauw. Another favorite place for picking up Delftware is at the pottery factories of De Delftse Pauw, which, although not as famous as De Porceleyne Fles, produce work of equally high quality. ⊠ *Delftweg 133* ☎ *015/212–4920* ⊕ *www. delftpottery.com* ☎ *Free tours* ⊗ *Apr.–Oct., daily 9–4:30; Nov.–Mar., weekdays 9–4:30, weekends 11–1.*

De Candelaer. This is a smaller pottery, and its city-center location makes it a convenient stop-off for comparisons of Delftware with other craftsmanship available in Delft. ⊠ *Kerkstraat 14* ☎ *015/213–1848* ⊕ *www.candelaer.nl.*

8

by visitors. At the top is the largest carillon bell in the Netherlands, weighing nearly 20,000 pounds and now is used only on state occasions. ⊠ *Heilige Geestkerkhof* ☎ *015/212–3015* ☎ *Combined ticket with Nieuwe Kerk €3.50* ⊗ *Apr.–Oct., Mon.–Sat. 9–6; Nov.–Jan., weekdays 11–4, Sat. 10–5; Feb and Mar., Mon.–Sat. 10–5.*

Fodor'sChoice ★ **Vermeer Centrum** (*Vermeer Center*). Housed in the former St. Lucas Guild, where Delft's favorite son was dean for many years, the Center takes visitors on a multimedia journey through the life and work of Johannes Vermeer. Touch screens, projections, and other interactive features are interspersed with giant reproductions of the master's work, weaving a tale of 17th-century Delft and drawing you into the mind of the painter. ☎ *015/213–8588* ⊕ *www.vermeerdelft.nl* ☎ *€7* ⊗ *Daily 10–5.*

WORTH NOTING

Legermuseum (*Netherlands Army Museum*). Delft's former armory makes an appropriate setting for an impressive military museum. Despite the gentle images of Dutch life, the origins of the Dutch Republic were violent. It took nothing less than the Eighty Years' War (1568–1648) to finally achieve independence from the Spanish crown. In addition

A view of the twin turrets of the Oostpoort in Delft, as seen from one of the many waterways.

to the guns, swords, and other implements of warfare, all periods of Dutch military history are explored in detail, from Roman times to the German occupation during World War II. ⊠ *Korte Geer 1* ☎ *015/215–0500* ⊕ *www.armymuseum.nl* 🖅 *€7.50* 🕓 *Tues.–Fri. 10–5, weekends noon–5.*

Nusantara Museum. In the same courtyard as the Prinsenhof Museum, the Nusantara has a colorful collection of ethnographic costumes and artifacts from the Dutch East Indies—most of it is ill-gotten gains from the 17th century by members of the Dutch East India Company. A large Javanese *gamelan* (percussion orchestra) takes center stage inside, and is surrounded by Indo-European batik, Hindu statuettes, shields and intricately carved spears, diamond-encrusted daggers, *wayang kulit* (shadow puppets), and a beautifully carved tomb. Other displays chart the history of the spice trade. ⊠ *Sint Agathaplein 4* ☎ *015/260–2358* ⊕ *www.nusantara-delft.nl* 🖅 *€3.50, combined ticket to Het Prinsenhof and Lambert van Meerten museums €10* 🕓 *Tues.–Sun. 11–5.*

Oostpoort (*East Gate*). At the southern end of the Oosteinde canal, the fairy-tale twin turrets of the Oostpoort form Delft's only remaining city gate. Dating back to 1400, with the spires added in 1514, parts of the structure are now a private residence, but you can still walk over the drawbridge. It is a short walk out of the center, but the effort of getting there is more than rewarded by the view.

Paul Tétar van Elven Museum. This 18th-century canal-side mansion was the former home of 19th-century painter Paul Tétar van Elven. The interior he created is charmingly redolent of Ye Olde Delft, complete with painted ceilings, antiques, and even a reproduction of an artist's atelier done up in the Old Dutch style. ⊠ *Koornmarkt 67* ☎ *015/212–4206* ⊕ *www.museumpaultetarvanelven.nl* ✉ *€4* ⊙ *Mid-Apr.–Oct., Tues.–Sun. 1–5.*

Prinsentuin (*Prince's Garden*). Between the Prinsenhof and the Nusantara Museum is Agathaplein, a Late Gothic leafy square built around 1400 and shaded by huge chestnut trees. At the center is the Prinsentuin, a cultivated garden that offers a calming respite from the city streets.

Stadhuis (*Town Hall*). At the west end of the Markt, the Town Hall is a gray-stone edifice with picturesque red shutters and lavish detailing, designed in 1618 by Hendrick de Keyser, one of the most prolific architects of the Golden Age. Inside is a grand staircase and Council Chamber with a famous old map of Delft. You can view the interior only by making arrangements through the Delft tourist office, which can also issue you a ticket to visit the torture chamber in Het Steen—this 13th-century tower is all that remains from Delft's original medieval Town Hall. ⊠ *Markt 87* ⊙ *By appointment.*

WHERE TO EAT

$$
CAFÉ ✗ **Café Vlaanderen.** At this extensive café, board games keep you entertained on a rainy day but sunny skies will make you head for the tables set under leafy lime trees out front on the Beestenmarkt. Out back is an equally shady garden. The deluxe fish wrap makes a delicious light lunch, while evening options include a delicious tuna and swordfish brochette. $ *Average main: €12* ⊠ *Beestenmarkt 16* ☎ *015/213–3311* ⊕ *www.vlaanderen.nl.*

$
DUTCH ✗ **De Nonnerie.** In the vaulted cellar of the famous Prinsenhof Museum, this luncheon-only tearoom has a sedate elegant atmosphere. If you can, get a table in the grassy courtyard under an umbrella, and—since you're within the House of Orange—order an Oranjeboom beer to wash down the fine *Delftsche Meesters palet* (three small sandwiches of pâté, salmon, and Dutch cheese). Entry is via the archway from Oude Delft into the Prinsenhof Museum, down a signposted path beside the gardens. $ *Average main: €7* ⊠ *Sint Agathaplein* ☎ *015/212–1860* ⊕ *www.de-prinsenkelder.nl/nonnerie* ▭ *No credit cards* ⊙ *Closed Mon. No dinner.*

$
CAFÉ ✗ **De Wijnhaven.** This Delft staple has loyal regulars, drawn by the many terrace tables on a small square overlooking a narrow canal—and a mean Indonesian satay. There's a smart restaurant on the first floor, but the bar and mezzanine have plenty to offer, with lunch snacks, a reasonable menu for dinner with the latest tracks on the speakers, and great

CLOSE UP

Vermeer: Sphinx of Delft

As one of the world's most adored artists, Johannes Vermeer (1632–75) has been the subject of blockbuster exhibitions, theater pieces, and best-selling novels (Tracy Chevalier's *Girl with a Pearl Earring,* also a sumptuous movie). He enjoys cult status, yet his reputation rests on just 35 paintings. Of course, those canvases—ordinary domestic scenes depicting figures caught in an amber light—are among the most extraordinary ever created. But Vermeer's fame is relatively recent. He died at age 42, worn out by economic woes. Only since the mid-19th century have critics rightfully revered his work. And when Proust proclaimed his *View of Delft* "the most beautiful painting in the world," audiences worldwide became enraptured.

How Vermeer painted scenes of such incomparable quietude, while living in a house filled with his 11 children, is a difficult question to answer, and little is known about his early life. We do know that his father ran an inn and was also an art dealer, as was Johannes himself. But that doesn't seem important—the "reality" that matters is the one Vermeer captured on his canvases. The way his light traps the most transient of effects is so perfect, you almost find yourself looking around to see where the sunlight has fallen, expecting it to be dappling your own face.

fries and salads. [$] *Average main: €9* ✉ *Wijnhaven 22* ☎ *015/214–1460* 🌐 *www.wijnhaven.nl.*

$$$$ FRENCH Fodor's Choice ★ 🍴 **De Zwethheul.** Delft's classiest restaurant is also its best hidden: set a little outside town, it can easily be reached by cab. In a restored 18th-century building, this award winner actually began as a humble pancake house. It's now run by top chef Mario Ridder, who took over when the former chef moved to the Parkheuvel in Rotterdam. In fine weather, you can eat on a beautiful terrace overlooking the Schie River. Specialties of the house include delights such as roasted Barbary duck with caramelized pistachio, date purée, beetroot, and balsamic sauce. [$] *Average main: €48* ✉ *Rotterdamseweg 480* ☎ *010/470–4166* 🌐 *www.zwethheul.nl* ✍ *Reservations essential* ⏲ *Closed Mon. and 2 wks in July–Aug. No lunch Sat.*

$$$ FRENCH 🍴 **Le Vieux Jean.** The tiny, family-run restaurant serves tasty meat-and-potatoes fare as well as good fish dishes such as *kabeljauw* (cod) with asparagus sauce. The adjoining Café de Oude Jean serves up somewhat cheaper fare. [$] *Average main: €23* ✉ *Heilige Geestkerkhof 3* ☎ *015/213–0433* 🌐 *www.levieuxjean.nl* ✍ *Reservations essential* ⏲ *Closed Sun. and Mon.*

$ CONTEMPORARY 🍴 **Stadscafé de Waag.** The ancient brick-and-stone walls of this cavernous former weigh house are adorned with hulking 17th-century balance scales. Tables on the mezzanine in the rear overlook the Wijnhaven canal, while those on the terrace in front nestle under the town's magnificent, looming clock tower. All the while, tastefully unobtrusive music creates a cool vibe for a mixed clientele. Happily, dishes such as Flemish asparagus with ham and egg, or *parelhoen* (guinea fowl) in a rich dark

Even the picturesque red shutters of the original town hall building in Delft make you want to set up an easel or snap a photo.

broth, are equal to the fabulous setting. $ *Average main: €10* ✉ *Markt 11* ☎ *015/213-0393* ⊕ *www.de-waag.nl.*

$$ ✕ **Van der Dussen.** Dining in this characterful candle-lit restaurant,
DUTCH located in one corner of the lovely centuries-old Bagijnhof, is like stepping back through time. Not that the food is old-fashioned in any way: it is modern Dutch, beautifully presented, and delicious—elegance on a plate that lives up to the grand surroundings. $ *Average main: €18* ✉ *Bagijnhof 118* ☎ *015/214-7212* ⊕ *www.restaurantvanderdussen.nl* ⊗ *Closed Sun. No lunch.*

$ ✕ **Willem van Oranje.** You might normally be wary of any large establish-
DUTCH ment on a main tourist crossroads that offers its menu in six languages, but what redeems this place, with its to-die-for view between the Town Hall and the New Church, is the wide selection of good-value Dutch pancakes. Fill up from a choice of around 50 sweet or savory (and sometimes both) flavor concoctions to suit every taste. Or if you still can't make up your mind, there are also all the usual Dutch café standards on the menu, including omelettes, rolls, and salads. A more sophisticated dinner menu with heartier fish and meat favorites appears on weekend evenings. $ *Average main: €8* ✉ *Markt 48a* ☎ *015/212-3059* ⊕ *www. willemvanoranjedelft.nl.*

WHERE TO STAY

For expanded hotel reviews, visit Fodors.com.

$$ HOTEL **Best Western Museumhotels Delft.** Several period touches stand out amid the chain stylings, helping these otherwise banally furnished rooms opposite Oude Kerk and adjacent to the Prinsenhof Museum retain some historic charm without sacrificing modern creature comforts. **Pros:** good location; some rooms have canal views. **Cons:** part of a chain; parking difficult. [$] *Rooms from: €105* ✉ *Phoenixstraat 50a* ☎ *015/215–3070* 🌐 *www.museumhotels.nl* *66 rooms.*

$$ HOTEL **Bridges House.** In this tastefully restored 17th-century inn, once the home of painter Jan Steen, antiques grace each spacious room, all adorned with extra-long beds with custom-made mattresses and some with cozy canal views. **Pros:** central location; canal views; bathrooms with tubs and enormous showerheads for a wake-up blast. **Cons:** parking is difficult. [$] *Rooms from: €113* ✉ *Oude Delft 74* ☎ *015/212–4036* 🌐 *www.bridges-house.nl* *10 rooms, 2 studio apartments* 🍴 *Breakfast.*

$ HOTEL **Hotel de Emauspoort.** Many of these simply furnished rooms just a stone's throw from the main market square overlook a canal, others a pretty courtyard, and some are "in" the courtyard in restored gypsy caravans. **Pros:** nice outlooks from many rooms; pleasant surroundings. **Cons:** furnishings are a bit standard, though the caravans are full of character. [$] *Rooms from: €95* ✉ *Vrouwenregt 9-11* ☎ *015/219–0219* 🌐 *www.emauspoort.nl* *26 rooms* 🍴 *Breakfast.*

$$ HOTEL ★ **Johannes Vermeer.** You'll be spoiled for choice of old-master views at the first Delft hotel to pay homage to the town's most famous son: the pleasant modern rooms (with beams and other nice touches) at the front overlook a canal, while those at the back have a sweeping city view that takes in three churches. **Pros:** historic building; nice garden. **Cons:** parking is difficult. [$] *Rooms from: €125* ✉ *Molslaan 18–22* ☎ *015/212–6466* 🌐 *www.hotelvermeer.nl* *25 rooms, 5 suites* 🍴 *Breakfast.*

$ HOTEL Fodor's Choice ★ **Leeuwenbrug.** Facing one of Delft's quieter waterways, this traditional and well-maintained hotel offers rooms that are large, airy, and tastefully contemporary in décor; those in the annex are particularly appealing, while those at the front have canal views. **Pros:** friendly; central; atmospheric lounge. **Cons:** some bathrooms are a little old. [$] *Rooms from: €99* ✉ *Koornmarkt 16* ☎ *015/214–7741* 🌐 *www.leeuwenbrug.nl* *36 rooms* 🍴 *Breakfast.*

PARTY TOWN

From February until December, there are festivals throughout Delft. Highlights include the De Koninck Blues Festival in mid-February; canalside concerts from the end of June through July and August; a week of chamber music during late August; the African Festival in early August; the Delft Jazz and Blues Festival at the end of August; a waiters' race in the Beestenmarkt in early September; and the City of Lights in mid-December.

Delft Tourist Information Point. ✉ *Hippolytusbuurt 4* ☎ *0900/515–1555* 🌐 *www.delft.com.*

$ B&B/INN 🏨 **Soul Inn.** The large '70s logo above the door of this 19th-century town house barely hints at the eclectic nature of this soul-inspired B&B, where rooms are individually bedecked with a chaotic mixture of chintz and glitz. **Pros:** quirky, quiet location; kitchens in suites. **Cons:** outside the historic center; décor not soothing—recalls a time when color coordination had yet to be invented. [$] *Rooms from: €60* ✉ *Willemstraat 55* ☎ *015/215-7246* 🌐 *www.soul-inn.nl* 🛏 *10 rooms, 2 suites, 7 apartments* 🍴 *Breakfast.*

NIGHTLIFE

Delft is home to one of the country's most important technical universities, and the large student population ensures the bars are always lively at night. Two good places to find a profusion of watering holes are the Markt and the Beestenmarkt. The latter is a peaceful little square where the discerning drinkers go on summery evenings to sit out under the leafy lime trees.

Café Vlaanderen. With its idyllic location on Delft's nicest square, Café Vlaanderen is not only a good place to eat, it's also a fine place to chill out with a cold one. ✉ *Beestenmarkt 16* ☎ *015/213-3311* 🌐 *www.vlaanderen.nl.*

Locus Publicus. For beer lovers looking to be pleasantly bewildered by a choice of around 200 different Belgian beers, Locus Publicus is the place to go. ✉ *Brabantse Turfmarkt 67* ☎ *015/213-4632* 🌐 *www.locuspublicus.nl.*

Speakers. The most humming nightspot—in fact, the only club (nearly all others are students only)—in Delft is Speakers. Each night there is something different going on. Friday night sees theme night (1970s, for instance); Saturday hosts the techno-beat crowd; and Sunday offers salsa parties. ✉ *Burgwal 45–49* ☎ *015/212-4446* 🌐 *www.speakers.nl.*

ROTTERDAM

Rotterdam looks to the future like almost nowhere else. The decision to leave the past behind wasn't made entirely through choice however—the old town disappeared overnight on May 14, 1940, when Nazi bombs devastated an area greater than one square mile, sweeping away more than 36,000 buildings in just a few torrid hours.

Since then, a new landscape of concrete, steel, and glass has risen like a phoenix from the ashes, and today this world port is home to some of the 21st century's most architecturally important creations. The city skyline—especially in the areas around the station and by the Maas on the Kop van Zuid development—is constantly changing, and as each year passes it lives up more and more to its billing as "Manhattan-on-the-Maas." Many of the new buildings are commissioned from top-drawer contemporary architects like Rem Koolhaas and Sir Norman Foster, and each has a striking identity.

That isn't to say the city is all glass and steel however. Areas such as historic Delfshaven—from where the pilgrim fathers set sail for the New World aboard the *Speedwell* in 1620—escaped the worst effects of the war, and still retain their old character and charm. And in between old and new, the large and leafy Het Park (simply "The Park") has a maze of paths weaving between small lakes and ponds to provide cool shade in summer and a welcome break from the urban sprawl at any time of year. As if that wasn't enough reason to visit, Rotterdam also boasts some of the country's best museums and top shopping opportunities.

Thanks to its location on the deltas of the Rhine and Maas rivers, Rotterdam has become the world's largest seaport. Through its harbors and the enormous Europoort pass more tons of shipping than through all of France combined. The rapid expansion of the port in the postwar years created a huge demand for labor, bringing waves of migrants from Italy, Spain, Greece, Turkey, Morocco, Cape Verde, and the Netherlands

Antilles, turning Rotterdam into one of the most ethnically diverse cities in Europe.

ORIENTATION

The city divides itself naturally into a number of main sectors. The **Central** area, south and east of the main railway station, is focused on the pedestrianized zone around the Lijnbaan and Van Oldenbarneveltstraat. This is where the city goes out to shop—all the major department stores and many exclusive boutiques are located here. Along the river are three old harbors, **Delfshaven, Oude Haven,** and **Leuvehaven.** Charming Delfshaven is so narrow it looks like a canal, and is lined with gabled houses dating back centuries, creating a classic Dutch scene. The Oude Haven, by contrast, is surrounded by modern buildings, some of which, like the Blaak Rail Station and Kijk-Kubus, are among Rotterdam's most iconic buildings. To the south of the river, across the Erasmus Bridge, the **Kop van Zuid** and **Entrepot** districts are where famous architects such as Sir Norman Foster and Renzo Piano have been given free rein to design housing projects, theaters, and public buildings to complete the area's transformation into a modern and luxurious commercial and residential district. **Museumpark** is the cultural heart of the city, and home to four museums and bordered by a Sculpture Terrace.

GETTING HERE AND AROUND

Direct trains leave Amsterdam Centraal Station for Rotterdam as often as six times an hour throughout the day, and hourly through the night—the journey time is around one hour. If driving, take the A10, A4, and A13 freeways south from Amsterdam. The drive will take about one hour, depending on traffic.

Because the different areas of Rotterdam are fairly spread out, to get between them you may want to make use of the efficient public transport network (taxis are expensive). Buses and trams fan out across the city above ground, while four underground Metro (subway) lines—one north–south, three east–west—offer an even faster way of getting about. All intersect at Beurs station in the city center for easy transfers. A fifth overground Metro line runs from Hofplein (east of the main train station) to The Hague, but this is of less interest to visitors as the main line trains are a much faster means of making the journey. To use the network you'll need an **OV-chipkaart** (public transport chip card). These credit card–size tickets can be loaded up with credit from machines in the railway and metro stations, and are debited as you board and leave trains, trams, metros, and buses. There are information and sales points

8

in the Beurs and Centraal Station metro stations, as well as in the main bus station. Or visit ⊕ *www.ov-chipkaart.nl* for more information.

Taxis are available at railway stations, major hotels, and at taxi stands in key locations. You can also order one by phone, but they cannot be hailed in the street. Expect to pay at least €40 for a 30-minute journey between Rotterdam and Delft.

Public Transportation Information ☎ *0900/9292* ⊕ *www.9292ov.nl.*

TOURS

Spido boat tours. The Nieuwe Maas River has flowed through Rotterdam for 700 years, dividing the city in two and acting as the city's lifeline. A continual procession of some 30,000 oceangoing ships and some 130,000 river barges passes annually through Rotterdam to and from the North Sea. A top option for visitors to see the city's waterfront is to take a 75-minute boat tour (€10.50) with the very popular Spido boat tours. They offer a range of excursions lasting from just over an hour to a full day, while a variety of water taxis and water buses also operates in the Waterstad (the docks and harbors along the banks of the river). ⊠ *Willemsplein 85* ☎ *010/275–9988* ⊕ *www.spido.nl.*

For those with an interest in Rotterdam's recent history, pick up a map from the tourist office called "Along the Fire Boundary." It has details of three self-guided walking routes that trace the edge of the area destroyed by the bombing of May 14, 1940, with detailed historical notes.

TIMING

With a day you can cover pretty much all of Rotterdam's sights. But don't forget to factor in extra time for shopping.

ESSENTIALS

Bicycle Rentals Rijwielshop Rotterdam CS ⊠ *Conradstraat 18, by Rotterdam Central Station* ☎ *010/412–6220.*

Emergency Services National Emergency Alarm Number ☎ *112 for police, fire, and ambulance.*

Hospitals Erasmus MC ⊠ *s-Gravendijkwal 230* ☎ *010/704–0704* ⊕ *www. erasmusmc.nl.*

Taxis Rotterdamse Taxi Centrale ☎ *010/462–6060* ⊕ *www.rtcnv.nl.*

Tourism Information VVV Rotterdam ⊠ *Binnenwegplein, Coolsingel 195–197* ☎ *010/271–0120* ⊕ *www.rotterdam.info.*

EXPLORING

TOP ATTRACTIONS

Fodor's Choice
★
Delfshaven. The last remaining nook of old Rotterdam is the old port area, reconstructed to appear just as it was when originally built—an open-air museum with rows of gabled houses lining the historic waterfront, trendy galleries, cafés, and restaurants. Walk along the Voorhaven, Achterhaven, and neighboring Piet Heynplein and marvel at the many historic buildings. For historic sights in the environs, check out the working mill of **Korenmolen de Distilleerketel** (open Wednesday and Saturday only), the fascinating **Museum de Dubbelde Palmboom**

Delfshaven, the historic port of Rotterdam, often hosts great ships recreated from the Netherlands' era of nautical supremacy.

on Rotterdam city history, and the **Oudekerk/Pilgrimvaders Kerk.** Tram No. 4 connects Delfshaven with the rest of the city, as does the nearby Delfshaven metro station. ⊠ *Achterhaven and Voorhaven, Delfshaven.*

Euromast. For a bird's-eye view of the contrast between Delfshaven and the majority of the city, as well as a spectacular panorama of city and harbor, visit the 600-foot-high Euromast. Designed by Rotterdam architect Huig Maaskant in 1960, this was the Netherland's tallest building for many years; when a new medical facility for the Erasmus University usurped the honor in 1970, an additional 25 feet were added to the tower in six days, restoring Euromast to its premier position. On a clear day, you can just about see the coast. The main observation deck is at 315 feet, but the **Euroscoop** is a rotating panoramic elevator that will carry you another 300 feet from there to the top of the mast. For the thrill seekers among us, on weekends from May to September you can skip the elevator and rappel down from the observation deck, or shoot down the rope slide in about 10 seconds on Europe's fastest "zip wire" (make reservations via the Web at ⊕ *www.abseilen.nl*). There's also a restaurant at the top. You can even stay up the tower overnight in one of two special suites, but be warned the prices are as high as the experience. Down below, the park at the base of the Euromast is where many Rotterdammers spend time when the weather is good. ⊠ *Parkhaven 20, Delfshaven* ☎ *010/436–4811* ⊕ *www.euromast.nl* ⊠ *€9.25; rappel or rope slide €49.50* ⊗ *Apr.–Sept., daily 9:30 am–11 pm; Oct.–Mar., daily 10 am–11 pm.*

Kunsthal. This "art house" sits at one end of the visitor-friendly museum quarter and hosts major temporary exhibitions. There is no permanent

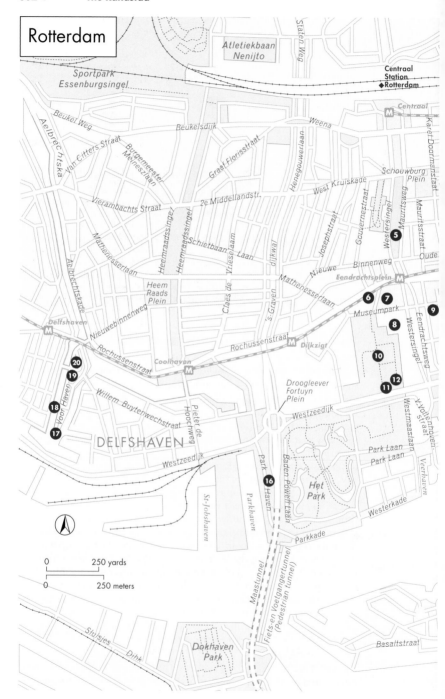

Rotterdam

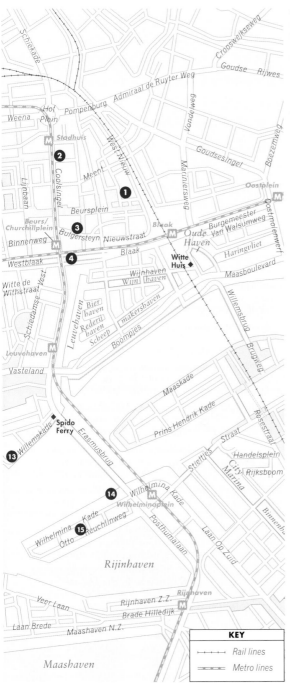

8

KEY

├──┼──┤ *Rail lines*

═ ═ ═ *Metro lines*

collection, other than the massive, multistory boxlike center itself, designed by architect-prophet Rem Koolhaas. Opinions about the building are sharply divided: some say the design bridging the gap between the Museumpark and the dike is a clever spatial creation; others consider it an ugly mix of facades (part glass, part brick, and part corrugated iron) that has led to rusted iron, stained concrete, and cracks in the central walkway. The biggest complaint is the lack of elevator, compounded by the hazards of the central ramp, whose steep angle makes this a potential ski slope for wheelchair users. Fortunately, the eclectic exhibitions, usually three or four at any one time, are always fascinating, regardless of the setting. ⊠ *Westzeedijk 341, Museumpark* ☎ *010/440–0301* ⊕ *www.kunsthal.nl* ☞ *€11* ☉ *Tues.–Sat. 10–5, Sun. 11–5.*

Fodor'sChoice   **Maritiem Museum Rotterdam.** A sea lover's delight, the Maritime Museum
★   is Rotterdam's noted nautical collection. Appropriately perched at the
☾   head of the Leuvehaven harbor, it was founded by Prince Hendrik in 1874. Set against the background of modern and historical maritime objects, the seafaring ways of old Rotterdammers make more sense. Star attraction of the ground floor is a large model of the Europoort, which shows how the Rotterdam area has developed over the centuries into the major seaport of today. The upper floors are mainly given over to rotating exhibitions on seafaring themes. Children have half a floor dedicated to them, called "Professor Plons" (Professor Plunge), where museum staff are on hand to help with looking through a real periscope, donning a hard hat and taking to the driving seat of a scaled-down crane, and engaging in many other activities dealing with the themes of water and ships. Kids will also love the museum's prize exhibit, the warship *De Buffel*, moored in the harbor outside, dating back to 1868. The ship has been perfectly restored and is fitted out sumptuously, as can be seen in the mahogany-deck captain's cabin. ⊠ *Leuvehaven 1, Witte de With* ☎ *010/413–2680* ⊕ *www.maritiemmuseum.nl* ☞ *€7.50* ☉ *July and Aug., Mon.–Sat. 10–5, Sun. 11–5; Sept.–June, Tues.–Sat. 10–5, Sun. 11–5.*

Fodor'sChoice   **Museum Boijmans van Beuningen.** Rotterdam's finest shrine to art, with
★   treasures ranging from Pieter Bruegel the Elder's 16th-century *Tower of Babel* to Mondriaan's extraordinary *Composition in Yellow and Blue*, ranks among the greatest art galleries in Europe. The top attraction here is the collection of old masters, which covers West European art from the 14th to the 19th century. In particular 15th- to 17th-century Dutch and Flemish art are well represented, including painters such as Van Eyck, Rubens, Hieronymous Bosch, and Rembrandt. The modern art section runs the gamut from Monet to Warhol and beyond, picking up Kandinsky, Magritte, and Dalí in between. In the Decorative Art and Design collection, both precious ornamental objects and everyday utensils dating from medieval times are displayed. In the museum café, note the fantastic collection of chairs, each by a different designer. More artworks embellish the museum gardens. ⊠ *Museumpark 18–20, Museumpark* ☎ *010/441–9400* ⊕ *www.boijmans.nl* ☞ *€12.50* ☉ *Tues.– Sun. 11–5.*

Museum de Dubbelde Palmboom (*Double Palm Tree Museum*). Devoted to the history of Rotterdam and its role as an international nexus, this museum traces the city's history from prehistoric times to the current day. The focus is on how exotic wares imported by the East India Company affected the city. The building itself is redolent of history: not only do its heavy beams and brick floors waft you back to yesteryear, but there even seems to be a faint smell of grains, recalling the many years the buildong spent as a warehouse. Ask for the informative guide in English, as all labeling is in Dutch. The first floor has some fascinating archaeological finds: one of the spouted ancient jugs has been traced to a town near Cologne, providing proof that traveling merchants were apparently very active in trading ceramics. ⊠ *Voorhaven 12, Delfshaven* ☎ *010/476–1533* ⊕ *www.museumrotterdam.nl* ✉ *€6, ticket also valid for a same-day visit to the Schielandshuis* ☉ *Tues.–Sun. 11–5.*

☾ **Natuurhistorisch Museum** (*Natural History Museum*). Located in a historic villalike structure with an enormous glass wing (echoing the hip Kunsthal next door), the Natural History Museum challenges its visitors with skeletal glimpses of creatures you'll be hard put to identify. As soon as you enter the foyer, you are face to face with a mounted scary-hairy gorilla. It doesn't stop there: in one room the skeleton of a giraffe stretches as far up as you can crane your own neck. Continue on to be met by a tiger and arching elephant tusks. There is an "ironic" re-creation of a trophy hunter's display, with turtles mounted on a wall, arranged according to size. In another area, a dinner table is set, with the skulls of a human, a cow, an anteater, a lion, a zebra, and a pig as guests. Before each of them is a plate laden with their respective dining preferences. Children, meanwhile, are drawn to the 40-foot-long skeleton of a sperm whale. ⊠ *Westzeedijk 345, Museumpark* ☎ *010/436–4222* ⊕ *www.nmr.nl* ✉ *€6* ☉ *Tues.–Sat. 10–5, Sun. 11–5.*

Nederlands Architectuurinstituut. Fittingly, for a city of exciting modern architecture, Rotterdam is the home of the **NAi,** or the Netherlands Architecture Institute. The striking glass-and-metal building—designed by Rotterdam local Joe Conen in 1993—hosts temporary displays on architecture and interior design in seven exhibition spaces, giving a holistic interpretation of the history and development of architecture, especially the urban design and spatial planning of Rotterdam. ⊠ *Museumpark 25, Museumpark* ☎ *010/440–1200* ⊕ *www.nai.nl* ✉ *€10* ☉ *Tues.–Sat. 10–5, Sun. 11–5.*

Oudekerk/Pilgrimvaders Kerk (*Pilgrim Fathers' Church*). On July 22, 1620, 16 men, 11 women, and 19 children sailed from Delfshaven on the *Speedwell.* Their final destination was America, where they helped found the Plymouth Colony in Massachusetts. Puritan Protestants fleeing England for religious freedom usually went to Amsterdam, but this group, which arrived in 1608, decided to live in Leiden, then 10 years later opted to travel on to the New World. On July 20, 1620, they left Leiden by boat, and via Delft they reached Delfshaven, where they spent their last night in Holland. After a sermon from their vicar, John Robinson, in what has since become this church, they boarded the *Speedwell,* sailing to Southampton, England, then left on the *Mayflower* on September 5, reaching Cape Cod 60 days later.

8

The church was built in 1417 as the Chapel of Sint Anthonius, then extended and restyled in the Late Gothic period. However, in 1761 the ceilings were raised, and the current style dates back to this Regency revamp, when an ornate wooden clock tower was also added. Next to the choir is a vestry from 1819, where you can find a memorial plaque to the Pilgrim Fathers on the wall. The bell tower has a tiny balcony. The church is now owned by the Trust for Old Dutch Churches. ⊠ *Aelbrechtskolk 20, Delfshaven* ☎ *010/477–4156* ⊕ *www.pelgrimvaderskerk. nl* ⊙ *July–Aug., weekdays 11–3, Sat. 1–4; Sept.–June, Sat. 1–4.*

★ **Schielandshuis** (*Schieland House*). Staunchly defending its position against the high-rise Robeco Tower and the giant Hollandse Banke Unie surrounding it, this palatial 17th-century mansion holds its own as a part of Rotterdam's historical museum (the other half is the Dubbelde Palmboom in Delfshaven). Built between 1662 and 1665 in Dutch Neoclassical style by the Schieland family, it burned down in 1864, but the facade survived, and the interior was carefully restored. Another renovation in 2010 has given it a new shine. Inside are Baroque- and Rococo-style rooms reconstructed from houses in the area, clothing from the 18th century to the present day, and the famous collection of maps, the Atlas von Stolk. Because of the frailty of the paper, only a tiny selection of these vintage documents is on display at any one time, usually under a specific theme. The museum's café is in a lovely garden. ⊠ *Korte Hoogstraat 31, Centrum* ☎ *010/217–6767* ⊕ *www. museumrotterdam.nl* 💶 *€6, ticket also valid for a same-day visit to the Dubbelde Palmboom Museum* ⊙ *Tues.–Fri. 10–5, weekends 11–5.*

Wereld Museum. On a corner of rustic Veerhaven, surrounded by old sailing boats moored alongside modern yachts, this museum is devoted to non-Western cultures, many of which have had a sizable influence on Rotterdam. The permanent collection features more than 2,000 art objects from Asia, the Americas, Africa, and Oceania. Most of the exhibition space, however, is given over to changing themed exhibitions—usually two each year. ⊠ *Willemskade 25, Scheepvaartkwartier* ☎ *010/270–7172* ⊕ *www.wereldmuseum.nl* 💶 *Exhibitions €12; permanent collection free* ⊙ *Tues.–Sun. 10:30–5:30.*

WORTH NOTING

Chabot Museum. This museum displays the private art collection of leading Dutch Expressionist painter and sculptor Henk Chabot, who was active between the two world wars, depicting peasants, market gardeners, and, later, refugees and prisoners. ⊠ *Museumpark 11, Museumpark* ☎ *010/436–3713* ⊕ *www.chabotmuseum.nl* 💶 *€6.50* ⊙ *Tues.–Fri. 11–4:30, Sat. 11–5, Sun. noon–5.*

Korenmolen de Distilleerketel. Set in the historic district of Delfshaven, this mill is the only working flour mill in the city. Formerly employed to grind malt to make jenever, the dusty-hair miller now mills grain for specific bakeries in the city, which means it is closed most of the week. ⊠ *Voorhaven 210, Delfshaven* ☎ *010/477–9181* 💶 *€2* ⊙ *Wed. 1–5 and Sat. 10–4.*

Museumpark. A project masterminded by Rem Koolhaas's Office for Metropolitan Architecture (OMA) in collaboration with French architect

Home to lengendary masterpieces by Breughel, Bosch, and Rembrandt, Museum Boijmans van Beuningen is a must-see in Rotterdam.

Yves Brunier, this modern urban garden is made up of different zones, extending from the Museum Boijmans van Beuningen to the Kunsthal. The idea is that each section is screened off from the last and creates a different impression—but each block of the garden isn't as radically different as this theory builds it up to be. The one part you should linger over is just before the bridge, where there is a memorial to city engineer G. J. de Jongh. Various artists had a hand in this, with Henk Chabot responsible for the inscription on the wall and Jaap Gidding designing the beautiful mosaic at the base of the monument, which represents Rotterdam and its surroundings at the end of the 1920s. Sculptor R. Bolle designed the bronze railings, with harbor and street scenes from the period when De Jongh was working in Rotterdam. ☒ *Museumpark to the north, Westersingel to the east, Westzeedijk to the south, and bounded by a canal on the west side, Museumpark.*

Nederlands Fotomuseum. The Dutch Photography Museum's permanent exhibit is its basement "Darkroom," where exhibits trace the history of photography in the Netherlands. Take a large white card at the entrance and place it in the developing trays scattered around the room to start the dozen or so video clips. (The cards are marked with flags for either Dutch or English commentary, so choose carefully.) Most of the rest of the museum is given over to changing exhibitions, which are always well worth a look. The museum is housed in the **Las Palmas** building in the Kop van Zuid neighborhood. ☒ *Wilhelminakade 332, Kop van Zuid* ☎ *010/203–0405* ⊕ *www.nederlandsfotomuseum.nl* ☑ *€7, free on Weds.* ⊙ *Tues.–Fri. 10–5, weekends 11–5.*

Sculpture Terrace. Set along the grassy bank of the Westersingel canal, this outdoor venue exhibits sculptures of the past 100 years. Highlights include Rodin's headless *L'homme qui marche* (Walking Man), Henri Laurens's *La Grande Musicienne* (The Great Musician), and Umberto Mastroianni's *Gli Amanti* (The Lovers), a fascinating jumble of triangular-shape points. ⊠ *Museumpark.*

Sint Laurenskerk. Built between 1449 and 1525, this church is juxtaposed against its modern surroundings. The main organ ranks as one of Europe's largest. Hendrick de Keyser's statue of Erasmus in the square was buried in the gardens of the Museum Boijmans van Beuningen during the war and miraculously survived. It's possible to to climb the church tower for a panoramic view, but only at specific times. ⊠ *Grotekerkplein 27, Sint Laurenskwartier* ☎ *010/411–6494* ⊕ *www. laurenskerkrotterdam.nl* ☜ *Church €1, tower €3.50* ☉ *Church: Tues.– Sat. 10–5; Tower: Wed. at 2, Sat. at 1 and 3.*

Stadhuis (*City Hall*). At the top of the Coolsingel, this elegant 1920s building is the hallowed seat of the mayor of Rotterdam and is open for guided tours on weekdays. A bronze bust of the architect, Henri Evans, is in the central hall. With the neighboring post-office building, the two early-1920s buildings are the sole survivors of their era. ⊠ *Coolsingel 40, Centrum* ☎ *14010 toll-free* ⊕ *www.rotterdam.nl.*

TENT Centrum Beeldende Kunst. The Rotterdam Center for Visual Arts, usually simply called TENT, showcases modern art by local artists of the last decade. Shows range from edgy, current-event type of stuff to tranquil designs for city gardens. The ground floor is devoted to up-and-coming artists, and the upper floor exhibits established artists' work. Artists also have a workplace to experiment with new projects. All exhibitions are temporary, lasting a maximum of three months. ⊠ *Witte de Withstraat 50, Witte de With* ☎ *010/413–5498* ⊕ *www.tentplaza.nl* ☜ *€4* ☉ *Tues.–Sun. 11–6.*

Toren op Zuid. An office complex by celebrated modern architect Renzo Piano, this structure houses the head offices of KPN Telecom. Its eye-catching billboard facade glitters with 1,000-odd green lamps flashing on and off, creating images provided by the city of Rotterdam, in addition to images provided by KPN and an art academy. The facade fronting the Erasmus Bridge leans forward by 6 degrees, which is the same as the angle of the bridge's pylon. It is also said that Piano could have been making a humorous reference to his homeland, as the Tower of Pisa leans at the same angle. ⊠ *Wilhelminakade 123, Kop van Zuid.*

WHERE TO EAT

Use the coordinate (⊕ A4) at the end of each listing to locate a site on the Where to Eat and Stay in Rotterdam map.

$ ✕ **Asian Glories.** Reputed to be the city's best Cantonese restaurant,
CHINESE   Asian Glories serves lunch, dinner, and Sunday brunch in a tasteful modern Asian interior or outdoors on its terrace. It's hard to choose what is most delicious; their dim sum, fresh oysters, mussels in black bean sauce, and Peking Duck consistently get raves from fussy eaters.

Leave room for an exotic dessert such as ice cream with rice and red bean sauce. $ *Average main: €10* ⊠ *Leeuwenstraat 15, Centrum* ☎ *010/411–7107* ⊘ *Closed Wed.* ✛ *D2.*

$$ ✕ **Bla Bla.** Just around the corner from the historic heart of Delf-
VEGETARIAN shaven, this restaurant is always lively and frequently crowded. There is always a choice of three or four main vegetarian dishes, inspired by cuisines from around the world, and the menu changes often. Make sure you're having dinner on the early side to get the freshest ingredi-ents—and a seat. $ *Average main: €18* ⊠ *Piet Heynsplein 35, Delf-shaven* ☎ *010/477–4448* ⊕ *www.bla-bla.nl* ⊘ *Closed Mon. and Tues. No lunch* ✛ *A4.*

$ ✕ **Café Dudok.** Lofty ceilings, a cavernous former-warehouse interior,
CAFÉ long reading tables stacked with international magazines and papers—little wonder this place attracts an artsy crowd. At its most mellow, the spot is perfect for a lazy afternoon treat of delicious homemade pastries, but you can come here for breakfast, lunch, high tea, dinner, or even a snack after midnight. They offer a small selection for vegetarians. The brasserie, on a mezzanine above the open kitchen at the back, looks out over the Rotte River. Since it's terribly crowded at times, you should get here unfashionably early to avoid disappointment—there's nowhere else like it in Rotterdam. $ *Average main: €10* ⊠ *Meent 88, Centrum* ☎ *010/433–3102* ⊕ *www.dudok.nl* ✛ *D2.*

$$ ✕ **Café Floor.** Adjacent to the Stadsschouwburg (Municipal Theater),
CONTEMPORARY this popular spot doesn't look too inviting from the outside, but the interior is modern, light, and airy; the staff are friendly; and the kitchen produces excellent food. Try the lamb brochette, so tender the meat practically dissolves on your tongue. There's also a good selection of tapas available and a delicious passion-fruit cheesecake. The beauti-ful garden at the back, and accompanying birdsong from the local fauna, make this a restful stop. This place is a favorite with local and international regulars, so be prepared to be patient if you go late-ish on a Saturday. $ *Average main: €12* ⊠ *Schouwburgplein 28, Centrum* ☎ *010/404–5288* ⊕ *www.cafefloor.nl* ✛ *C2.*

$$$ ✕ **De Engel.** The international kitchen of this former town house has cre-
ECLECTIC ated a loyal following, who flock here for excellent food, a view over the Westersingel, and an intimate setting (tables are very close together). The very friendly staff is more than helpful with recommendations, as are your next-table neighbors. For a special taste treat, try the truffle soup, or the skate wing with garlic sauce. While there is a menu, daily changing seasonal specialties are always available, and often the best choice. The house recommends you simply let the chef "surprise" you, and rest assured you won't be disappointed. $ *Average main: €25* ⊠ *Eendrachtsweg 19, Centrum* ☎ *010/413–8256* ⊕ *www.restaurant-deengel.nl* ⌕ *Reservations essential* ⊘ *Closed Sun. No lunch Sat.* ✛ *C3.*

$$ ✕ **Dewi Sri.** This restaurant has *rijsttafel* (rice table) to dream about,
INDONESIAN with creative takes on traditional Indonesian dishes. Rice table is like Indonesian smorgasbord with samplings from the menu. Choose from a multitude of tantalizing options from Indonesian, Javanese, and Suma-tran menus. Some diners may find the mock woodcarvings a little heavy, given the subtle flavors of the food being served. All in all, though, this

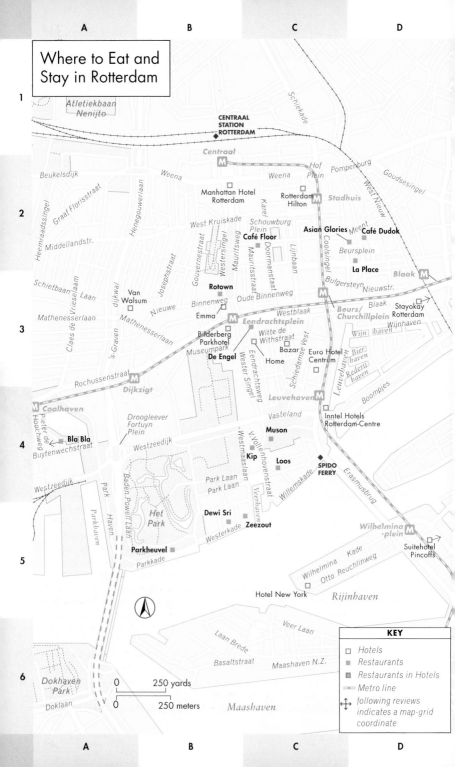

Where to Eat and Stay in Rotterdam

A **B** **C** **D**

1

Atletiekbaan
Nenijto

Schiekade

CENTRAAL
STATION
ROTTERDAM

Beukelsdijk

Weena

Centraal Ⓜ

Weena

Hof
Plein

Pompenburg

Goudsesingel

West Nieuw

Stadhuis

2

Graaf Florisstraat

Henegouwerlaan

Manhattan Hotel
Rotterdam

Rotterdam
Hilton Ⓜ

Meent

Asian Glories

Café Dudok

Heemraadssingel

Middellandstr.

West Kruiskade

Schouwburg
Plein

Karel

Coolsingel

Beursplein

Gouvernestraat

Café Floor

Doormanstraat

Lijnbaan

La Place

Schietbaan Laan

Josephstraat

Mauritsweg

Westersingel

Mauritsstraat

Bulgersteyn

Nieuwstr.

Blaak Ⓜ

Mathenesserlaan

Van
Walsum

dijkwal

Nieuwe

Rotown

Binnenweg

Oude Binnenweg

Westblaak

Blaak

Stayokay
Rotterdam

Claes de Vrieselaan

's Graven

Mathenesserlaan

Emma

Ⓜ Eendrachtsplein

Beurs/
Churchillplein

Wijn haven

Wijnhaven

3

Rochussenstraat Ⓜ
Dijkzigt

Bilderberg
Parkhotel
Museumpark

De Engel

Witte de
Withstraat

Home

Schiedamse Vest

Bazar

Euro Hotel
Centrum

Bier
haven

Rederij

Boompjes

Wester Singel

Eendrachtsweg

Leuvehaven

Ⓦ Coolhaven

Droogleever
Fortuyn
Plein

Ⓜ Leuvehaven

4

Pieter de
Hoochweg

Bla Bla

Westzeedijk

Vasteland

Inntel Hotels
Rotterdam-Centre

Buytenwechstraat

Park Laan
Park Laan

v.Vollenhovenstraat

Muson

Westmaaslaan

Kip

Loos

◆ SPIDO
FERRY

Erasmusbrug

Westzeedijk

Park

Haven

Baden Powell'laan

Veerhaven

Willemskade

Wilhelmina
-plein Ⓜ

Het
Park

Dewi Sri

Zeezout

Westerkade

Wilhelmina
Kade

Otto Reuchlinweg

Suitehotel
Pincoffs

5

Parkheuvel

Parkkade

Hotel New York

Rijnhaven

Dokhaven
Park

Veer Laan

Doklaan

Laan Brede

Basaltstraat

Maashaven N.Z.

Maashaven

6

0 ___ 250 yards

0 ___ 250 meters

KEY	
□	Hotels
■	Restaurants
■	Restaurants in Hotels
⚍	Metro line
⟷	following reviews indicates a map-grid coordinate

A **B** **C** **D**

place probably has the best Indonesian food in Rotterdam, so don't let the décor faze you. The large restaurant upstairs could feel quite empty midweek, but the staff is incredibly polite, appearing discreetly at your table just as soon as you feel the need to ask for something. If you can't find space in the Dewi Sri, try the adjacent Warisan restaurant, which serves similarly priced and equally mouthwatering Thai food. $ *Average main: €15* ⊠ *Westerkade 20, Scheepvaartkwartier* ☎ *010/436–0263* ⊕ *www.dewisri.nl* ☾ *No lunch weekends* ✢ *B5.*

$$$ ✕ **Kip.** Dark wooden floors, unobtrusive lighting, and a big fireplace
DUTCH make Kip's traditional interior warm and cozy. As befits the restaurant's name (which means chicken), the chicken breast (from a special Dutch breed called *Hollandse blauwhoender*) with truffles is the most popular dish, but the kitchen offers a whole lot more. There's always a daily-changing fish option, such as cod with saffron-and-fennel sauce, and plenty of meatier fare, such as veal in wild mushroom sauce. The menu must work, because this spot is always packed. In summer, a leafy garden at the back provides welcome respite from the bustle of the big city. $ *Average main: €24* ⊠ *Van Vollenhovenstraat 25, Scheepvaartkwartier* ☎ *010/436–9923* ⊕ *www.kip-rotterdam.nl* ⊜ *Reservations essential* ☾ *No lunch* ✢ *C4.*

$ ✕ **La Place.** This large self-serve café on the top floors of the V&D
DUTCH department store offers everything from simple rolls to grilled meats at reasonable prices. The salad bar is a pretty good lunch option. The roof transforms into a sunny terrace in summer. On the ground floor, La Place Express offers a lunch option for those in a hurry: a tempting variety of reasonably priced sandwiches, but it's takeout only. $ *Average main: €8* ⊠ *Hoogstraat 185, Centrum* ☎ *0900/235–8363* ⊕ *www.laplace.nl* ▭ *No credit cards* ☾ *Closed Mon.* ✢ *D2.*

$$ ✕ **Loos.** In the grand style of Rotterdam's cafés, Loos has a range of
DUTCH international magazines and newspapers on its reading racks, and in a fun gesture, six clocks with different time zones decorate one wall. You enter and see what looks like a forest of tables, but this trompe l'oeil effect is largely caused by a wall-size mirror. As for the food, some dishes are excellent, including such delights as roasted-pepper-and-smoked-apple soup with aniseed cream, monkfish with truffle-butter sauce, and steak with Armagnac-soaked raisins and a duck-liver-and-truffle sauce. If you want to eat less luxuriously, try the bar menu. $ *Average main: €18* ⊠ *Westplein 1, Scheepvaartkwartier* ☎ *010/411–7723* ⊕ *www.loos-rotterdam.nl* ☾ *No lunch weekends (restaurant)* ✢ *C4.*

$$$$ ✕ **Parkheuvel.** Overlooking the Maas, this posh restaurant is run by chef-
ECLECTIC owner Erik van Loo. It is said to be popular among the harbor barons,
Fodor's Choice who can oversee their dockside territory from the bay windows of this
★ tastefully modern, semicircular building. Tables are covered with cream-colored linens, and wood-frame chairs are elegantly upholstered. The service here is as effortlessly attentive as you would expect from one of Holland's top five restaurants. Luxuries such as truffles are added to the freshest ingredients, with the day's menu dictated by the availability of the best produce at that morning's markets. Kudos and salaams are offered up by diners to many of the chef's specialties, including the ravioli of black Bresse chicken with pan-fried langoustines. $ *Average main:*

8

€45 ✉ Heuvellaan 21, Centrum ☎ 010/436–0530 🌐 www.parkheuvel.nl ✍ Reservations essential ⏲ Closed Sun. and 3 wks in Aug. No lunch Sat. ✥ B5.

$ CAFÉ 🍴 **Rotown.** This arts-center venue is more celebrated for its funky bar than for its restaurant proper. A buzz fills the dining area, a spillover from the crowd up front. The menu is quite extensive, ranging from burgers to dim sum, although the service can be a bit hit-or-miss. But if you like a stylish, party-hearty atmosphere (bands often play at the bar), this could be worth it. [$] *Average main: €10 ✉ Nieuwe Binnenweg 17–19, Centrum ☎ 010/436–2669 🌐 www.rotown.nl ✥ B3.*

$$$ SEAFOOD 🍴 **Zeezout.** On an elegant riverfront terrace, the charming "Sea Salt" mirrors the freshness of its sea-based menu in crisp linen tablecloths and its spotlessly clean, open kitchen, where the bustle of the staff whets your appetite. A large fish mosaic on the wall looks out across the river to the floodlighted Erasmus Bridge; a window awning adds to the romance of the view. Try the turbot accompanied by shrimp, aubergine cream, and *rösti* (potato pancakes). [$] *Average main: €27 ✉ Westerkade 11b, Scheepvaartkwartier ☎ 010/436–5049 🌐 www.restaurantzeezout.nl ✍ Reservations essential ⏲ Closed Mon. No lunch Sun. ✥ C5.*

WHERE TO STAY

Use the coordinate (✥ A4) at the end of each listing to locate a site on the Where to Eat and Stay in Rotterdam map.

For expanded hotel reviews, visit Fodors.com.

$ HOTEL ★ 🏨 **Bazar.** The well-traveled owner has created havens from his wanderings, with hot, deep colors evoking Turkey and Morocco throughout the individually styled rooms on the second floor, and motifs conjuring up Africa and South America on the third and fourth floors. **Pros:** top-floor rooms have balconies. **Cons:** elevator stops at the third floor. [$] *Rooms from: €80 ✉ Witte de Withstraat 16, Witte de With ☎ 010/206–5151 🌐 www.hotelbazar.nl 🛏 27 rooms 🍽 Breakfast ✥ C3.*

$ HOTEL 🏨 **Bilderberg Parkhotel.** The town-house facade is dramatically yoked to a metallic skyscraper, and rooms have been renovated in uncluttered modern styles; the best are those at the back overlooking a quiet, grassy garden. **Pros:** convenient for museums; excellent service; good restaurant. **Cons:** rooms lack character. [$] *Rooms from: €119 ✉ Westersingel 70, Centrum ☎ 010/436 🌐 www.bilderberg.nl 🛏 189 rooms ✥ B3.*

$ HOTEL 🏨 **Emma.** The third generation of the Orsini family sees to the comfort of guests at this pleasanty modern retreat on social, busy Nieuwe Binnenweg, where plenty of shops and nightspots are conveniently close; the nearest sidewalk café is right opposite the hotel. **Pros:** friendly; good value; elevator; good breakfast; smoke-free environment. **Cons:** on noisy junction. [$] *Rooms from: €85 ✉ Nieuwe Binnenweg 6, Centrum ☎ 010/436–5533 🌐 www.hotelemma.nl 🛏 24 rooms 🍽 Breakfast ✥ B3.*

$ HOTEL 🏨 **Euro Hotel Centrum.** Despite the businesslike, anonymous name, this is a welcoming and comfortable modern hotel with snug, stylish rooms and lots of flowers and plants, so the overall feeling is spruce and nicely kept. **Pros:** friendly; quiet; good buffet breakfast. **Cons:** situated on a

The Stayokay Rotterdam is housed in a few of Rotterdam's most iconic and eye-catching buildings: the Piet Blom–designed "cube houses."

drab street. $ *Rooms from: €85 ⊠ Baan 14–20, Centrum* ☎ *010/214–1922* ⊕ *www.eurohotelcentrum.nl* ↝ *53 rooms, 2 suites* ⊺◉⊺ *Breakfast* ✛ *C3.*

$$ 🖵 **Hotel New York.** An atmospheric standout on Rotterdam's business-
HOTEL oriented hotel scene occupies the former twin-towered, waterside head-
quarters of the Holland America Line, offering individually decorated
rooms with high ceilings that contrast with the modernist, vaguely nau-
tical décor, and excellent views. **Pros:** great riverside location; historic
building; nice room décor. **Cons:** away from main sights. $ *Rooms
from: €110 ⊠ Koninginnenhoofd 1, Kop van Zuid* ☎ *010/439–0500*
⊕ *www.hotelnewyork.nl* ↝ *71 rooms, 1 suite* ✛ *C5.*

$ 🖵 **Inntel Hotels Rotterdam Centre.** The majority of the rooms in this mod-
HOTEL ern high-rise, built at the opening to the Leuvehaven inner harbor,
have water views and all are simply but tastefully decorated, wearing a
designer-look edge. **Pros:** friendly; central; pool and sauna. **Cons:** not
for those who shun big hotels. $ *Rooms from: €85 ⊠ Leuvehaven 80,
Centrum* ☎ *010/413–4139* ⊕ *www.inntelhotelsrotterdamcentre.com*
↝ *239 rooms, 24 suites* ✛ *C4.*

$$$ 🖵 **Manhattan Hotel Rotterdam.** The only five-star hotel in the city draws
HOTEL celebrity guests, and the regal purple corridors, lined with copies of
Fodor'sChoice Dutch masterpieces, and bright spacious rooms fitted out with luxuri-
★ ously huge beds will make you feel like a member of the glitterati yourself.
Pros: sky-high luxury; slick-yet-friendly service; CD players and every
other amenity. **Cons:** sky-high prices. $ *Rooms from: €189 ⊠ Weena
686, Centrum* ☎ *010/430–2000* ⊕ *www.manhattanhotelrotterdam.com*
↝ *224 rooms, 7 suites* ✛ *B2.*

$$$ ⊞ **Rotterdam Hilton.** A business-oriented chain hotel offers all the
HOTEL   expected luxury appointments and modern amenities and caters to
visitors, businessfolks as well as tour groups, who want a name they
can rely on. **Pros:** centrally located. **Cons:** lacks character. $ *Rooms
from: €175* ⊠ *Weena 10, Centrum* ☎ *010/710–8000* ⊕ *www.rotterdam.
hilton.com* ⌁ *246 rooms, 8 suites* ✛ *C2.*

$ ⊞ **Stayokay Rotterdam.** If you're running on a budget, this modern hos-
tel right in the middle of the city is just the ticket, and it occupies sev-
eral of Rotterdam's most iconic and eye-catching buildings: the Piet
Blom–designed "cube houses" built in 1984 between Blaak train and
metro station and the Oude Haven. **Pros:** great location; good value;
unusual building; some double rooms. **Cons:** as with other hostels, you
can't always choose your roommates. $ *Rooms from: €60* ⊠ *Overblaak
85–87, Centrum* ☎ *010/436–5763* ⊕ *www.stayokay.com* ⌁ *5 double
rooms, 44 dorm rooms* ⊖⚮ *Breakfast* ✛ *D3.*

$$ ⊞ **Suitehotel Pincoffs.** Spacious high-ceilinged rooms are individually
furnished, tastefully decked out in modern styles but also manage a
respectful nod to the historic surroundings—and overlook the Maas
river and the iconic Erasmus bridge. **Pros:** a short tram ride from sights;
occupies lovely old customs building in trendy Kop van Zuid district;
pleasant bar serves light meals. **Cons:** breakfast is extra. $ *Rooms from:
€125* ⊠ *Stieltjesstraat 34, Kop van Zuid* ☎ *010/297–4500* ⊕ *www.
hotelpincoffs.nl* ⌁ *17 rooms* ✛ *D5.*

$ ⊞ **Van Walsum.** The friendly and gregarious owner proudly restores and
HOTEL   reequips his rooms, floor by floor, on a continuously rotating basis,
with the always-modern décor of each floor determined by that year's
best buys in furniture, carpeting, and bathroom tiles. **Pros:** friendly;
within walking distance of the Museum Boijmans van Beuningen and
other major attractions. **Cons:** away from the nightlife. $ *Rooms from:
€89* ⊠ *Mathenesserlaan 199–201, Centrum* ☎ *010/436–3275* ⊕ *www.
hotelvanwalsum.nl* ⌁ *28 rooms* ⊖⚮ *Breakfast* ✛ *A3.*

NIGHTLIFE AND THE ARTS

THE ARTS

Rotterdam's arts calendar extends throughout the year.

VVV Rotterdam Info. You can book tickets and find out what's going on
around town through the local tourist information office. ⊠ *Coolsingel
195–197, Centrum* ☎ *010/271–0120* ⊕ *www.rotterdam.info.*

FILM

Partly because of the annual avant-garde **International Film Festival Rotterdam** (⊕ www.filmfestivalrotterdam.com), held in late January–early
February, there is a lot of general interest in film in this city—as a result,
you have many screens to choose from.

Pathé. The Pathé is the place to head for blockbusters. ⊠ *Schouwburgplein 101, Centrum* ☎ *020/575–1751.*

There's an open-air cinema at the Museumpark in September.

THEATER

Nieuwe Luxor Theater. With 1,500 seats, this theater was specifically designed to host major stage musicals and other popular events. The theater, one of the Netherlands' largest, was designed by Australian architect Peter Wilson and has a marvelous view of Rotterdam's harbor and skyline. Performances are often in English. ✉ *Posthumalaan 1, Kop van Zuid* ☎ *010/496–0000* ⊕ *www.luxortheater.nl.*

Theater Lantaren/Venster. The Theater Lantaren/Venster has an interesting program that shows art films in addition to hosting small-scale dance and theater performances. ✉ *Otto Reuchlinweg 996, Kop van Zuid* ☎ *010/277–2266* ⊕ *www.lantarenvenster.nl.*

Theater Zuidplein. Rotterdam's cultural climate facilitates the staging of productions from many semiprofessional groups, such as Turkish folk dance, classical Indian dance, and capoeira Brazilian martial art troupes. The Theater Zuidplein is particularly known for its multicultural program. ✉ *Zuidplein 60–64, Charlois* ☎ *010/203–0203* ⊕ *www. theaterzuidplein.nl.*

NIGHTLIFE

To get your bearings and find your way around the party scene, look out for glossy party fliers in cafés, record stores, and clothes shops selling clubbing gear. The best nights tend to be Thursday to Saturday, 11 pm to 5 am. Most venues have a clubbing floor, with DJs working the crowd, and more ambient rooms for smoking or just plain relaxing. From hard-core techno—which has been popular here since the early '90s—to early-hour chill-out cafés, there is a wide gamut of nighttime entertainment. West Kruiskade (also known as Chinatown) is the place to go if you want lively bars and music from around the world. Nieuwe Binnenweg and Witte de Withstraat have many busy late-night cafés and clubs. Oude Haven is particularly popular with students, and the Schouwburgplein is favored by visitors to the nearby theaters and cinemas. Stadshuisplein has a number of tacky discos and bars.

CAFÉS

Breakaway. Busy and with a young international crowd, this is the nearest you'll get to a Dutch take on an American bar. ✉ *Karel Doormanstraat 1, near Centraal Station, Centrum* ☎ *010/233–0922* ⊕ *www. breakaway.nl.*

De Schouw. An erstwhile brown café and former journalists' haunt, De Schouw is now a trendy brown bar with a mix of artists and students. ✉ *Witte de Withstraat 80, Witte de With* ☎ *010/412–4253.*

Locus Publicus. With a menu that tops 200 varieties of Belgian beer, Locus Publicus is a favorite with enthusiasts. Best of all, this one-room café a few minutes' walk east from Blaak station has an open log fire in winter. ✉ *Oostzeedijk 364, Blaak* ☎ *010/433–1761* ⊕ *www. locus-publicus.com.*

NRC (*Nieuw Rotterdams Café*). The NRC, opposite De Schouw, is a brand-new and altogether grander grand café in a building that formerly housed the editorial offices and print room of the eponymous Dutch national paper. ✉ *Witte de Withstraat 63, Witte de With* ☎ *010/414–4188* ⊕ *www.nieuwrotterdamscafe.nl.*

Spanning the Meuse, Rotterdam's Erasmus Bridge makes a spectacular sight at night.

CLUBS

Club Vibes. The long, narrow Club Vibes has a friendly staff who chat up night owls at the bar—you shouldn't arrive here before 1:30 am. Music is mostly 1970s and 1980s, with some more mainstream 1990s nights. It's open Thursday to Saturday only. ⊠ *Westersingel 50a, Museumpark* ☏ *010/436–1655* ⊕ *www.clubvibes.nl.*

Rotown. A high-style restaurant, Rotown has new-talent bands playing on Saturday night. ⊠ *Nieuwe Binnenweg 19, Museumpark* ☏ *010/436–2669* ⊕ *www.rotown.nl.*

Toffler. In a former pedestrian tunnel, Toffler opens late and music really kicks off into the early hours with changing guest and house DJs every Friday and Saturday night (cover charge varies). ⊠ *Weena-Zuid 33, Centrum* ⊕ *toffler.nl.*

GAY AND LESBIAN BARS

Gay Palace. Very much part of the late-night scene, Gay Palace attracts crowds of young gay and lesbian Rotterdammers to its large dance floor on Saturday and some Friday nights. ⊠ *Schiedamsesingel 139, Centrum* ☏ *010/414–1486* ⊕ *www.gay-palace.nl.*

JAZZ

Dizzy. If you appreciate live performances, Dizzy is *the* jazz café in Rotterdam. A big terrace out back hosts both Dutch and international musicians every Tuesday and Sunday. The café also serves good, reasonably priced food. Come early if you want a seat. Concerts and jam sessions are free. ⊠ *'s-Gravendijkwal 127, 's-Gravendijkwal* ☏ *010/477–3014* ⊕ *www.dizzy.nl.*

North Sea Jazz Festival. For three days in mid-July, jazz lovers from around the world descend on Rotterdam for the North Sea Jazz Festival, which fills the Ahoy' arts complex with music. Around 180 artists perform on 15 different stages in what is one of Europe's largest and most popular celebrations of jazz. ⊕ *www.northseajazz.com.*

POP AND ROCK

For mega-events, choose between the 13,500-seater **Ahoy'**, which holds pop concerts and large-scale operas, and **De Kuip**, Rotterdam's major football stadium, which boasts of its Bob Dylan, Rolling Stones, and U2 concerts. Tickets for both venues often sell out quickly, but De Kuip has a better sound system.

Ahoy'. Ahoy' hosts major pop concerts for big names such as Lady Gaga, Green Day, and Neil Young, but also hosts classical philharmonic orchestras, top jazz musicians, and performance companies like Cirque du Soleil. ⊠ *Ahoyweg 10, Zuidplein* ☎ *010/293–3300* ⊕ *www.ahoy.nl.*

De Kuip/Feyenoord Stadion. Despite being able to seat more than 51,000 people, De Kuip/Feyenoord Stadion usually sells out for concerts. ⊠ *Van Zandvlietplein 1, Kop van Zuid* ☎ *010/492–9444.*

SHOPPING

Rotterdam is the number-one shopping city in South Holland. Its famous Lijnbaan and Beurstraverse shopping centers, as well as the surrounding areas, offer a dazzling variety of shops and department stores. Here you'll find all the biggest chains in Holland, such as Mango, MEXX, Morgan, Invito, and Sacha. The archways and fountains of the Beurstraverse—at the bottom of the Coolsingel—make this newer, pedestrianized area more pleasing to walk around. It is now one of the most expensive places to rent shop space, and has a nickname: *Koopgoot,* which can mean "shopping channel" (if you like it) or "shopping gutter" (if you don't). The Bijenkorf department store has an entrance here on the lower-street level. Van Oldenbarneveldtstraat and Nieuwe Binnenweg are the places to be if you want something different. There is a huge variety of alternative fashion to be found here.

DEPARTMENT STORES

De Bijenkorf. The best in Rotterdam, De Bijenkorf is a favorite department store, designed by Marcel Breuer (the great Bauhaus architect) with an exterior that looks like its name, a beehive. There's a good range of clothing and shoes from both designers and the store's own label, plus a selection of cosmetics and perfume on the ground floor, with a Chill Out department on the same floor geared toward street- and clubwear; here, on some Saturdays a DJ keeps it mellow, and you can even get a haircut at in-store Kinki Kappers. De Bijenkorf is well-known for its excellent household-goods line, ranging from lights and furniture to sumptuous fabrics and rugs. Check out the second-floor restaurant with its view out over the Coolsingel and Naum Gabo's sculpture *Constructie.* ⊠ *Coolsingel 105, Centrum* ☎ *0800/0918* ⊕ *www.debijenkorf.nl.*

V&D. V&D is great for household goods, stationery, and other everyday necessities. Rest your tired tootsies and admire the city view from the rooftop café, La Place, where you can indulge in a wide selection of snacks and full meals. ⊠ *Hoogstraat 185, Centrum* ☎ *0900/235–8363* *€0.18 per min.* ⊕ *www.vd.nl.*

SHOPPING DISTRICTS AND STREETS

Exclusive shops and boutiques can be found in the Entrepotgebied, Delfshaven, Witte de Withstraat, Nieuwe and Oude Binnenweg, and Van Oldenbarneveldtstraat. West Kruiskade and its vicinity offer a wide assortment of multicultural products in the many Chinese, Surinamese, Mediterranean, and Arabic shops. The shops in the city center are open every Sunday afternoon, and there is late-night shopping—until 9—every Friday.

SPECIALTY STORES

There are numerous specialty stores all across town, and depending on what you are looking for, you should be able to find it somewhere. If in doubt, ask a fellow shopper or the tourist office.

ANTIQUES

Look along the **Voorhaven** and its continuation **Aelbrechtskolk,** in Delfshaven, for the best antiques. On Sunday head to the **Schiedamsdijk,** where you can expect to find a market that specializes in antiques and old books, open noon–5.

ART GALLERIES

Many galleries provide the opportunity both to look at art and buy it. These can be found along the Westersingel and in the Museumpark area, but the top galleries are on Witte de Withstraat, also lined with numerous cafés, making it an ideal street to spend some time window-shopping.

MAMA. If you're looking for new, exciting, and innovative art with high standards, you'll find it here. MAMA encourages the collaboration of emerging experimental artists. Some of the work may shock; some might make you laugh out loud in delight; but all of it is art-critic-worthy. Consider film- and video-based art by the Dutch Galleon of Mayhem or the inflatable sculptures by a group of "artoonists," including a giant rabbit by Florentijn Hofman. The gallery is open Wednesday–Sunday 1–6. ⊠ *Witte de Withstraat 29–31* ☎ *010/233–2022* ⊕ *www.showroommama.nl.*

BOOKS

Selexyz Donner. The biggest bookstore in Rotterdam, its 10 floors include an excellent selection of English-language books, which are distributed throughout the shop under specific headings. ⊠ *Lijnbaan 150, Centrum* ☎ *010/413–2070* ⊕ *www.selexyz.nl.*

DESIGN

Dille & Kamille. From herbs to sturdy wooden spoons to recipe books, this is a browser's heaven for anyone interested in cooking. It is one of the few shops in the Netherlands that still carries traditional Dutch household items, such as a huge water kettle to make tea for 25, a nutmeg mill, or a *zeepklopper,* a device that holds a bar of soap and can whip up bubbles—a forerunner to liquid dish-washing detergent. ⊠ *Korte Hoogstraat 22-24, Centrum* ☎ *010/411–3338* ⊕ *www.dille-kamille.nl.*

Entrepot Harbor design district. There are several interior-design stores alongside the city marina at Kop van Zuid.

Galerie ECCE. More like a museum of modern art and home furnishings than a mere gallery, the Galerie ECCE has an exclusive collection of ultramodern furniture, lamps, and glassware from Dutch and European designers and offers a custom-design service. You'll find a variety of smaller unique design items, suitable for gifts, such as coasters and wall sconces. The gallery has a new exhibition of paintings and sculpture every two months, and also specializes in the production of trompe l'oeil wall paintings. ⊠ *Witte de Withstraat 17a–19a, Witte de With* ☎ *010/413–9770* ⊕ *www.galerie-ecce.nl.*

FASHION

Sister Moon. For fashion suggestions, start with Sister Moon, which has a small collection of exclusive, hip clothing for men and women in the party scene; part of the boutique is devoted to trendy secondhand togs. ⊠ *Nieuwe Binnenweg 89b, Centrum* ☎ *010/436–1508* ⊕ *www. sister-moon.nl.*

Urban Unit. Graffiti artists favor Urban Unit, loving the look of the men's sneakers and street wear on sale (while stocking up on spray cans and other graffiti supplies). ⊠ *Nieuwe Binnenweg 63b, Centrum* ☎ *010/436–3825* ⊕ *www.urban-unit.nl.*

Van Dijk. On Van Oldenbarneveldtstraat the prices rise as the stores get more label based. Van Dijk stocks Stella McCartney, Paul Smith, and many others, and the owner, Wendela, has two of her own design labels. You can find trendy shoes, bags, and accessories here and have plenty of room to try on clothes in the *paskamers* (fitting rooms). ⊠ *Van Oldenbarneveldtstraat 105, Centrum* ☎ *010/411–2644* ⊕ *www. wendelavandijk.nl.*

Where there's fashion, there's music: keep in mind that Holland's largest concentration of international music stores can be found on the Nieuwe Binnenweg, ranging from techno to ambient, rock to Latin and African.

STREET MARKETS

Binnenrotteplein. The expansive Binnenrotteplein, between Sint Laurenskerk and Blaak railway station, is home to one of the largest street markets in the country, every Tuesday and Saturday from 9 to 5 and Friday from noon to 5. Among the 520 stalls you can find a flea market, book market, household items, used goods, food, fish, clothes, and flowers. From April to December, a fun shopping market with 200 stands is held on Sunday from noon to 5.

Travel Smart Amsterdam and the Netherlands

WORD OF MOUTH

"Depending on the time of day there are about 10 trains an hour from Schiphol Airport into Amsterdam's main train station, Centraal. Two of which are Fyra trains, which you should pay a supplement for, so should be avoided. These leave at 18 and 48 minutes past the hour. Two make a stop at Sloterdijk. These leave at 15 and 45 past the hour. The rest are direct and take on average 17 minutes to get to Centraal. In the Spring of 2012, one paid €3.80 for a single ticket at the machine, €4.30 at the window. There are no discounts for seniors. There are generally a couple of NS staff around to help with machines or direct you to the windows, station etc. but the signs are pretty clear."
—hetismij2

GETTING HERE AND AROUND

▌ AIR TRAVEL

The least expensive airfares to the Netherlands originate from the United Kingdom and other European countries, are priced for round-trip travel, and must usually be purchased in advance online. Airlines generally allow you to change your return date for a fee; most low-fare tickets, however, are nonrefundable.

EasyJet has low fares to Amsterdam flying in from Belfast, Edinburgh, Geneva, Glasgow, Liverpool, London (Gatwick and Luton), and Nice. Transavia flies to Amsterdam and Rotterdam from Barcelona, Nice, and numerous other cities. Ryanair flies to the southern Dutch city of Eindhoven from London, Stansted, and a dozen other cities around Europe. BMIBaby flies to Amsterdam from its hub in Nottingham (East Midlands Airport).

Consolidators and Low-Cost Airlines
BMIBaby ⊕ *www.bmibaby.com.* **EasyJet**
⊕ *www.easyjet.com.* **Ryanair** ⊕ *www.ryanair.com.*

Air Pass Info FlightPass ⊠ *EuropebyAir*
☎ *888/321-4737* ⊕ *www.europebyair.com.* **oneworld Visit Europe Pass** ⊕ *www.oneworld.com.* **SkyTeam Go Europe Pass**
⊕ *www.skyteam.com.* **Star Alliance Europe Airpass** ⊕ *www.staralliance.com.*

Flying time to Amsterdam is 7 hours from New York, 8 hours from Chicago, 10½ hours from Los Angeles, 9 hours from Dallas, 6½ hours from Montreal, 9½ hours from Vancouver, and 20 hours from Sydney.

Always ask your carrier about its check-in policy. Plan to arrive at the airport about two hours before your scheduled departure time—and don't forget your passport. If you are flying within Europe, check with the airline to find out whether food is served on the flight. If you have dietary concerns, request special meals when booking. Low-cost airlines don't provide a complimentary in-flight service, but snacks and drinks can be purchased on board. For help picking the most comfortable seats, check out SeatGuru.com, which has information about specific seat configurations for different types of aircraft.

Smoking is prohibited on flights to and from Amsterdam. You are not required to reconfirm flights, but you should confirm the departure time by telephone if you made your reservation considerably in advance, as flight schedules are subject to change without notice.

Airlines and Airports Airline and Airport Links.com. This helpful website has links to many of the world's airlines and airports. ⊕ *www.airlineandairportlinks.com.*

Airline Security Issues Transportation Security Administration. This agency has answers for almost every question that might come up. ⊕ *www.tsa.gov.*

A 2004 European Union (EU) regulation standardized the rights of passengers to compensation in the event of flight cancellations or long delays. The law covers all passengers departing from an airport within the EU, and all passengers traveling into the EU on an EU carrier, unless they received assistance in the country of departure. Full details are available from the airlines, and are posted prominently in all EU airports.

AIRPORTS

Located 17 km (11 miles) southeast of Amsterdam, **Schiphol** (pronounced "Shhkip-hole") is the main passenger airport for Holland. With the annual number of passengers using Schiphol exceeding 45 million, it is ranked among the world's top five best-connected airports. Several hotels, a service to aid passengers with disabilities, parking lots, and a main office of the Netherlands tourist board (in Schiphol Plaza and known as "HTi"— Holland Tourist Information) can all prove most useful. The comprehensive

Schiphol telephone service, charged at €0.40 per minute, provides information about flight arrivals and departures as well as all transport and parking facilities.

Rotterdam is the biggest of the regional airport options and provides daily service to many European cities; another regional airport is **Eindhoven.** An increasing number of international charter flights and some budget carriers choose these airports, as benefits include shorter check-in times and ample parking. However, there are no rail links that connect such regional airports with their respective nearby cities, so passengers must resort to taking buses or taxis.

Airport Information Holland Amsterdam Schiphol Airport ✉ *17 km [11 miles] southwest of Amsterdam* ☎ *0900/0566 [€0.40 per min], 31/207940800 Calls from outside the Netherlands only.* ⊕ *www.schiphol.nl.* **Eindhoven Airport** ✉ *8 km [5 miles] west of Eindhoven, Eindhoven* ☎ *0900/9505 [€1.30 per call], +35-22/700-0767 Calls from outside the Netherlands only.* ⊕ *www.eindhovenairport. nl.* **Rotterdam The Hague Airport** ✉ *17 km [11 miles] northwest of Rotterdam, Rotterdam* ☎ *010/446-3444* ⊕ *www.rotterdam-airport.nl.*

GROUND TRANSPORTATION

The Schiphol Rail Link operates between the airport and the city 24 hours a day, with service to Amsterdam Centraal Station (usually abbreviated to Amsterdam CS), and to stations in the south of the city. From 6:30 am to 12:30 am, there are up to eight trains each hour to Centraal; at other times, there is one train every hour. The trip takes about 15–20 minutes and costs €3.80. Schiphol Station is beneath Schiphol Plaza. From Centraal Station, Trams 1, 2, and 5 go to Leidseplein and the Museum Quarter. Keep in mind that Schiphol Station is one of Holland's busiest—make sure you catch the shuttle to Amsterdam and not a train heading to The Hague! As always, when arriving at Amsterdam's Centraal Station, keep an eye out for pickpockets. You may wish to hop aboard a tram or bus to get to your

hotel, so go to one of the **Gemeentevervoerbedrijf (GVB) Amsterdam Municipal Transport** booths found in front of the Centraal Station. Here you can find directions, fare information, and schedules.

Connexxion Schiphol Hotel Shuttle operates a shuttle bus service between Amsterdam Schiphol Airport and all of the city's major hotels. The trip takes about a half hour and costs €16 one-way, or €26 round-trip. Hours for this shuttle bus are 6:30 am to 9 pm, every half hour.

Finally, there is a taxi stand directly in front of the arrival hall at Amsterdam Schiphol Airport. A service charge is included, but small additional tips are not unwelcome. New laws determine that taxi fares are now fixed from Schiphol to Amsterdam; depending on the neighborhood, a trip will cost around €40 or more. A new service that might be convenient for budget travelers who count every euro is the Schiphol Travel Taxi. The taxi needs to be booked at least 24 hours in advance and rides are shared, so the trip will take a bit longer as the taxi stops to pick up and drop off passengers. Make bookings via the Schiphol website. A shared taxi ride costs around €21.

Contacts Connexxion Schiphol Hotel Shuttle ☎ *038/339-4741* ⊕ *www. schipholhotelshuttle.nl.* **Schiphol Rail Link** ☎ *0900/9292 [€0.70 per min]* ⊕ *9292.nl.* **Schiphol Travel Taxi** ⊕ *www.schiphol.nl.*

FLIGHTS

When flying internationally to the Netherlands, you usually choose between a domestic carrier, the national flag carrier of the country, and a foreign carrier from a third country. You may, for example, choose to fly KLM Royal Dutch Airlines to the Netherlands for the basic reason that, as the national flag carrier, it has the greatest number of nonstop flights. Domestic carriers offer connections to smaller destinations. Third-party carriers may have a price advantage.

KLM and its global alliance partner Delta Air Lines—together with their regional partner airlines—fly from Amsterdam's Schiphol Airport to more than 400 destinations in more than 80 countries. Nearly 100 of those are European destinations, with three to four daily flights to most airports and up to 17 flights a day to London alone. Delta now handles all reservations and ticket office activities on behalf of KLM in the United States and Canada, with KLM's biggest North American hubs in Detroit and Minneapolis, and Memphis, New York, and Washington, D.C., among its gateways. KLM's direct flights connect Amsterdam to Atlanta, Los Angeles, Miami, and numerous others. Including connections via KLM's hubs, the airline flies to more than 120 destinations in the United States from Amsterdam. In Canada, KLM serves Montreal, Toronto, and Vancouver. For more information, contact the airline at one of the reservation numbers below. For further information about schedules and special fare promotions, go to KLM's website.

Other international carriers include American Airlines, United Airlines, and US Airways. Dutch charter airline Martinair has direct flights to Amsterdam from Orlando and Miami. None of these carriers makes a transatlantic flight to any of the Netherlands' regional airports. If your carrier offers Rotterdam as a final destination, for example, you fly into Amsterdam, then transfer. KLM Cityhopper offers flights connecting Amsterdam with the smaller regional airports. Transavia Airlines flies from Amsterdam and Rotterdam to a number of European destinations, and many other carriers link European capitals with Amsterdam. EasyJet has budget flights to Amsterdam from several European destinations; Ryanair offers a similar service out of Eindhoven Airport. Check online or with your travel agent for details.

SN Brussels Airlines is Belgium's foremost carrier, with routes to the United States, Africa, and all over Europe. Low-cost carrier Ryanair operates an ever-expanding network of routes out of its hub at Brussels South Charleroi Airport. This can be a very economical way of getting around Europe, and you'll get the best deals if you book well ahead.

Airline Contacts American Airlines
☎ 800/433–7300, 0900/555–7770 in the Netherlands, 0844/499–7300 in U.K. ⊕ www. aa.com. **British Airways** ☎ 800/247–9297 in U.S., 0844/493–0787 in U.K., 020/346–9559 in the Netherlands ⊕ www.britishairways. com. **Brussels Airlines** ☎ 516/296–9500 in U.S., 0905/609–5609 in U.K., ⊕ www. brusselsairlines.com. **Delta Airlines** ☎ 800/221–1212 for U.S. reservations, 800/241–4141 for international reservations, 0871/22–11–222 in U.K., 020/721–9128 in the Netherlands ⊕ www.delta.com. **KLM Royal Dutch Airlines** ☎ 0130/039–2192 in Australia, 020/474–7747 in the Netherlands, 09/921–6040 in New Zealand, 0871/231–0000 in U.K. ☎ 800/618–0104 in U.S. and Canada ⊕ www. klm.com. **United Airlines** ☎ 800/864–8331 in U.S. and Canada, 020/346–9381 in the Netherlands ⊕ www.united.com.

▮ BOAT TRAVEL

International ferries link Holland with the United Kingdom. There are two daily Stena line crossings between the **Hoek van Holland** (Corner of Holland, an industrial shipping area west of Rotterdam) and Harwich, on the car ferry, taking approximately six and a half hours. The overnight crossing takes about seven hours. These are the only ferry crossings that can be booked at the international travel window in large railway stations. There is one P&O Ferries overnight crossing between the Europoort in Rotterdam and Hull, which takes about 12 hours, and one DFDS Seaways overnight crossing from Newcastle to IJmuiden, in Amsterdam, taking 15 hours.

Hire your own boat or take a guided city canal tour of Amsterdam, Leiden, or Delft; alternatively, take a harbor tour to **check out Rotterdam's extensive Europoort,** the world's biggest harbor, and the flood barrier. There are pedestrian ferries behind Amsterdam's Centraal Station across the IJ. *For more specific information about guided tours, see individual regional chapters.*

Passenger Terminal Amsterdam (*PTA*). Passengers visiting Amsterdam as part of a cruise will find themselves arriving at the shiny new Passenger Terminal, 400 yds east of the city's Central Station. After entering Holland's great North Sea Canal at the port city of IJmuiden, most passenger ships then head south to Amsterdam. Once there, besides the usual embarkation and disembarkation facilities, the new terminal has a number of food outlets, along with several souvenir shops offering you that last-minute chance to stock up with those indispensible Delftware clogs and "I Heart Holland" T-shirts. ✉ *Piet Heinkade 27* ☎ *020/509–1000* ⊕ *www.ptamsterdam.com.*

To/from the U.K. and Holland DFDS Seaways ✉ *Sluisplein 33, IJmuiden* ☎ *0255/546–666 in the Netherlands, 0871/522–9955 in U.K.* ⊕ *www.dfdsseaways.com.* **P&O Ferries** ✉ *In Holland Beneluxhaven, Havennummer 5805, Rotterdam/Europoort, Rotterdam* ☎ *020/200–8333* ⊕ *www.poferries.com.* **Stena Line** ✉ *In Holland: Hoek van Holland Terminal, Stationsweg 10, Hoek van Holland* ☎ *0844/770–7070 in U.K., 0900/8123 in the Netherlands [€0.10 per min]* ⊕ *www.stenaline.nl.*

▌ BUS TRAVEL

The bus and tram systems within Holland provide excellent transport links within cities. Frequent bus services are available in all towns and cities; trams run in Amsterdam, The Hague, between Delft and The Hague, and in Rotterdam. Amsterdam and Rotterdam also have subways, referred to as the metro. Amsterdam's metro system has four lines, running southeast, northwest and southwest; Rotterdam's metro system has five lines (three east to west, one north to south, and one connecting to The Hague), which extend into the suburbs and cross in the city center for easy transfers.

Several large companies provide bus and tram services across the country, including Connexxion, BBA, and Arriva. GVB provides additional services in Amsterdam, HTM in The Hague, GVU in Utrecht, and RET in Rotterdam. There are maps of each city's network in most shelters. Buses are clean and easy to use, and bus lanes (shared only with taxis) remain uncongested, ensuring that you travel more swiftly than other traffic during rush hour.

To get around by bus, tram, or metro you'll need an *OV-chipkaart* (public transport chip card)—an electronic payment system, which you hold up to a detector each time you board and leave any bus or tram. Bought preloaded from metro, train, and bus stations, from some magazine kiosks, or from drivers, these credit card–size tickets can be topped up with credit from machines in the stations and are debited according to the distance traveled. Visit the OV-chipkaart website (⊕ www.ov-chipkaart.nl) or call the help desk (☎ 0900/500–6010) for more information. You can also buy tickets for individual journeys from bus/tram drivers, although this works out to be more expensive.

The OV-chipkaart can also be used on trains (note that the check-in/check-out detectors for the trains are clearly marked and in the railway stations, not on board).

Teams of ticket inspectors occasionally make spot checks on trams and buses. This doesn't happen often, but if you are checked and your OV-chipkaart hasn't been checked in, you face a fine.

Bus Information for the Netherlands
Trains, Buses, Trams, and Ferries. Information on all public transportation, including schedules, fares for trains, buses, trams, and ferries in the Netherlands. ☎ 0900/9292 [€0.70 per min] ⊕ 9292.nl. **De Lijn** ☎ 070/220–200 [€0.30 per min] ⊕ www.delijn.be. **STIB/MIVB** ☎ 070/232–000 ⊕ www.stib.be.

▐ CAR TRAVEL

A network of well-maintained highways and other roads covers the Netherlands, making car travel convenient, although traffic is exceptionally heavy around the bigger cities, especially on the roads in the Randstad, and those approaching the North Sea beaches on summer weekends. There are no tolls on roads or highways. Major European highways leading into Amsterdam from the borders are E19 from western Belgium; E25 from eastern Belgium; and E22, E30, and E35 from Germany. Follow the signs for *Centrum* to reach the center of the city. At rush hour, traffic is dense but not so dense as to become stationary.

In Canada Canadian Automobile Association (CAA) ☎ 800/992–8143 ⊕ www.caa.ca.

In the U.S. American Automobile Association (AAA) ☎ 800/564–6222 ⊕ www.aaa.com.

RENTAL CARS

The major car-rental firms have convenient booths at Schiphol and all the region's airports, but the airports charge rental companies a fee that is passed on to customers, so you'll get a better deal at downtown locations. Consider also whether you want to get off a transatlantic flight and into an unfamiliar car in an unfamiliar city. You must be at least 21 years old to rent cars from most agencies. Some agencies require renters to be 25. You can drive in the Netherlands and Belgium with a valid U.S. driver's license.

Most major American rental-car companies have offices or affiliates in the Netherlands, but the rates are generally better if you make an advance reservation from abroad rather than from within Holland. Rates vary from company to company; daily rates start at approximately €35 for a one-day rental, €70 for a three-day rental, and €160 for a week. This may not include collision insurance or airport fee. Tax is included and weekly rates often include unlimited mileage. Most cars in Europe are stick-shift. An automatic transmission will cost a little extra. Rental cars are European brands and range from economy, such as a Ford Ka, to luxury, such as a Mercedes. They will always be in good condition. It is also possible to rent minivans.

Autoverhuur (car rental) in Holland is best for exploring the center, north, or east of the country, but is to be avoided in the heavily urbanized northwest, known as the Randstad, where the public transport infrastructure is excellent. Signage on country roads is usually pretty good, but be prepared to patiently trail behind cyclists blithely riding two abreast (which is illegal), even when the road is not wide enough for you to pass.

GASOLINE

Many of the gas stations in the Netherlands (especially those on the high-traffic motorways) are open 24 hours. Those that aren't open 24 hours generally open early in the morning, around 6 or 7, and close late at night, around 10 or 11. Unleaded regular costs about €1.70 per liter, and major credit cards are widely accepted. If you pay with cash and need a receipt, ask for a *bon*.

PARKING

Parking space is at a premium in Amsterdam as in most towns, especially in the Centrum (historic town center), which has narrow, one-way streets and large areas given over to pedestrians. Most neighborhoods are metered from 9 am to 7 pm, so it is a good idea (if not the only option) to leave your car only in designated parking areas. *Parkeren* (parking lots) are indicated by a white P in a blue square. Illegally parked cars in Amsterdam get clamped by the **Dienst Parkeerbeheer** (Parking Authority) and, after 24 hours, if you haven't paid for the clamp to be removed, towed. You'll be towed immediately in some areas of the city. If you get clamped, a sticker on the windshield indicates where you should go to pay the fine (which can be more than €100).

ROAD CONDITIONS

Holland has an excellent road network, but there is a great deal of traffic using it every day, as you might expect from a country with a high population density. In cities, you will usually be driving on narrow one-way streets and sharing the road with other cars, buses, trams, and bicyclists, so remain alert at all times. When driving on smaller roads in cities, you must yield to traffic coming from the right. Traffic lights are located before intersections, rather than after intersections as in the United States. Traffic circles are very popular and come in all sizes. Driving outside of cities is very easy; roads are very smooth and clearly marked with signs. Traffic during peak hours (7–9 am and 4–7 pm) is constantly plagued with *files* (traffic jams), especially in the western part of the country. If you are going to drive here, you must be assertive. Drivers are very aggressive; they tailgate and change lanes at very high speeds. All road signs use the international driving symbols. Electronic message boards are used on some freeways to warn of traffic jams and to slow traffic down to 90, 70, or 50 kph.

ROADSIDE EMERGENCIES

If you haven't joined a motoring organization, the **ANWB** (Royal Dutch Touring Club) offers 24-hour road assistance in the Netherlands. If you aren't a member, you can call the ANWB after breaking down, but you must pay a €150 on-the-spot membership charge. Emergency crews may not accept credit cards or checks when they pick you up. If your automobile association is affiliated with the **Alliance International du Tourisme** (AIT), and you have proof of membership, you are entitled to free help. To call for assistance push the help button on any yellow ANWB phone located every kilometer (½ mile) on highways, and a dispatch operator immediately figures out where you are. Alternatively, ring their 24-hour emergency line or their information number for details about their road rescue service.

Contacts in Amsterdam ANWB (Royal Dutch Touring Club) ☎ *088/269–2888 emergency number, 088/269–2222 office number* ⊕ *www.anwb.nl.*

RULES OF THE ROAD

Driving is on the right in the Netherlands, and regulations are largely as in the United States. Speed limits are 120 kph (75 mph) on superhighways and 50 kph (30 mph) on urban roads. Some cities also have 30 kph (20 mph) zones around schools. In the Netherlands the limit on standard rural highways is 80 kph (50 mph), or 100 kph (62 mph) if the traffic in each direction is separated by a central barrier. For safe driving, go with the flow, stay in the slow lane unless you want to pass, and make way for faster cars wanting to pass you. In cities and towns, approach crossings with care; local drivers may exercise the principle of priority for traffic from the right with some abandon. Although the majority of cyclists observe the stoplights and general road signs, many expect you, even as a driver, to give way. The latest ruling states that unless otherwise marked, all traffic coming from the right has priority, even bicycles. The driver and front-seat passenger are required to wear seat belts, and other passengers are required to wear available seat belts.

Using a handheld mobile phone is illegal while driving, but you are allowed to drive while using a headset or earpiece. Turning right on a red light is not permitted. Fines for driving after drinking are heavy, including the suspension of license and the additional possibility of six months' imprisonment.

Fog can be a danger on highways in late fall and winter. In such cases, it is obligatory to use your fog lights.

▌ PUBLIC TRANSPORTATION IN AMSTERDAM

METRO

Amsterdam has a full-fledged subway system, called the metro, but travelers will usually find trams and buses more convenient for getting around, as most metro stops are geared for city residents traveling to the outer suburbs. However, the Amsterdam metro can get you from point A to point C in a quantum leap—for instance, from Centraal Station (at the northern harbor edge of the city) to Amstel Station (a train station at the southeastern area of the city, with connections to many buses and trams)—much faster than a tram, which makes many stops along the way. You'll need an OV-chipkaart, used the same way as for other public transport.

Four metro lines, including the express tram (*sneltram*), serve Amsterdam and the surrounding suburbs. A fifth, the much-vaunted Nord-Zuid metro line, is still some years away after lengthy delays—and is the cause of all the heavy construction work you may see around Amsterdam Centraal railway station. Although many stops on the existing metro lines will not be of use to the tourist, several can prove handy. Nieuwmarkt lets you off near the Red Light District and is near the famous sights of the Oude Zijde area. Waterlooplein is near the eastern edge of the Oude Zijde, stopping at the square where the Stadhuis-Muziektheater is located, and offers access to sights of the Jewish Quarter and the Plantage; a walk several blocks to the south leads you to the Eastern Canal Ring and its many historic houses. Wibautstraat is not too far from the Amstel River and provides access to the southern sectors of the city, including De Pijp. Amstel Station is a train station near the Amstel River in the southeastern area of the city, with connections to many buses and trams. Amsterdam Zuid/WTC (South/World Trade Center)

is at the southern edge of Amsterdam Zuid (South) and rarely used by tourists. VU (Vrije Universiteit) is in the suburb of Buitenveldert. It's possible to transfer from the metro to trains at several shared stops, either by crossing the platform or merely going outside to an adjacent train station. Line 50 (Ringlijn) travels from Isolaterweg in the northeastern part of the city to Gein, a southeastern suburb. Lines 51, 53, and 54 all start at Centraal Station and follow the same routes until they head into the suburbs. They ride as a subway from Centraal Station to Amstel Station, then whiz along the rest of the routes above ground, parting ways at Spaklerweg. The No. 51 passes through Buitenveldert, stopping at the VU and continuing south into Amstelveen. The 53 passes Diemen and ends up southeast in Gaasperplas. The 54 also travels southeast and shares the rest of its route with the 50, passing through Holendrecht and ending at Gein.

TRAMS AND BUSES

Many tram and bus routes start from the hub at Centraal Station. A large bus depot is on the Marnixstraat, across from the main police station, and there's another one at Harlemmermeer station in the Overtoomseveld neighborhood of western Amsterdam. Trams and buses run from about 6 am to midnight daily. The tram routes, with a network of 130 km (80 miles) of track, make this characteristic form of transport more useful than the bus for most tourists. Night owls can make use of the hourly night-bus services, with double frequency on Friday and Saturday night, but routes are restricted.

Between stops, trams brake only when absolutely necessary, so listen for warning bells if you are walking or cycling near tramlines. Taxis use tramlines, but other cars are allowed to venture onto them only when turning right. The newer fleets of buses are cleaner, and therefore nicer to use, and bus lanes (shared only with taxis) remain uncongested, ensuring that you travel more swiftly than the rest of the traffic in rush hour. If the bus is very crowded, you may have to stand, so hold on to a handrail, as the buses can travel quite fast; to **avoid rush hour,** don't travel between 7:30 and 9 in the morning or between 4 and 6 in the afternoon. As with all urban systems of transportation, keep an eye out for pickpockets.

There are 16 tramlines servicing the city. Trams 1, 2, 4, 5, 9, 13, 16, 17, 24, and 25 all start and end their routes at Centraal Station. The most frequently used trams by visitors are the 1, 2, and 5, which stop at the big central Dam Square and, along with 6, 7, and 10, also stop at Leidseplein square. The numbers 2, 3, 5, and 12 will get you to Museumplein and the Museum District. Trams 5, 16, 24, and 25 travel through Amsterdam's chic Zuid district. The No. 4 tram stops at the RAI convention center and the No. 5 will take you to Station South/World Trade Center. The remaining lines pass through East and West Amsterdam and take you farther outside the center city (Centrum) to areas generally more off-the-beaten-track for tourists.

More than 30 GVB buses cover all the city's neighborhoods and are a good way to get closer to specific addresses. The Conexxion bus company operates about 50 different buses that will take you from Amsterdam to all areas of Holland. Most of these depart from Centraal Station. Buses 110 to 117 travel to the "folkloric" area of North Holland, just to the north of the city, where favorite tourist destinations include Volendam, Marken, Edam, Hoorn, and Broek in Waterland.

FERRIES

Four GVB ferry lines leave from Centraal Station, but not all are of interest to tourists. The Buiksloterwegveer leaves from Pier 7 behind Centraal Station every eight to 15 minutes, day and night. The ferry transports pedestrians, cyclists, and motorcyclists across the IJ channel to North Amsterdam. There is no fee for the service. North Amsterdam may prove to be less interesting than the refreshing trip, which takes about five minutes.

TICKETS

Besides the OV-chipkaart system, *covered above,* in Amsterdam you can also buy 24-, 48-, 72-, and 96-hour travel-anywhere tickets (€7.50 for one day, €12 for two days, €16 for three days, €20.50 for four days), which cover all urban bus and streetcar routes. You can also buy chip cards from the driver that are valid for one hour of unlimited travel. Fares are often reduced for children ages 4 to 11 and for people who are 65 years or older.

The electronic *I amsterdam Card* provides free or discounted admission to many top attractions, plus a free canal round-trip, and free use of public transport. These can be bought online or from tourist offices in Amsterdam, and cost €40, €50, or €60 for 1, 2 or 3 days, respectively.

Contacts GVB ✉ *Prins Hendrikkade 108–114, Centrum* ☏ *0900/9292* ⊕ *www.gvb.nl.*

▮ TAXIS IN AMSTERDAM

Vacant taxis on the move through the streets are often on call to their dispatcher. Occasionally, if you get lucky, they'll stop for you if you hail them, but officially the regular practice is to wait by a taxi stand or phone them. Taxi stands are at the major squares and in front of the large hotels. You can also call Taxicentrale, the main dispatching office. A 5-km (3-mile) ride will cost about €20. A new initiative in the city is the *Wieler Taxi* (bike taxi), which resembles a larger version of a child's pedal car and isn't very practical in the rain.

Contacts Taxicentrale Amsterdam ☏ *020/777-7777* ⊕ *www.tcataxi.nl.* **Wielertaxi** ☏ *06/2824-7550* ⊕ *www.wielertaxi.nl.*

▮ TRAIN TRAVEL

Dutch trains are modern and the quickest way to travel between city centers. Services are relatively frequent, with a minimum of two departures per hour for each route, and often more. Although many Dutch people complain about delays, the trains usually run roughly on time. Most staff speak English. Reserving a seat is not possible.

Intercity trains can come double-decker; they stop only at major stations. *Sneltreins* (express trains) also have two decks but take in more stops, so they are a little slower. *Stoptreins* (local trains) are the slowest. Smoking is not permitted on trains and permitted only in designated zones in stations.

On the train you have the choice of first or second class. First-class travel costs 50% more, and on local trains gives you a slightly larger seat in a compartment that is less likely to be full. At peak travel times, first-class train travel is worth the difference.

Train tickets for travel within the country can be purchased at the last minute. Normal tickets are either *enkele reis* (one-way) or *retour* (round-trip). Round-trip tickets cost approximately 75% of two single tickets. They are valid only on the day you buy them, unless you ask specifically for a ticket with a different date. You can get on and off at will at stops in between your destinations until midnight. You can also use the OV-chipkaart *covered above*, but remember to check in on the platform before you board, and to check out when you leave the train.

You cannot buy domestic train tickets in the Netherlands with credit cards or traveler's checks. If you don't have euros, bureau de change GWK has a branch at Amsterdam Centraal Station and all major stations throughout the country. You can also buy tickets at the yellow touch-screen ticket machines in every railway station. These machines accept debit cards with a four-digit PIN code but not credit cards. Fares are slightly lower than if you visit a manned ticket desk. Note that you can't buy tickets aboard the trains, and you

risk a hefty fine if you board and travel without one.

Train fares in Holland are lower than in most other European countries, but you can still save money by looking into rail passes—there is a host of special saver tickets that make train travel even cheaper. Be aware, however, that if you don't plan to cover many miles, then you may as well buy individual tickets; a *dagkaart* (unlimited travel pass for one day) costs €47 second class, €80 first class, but it is almost impossible to rack up enough miles to make it worthwhile. Short of flying, taking the Channel Tunnel is the fastest way to cross the English Channel: 35 minutes from Folkestone to Calais, 60 minutes from motorway to motorway, or two hours and 15 minutes from London's St. Pancras Station to Paris's Gare du Nord.

Contacts NS–Nederlandse Spoorwegen/ Dutch Railways ⊕ www.ns.nl. SNCB/NMBS ⊕ www.b-rail.be. Thalys ⊕ www.thalys.com.

Information and Passes Eurail ⊕ www. eurail.com. Rail Europe ⊠ 44 S. Broadway, No. 11, White Plains, New York, USA ☎ 800/622–8600 in U.S., 800/361–7245 in Canada ⊕ www. raileurope.com/us.

Train Information Public Transport Information. Holland-wide Public Transport Information, including schedules and fares. ☎ 0900/9292 at €0.70 per min. ⊕ 9292.nl. Lost and Found. For lost and found on train lines and in stations, ask for a form at the nearest station. ☎ 0900/321–2100 at €0.80 per min. Nederlandse Spoorwegen (*Dutch Rail*). Information from Dutch Rail's Customer Service. ☎ 0900/202–1163 calls cost 10¢ per minute ⊕ www.ns.nl.

ESSENTIALS

▮ ACCOMMODATIONS

The Netherlands offers a range of options, from the major international hotel chains and small, modern local hotels to family-run restored inns and historic houses. Accommodations in Amsterdam are at a particular premium at any time of year, so you should book well in advance. Should you arrive without a hotel room, head for one of the city's four VVV (Netherlands Board of Tourism) offices, which have a same-day hotel booking service and can help you find a room. A small fee is charged for this service.

The hotel situation elsewhere in the Netherlands is less tight outside of the summer months, but hotels in larger cities often fill with business customers during the week. Most hotels that do cater to business travelers sometimes grant substantial weekend rebates. These discounted rates are often available during the week, as well as in July and August, when business travelers are thin on the ground. Wherever you go, you will have a wider choice if you plan ahead.

APARTMENT AND HOUSE RENTALS

If you travel with a group of friends, or with children, or if you plan to stay for more than 2 nights, you may want to consider renting an apartment. Not only will you probably spend less money per person per night, you can also save by cooking your own meals. On top of that, staying in an apartment will offer you the opportunity to experience the city as a local. The Amsterdam tourist information website (⊕ *www.iamsterdam.com*) offers a list of trustworthy companies as well as private home-owners that offer accommodation for rent.

A reliable organization with a varied choice of rentals is **Amsterdam City Mundo** (⊕ *www.amsterdam.citymundo.com*). Their carefully selected accommodations include apartments, studios, houseboats, and even a few multi-storied houses. Most apartments sleep up to four people. All accommodations are privately owned and fully furnished, which makes for a homey feel. The minimum stay is 3 nights, the maximum stay 21 nights (the more nights you stay, the better the rates). Linen and towels are included in the price. The rate for one person per night lies between €25 and €54, depending on the state of the apartment, the location, the amount of people, and the amount of nights.

For a special and stylish stay you can book **Maison Rika** (⊕ *www.rikaint.com*), a charming two-story guesthouse on the Oude Spiegelstraat with canal views. The beautiful 17th-century house is modernized and decorated by Ulrika Lundgren, the Swedish-born designer behind Amsterdam-based fashion label Rika. The apartment sleeps up to four people and costs €195 per night.

De Blauwe Polder (⊕ *www.blauwepolder. nl*) offers 4 modern cottages in the countryside, just outside Amsterdam. The comfortable accommodations guarantee a peaceful stay amidst green fields. The rent includes bikes to explore the beautiful surroundings, or to cycle to the city center of Amsterdam, which is only 15 minutes away. Each apartments sleeps 2 people. A minimum stay of 2 nights is required and with a week's stay you get 20% discount. Rates are per apartment per night and depend on the season. In high season (July 15 to September 15) rates are between €90 and €75, in mid-season (April 15 to July 14 and September 16 to November 1) between €75 and €65, and in low season (November 1 to April 14) between €65 and €55.

Remember that the VVVs (tourist offices) in each region you plan to visit all have extensive accommodations listings. They can book reservations for you according to your specific requirements. For more information, see our special section in the Where to Stay chapter.

Local Agents in the Netherlands Center Parcs ☎ 010/498–9754, 0900/660–6600 [€0.50 per min] ⊕ www.centerparcs.com. **City Mundo** ⊠ Schinkelkade 30 ☎ 020/470–5705 ⊕ amsterdam.citymundo.com. **Landal Green Parks** ☎ 070/300–3506 ⊕ www.landalgreenparks.com. **VVV Tourist Offices for the Netherlands** ⊕ www.vvv.nl.

BED-AND-BREAKFASTS

A pleasant alternative to getting accommodations in a hotel is to stay at a B&B. You'll find a large assortment scattered throughout the Netherlands. The best way to track down B&Bs in Amsterdam is either through creative city accommodations specialist City Mundo or Holiday Link, both of which deal with private houses and longer stays. Prices vary widely from €25 to €40 per person.

Reservation Services in the Netherlands Bed & Breakfast Holland ☎ 020/615–7527 ⊕ www.bbholland.com. **Bed and Breakfast Service Nederland** ⊠ Zandkasteel 43, Eindhoven ☎ 040/762–0600 ⊕ www.bedandbreakfast.nl. **City Mundo** ⊠ Schinkelkade 30 ☎ 020/470–5705 ⊕ amsterdam.citymundo.com.

HOME EXCHANGES

With a direct home exchange you stay in someone else's home while they stay in yours. Some outfits also deal with vacation homes, so you're not actually staying in someone's full-time residence, just their vacant weekend place.

Exchange Clubs Home Exchange.com. From $7.95 per month for a 1-year online membership listing. ☎ 800/877–8723 ⊕ www.homeexchange.com. **HomeLink International.** Yearly fee is $119. ☎ 800/638–3841 ⊕ www.homelink.org. **Intervac U.S.** Monthly fee is $8.33. ☎ 800/756–4663 ⊕ www.intervac-homeexchange.com.

HOSTELS

Many hostels are affiliated with Hostelling International (HI), an umbrella group of hostel associations with some 4,500

member properties in more than 70 countries. Other hostels are completely independent and may be nothing more than a really cheap hotel.

Membership in any HI association, open to travelers of all ages, allows you to stay in HI-affiliated hostels at member rates. One-year membership is about $28 for adults; hostels charge about $10–$30 per night. Members have priority if the hostel is full; they're also eligible for discounts around the world, even on rail and bus travel in some countries.

The Dutch national hostel association, Nederlandse Jeugdherberg Centrale (NJHC), better known as Stayokay, and the Belgian Auberges de Jeunesse and Vlaamse Jeugdherbergen associations are all affiliated with HI. NJHC has an excellent website with visuals and information about the many hostels in Holland.

Amsterdam is world famous for two beloved hostels: the Flying Pig Palace and the Stayokay Hostel in Vondelpark, open to travelers of all ages. Hostels elsewhere in the Netherlands and in Belgium are also well organized and clean. Rooms with one to 10 beds are available, and hostels are suitable for family stays. Many are near train stations.

Organization in Holland Stayokay (Nederlandse Jeugdherberg Centrale) ☎ 020/551–3155 ⊕ www.stayokay.com.

Information Hostelling International—USA ☎ 301/495–1240 ⊕ www.hiusa.org.

HOTELS

In line with the international system, Dutch hotels are awarded stars (one to five) by the Benelux Hotel Classification System, an independent agency that inspects properties based on their facilities and services. Those with three or more stars feature en suite bathrooms where a shower is standard, whereas a tub is a four-star standard. Guest rooms in lodgings listed in this guide have a shower unless otherwise indicated.

One Dutch peculiarity to watch out for is having twin beds pushed together instead of having one double. If you want a double bed (or *tweepersoonsbed*), you may have to pay more. Keep in mind that the star ratings are general indications and that a charming three-star might make for a better stay than a more expensive four-star. During low season, usually November to March (excluding Christmas and the New Year) when a hotel is not full, it is sometimes possible to negotiate a discounted rate, if one is not already offered. Prices in Amsterdam are higher over the peak summer period, while those in less touristed cities may actually fall at this time when the core business trade tails off. Room rates for deluxe and four-star rooms are on a par with those in other European cities, so in these categories, ask for one of the better rooms, since less desirable rooms—and there occasionally are some—don't measure up to what you are paying for. Most cheaper hotels quote room rates including breakfast, while for those at the top end it usually costs extra. When you book a room and are in any doubt, specifically ask whether the rate includes breakfast.

Check out your hotel's location, and ask your hotelier about availability of a room with a view, if you're not worried about the extra expense: hotels in the historic center with a pretty canal view are highly sought after. Always ask if there is an elevator (called a "lift") or whether guests need to climb any stairs. Even if you are fairly fit, you may find traditional Dutch staircases in older buildings intimidating and difficult to negotiate. Keep that in mind if you're planning on making reservations in a listed monument, such as a historic canalside town house. The alternative is to request a ground-floor room. In older hotels, the quality of the rooms may vary; if you don't like the room you're given, request another. This applies to noise, too. Front rooms may be larger or have a view, but they may also have a lot of street noise—so if you're a light sleeper, request a quiet room when making reservations. Remember to specify whether you care to have a bath or shower, since many bathrooms do not have tubs. It is always a good idea to have your reservation, dates, and rate confirmed by fax.

Taking meals at a hotel's restaurant sometimes provides you with a discount. Some restaurants, especially country inns, require that guests take half board, at least lunch or dinner, at the hotel. Full pension entitles guests to both lunch and dinner. Guests taking either half or full board also receive breakfast. If you take a *pension,* you pay per person, regardless of the number of rooms.

Many hotels in Amsterdam appear to be permanently full, so book as far in advance as you can to be sure of getting what you want.

Aside from going directly to the hotels or booking a travel-and-hotel package with your travel agent, there are several ways of making reservations. The VVV offers a room reservation service; branches of the VVV can be found in Schiphol Airport, Amsterdam Centraal Station, and at Leidseplein. Contact the VVV's office, or go to their website. Hotel reservations made via the I amsterdam website are free; those made in person or by phone/fax incur a €15 booking fee. Hotels will sometimes ask you to confirm your reservation by fax or e-mail. If you are having an extended stay, the property may request a deposit either in the local currency or billed to your credit card.

Reservation Services in Amsterdam **VVV Amsterdam Hotel Reservations** ☎ *020/201–8800* ⊕ *www.iamsterdam.com.* **VVV Netherlands Board of Tourism Switchboard.** First stop for many travelers' queries and questions. ☎ *070/370–5705.*

▮ ADDRESSES

With a history as venerable as Holland's, it's no surprise that many of the country's *straten,* or streets, take their names from its famous sons and daughters. In Amsterdam, for one example, Hugo de Grootstraat honors Delft's noted lawyer-philosopher (*straat* is "street"). In addition, you get all the variations: Hugo de Grootkade (*kade* is a street running parallel to a canal), Hugo de Grootplein (*plein* is "square"), ad infinitum. In Amsterdam, there's even an Eerste, Tweede, and Derde (first, second, and third) Hugo de Grootstraat. Of course, kings and queens feature too: Wilhelminastraat is named after Queen Wilhelmina, the grandmother of the current queen, Beatrix.

Other geographical terms to keep in mind are a *dwarsstraat,* which runs perpendicular to another street or canal, such as Leidsestraat and Leidsedwarsstraat. A *straatje* is a small street; a *weg* is a road; a *gracht* a canal; a *steeg* a very small street; a *laan* is a lane or avenue. *Baan* is another name for a road, not quite a highway, but busier than an average street. Note that in the Netherlands, the house number always comes after the street name on addresses.

The Dutch also have an infinite range of names for bodies of water, from *gracht* to *singel* to *kanaal* (all meaning "canal"). The difference between a singel and a gracht is hard to define, even for a Dutch person. In fact, the names can be doubly confusing because sometimes there is *no* water at all—many grachten have been filled in by developers to make room for houses, roads, and so on. Near harbor areas you'll notice *havens* (harbors), named after the goods that ships used to bring in, like *Wijnhaven* (Wine Harbor) and *Vishaven* (Fish Harbor) in Rotterdam.

Amsterdam streets radiate outward from Centraal Station; in general, street numbers go up as you move away from the station. Don't let common address abbreviations confuse you. BG stands for *Begane Grond* (ground floor); SOUT for *Soutterrain* (basement); HS for *Huis* (a ground-floor apartment or main entry). Common geographical abbreviations include *str.* for *straat* (street); *gr.* for *gracht* (canal); and *pl.* for *plein* (square). For example: Leidsestr. or Koningspl.

▮ COMMUNICATIONS

INTERNET

If you're traveling with a laptop, take a spare battery and an electrical-plug adapter with you, as new batteries and replacement adapters are expensive. Many hotels are equipped with jacks for computers with Internet connections, and almost all have Wi-Fi. Some offer this service to hotel guests for free; others may charge up to €15 per hour for access.

PHONES

The country code for the Netherlands is 31. The area code for Amsterdam is 020. To call an Amsterdam number within Amsterdam, you don't need the city code: just dial the seven-digit number. To call Amsterdam from elsewhere in the Netherlands, dial 020 at the start of the number. In addition to the standard city codes, there are three other prefixes used: public information numbers starting with 0800 are free phone numbers, but be aware that information lines with the prefix 0900 are charged at premium rates (35¢ a minute and more). Numbers starting with 06 indicate mobile (cell) phones. Mobile signal strength is good throughout the country.

The area codes for other Dutch cities are: Delft, 015; Rotterdam, 010; Utrecht, 030; Haarlem, 023; The Hague, 070.

LOCAL DO'S AND TABOOS

CUSTOMS OF THE COUNTRY

The Dutch are generally warm and welcoming. Most are multilingual and proud of it. They are also open and direct when it comes to speaking their mind, and are not afraid of making personal remarks. This can sometimes come across as a bit abrupt, or even rude, but there is certainly no offense intended.

GREETINGS

When greeting people, you should shake their hand and say your name if you have not already done so. It is usual to greet family and close friends of the opposite sex with a three-cheek kiss.

Common phrases are: *goede dag* (good day), *graag* (please), and *dank U wel* (thank you).

SIGHTSEEING

When visiting a Catholic or Protestant church service, you should not wear shorts. When visiting a mosque, women should wear long sleeves and pants or a knee-length skirt, and a scarf on their heads.

OUT ON THE TOWN

If you are visiting a Dutch person's home, bring a bouquet of flowers or a bottle of wine as a gift. It is polite to arrive about 10 minutes late, to allow your host time for last-minute preparations.

Don't be surprised if you arrive for dinner and are offered coffee before any alcoholic aperitifs appear. During the meal, keep both hands above the table.

DOING BUSINESS

Arrive on time for business appointments. Shake hands, and use family names rather than first names.

The pace of business meetings is more relaxed than in the United States, so don't rush into business too promptly; instead spend a few minutes chatting about weather or travel. If you have met your associate's family previously, ask about them before beginning business. If you are in a meeting with several Dutch people, expect negotiations to drag on.

In Dutch business it is important that everyone has a chance to air their views, even if it means discussing trivial points ad nauseam. It is a very fair system, but can also be long-winded and frustrating if you are used to quick decision-making.

Breakfast meetings are not popular in Holland, as most businesspeople take a light breakfast at home. Business lunches are far more popular. Don't be surprised if your Dutch colleagues drink milk with their lunch.

LANGUAGE

Try to learn a little of the local language. You need not strive for fluency; even just mastering a few basic words and terms is bound to make chatting with the locals more rewarding.

There are two official Dutch languages: Dutch, used widely across the country, and Friese, used only in the north. In Amsterdam, and in all other cities and towns, English is widely spoken.

State schools teach English to pupils as young as eight. Not only is it the country's strong second language, but the general public is very happy to help English-speaking visitors, to the extent that even if you ask in Dutch they answer cheerfully in English. Signs and notices often have duplicated information in English, if not more languages. Even in small villages you can usually find someone who speaks at least a little English.

When dialing a Dutch number from abroad, drop the initial zero from the local area code, so someone calling from New York, for example, to Amsterdam would dial 011 + 31 + 20 + the seven-digit phone number. When dialing from the Netherlands overseas, the country code is 00–1 for the United States and Canada, 00–61 for Australia, and 00–44 for the United Kingdom. All mobile and landline phones in Holland are 10 digits long (although some help lines and information centers have fewer digits).

Since hotels tend to overcharge for international calls, it is best to use a public phone. When making a call, listen for the dial tone (a low-pitched hum), insert a credit card, then dial the number. Since the increase in cellular phones, the number of phone cells, or phone booths, is decreasing. At every railway station there are still plenty of pay phones, either in the ticket hall or on the platforms.

To ask directory assistance for telephone numbers outside the Netherlands, dial 0900/8418 (calls are charged at €1.15 per call). For numbers within the Netherlands, dial 0900/8008 (calls are charged at €1.15 per call).

To reach an operator, dial 0800/0410. To make a collect call, or dial toll-free to a number outside the Netherlands, dial 0800/0101.

CALLING OUTSIDE

The country code for the United States is 1.

Access Codes in Holland AT&T Direct ☎ *0800/022–9111.* **MCI WorldPhone** ☎ *0800/023–5103* ⊕ *consumer.mci.com.*

CALLING CARDS

Telephone cards are no longer used in public phone booths in the Netherlands. They accept credit cards instead, or local chip cards (available only with Dutch bank passes).

MOBILE PHONES

British standard cell phones work in the Netherlands, but American and Canadian standard (nonsatellite) cell phones may not. If you have a multiband phone (some countries use different frequencies than what's used in the United States) and your service provider uses the world-standard GSM network (as do T-Mobile, Cingular, and Verizon), you may be able to use your phone abroad. Roaming fees can be steep, however: 99¢ a minute is considered reasonable. And overseas you normally pay the toll charges for incoming calls. It's almost always cheaper to send a text message than to make a call, since text messages have a low set fee. If you'd like to rent a cell phone while traveling, reserve one at least four days before your trip, as most companies will ship it to you before you travel. Cellular-Abroad rents cell phones packaged with prepaid SIM cards that give you a local cell phone number and calling rates. Planetfone rents GSM phones, which can be used in more than 100 countries. If you just want to make local calls, your best bet may be to consider buying a new SIM card (note that your provider may have to unlock your phone for you to use a different SIM card) and a prepaid service plan in the destination. You'll then have a local number and can make local calls at local rates. If your trip is extensive, you could also simply buy a new cell phone in your destination, as the initial cost will be offset over time.

■TIP➔ If you travel internationally frequently, save one of your old mobile phones or buy a cheap one on the Internet; ask your cell phone company to unlock it for you, and take it with you as a travel phone, buying a new SIM card with pay-as-you-go service in each destination.

Contacts Cellular Abroad. This company rents and sells GSM phones and sells SIM cards that work in many countries. ☎ *800/287–5072* ⊕ *www.cellularabroad.com.* **Mobal.** With per-call rates that vary throughout the world, Mobal rents mobiles and sells GSM phones that will operate in 140 countries. ☏ *888/888–9162* ⊕ *www.mobalrental.com.* **Planet Fone.** This firm rents cell phones, but the per-minute rates are expensive. ☏ *888/988–4777* ⊕ *www.planetfone.com.* **rent2connect** ☏ *+32/2/652–1414* ⊕ *www.locaphone.be.*

▌ EATING OUT

MEALS AND MEALTIMES

Traditional Dutch cuisine is very simple and filling. A typical Dutch *ontbijt* (breakfast) consists of *brood* (bread), *kaas* (cheese), *hard gekookte ei* (hard-boiled eggs), ham, yogurt, jams, and fruit.

Lunch is usually a *boterham* (sandwich) or a *broodje* (soft roll or a baguette). Salads and warm dishes are also popular for lunch. One specialty is an *uitsmijter*: two pieces of bread with three fried eggs, ham, and cheese, garnished with pickles and onions. *Pannenkoeken* (pancakes) are a favorite lunch treat topped with ham and cheese or fruit and a thick *stroop* (syrup).

A popular afternoon snack is *frites* (french fries); try them with curry ketchup and onions, called *frites speciaal*, with a *kroket* (a fried, breaded meat roll) on the side. Another snack is whole *haring* (herring) served with raw onions. Stay away from *frikandel*, a long hot dog that can contain anything.

Diner (dinner) usually consists of three courses: an appetizer, main course, and dessert, and many restaurants have special prix-fixe deals. Beverages are always charged separately. Dutch specialties include *erwtensoep* (a thick pea soup with sausage), *zalm* (salmon), *gerookte paling* (smoked eel), *hutspot* (beef stew), *aardappel au gratin* (potato au gratin), and *lamsvlees* (lamb). Steamed North Sea mussels are almost as popular in Holland as they are in Belgium. In general, the standard of the once-dull Dutch cuisine is improving steadily. Chefs have in recent years become more adventurous, and you will find many other more exciting choices (usually French-influenced) on menus than were seen a decade ago.

An oft-seen dessert is *Dame Blanche,* meaning White Lady, made of vanilla ice cream with hot dark chocolate and whipped cream. Holland is famous for its cheeses, including Gouda, Edam, and Limburger. Indonesian cuisine is also very popular here, and a favorite lunch or dinner is *rijsttafel,* which literally means "rice table" and refers to a prix-fixe meal that includes a feast of 10–20 small spicy dishes.

Restaurants open for lunch starting at 11 am, while restaurants opening for dinner will accept guests as early as 5 or 6 pm, closing at 11. Most restaurants are closed Monday.

PAYING

Major credit cards are accepted in most restaurants. Visa and MasterCard are the most widely used; smaller establishments may not accept American Express or Diners Club. Some bars and cafés won't accept credit cards, though most will. Don't rely on traveler's checks for paying restaurant bills.

Tipping 15% to 20% of the cost of a meal is not common practice in the Netherlands. Instead, it is customary to round off the total to a convenient figure, to reward good service. If paying with a credit card, pay the exact amount of the bill with your card, and leave a few euros in cash on the table for the waiting staff.

RESERVATIONS AND DRESS

Regardless of where you are, it's a good idea to make a reservation if you can. We only mention them specifically when reservations are essential (there's no other way you'll ever get a table) or when they are not accepted. For popular restaurants, book as far ahead as you can (often 30 days), and reconfirm as soon as you arrive. (Large parties should always call ahead to check the reservations policy.) We mention dress only when men are required to wear a jacket or a jacket and tie.

The Dutch favor relatively casual dress when dining out; men in open-neck shirts are far more common than a dining room full of suits. Jackets and ties are a rarity, except in the very top establishments. If in any doubt, check ahead with the restaurant in question.

WINES, BEER, AND SPIRITS

When you just ask for a "beer" in the Netherlands, you will get a small (200 milliliters) glass of draft lager beer with 5% alcohol content, known as *pils*. There are a number of national breweries that turn out similar fare—in Amsterdam it will usually be Heineken, but you may also encounter Amstel, Oranjeboom, Grolsch, Bavaria, or a number of smaller outfits. The argument for serving beer in small glasses is that you can drink it before it gets warm, and that you can also drink more of them. Many bars will also serve you a pint (500 milliliters) if you ask them. There are a number of smaller artisanal breweries that attempt different beer styles with ever-improving results—look out for the La Trappe, De Prael, Emelisee, De Molen, Jopen, and 't IJ names in particular. Many Dutch bars serve fine Belgian beers, including white (wheat) beer, Westmalle (a Trappist brew, which comes in brown and strong blond "triple" versions), kriek (a fruit-flavored beer), and Duvel, a very strong blond beer. All the major cities also have a few specialist beer cafés, for real connoisseurs, with beer lists stretching into the hundreds. In Amsterdam, the In De Wildeman café is one of the best places to head on that score. To discover Amsterdam's true beer culture in more depth, check out *Around Amsterdam in 80 Beers* (www. booksaboutbeer.com), by Fodor's expert Tim Skelton. Keep in mind that many Dutch and Belgian beers have a high alcohol content; 8%–9% alcohol per volume is not unusual.

Be sure to try locally produced *genièvre* or *jenever*, a strong, ginlike spirit taken neat. Sometimes its edge is taken off with sweeter fruit flavors like apple, lemon, and red currant. In some bars, bartenders fill the small glass to the brim, so that only surface tension keeps it from overflowing. Faced with such a delicate balance, you have to lean over and take the first sip from the bar, rather than pick up the glass.

ELECTRICITY

The electrical current in the Netherlands is 220 volts, 50 cycles alternating current (AC); wall outlets take Continental-type plugs, with two round prongs.

Consider making a small investment in a universal adapter, which has several types of plugs in one lightweight, compact unit. Most laptops and mobile phone chargers are dual voltage (i.e., they operate equally well on 110 and 220 volts), so require only an adapter. These days the same is true of small appliances such as hair dryers. Always check labels and manufacturer instructions to be sure. Don't use 110-volt outlets marked "for shavers only" for high-wattage appliances such as hair dryers.

Contacts Walkabout Travel Gear. This source has a good coverage of electricity under "adapters." ⊕ *www.walkabouttravelgear. com.*

EMERGENCIES

Police, Ambulance, and Fire ☎ *112 Europe-wide toll-free 24-hour switchboard for emergencies.*

Afdeling Inlichtingen Apotheken. The 24-hour help-line service Afdeling Inlichtingen Apotheken (*apotheken* means "pharmacy") can direct you to your nearest open pharmacy; there is a rotating schedule to cover evenings, nights, and weekends—details are also posted at your local *apotheken*, and in the city newspapers. ☎ *020/694–8709.*

Centrale Doktersdienst (*Central Doctor Services*). The Centrale Doktersdienst offers a 24-hour English-speaking help line providing advice about medical symptoms. ☎ *020/592–3434.*

Directory Inquiries. In the case of minor accidents, phone the Directory Inquiries service to get the number for the outpatients' department at your nearest *ziekenhuis* (hospital). ☎ *0900/8008*.

TBB. A 24-hour dental service that refers callers to a dentist (or *tandarts*), TBB also has operators that can give details of pharmacies open outside normal hours. ☎ *020/506–3841, 0900/821–2230* ⊕ *www.tandartsbemiddelingsbureau.nl*.

Central Number. For non-urgent police matters, call the central number. ☎ *0900/8844*.

Police Headquarters. Amsterdam's police headquarters is at the crossing Marnixstraat/Elandsgracht and can be reached with Tramline 3, 7, 12, or 17.

For car breakdowns and other car-related emergencies, call the big automobile agency in the Netherlands, the ANWB (⇨ *Car Travel, Emergency Services*).

Note that all numbers quoted above with the code 020 are for Amsterdam and surrounding area only.

Contacts in Amsterdam and the Netherlands **Medical Emergencies, Police, Fire, Accidents, and Ambulance** ☎ *112*.

HOSPITALS IN AMSTERDAM
For emergency treatment, the **AMC** and **Sint Lucas Andreas** hospitals have first-aid departments.

Contacts **AMC (Academisch Medisch Centrum).** The largest, most modern hospital serving Amsterdam and surroundings is the AMC. It's actually outside the city proper, in the Holendrecht area. ✉ *Meibergdreef 9, Amsterdam Zuidoost* ☎ *020/566–9111* ⊕ *www.amc.nl*. **Sint Lucas Andreas Ziekenhuis.** Located in the Geuzenveld district, the Sint Lucas Andreas Ziekenhuis is in the western part of Amsterdam. ✉ *Jan Tooropstraat 164* ☎ *020/510–8911* ⊕ *www.sintlucasandreasziekenhuis. nl*. **Slotervaart Ziekenhuis.** This hospital is located in the southwestern part of the city. ✉ *Louwesweg 6* ☎ *020/512–9333* ⊕ *www. slotervaartziekenhuis.nl*. **VU Medisch Centrum.** The VU Medisch Centrum is a university teaching hospital in the Buitenveldert

area. ✉ *De Boelelaan 1117* ☎ *020/444–4444* ⊕ *www.vumc.nl*.

▌HEALTH

SHOTS AND MEDICATIONS
Standards of health in the Netherlands are generally very good. You won't need any immunizations and you are unlikely to get sick. Older visitors, however, may wish to consider immunization against influenza if traveling over the winter months. If you do fall ill, you've picked the right place, as Dutch health care is generally acknowledged to be one of the best in the world.

SPECIFIC ISSUES IN AMSTERDAM AND THE NETHERLANDS
While you are traveling in the Netherlands, the Centers for Disease Control and Prevention (CDC) in Atlanta recommends that you observe health precautions similar to those that would apply while traveling in the United States. The main Dutch health bureau is the GGD, which stands for Gemeentelijke Gezondheidsdienst (Communal Medical Health Service). English-speaking medical help is easy to find. Most doctors have a good English vocabulary and are familiar with English medical terms. *Drogists* (drugstores) sell toiletries and nonprescription drugs (⇨ *Emergencies*). For prescription drugs, go to an *apotheek* (pharmacy).

Health Warnings **National Centers for Disease Control & Prevention (CDC)** ☎ *800/232–4636 international travelers' health line* ⊕ *www.cdc.gov/travel*. **World Health Organization (WHO)** ⊕ *www.who.int*.

OVER-THE-COUNTER REMEDIES
You will find most standard over-the-counter medications, such as aspirin and acetaminophen, in the *drogisterij* (drugstore). You will have difficulty finding antihistamines and cold medications, like Sudafed, without a prescription.

Medical Care in Holland **GGD Nederland.** For inquiries about medical care, contact the national health service agency: GGD

Nederland. ⊠ *Nieuwe Achtergracht 100*
☎ *020/555–5911* ⊕ *www.ggd.nl.*

▌HOURS OF OPERATION

Banks are open weekdays 9:30 to 4 or 5, with some extending their business hours to coordinate with late-night shopping. Some banks are closed Monday mornings.

The main post office is open weekdays 9 to 6, Saturday 10 to 1:30. In every post office you'll also find the Postbank, a money-changing facility, which has the same opening hours.

Apotheken (pharmacies) are open weekdays from 8 or 9 to 5:30 or 6. There are always pharmacies on call during the weekend. The after-hours emergency pharmacy telephone number is ☎020/694–8709. Operators always speak English.

Most shops are open from 1 to 6 on Monday, 9 to 6 Tuesday through Saturday. Hairdressers are generally closed Sunday and sometimes Monday. If you really need a haircut on those days, try a salon at one of the larger hotels. Thursday or Friday (Thursday in Amsterdam) is a designated late-night shopping night—*Koopavond* (buying evenings)—with stores staying open until 9. *Markten* (markets) selling fruit, flowers, and other wares run from 10 to 4 or sometimes 5. Small *nachtwinkels* (late-night shops) selling food, wine, and toiletries, are open from afternoon to midnight or later. Supermarkets are open weekdays until 8 or 10 pm, Saturday until 6 or 8 pm, with most open on Sundays either from 11 to 7 or from 4 to 10 pm.

▌MONEY

The price tags in Amsterdam are considered reasonable in comparison with those in main cities in neighboring countries, although with the strength of the euro versus the dollar, they may feel expensive to North American visitors. Good value for the money can still be had in many places, and as a tourist in this Anglophile country, you are a lot less likely to get ripped off in the Netherlands than in countries where English is less widely embraced.

Here are some sample prices: admission to the Rijksmuseum is €14; the cheapest seats at the Stadsschouwburg theater run €20 for plays, €25 for opera; €7.50–€11.50 for a ticket at a movie theater (depending on time of show). Going to a nightclub might set you back €5–€20. A daily English-language newspaper is €3–€5. A taxi ride (1⅓ km, or ¾ mile) costs about €8. An inexpensive hotel room for two, including breakfast, is about €60–€110, an inexpensive dinner is €25–€40 for two, and a half-liter carafe of house wine is €10. A simple sandwich item on the menu runs about €3.50, a cup of coffee €1.80. A Coke is €2.50, and a half-liter of beer is €5.

Prices throughout this guide are given for adults. Substantially reduced fees are almost always available for children, students, and senior citizens.

▌TIP➜ Banks never have every foreign currency on hand, and it may take as long as a week to order. If you're planning to exchange funds before leaving home, don't wait until the last minute.

ATMS AND BANKS

Your own bank will probably charge a fee for using ATMs abroad; the foreign bank you use may also charge a fee. Nevertheless, you'll usually get a better rate of exchange at an ATM than you will at a currency-exchange office or even when changing money in a bank. And extracting funds as you need them is a safer option than carrying around a large amount of cash.

▌TIP➜ PINs with more than four digits are not recognized at ATMs in many countries. If yours has five or more, remember to change it before you leave.

The Dutch word for ATM is *Geldautomaat*. They are widespread, and accessible 24 hours a day, seven days per week. The majority of machines work with Maestro, Cirrus, and Plus.

CREDIT CARDS

It's a good idea to inform your credit-card company before you travel, especially if you're going abroad and don't travel internationally very often. Otherwise, the credit-card company might put a hold on your card owing to unusual activity—not a good thing halfway through your trip. Record all your credit-card numbers—as well as the phone numbers to call if your cards are lost or stolen—in a safe place, so you're prepared should something go wrong. Both MasterCard and Visa have general numbers you can call (collect if you're abroad) if your card is lost, but you're better off calling the number of your issuing bank, since Master-Card and Visa usually just transfer you to your bank; your bank's number is usually printed on your card.

If you plan to use your credit card for cash advances, you'll need to apply for a PIN at least two weeks before your trip. Although it's usually cheaper (and safer) to use a credit card abroad for large purchases (so you can cancel payments or be reimbursed if there's a problem), note that some credit-card companies *and* the banks that issue them add substantial percentages to all foreign transactions, whether they're in a foreign currency or not. Check on these fees before leaving home, so there won't be any surprises when you get the bill.

■ TIP→ Before you charge something, ask the merchant whether or not he or she plans to do a dynamic currency conversion (DCC). In such a transaction the credit-card *processor* (shop, restaurant, or hotel, not Visa or MasterCard) converts the currency and charges you in dollars. In most cases you'll pay the merchant a 3% fee for this service in addition to any credit-card company and issuing-bank foreign-transaction surcharges.

Dynamic currency conversion programs are becoming increasingly widespread. Merchants who participate in them are supposed to ask whether you want to be charged in dollars or the local currency, but they don't always do so. And even if they do offer you a choice, they may well avoid mentioning the additional surcharges. The good news is that you *do* have a choice. And if this practice really gets your goat, you can avoid it entirely thanks to American Express; with its cards, DCC simply isn't an option.

Major credit cards are accepted in most hotels, gas stations, restaurants, cafés, and shops. Be aware, however, that you cannot use credit cards to purchase train tickets in the Netherlands.

Reporting Lost Cards American Express ☎ 800/528–4800 in the U.S., 1–336/393–1111 collect from abroad ⊕ www.americanexpress. com. **Diners Club** ☎ 800/234–6377 in the U.S., 1–514/877–1577 collect from abroad ⊕ www.dinersclub.com. **MasterCard** ☎ 800/307–7309 in the U.S., 636/722–7111 collect from abroad ⊕ www.mastercard.com. **Visa** ☎ 800/847–2911 in the U.S., 0800/022–3110 toll-free in the Netherlands ⊕ www.visa. com.

Reporting Lost Cards in Amsterdam and the Netherlands: American Express ☎ 020/504–8000. **Diners Club** ☎ 020/654–5511. **MasterCard** ☎ 0800/022–5821. **Visa** ☎ 0800/022–3110.

CURRENCY AND EXCHANGE

The single euro is the official currency of the Netherlands. At press time, 1 euro = 1.29 US$. Shop around for the best exchange rates (and also check the rates before leaving home).

There are eight coins—1 and 2 euros, plus 1, 2, 5, 10, 20, and 50 cents. Bills are 5-, 10-, 20-, 50-, 100-, 200-, and 500-euro notes. Note that because of counterfeiting concerns, few shops and restaurants will accept notes higher in value than 50 euros. If you do find yourself with higher denominations, change them in a bank. The Dutch also consider the 1- and 2-cent coins to be an irritation, and many shops round prices up or down to the nearest 5 cents.

These days, the easiest way to get euros is through an ATM, called a *geldautomaat* in the Netherlands. You can find them in airports, train stations, and throughout the cities. ATM rates are excellent because they are based on wholesale rates offered only by major banks. At exchange booths always confirm the rate with the teller before exchanging money—you won't do as well at exchange booths in airports, or in hotels, restaurants, or stores. To avoid lines at airport exchange booths, get some euros before you leave home.

GWK Travelex is a nationwide financial organization specializing in foreign currencies, where travelers can exchange cash and traveler's checks, receive cash against major credit cards, and receive Western Union money transfers. Many of the same services are available at banks.

▓ TIP➔ **Even if a currency-exchange booth has a sign promising no commission, rest assured that there's some kind of huge, hidden fee. (Oh . . . that's right. The sign didn't say no *fee*.) And as for rates, you're almost always better off getting foreign currency at an ATM or exchanging money at a bank.**

Exchange Services in Amsterdam
GWK Travelex (bureau de change). Throughout the Netherlands, GWK Travelex (bureau de change) branches are found in or near railway stations. ☎ *0900/0566* ⊕ *www. gwktravelex.nl.* **Amsterdam Schiphol Airport**. The exchange service offices at Amsterdam Schiphol Airport are open 24 hours a day, seven days a week. ☎ *0900/0141 €0.40 per min.* ⊕ *www.schiphol.com*

▐ PACKING

When coming to the Netherlands, be flexible: pack an umbrella (or two—the topography results in a blustery wind, which makes short work of a lightweight frame); bring a raincoat, with a thick liner in winter; and always have a sweater or jacket handy. For daytime wear and casual evenings, turtlenecks and thicker shirts are ideal for winter, under a sweater. Unpredictable summer weather means that a long-sleeved cotton shirt and jacket could be perfect one day, whereas the next, a T-shirt or vest top is as much as you can wear, making it hard to pack lightly. Bring a little something for all eventualities and you shouldn't get stuck.

Essentially, laid-back is the norm. Stylewise, anything goes. Men aren't required to wear ties or jackets, except in some smarter hotels and exclusive restaurants; jeans are very popular and worn to the office. Cobblestone streets make walking in high heels perilous—you don't want a wrenched ankle—and white sneakers are a dead giveaway that you are an American tourist; a better choice is a pair of dark-color, comfortable walking shoes.

Women wear skirts more frequently than do women in the United States, especially those over 35. Men need only include a jacket and tie if you're planning to visit one of the upper-echelon restaurants.

▐ PASSPORTS

All U.S., Canadian, and U.K. citizens, even infants, need only a valid passport to enter the Netherlands for stays of up to 90 days.

It's a good idea to always carry your passport with you, even if think you don't need one, for example if traveling between the Netherlands and other countries within the European Schengen agreement (which includes Belgium, France, and Germany, but not the United Kingdom). You are required to carry valid ID at all times in the Netherlands, and although it's very unlikely that you'll be asked for it, it's better to be safe than risk a fine.

▓ TIP➔ **Before your trip, make two copies of your passport's data page (one for someone at home and another for you to carry separately). Or scan the page and e-mail it to someone at home and/or yourself.**

▮ RESTROOMS

Restrooms (*toiletten* or *WC* in Dutch) in restaurants, bars, and other public places in the Netherlands are generally very clean, and most are free, although you may have to pay a few cents to an attendant in some cafés, and up to 50 cents in stations. A few older cafés and bars here may have only one unisex restroom. Women shouldn't be surprised to find a urinal, possibly in use, beside the washbasin in such establishments.

Find a Loo **The Bathroom Diaries.** Flush with unsanitized info, the Bathroom Diaries has the lowdown on restrooms the world over—each one located, reviewed, and rated. ⊕ *thebathroomdiaries.com.*

▮ SAFETY

Amsterdam is unlike any other modern metropolis: although it has had certain problems with crime, and with abuse of legalized prostitution and soft drugs, the serious crime rate is exceptionally low, so having your bike stolen is the worst thing most likely to happen to you. Still, in crowded intersections and dark alleys, it is always best to be streetwise and take double safety precautions; it may be best to keep your money in a money belt and not flaunt your expensive camera. Be especially wary of pickpockets in crowds and while riding the tram. And use common sense when going out at night. Keep to well-lighted areas and take a taxi if you are going a long distance. Although it is easy to lose yourself in a romantic 18th-century haze taking a midnight stroll along the canals in Amsterdam, remember that muggings do very occasionally occur. Late at night, it may be best to keep to the main thoroughfares and not venture down deserted streets.

▮▮TIP➡ Distribute your cash, credit cards, IDs, and other valuables between a deep front pocket, an inside jacket or vest pocket, and a hidden money pouch. Don't reach for the money pouch once you're in public.

▮ TAXES

Hotels in Holland always include the service charge, and the 6% V.A.T. (B.T.W. in Dutch), in the room rate. Tourist tax is never included and is a few euros extra. If in doubt, inquire when booking. In restaurants you pay a 5% service charge, 6% V.A.T. on food items, and 19% V.A.T. on all beverages, all of which are included in the quoted menu prices. V.A.T. is 19% on clothes and luxury goods, 6% on basic goods. On consumer goods, it is always included in the amount on the price tag, so you can't actually see what percentage you're paying.

When making a purchase, ask for a V.A.T. refund form and find out whether the merchant gives refunds—not all stores do, nor are they required to. Have the form stamped like any customs form by customs officials when you leave the country or, if you're visiting several EU countries, when you leave the EU. After you're through passport control, take the form to a refund-service counter for an on-the-spot refund (which is usually the quickest and easiest option), or mail it to the address on the form (or the envelope with it) after you arrive home. You receive the total refund stated on the form, but the processing time can be long, especially if you request a credit-card adjustment.

Global Refund is a Europe-wide service with 225,000 affiliated stores and more than 700 refund counters at major airports and border crossings. Its refund form, called a Tax Free Check, is the most common across the European Continent. The service issues refunds in the form of cash, check, or credit-card adjustment.

VAT Refunds **Global Refund.** ☎ *866/706–6090* ⊕ *www.globalrefund.com.*

▮ TIME

The Netherlands is on Central European Time (CET), one hour ahead of Greenwich Mean Time (GMT). Daylight saving time begins on the last Sunday in March, when clocks are set forward one hour; on the last Sunday in October, clocks are set back one hour. Holland operates on a 24-hour clock, so am hours are listed as in the United States and Britain, but pm hours continue through the cycle (1 pm is 13:00, 2 pm is 14:00, etc.). When it's 3 pm in Amsterdam, it is 2 pm in London, 9 am in New York City, and 6 am in Los Angeles.

Speaking Clock. A telephone call will get you the speaking clock in Dutch. ☎ *0900/8002.*

❚ TIPPING

In Dutch restaurants, a service charge of about 5% is often included in menu prices. Round the bill up to a convenient figure, or leave a few euros extra, if you've really enjoyed the meal and you got good service, and leave the tip as change rather than putting it on your credit card. If you're not satisfied, don't leave anything. Though a service charge is also included in hotel, taxi, bar, and café bills, the Dutch mostly round up the change to the nearest two euros for large bills and to the nearest euro for smaller ones. Consider tipping in bars only if you were served at a table. Restroom attendants and cloakroom attendants usually have fixed charges that are clearly displayed and do not require tipping.

If service is not included, people often round up a bit when paying, but it isn't offensive to pay the exact amount. Taxi drivers also appreciate a rounding up of the bill, but again, paying the exact amount is perfectly acceptable. Railway porters expect €1 per item. For bellhops and doormen at both hotels and night-spots, a few euros is adequate. Bartenders are tipped only for notably good service; again, rounding off is sufficient.

❚ TOURS

BICYCLE TOURS

From April through October, guided two- to three-hour bike trips through the central area of Amsterdam are available through Yellow Bike. Let's Go self-guided tours (contact the VVV or visit the website for further details) takes you out of the city center by train before introducing you to the safer cycling of the surrounding countryside. Its tours include Edam and Volendam, Naarden and Muiden, and, in season, a Tulip Tour.

Contacts Let's Go ✉ *Tours start from VVV Netherlands Board of Tourism, Centraal Station, Centrum* ⊕ *www.letsgo-amsterdam.com.* **Yellow Bike** ✉ *Nieuwezijds Kolk 29, Centrum* ☎ *020/620–6940* ⊕ *www.yellowbike.nl.*

BOAT TOURS

The quickest, easiest, and (frankly) most delightful way to get your bearings in Amsterdam is to take a canal-boat cruise. Trips last from one to one-and-a-half hours and cover the harbor as well as the main canal district; there is a taped or live commentary available in four languages. Excursion boats leave from *rondvaart* (excursion) piers in various locations in the city every 15 minutes from March to October, and every 30 minutes in winter. Departures are frequent from Prins Hendrikkade near the Centraal Station, along the Damrak, and along the Rokin (near Muntplein), at Leidseplein, and Stadhouderskade (near the Rijksmuseum). For a tour lasting about an hour, the cost is around €14, but the student guides expect a small tip for their multilingual commentary. A free trip is included in the I amsterdam card *(see above)*. For a truly romantic view of Amsterdam, opt for one of the special dinner and candlelight cruises offered by some companies, notably Holland International. A candlelight dinner cruise costs upward of €30. Trips for all boat tours can also be booked through the tourist office.

Operators of canal cruises include Holland International, Gray Line Amsterdam,

Rederij Lovers, Rederij P. Kooij, Rederij Noord/Zuid, and Rederij Plas.

A popular option for exploring the city's canals, and some of the attractions that lie along them, is to hop on board one of Canal Company's Canal Buses (actually ferrylike passenger boats). Canal Buses, which leave from Centraal Station and travel along the canals by three different routes, allow you to disembark at points of interest along the way. Stops along the Green Line include the Anne Frank House, Rembrandtplein, and Rembrandt's House; the Red Line stops at the Rijksmuseum, City Hall, and the Westerkerk; and the Blue Line stops at the Tropenmuseum, NEMO, and the Scheepvaartmuseum. A Canal Bus Day Pass, which costs €22, is valid from the time you buy it until noon the following day; you can hop on and off the boats as many times as you like within that time. Buying a day pass also gets you reduced entry rates at some museums along the routes.

The Canal Bike *Waterfiets* is a pedal-powered boat that seats up to four. You can tour the Grachtengordel ring of canals at your own pace. For one or two people, the hourly fee is €8 per person, and for three to four people, it costs €8 per person, per hour. Rental hours are between 10 and 6:30 daily. There are five landing stages throughout the city, with two of the most popular ones across from the Rijksmuseum and across from the Westerkerk.

Fees and Schedules Amsterdam Canal Cruises ⊠ *Stadhouderskade, opposite the Heineken Experience, The Pijp* ☎ *020/679–1370* ⊕ *www.amsterdamcanalcruises.nl.* **Canal Bus** ⊠ *Weteringschans 26–1, Leidseplein* ☎ *020/623–9886* ⊕ *www.canal.nl.* **Gray Line Amsterdam** ⊕ *www.grayline.com.* **Holland International** ⊠ *Prins Hendrik-kade, opposite Centraal Station, Centrum* ☎ *020/625–3035* ⊕ *www.hir.nl.* **Rederij Lovers** ⊠ *Prins Hendrikkade, opposite Centraal Station, Centrum* ☎ *020/530–1090* ⊕ *www.lovers.nl.* **Rederij P. Kooij** ⊠ *Rokin, near Spui, Centrum* ☎ *020/623–3810* ⊕ *www.rederijkooij.*

nl. **Rederij Plas** ⊠ *Damrak, quays 1–3, Dam* ☎ *020/624–5406* ⊕ *www.rederijplas.nl.*

BUS TOURS

Afternoon bus tours of Amsterdam operate daily. Itineraries vary, and prices start at €17. A hop-on, hop-off city tour that includes nine stops is offered by Key Tours. However, it must be said that this city of narrow alleys and canals is not best appreciated from the window of a coach. Also, a number of visitors feel unhappy that part of some tours involves a visit to a diamond factory, where they feel pressured into listening to a sales pitch. The same bus companies operate scenic trips to attractions outside the city.

Fees and Schedules Key Tours ⊠ *Paulus Potterstraat 8, Museum District* ☎ *020/305–5333* ⊕ *www.keytours.nl.* **Lindbergh Excursions** ⊠ *Damrak 26, Dam* ☎ *020/622–2766* ⊕ *www.lindbergh.nl.*

SPECIAL-INTEREST TOURS

ART AND ARCHITECTURE

From quaint to grandiose, Golden Age to Modernism, art and architecture in the Netherlands has never been anything less than visionary.

Contacts ARCHITECTURE tours.nl. This firm offers customized architecture tours. ☎ *06/2884-7075* ⊕ *www.architecturetours.nl.*

WALKING TOURS

The Netherlands Tourist Board (VVV) maintains lists of personal guides and guided walking and cycling tours for groups in and around Amsterdam and can advise you on making arrangements. You can also contact Guidor, Nederlandse Gidsen Organisatie (Dutch Guides Organization). Typical costs range from €150 for a half day to €250 for a full day. The tourist office also sells brochures outlining easy-to-follow self-guided theme tours through the central part of the city. Among them are "A Journey of Discovery Through Maritime Amsterdam," "A Walk Through the Jordaan," "Jewish Amsterdam," and "Rembrandt and Amsterdam."

Walking tours focusing on art and architecture are organized by Stichting Arttra and Architectour. For walking tours of the Jewish Quarter, contact Joods Historisch Museum. Yellow Bike Tours organizes two-hour walking tours of the Jordaan and the Red Light District.

Probably the best deal in town is Mee in Mokum, which offers walking tours led by retired longtime residents. For a mere €7.50, you are given an entertaining three-hour educational tour of the inner city or the Jordaan, focusing on architecture and surprising facts. These tours are also popular with Amsterdammers who wish to discover new things about their city. The admission fee entitles you to reduced fees to a choice of museums and a reduction in the price of a pancake at a nearby restaurant. Tours are held daily and start promptly at 11 am. You must reserve at least a day in advance. Tours are limited to eight people; private arrangements can also be made for other times of the day.

Fees and Schedules Architectour ⊠ *Touwslagerstraat 13* ☎ *020/625-9123.* **Arttra Cultureel Orgburo** ⊠ *Tweede Boomdwarsstraat 4* ☎ *020/625-9303* ⊕ *www.arttra.com.* **Guidor, Nederlandse Gidsen Organisatie** ⊠ *Leidseplein 33* ☎ *020/624-6072* ⊕ *www.guidor.nl.* **Joods Historisch Museum** ⊠ *Nieuwe Amstelstraat 1, Postbus 16737, Plantage* ☎ *020/531-0310* ⊕ *www.jhm.nl.* **Mee in Mokum** ⊠ *Tours start from Museumcafé Mokum, Kalverstraat 92, Dam* ☎ *020/625-1390 call between 1 and 4.* **Yellow Bike** ⊠ *Nieuwezijds Kolk 29, Centrum* ☎ *020/620-6940* ⊕ *www.yellowbike.nl.*

▮ VISITOR INFORMATION

AMSTERDAM AND BEYOND

The VVV (Netherlands Board of Tourism) has several offices around Amsterdam. The office on Stationsplein, opposite Centraal Station, is open Mon.–Fri. 9–7, Sun. 10–5 in summer; on Leidseplein, Mon.–Fri. 10–7, Sat. 10–6, Sun. 12–6; and at Schiphol Airport, daily 7 am–10 pm. Hours at all offices except Schiphol

may vary slightly with the seasons. Each VVV within Holland has information principally on its own region.

ONLINE TRAVEL TOOLS
AMSTERDAM AND THE
NETHERLANDS

For a guide to what's happening in Holland, the official site for the Netherlands Board of Tourism is ⊕ *www.holland.com.* The official Amsterdam site is ⊕ *www.iamsterdam.com.* More information is found at ⊕ *www.visitamsterdam.nl.* Other general sites are ⊕ *www.amsterdamhotspots.nl* and ⊕ *www.amsterdam.info.* The website ⊕ *www.channels.nl* guides you through the city with the help of many colorful photographs. The American Society of Travel Agents is at ⊕ *www.asta.org.* For rail information and schedules, go to ⊕ *www.ns.nl.* For airport information, go to ⊕ *www.schiphol.com.* For flight information and reservations on KLM, the national carrier, go to ⊕ *www.klm.com;* check out the low tariffs to other European destinations on ⊕ *www.easyjet.com,* or ⊕ *www.ryanair.com.*

One of the most informative English-language websites about the Netherlands is at ⊕ *www.expatica.com.* At ⊕ *www.dutchnews.nl* you'll find a daily digest in English of the top domestic news stories in the Netherlands. *Shark* is a free newspaper with alternative listings; their site is at ⊕ *www.underwateramsterdam.com.* Go to ⊕ *amsterdam.citymundo.com* to view City Mundo's creative city-specialist directory of accommodations. Make accommodation bookings online with ⊕ *www.booking.com* or ⊕ *www.hotels.com.* For budget accommodations, try ⊕ *www.stayokay.com,* which provides comprehensive information for the Netherlands—just click on "English" to access all information. Hostelling International has a site for worldwide reservations at ⊕ *www.iyhf.org.* For information on car-breakdown rescue service, camping, biking, hiking, and water sports, go to ⊕ *www.anwb.nl,* the Dutch Touring

Club. Go to ⊕ *www.raileurope.com* for pan-Europe ticket sales, for U.S. residents, which also has links to sites for Australian, Canadian, New Zealand, and British residents. You'll find these at the top of the screen. At ⊕ *www.weer.nl* you can find weather forecasts for the Netherlands (in Dutch but with figures and visuals so it's accessible). For a fun site where you can learn a bit of Dutch, go to ⊕ *www.learndutch.org*.

Virtually all cities and towns have individual tourism websites; see the Essentials listings near the beginning of many of our town write-ups.

INDEX

PHOTO CREDITS

1, Amanda Hall / age fotostock. Chapter 1: Experience Amsterdam and the Netherlands: 6-7, JacobH/ istockphoto. 9 (left), Amsterdam Tourism & Convention Board. 9 (right), jan kranendonk/shutterstock. 10, aniad/shutterstock. 11 (left), diego cervo/iStockphoto. 11 (right), Nikonaft/shutterstock. 12, Bjorn Svensson / age fotostock. 13, Will Salter / age fotostock. 14 (top left), Meg Zimbeck/Flickr. 14 (bottom left),suvodeb/Suvodeb Banerjee. 14 (right), Andresr/shutterstock. 15 (top left), William Allum/shutterstock. 15 (bottom left), ROOS ALDERSHOFF FOTOGRAFIE/State Hermitage Museum St Petersburg. 15(right), Amsterdam Tourism & Convention Board. 16 (left), Jarno Gonzalez Zarraonandia/ shutterstock. 16 (top center), Rob Bouwman/shutterstock. 16 (top right), Rex Roof/Flickr. 16 (bottom right) Chris Warren/ age footstock. 17 (left), Peng Chau/Flickr. 17 (top center), jan kranendonk/ shutterstock. 17 (bottom center) FAN/ age footstock. 17 (right), Margareta Svensson, Amsterdam. 19, jan kranendonk/shutterstock. 21, lillisphotography/iStockphoto. 23, jan kranendonk/shutterstock. 24, Amsterdam Tourism & Convention Board. 25 (left), Henkje/shutterstock. 25 (right), jhorrocks/ istockphoto. Chapter 2: Exploring Amsterdam: 27, Michael Zegers / age fotostock. 28 (top), lillisphotography/iStockphoto. 28 (bottom), Yvwv/wikipedia.org. 29, Ricardo De Mattos/iStockphoto. 30, April Gertler. 33, Martin Moos / age fotostock. 35, mattmangum/wikipedia. org. 39, Bob Turner / age fotostock. 44, PATRICK FORGET / age fotostock. 47, Ingolf Pompe /age fotostock. 55, Jochen Tack / age fotostock. 56, McPHOTO / age fotostock. 59, ROOS ALDERSHOFF FOTOGRAFIE/State Hermitage Museum St Petersburg. 61, Postman81/wikipedia. org. 65, Richard Wareham / age fotostock. 67, Eric Gevaert/shutterstock. 70, Atlantide S.N.C. /age fotostock. 72, Sergio Pitamitz / age fotostock. 75, Dina Litovsky. 76, Ingolf Pompe / age fotostock. 78 and 79, Alexei Profokiev. 80, Javier Larrea / age fotostock. 82, April Gertler. 84-85, Ingolf Pompe /age fotostock. 87, Will Salter / age fotostock. 89, Amsterdam Tourism & Convention Board. 91, RABOUAN Jean-Baptiste / age fotostock. 92-93, Public Domain. 96, Atlantide S.N.C./age fotostock. 98 Kevin Gessner/Flickr. 99,Ingolf Pompe / age fotostock. Chapter 3: Where to Eat: 101, Javier Larrea / age fotostock. 102, Suzette Pauwels/Flickr. 106, Sabine Lubenow / age fotostock. 111, boo_licious/Flickr. 114, AMIT_GERON/Design Hotels. 117, serge ligtenberg. 120, Apus apus via Wikimedia Commons [Creative Commons Attribution-Share Alike 3.0 Unported, 2.5 Generic, 2.0 Generic and 1.0 Generic license]. 125, Sea Palace Chinese restaurant by www.flickr.com/photos/ctsnow/7914140804/ Attribution License. 135, MAISANT Ludovic / age fotostock. 137, Restaurant Greetje. Chapter 4: Where to Stay: 141, Merten Snijders / age fotostock. 142, rob terbekke | fotografi e. 145, Will Salter / age fotostock. 151 (top), Matthew Shaw. 151 (bottom), Sofitel Legend The Grand Hotel. 160 (top), Hotel V. 160 (bottom), rob ter bekke | fotografi e. 163 (top), Amit Geron/Design Hotels. 163 (bottom), Sandton Hotel de Filosoof en Malie Hotel. 166 (top), Okura Hotels & Resorts. 166 (bottom), Allard van der Hoek. Chapter 5: Nightlife and the Arts: 169, Ingolf Pompe / age fotostock. 170, TrouwAmsterdam. 172, Amsterdam Tourism & Convention Board. 175 gen gibson/flickr. 176, Alper .uğun/Flickr. 179, Hotel Okura Amsterdam. 184, Ingolf Pompe / age fotostock. 186, Jeroen van der Goorbergh/Flickr. 197, sergio pitamitz / age fotostock. 199, Ton Koene / age fotostock. Chapter 6: Shopping: 203, Caroline Penn / age fotostock. 204, Ingolf Pompe / age fotostock. 205 (top), alljan moehamad. 205 (bottom), THOMAS ZUM VORDE SIVE VORDING. 206, JEANNETTE HUISMAN. 209, Ingolf Pompe / age fotostock. 212, FORGET Patrick/ SAGAPHOTO.COM / Alamy. 214, Sergio Pitamitz / Alamy. 217 (top), Lourens Smak / Alamy. 217 (bottom), Hans van der Mars. 220, Meg Zimbeck/Flickr. 222, Michael Zegers / age fotostock. Chapter 7: Day Trips from Amsterdam: 229, Rene van der Meer / age fotostock. 230, Bas Lammers/Flickr. 233, Ton Koene / age fotostock. 234-35, Chris Warren / age fotostock. 240, Jeremy Burgin/Flickr. 244, FAN / age fotostock. 246-47, Jose Fuste Raga / age fotostock. Chapter 8: The Randstad: 249, Atlantide S.N.C. / age fotostock. 250, Gastev/Mirko Tobias Schaefer/Flickr. 251 (top), Styve Reineck/Shutterstock. 251 (bottom), Worldpics/Shutterstock. 252, lynnlin/Shutterstock. 255, wikipedia.org. 256, CMB / age fotostock. 260, Joost J. Bakker IJmuiden/Flickr. 263, P. Narayan / age fotostock. 264, Ian Murray / age fotostock. 266, Rob Hogeslag/Flickr. 270, Javier Larrea / age fotostock. 273, Pixel Addict/Toni/ Flickr. 276, Javier Larrea /age fotostock. 282, Jochen Tack / age fotostock. 285, W. de Jonge/wikipedia. org. 289, Michele Falzone / age fotostock. 292, Wilmar / age fotostock. 295, Mark Sunderland / age fotostock. 298, MAISANT Ludovic / age fotostock. 301, Ingolf Pompe / age fotostock. 307, Michael Zegers / age fotostock. 313, Javier Larrea / age fotostock. 316, Ljupco Smokovski/Shutterstock.

NOTES

NOTES

NOTES

NOTES

NOTES

ABOUT OUR WRITERS

Floris Dogterom emigrated from The Hague to Amsterdam in the 1980s, a move that still raises some eyebrows in his rather chauvinistic place of birth. In the equally chauvinistic Dutch capital, after myriad odd jobs, he finally sat down at a keyboard to pursue a career in writing. Over the years he contributed as a writer, editor, and columnist to publications like *Time Out Amsterdam, Unfold Amsterdam, Radio Netherlands Worldwide*, and the now-legendary *Amsterdam Weekly*. Floris claims he learned English from watching televised pool games on the BBC. For this edition he updated our Exploring Amsterdam and Day Trips from Amsterdam chapters.

When **Karina Hof** left New York City, she intended to spend just a year abroad. But nearly a decade later, Holland has become home. When not writing about Dutch ephemera for readers in the United States or editing news at Radio Netherlands Worldwide, she can be found dog-watching in the green spaces of Amsterdam Zuid. For this edition, she updated our Experience Amsterdam chapter, rolling up her sleeves to refashion our What's New section and write our new Biking in Amsterdam feature.

Liz Humphreys is a recent transplant to Amsterdam from New York City, where she spent a decade in senior editorial positions for fashion, lifestyle, and health publications and websites including *Lucky*, iVillage, and Everyday Health. To indulge her obsessions with food, wine, and travel, she has also covered NYC restaurants and sights for *USA Today* and has written and edited for Fodors.com and Forbes Travel Guides. In between eating and drinking, Liz found time to earn intermediate and advanced certificates in wine studies from the WSET (Wine & Spirit Education Trust) and now attempts to visit as many wine regions around the world as possible, which she chronicles on her blog, ⊕ *winederlust.com*. Liz updated our Where to Eat chapter.

Marie-Claire Melzer grew up in a leafy Dutch village and moved to Amsterdam in the early 1990s to study art history and cinema. After years of exploring the city's culture and nightlife she made a career writing about it for papers and periodicals such as *Het Parool, VARA TV Magazine, Amsterdam Weekly,* and *De Groene Amsterdammer*. Currently she keeps an eye on the local jazz scene for music magazine *Jazzism*. For this edition Marie-Claire updated our Where to Stay, Shopping, and Nightlife and Arts chapters.

After more than 20 years in the Netherlands, and thoroughly addicted to *uitsmijters* and *pannekoeken* (pancakes), British-born **Tim Skelton** considers himself a true Eindhovenaar. When not repairing his rusty Dutch bicycle, he writes magazine features on a range of subjects from travel to environmental issues, and is the author of *Around Amsterdam in 80 Beers*, the essential guide for any beer lover visiting the capital. He has also written a guidebook to Luxembourg for Bradt Travel Guides. For this edition he updated our Randstad and Travel Smart chapters and also updates the Belgium section on Fodor's website.